THE MAN
ROBERT BURNS

your gratefully indebted, humble servant
Robert Burns

PORTRAIT OF BURNS
After Beugo's celebrated vignette

Your portrait of Burns I showed a few days ago to Mrs. Begg, the surviving sister of the Bard, who emphatically pronounced it, after a minute examination, to be "an extremely good representation" of her immortal brother. All the features of the Poet, Mrs. Begg remarked, were most correctly delineated. (*Extract from a letter to the Publishers from Dr. Rogers, Stirling.*)

THE MAN
ROBERT BURNS

BY
GRANT F. O. SMITH

INTRODUCTION BY
H. B. ANDERSON, M.D.

*I was born a poor dog; and however I may occasionally pick up a
better bone than I used to do, I know I must live and die poor; but
I will indulge the flattering faith that my poetry will considerably
outlive my poverty.*—ROBERT BURNS (1791).

THE RYERSON PRESS ～ TORONTO

PRINTED AND BOUND IN CANADA
BY THE RYERSON PRESS, TORONTO

TO

MY STAUNCH FRIEND

THOMAS A. GILLEN

PAST PRESIDENT OF THE BURNS LITERARY SOCIETY,
TORONTO,

WHOSE DEEP APPRECIATION OF THE GENIUS OF ROBERT BURNS AND
WHOSE READY AND CONSTANT ASSISTANCE TO THE AUTHOR HAVE BEEN
OF THE GREATEST VALUE IN MAKING THIS WORK POSSIBLE.

ACKNOWLEDGMENTS

This work has been in preparation for many years, during which the author has been under obligation to many sources, both in the hands of descendants of the Poet, and in a remarkable collection of Burnsiana made by the author's parents. Whilst every reasonable care has been taken to trace and acknowledge ownership of copyright material, information which will enable the publishers to rectify any reference or credit in subsequent editions will be welcomed.

Foreword

ROBERT BURNS is a part of daily life, he has sung his way into all the lovely common things of life. He is not a tradition, he is a living force. His songs are in the air.

The Man Robert Burns is the result of intensive research during many years. It brings together an unprecedented collection of interesting and valuable material, never hitherto comprised in one volume. This compendious work contains an unequalled record of authentic letters, criticisms and opinions (both contemporary and subsequent to his decease) bearing on the life and work of Robert Burns, as well as many reproductions of rare pictures, some never before published, and a unique genealogical tree of the direct descendants of the Poet. Therefore it should be of absorbing interest and great value to Scotsmen and other lovers of the Poet everywhere.

The writer felt impelled to begin such a volume because, though a North of England man, he had since childhood been intimately associated with lovers and admirers of the great bard. The association had its genesis through the author's father, who, as a shipowner of Sunderland in sailing ship days, visited the Burns country, his boats often being chartered to Leith and other places from which access could be had to the land of Burns and that of the Bard's forebears farther North.

The writer's sister distinctly recalls that, as a little girl, she was taken by her father on such a trip, a visit being paid to the Poet's

cottage.   That would be roughly sixty-eight years after Burns'
death.   This ship-owning Burns enthusiast lost no opportunity
on these excursions of getting first-hand information, as far as he
could, about the Poet's career.   The results of these contacts
would be related to his family and the visitors to the home in
Sunderland.   Thus it came about, that this present scribe from
his earliest years breathed the Burns atmosphere, and was nurtured
in the Burns spirit and tradition.

The introduction by Dr. H. B. Anderson of Toronto, renowned
Burns lover and author of *Robert Burns: His Medical Friends,
Attendants and Biographer*, will be greatly appreciated.

GRANT F. O. SMITH.

TORONTO,
July 1, 1940.

Introduction

Over a century ago Lockhart proffered an apology on the publication of the sixth narrative of the life of Robert Burns, but Carlyle acquitted him of blame with the reflection that it was not the choice of the task but the manner of its performance that might call for criticism. In his opinion the character of Burns was a theme that could never become either trite or exhausted. His prophetic vision of the enduring fame and increasing popularity of the national poet of Scotland has been abundantly verified, yet with each addition to the long list of works dealing with his writings and with every phase of his life and character, the question still arises, what is there to justify its appearance?

Mr. Grant F. O. Smith, of Toronto, now challenges the question by presenting for the approbation of lovers of Burns and the reading public in general, an attractive volume entitled *The Man Robert Burns*.

The title itself is well chosen, for assuredly "it is not chiefly as a poet, but as a man, that he interests and affects us." The significance of the title is apparent in the choice of topics, as well as in the selection and arrangement of the material contained in the twenty-one sections into which the book is divided. The man Robert Burns is constantly kept in view, not only in what the author writes about his subject but in his extensive use of authenticated material written by the Poet himself and by others who knew him best. For this reason he includes in the book the autobiography and many letters of the Poet, the biographical narratives of his brother, Gilbert, and his schoolmaster, John Murdoch, the constitution and proceedings of the Bachelors' Club, organized by Burns in 1780, and other source material not usually found in single volume editions.

The sections dealing with the origin of the family surname, the ancestry and descendants of the Poet, alone contain sufficient new and important information to afford ample justification for the publication. Whether based on tradition or verifiable fact, the story of the surname and the various changes in its form, until the Poet in 1786 adopted the surname of Burns, is full of interest; and if the suggestion that the family name originally was Campbell is confirmed by further investigation, it is highly important.

The new and more detailed information concerning the ancestry and the descendants of the Poet indicates a generous amount of talent and distinction among both, and will be read with satisfaction by many who have felt that undue emphasis has been attached by certain writers to his peasant birth, though, on grounds of heredity, it may not be an inexplicable phenomenon that the greatest genius in the history of Scotland should be traced to humble forebears.

A genealogical tree of the descendants of the Poet and Jean Armour is another new and important feature of the work. In its preparation as well as in the collection of other material, the author has been fortunate in having had the collaboration of a distant kinsman of Burns, in the person of Mr. Charles Stuart Burness, of Toronto. It will be of interest to Canadians in general to learn that so many of the Poet's descendants are now residents of this country.

The book contains, as one would anticipate, the poems which have endeared the Poet to countless readers and which serve best to reveal his personality and character.

An account is given of Burns' Masonic associations and activities; brief biographies introduce the reader to his correspondents, and a most impressive assemblage of opinions and tributes of world renowned authors of his own period and later, of eminent statesmen, scientists, professors, professional men and men of affairs, bear eloquent testimony to his genius and character.

The attractiveness and value of the book are greatly enhanced by the sixty-eight excellent pictures used in its illustration.

Altogether, the author may be congratulated on the success of his efforts to present, within the compass of a single volume, an unprecedented amount of relevant material, upon which readers may arrive at a personal judgment on the life, character and works of the man Robert Burns. It is hoped and believed that the work will meet with the cordial reception that its merits deserve.

H. B. ANDERSON.

TORONTO,
July 1, 1940.

Contents

		PAGE
INTRODUCTION BY H. B. ANDERSON, M.D.		ix
I.	ORIGIN OF NAME	1
II.	ANCESTRY	9
III.	DESCENDANTS OF ROBERT BURNS AND JEAN ARMOUR	14
IV.	THE LIFE OF ROBERT BURNS WRITTEN BY THE POET HIMSELF	19
V.	THE LIFE OF ROBERT BURNS WRITTEN BY THE POET'S BROTHER GILBERT	29
VI.	THE LIFE OF ROBERT BURNS WRITTEN BY HIS ONLY SCHOOLMASTER, JOHN MURDOCH	39
VII.	DEATH AND FUNERAL OF ROBERT BURNS	45
VIII.	THE MOTHER OF ROBERT BURNS	50
IX.	THE POET'S BROTHER WILLIAM	53
X.	THE BACHELORS' CLUB	58
XI.	ROBERT BURNS AND FREEMASONRY	63
XII.	THE CORRESPONDENTS OF ROBERT BURNS	91
XIII.	RELIGION	143

PAGE

XIV. "Highland Mary" [Mary Campbell, 1763-1786] 148

XV. Poems and Epistles [1773-1796] 153

XVI. The Burns Festival—Ayr, 1844 280

XVII. Humour 303

XVIII. Memories of Burns: Dorothy Wordsworth . . 309

XIX. Memories of Burns: Sir Walter Scott . . . 311

XX. Tributes 314

Genealogical Tree of the Direct Descendants
of Robert Burns 390

List of Subscribers 391

List of Illustrations

FACING PAGE

Frontispiece—Portrait of Burns after Beugo's Celebrated Vignette

Robert, the Eldest Son of the Poet 14

Col. William Nicol Burns, Third Son of the Poet . . . 14

Lieut.-Col. James Glencairn Burns, Fourth Son of the Poet 14

Annie Burns Burns, Daughter of James Glencairn Burns (Second Marriage) 14

George Ian Burns Gowring, Only Son of Violet Burns Gowring 15

Mabel Burnand Hutchinson, Wife of Robert Burns Hutchinson, 1937 15

Robert Burns Hutchinson and His Youngest Daughter Jean, 1938 15

Robert Burns Hutchinson and His Youngest Son, Beverley, 1937 15

Robert Burns Hutchinson, Great-Grandson of Burns, in His Home in Vancouver, British Columbia . . . 15

The Birthplace of Burns 30

FACING PAGE

Room in which Burns was Born 30

Agnes Brown, the Mother of Burns 31

Gilbert Burns, Brother of the Poet 31

Isabella Burns (Mrs. Begg), the Poet's Youngest Sister . 31

Violet Burns Gowring, Great-Granddaughter of Burns . . 31

The Burns Statue, Toronto, Ontario 46

Tombstones of the Poet's Ancestors in Glenbervie
    Churchyard 46

The House where Burns Died, Dumfries 47

Burns Mausoleum, Dumfries 47

The Funeral of Burns, Dumfries, July 25, 1796 47

Robert Burns, Depute Master, by W. Stewart Watson . . 62

Tarbolton, House in which Burns was Made a Freemason . 63

Tarbolton Procession of St. James' Lodge 63

Lodge Canongate Kilwinning No. 2, Looking S.E. . . . 78

Lodge Canongate Kilwinning No. 2, Looking N.E. . . . 79

Burns Reciting "A Winter Night" in the Home of the
    Duchess of Gordon 94

Dumfries, Market Place 94

Portrait of Thomas Blacklock, D.D. 95

Portrait of Elizabeth Burnett of Monboddo 95

Portrait of Mrs. Dunlop of Dunlop 95

Portrait of Captain Francis Grose, F.S.A. 95

Burns and Sir Walter Scott at Dr. Adam Ferguson's
    House 126

Burns at Lord Monboddo's House 126

FACING PAGE

Portrait of Burns by Sir Henry Raeburn (Age about 18, Lochlea Period) 127

Portrait of Burns after Nasmyth 127

Portrait of Burns after Skirving 127

The Hero and Heroine 142

Robert Burns in the Fox Livery after Nasmyth . . . 142

Burns and Bonnie Jean (Married) 142

Letter of Robert Burns to His Brother Gilbert 143

Death and Doctor Hornbook 174

Tam o' Shanter Inn (1938) 174

Portrait of Jean Armour and Her Grand-daughter, Sarah Elizabeth Maitland Tombs 174

Facsimile of Burns' Hand-writing 175

Portrait of James Cunningham, Earl of Glencairn . . . 175

Kilmarnock. Market Cross 175

The Jolly Beggars 190

"John Anderson, my Jo" 190

"Willie Brew'd a Peck o' Maut" 190

The Cotter's Saturday Night 191

Burns' First Love, Nelly Kilpatrick 191

Nithsdale 238

The Bonnie Lass o' Ballochmyle 238

Ayr. The Twa Brigs 239

Edinburgh Castle from the Gray Friar's Churchyard . . 239

"And we'll tak' a cup o' kindness yet . . . . . . 254 For Auld Lang Syne"

FACING PAGE

"We twa ha'e paidl'd i' the burn 254
Frae morning sun till dine"

Willie's Mill. Tarbolton 255

To Mary in Heaven 255

"Nursing her wrath to keep it warm" 270

"The Souter tauld his queerest stories" 270

"Nae man can tether time or tide" 271

"And, wow! Tam saw an unco sight!" 271

"But scarcely had he Maggie rallied" 286

"Ae Spring brought off her master hale" 286

The Horrors of War 287

The Soldier's Return 287

I

Origin of Name

IT HAS long been a subject of dispute between Highlanders and Lowlanders whether Burns was to be set in the one hand or the other. There is much of the Celtic spirit in Burns' poems, and a vague tradition of his Highland ancestry has long persisted. All that has hitherto been known with certainty are the statements of the Poet himself and of his brother Gilbert:

"My father was of the north of Scotland, the son of a farmer who, like his ancestors, had rented lands of the noble Keiths of Marischal.[1]" —ROBERT BURNS.

"The father of Dr. Paterson, now physician at Ayr, was, I believe, a native of Aberdeenshire, and was one of the established teachers in Ayr, when my father settled in the neighbourhood. He early recognized my father as a fellow-native of the north of Scotland, and a certain degree of intimacy subsisted between them during Mr. Paterson's life."—GILBERT BURNS [A letter to Mrs. Dunlop after the Poet's death].

The late Alexander Carmichael (1833-1912), a well-known Celtic enthusiast, disinterred the story of Burns' ancestry.

1. James Keith, Marshal Keith, was born at the castle of Inverugie. near Peterhead, June 11, 1696. He came of a family which from the twelfth century had held the hereditary office of Great Marischal of Scotland. Sir William Keith was created Earl Marischal in 1458; and George, fifth Earl (1553-1623), in 1593 founded the Marischal College in Aberdeen. The family is now represented by the Earl of Kintore.

"The Land of Lorne," according to him, "was not only the ancestral home of Lord Macaulay, of David Livingstone, of Thomas Campbell, but . . . of the forebears of Robert Burns and John Ruskin."

Tradition has assigned as the root of the family tree planted in Kincardineshire, a certain Walter Campbell from Muckairn, Argyllshire, who had in the early part of the seventeenth century, for political or prudent reasons, abandoned his native district and settled in the parish of Glenbervie in the Mearns, dropping his proper surname and assuming that of Burnhouse from the name of the property he held in his county of origin.

The house of Walter Campbell in Argyllshire was called "Taigh-an-uillt," the house of the burn—burn house; while Walter Campbell himself was known as "Ualtair Taigh-an-uillt," Walter of the burn house, that is Walter Burnhouse, because the knoll upon which his house stood was skirted by the burn Lauchragan. The name Ualtair (Walter) is confined in the Highlands to Campbells or to immediate Campbell connections. The fact that he was "air taigh dha fhein" on a house of his own suggests that Walter Campbell was married.

In the Mearns (i.e. Kincardine), Walter Campbell found people of the name of Burness, singularly like his own familiar cognomen of Burn-house, at home in Muckairn. As a slight disguise, he called himself by this designation of Burnhouse, dropping his clan name of Campbell. It was an easy transition from Walter Burnhouse to Walter Burness, Burnus, Burnes, Burns. The Poet spelt it Burness for a time and finally, in 1786, spelt it Burns. Burness was the form usually adopted in Kincardineshire in the early part of the eighteenth century and probably before that time. In the Kirk session records of Glenbervie the name is invariably spelled Burness.

A relative of Burns, Dr. James Burnes (1801-1862), the learned educationist of India, on being made a Knight of the Royal Hanoverian Guelphic order, conferred on him by King William IV (1765-1837), had to produce his pedigree and to register his arms. He published a pamphlet giving the result of his researches. He began his pedigree with a certain Walter Campbell of Burnhouse in Argyll, who had fled to the north country in the seventeenth century, assuming the name of "Burnhouse." He stated that he did so on the authority of his relative, John Burness of Stonehaven, the author of Thrummy Cap, and also on the authority of the "Rev. Alexander Greig, Episcopal minister, Stonehaven, who was born in 1707, and died in 1793, and who was well versed in the records of the family, his mother having been a Burness and a grand-daughter of the said Walter Campbell."

Mr. Greig said that:

Walter Campbell had been the proprietor of a small domain called Burnhouse in Argyllshire, but that he had taken part with James II at the Revolution, and incurred the displeasure of his chief, and had to flee, taking with him his only son Walter, then a boy; that he dropped the name of Campbell, and became known by that of Burness, probably a corruption of Burnhouse, the place of his birth, and that he settled in the parish of Glenbervie.

James Taylor (aged eighty-seven), Drumlithie, records that, "his grandmother had been a Burness, and he had heard that the original name of the family had been Campbell, but that it had been changed in consequence of a duel." Mary Burness, an old woman in Stonehaven, and a near relative of Dr. Burnes, also said the family had been Campbells. Dr. Burnes gave these details to the Heralds College, and registered arms embodying the Campbell arms. Then he went back to India, and on his return he set to work to disprove all he had already written, and wrote another pamphlet to prove that Burnes or Burns was an English name, and that the family were descended from a certain King of Mercia of the eleventh century. His own relations ridiculed and disowned this absurd attempt.

In the *Scots Magazine* of 1889-1890, there is an article on "The Land of Burns" from Mr. Crabbe Watt, K.C., which shows great research. In it he quotes from Dr. Burnes as to the Campbell origin of the family, and says that Dr. Burnes' own investigations in the churchyard of Glenbervie to some extent confirm it. He considers Dr. Burnes' first attempt at a pedigree to have been the more correct, and says that Walter Campbell of Burnhouse is recognized by the Heralds College and by Scottish antiquaries as the root of the family. Mr. Crabbe Watt says, that Walter Campbell settled in Glenbervie as a small leaseholder; and that his son Walter, who as a boy had accompanied his father from Argyllshire, learnt the trade of shoemaking in Aberdeen. After a time he returned to Kincardine, married and took the farm of Bogjorgan. He had four sons: William, John, James and Robert. James, the third son, was born in 1656 and became tenant of the farm of Brawlinmuir.

Chambers, in his *Life of Burns*, fixes upon the weak point in the traditions given by Dr. James Burnes. He says:

The story requires some correction in point of date, for it is inadmissible that the grandfather of a man born in 1656, which was the case of James Burnes of Brawlinmuir, could be liable, after the Revolution, to change his residence on account of his political principles. It is, however, not impossible that in the course of transmission from mouth to mouth, the tradition suffered to this extent, and that the time of the Civil War was actually referred to. . . . On the other hand it is certain that, however Walter Burness acquired his name, it was one that did not take its rise in that manner, for it occurs in public documents of the age of Bruce. What is more to the purpose, the name of James Burnes, servitor to Sir Alexander Strachan of Thornton, Knight Baronet, appears as a witness to a deposition granted in 1637 by the Earl of Traquair, Treasurer of Scotland, in the name of the Scottish Exchequer. Thornton is situated within ten miles of Bogjorgan and Brawlinmuir. Our finding a Burness in the district in 1637 certainly reduces the likelihood of the family being Argyllshire refugees of the time of the Civil War. It must at the same time be admitted as not impossible that the supposed Walter Campbell might be the more ready to adopt his territorial appellation as a surname in consequence of finding men of that name already in the country.

This was undoubtedly one reason why Walter Campbell retained his designation of Burnhouse and dropped his clan name of Campbell. The fact that such clear and similar traditions existed in two districts which have so little communication as Muckairn and Glenbervie, appears to be strong evidence in favour of the descent of the poet, Robert Burns, from Walter Campbell, the fugitive son of Muckairn.

The first Duke of Argyll and Greenwich was the ablest man of his time. It was of him that Pope said:

> The great Argyll whose powers are known to wield
> And shake alike the senate and the field.

He was as patriotic as he was great, and championed his country and his people when their liberties was threatened. It was he who commanded the Hanoverian army at the battle of Sheriffmuir, when the curious and suggestive sight was seen of the Highlanders of the two opposing armies cutting down and defeating all before them. The Duke of Argyll was commander-in-chief of the British army. He was quietly relieved of this, however, because of the patriotic stand he made against the insults offered to Scotland on account of the Porteous Riot.

When the arrogant Queen Caroline declared that she was going to reduce Edinburgh to ashes and Scotland to a hunting-ground, the Duke replied: "Then, Your Majesty, it is time for me to go home and prepare my hounds." "What do you mean by that?" angrily demanded the Queen. "Oh, Your Majesty, that I may be ready for the chase when it comes." It was probably in consequence of this that the Duke, notwithstanding he had been opposed to him, was in secret correspondence with the exiled king, James VIII, the father of Prince Charlie.

Horace Walpole, in his letter of June 30, 1742, to Sir Horace Mann, mentions the curious fact that in this correspondence the Duke signed himself "Burnus." Probably the Duke could have been aware of the name which his relative, Walter Campbell, had adopted in Kincardine.

Mr. Charles Macdonald, Barrachaenndoir, says that the last of the Campbells of Inverliver who left Muckairn were tall, sinewy, black-haired people, and so singularly like the portraits of Burns that they and Burns might have been brothers. They were highly endowed, and yet somehow things never seemed to thrive with them.

Walter Campbell himself was a poet, and many of his songs used to be sung in Muckairn till the old people were removed to make room for the sheep-breeding strangers. Speaking of the descent of Burns from Walter Campbell, one aged informant said:

"Bu dual do Bhurns bardachd a bhi ann—Bu mhath am bard bho'n do shiolaich e." ["Bardism was natural in Burns—good was the bard from whom he was descended."]

The following verses by Walter Campbell describe the salient features of Glenlonan. They are as true to nature as they are to music and to rhythm:

GAELIC	ENGLISH
Clacha dubh	Clacha dubh
An aghaidh sruth	Against the stream
Am bun a bhruth—	At the foot of the brae
—aich bhoidheich.	So beauteous.
Barra-goille	Barra-goill
An oir na coille	On the edge of the copse
Am moch an goir	Where early sings
Na smeoraich.	The mavis.
Barra-glas	Barra-glas
A bhruthaich chas	On the steep brae,
'S e laiste leis	And it aflame
Na neoinein.	With daisies.
'S Duntannachan	And Duntannachan
Nan samhnachan	Of the lusty trout,
Far nach gann	Where plenty are
An lon-dubh.	The blackbirds.
Bail-an-deoir	Bail-en-deoir
An uchd na treoir	In the lap of the strong,
An ceo-achadh	In the mistiness
Mhuc-arna.	Of Muckairn.
Agus Luachragan	And Luachragan
Nan cluanagan	Of the little meadows
A tuathachadh	A-northing to
Gu sala.	The sea.

The verses, said to have been composed by Walter Campbell when leaving Muckairn, are very tender and beautiful, and such as may well have been composed by one in his unhappy condition:

Soiridh le Lonan nan gleann,
Is leis an Neannd is glaine sruth,
Soiridh dha'n Mhuic is dha h-all
    Mo chreach leir, mo chradh an diugh!

Soiridh le Cruachan nam beann,
Is tric a sheall mi ort gu moch,
Soiridh le Atha nan ath,
    Is lionar bradan tarra-gheal ort.

Soiridh dha'm chomhalta chaomh,
Is ioma caochladh thig air sruth,
Thig caochladh air gach ni's an t-saoghal,
Ach cha chaochail mo ghaol-sa dhut.

[Translation]

Farewell to thee, Lonan of the glens,
And to thee, Nant, purest of streams,
Farewell to thee, Muckairn, and to thy people:
    Alas, my grief! mine agony this day!

Farewell to thee, Cruachan of the peaks,
Oft I gazed on thee at early morn;
Farewell to thee, Awe of the fords,
    Many the white-bellied salmon dwelling in thee.

Farewell to thee, co-fosterer of my love—
Many are the changes that come upon a stream;
Change shall come on all things in the world,
    But change shall my love for thee never.

One cannot fail to see the strong family resemblance between these fragments and passages in the poems of Robert Burns. The poetic affinity is striking and touching.

The view taken by Rev. Charles Rogers, LL.D. (1825-1890) is worthy of being read with care.

That Robert Burns was, in respect of his great powers, directly indebted to his ancestors may not be affirmed. Neither may we venture to assert that he arose in a soil that had no preparation. So to speak would be to substitute for providential pre-arrangement the government of chance. As in the meadow there are spots more especially efflorescent, so from certain races, or certain combination of races, descend those who by their thought and activities tend to renovate and ennoble. . . . I, for one, incline to believe the strong influence of heredity. Like oil in water, mental power rises to the surface, and though beclouded for many generations, will emerge itself.

II

Ancestry

D R. JAMES BURNES (1801-1862) and Adam Burnes (1802-1872), sons of Provost James Burnes (1780-1852), Montrose, visited Glenbervie Churchyard between eighty-three and eighty-eight years ago (1850-1855), and found the graves of their and the Poet's ancestors almost hidden under an overgrowth of grass, moss and weeds, and the stones placed over them fast crumbling to decay. Two flat or thorough stones rested upon the soil. One bore the dates 1715 and 1719, and marked the resting-place of William Burnes, tenant in Bogjorgan, great-grand-uncle of the Poet, and his wife, Christian Fotheringham; the other commemorated James Burnes, tenant in Brawlinmuir, and his wife, Margaret Falconer, the great-grandparents of Burns. The latter stone was lying upon its face. Upon being turned over, it was found to bear, under the conventional death's head, the following inscription:

MEMENTO MORI

J. B.	17-42	M. F.

HERE UNDER LYES THE BODY OF JAMES BURNES, WHO WAS TENANT IN BRAWLINMUIR, WHO DIED YE 23 OF JANUARY, 1743. AGED 87 YEARS.

ALSO THE BODY OF MARGARET FALCONER, HIS SPOUSE, WHO DEPARTED THIS LIFE THE 28TH OF DEC. 1749, AGED 90 YEARS.

ALTHOUGH OUR BODYS WORMS DESTROY—OUR REINS CONSUMED BE,
YET IN OUR FLESH AND WITH OUR EYES SHALL OUR REDEEMER SEE.

HERE IS THE GRAVE OF THOMAS BURNES, SON TO THE ABOVE, WHO DEPARTED THIS LIFE JUNE YE 8, 1734, AGED 29 YEARS. ALSO HIS LAWFUL AND ONLY DAUGHTER, MARGARET, WHO DEPARTED THIS LIFE MARCH YE 24TH, 1741, AGED 8 YEARS.

9

JAMES BURNES: great-grandfather of the Poet, was tenant in Brawlinmuir, born 1656, died January 23, 1743, aged 87 years, buried in Glenbervie Churchyard. For the farm at Brawlinmuir, he paid a rent equal to £300 sterling. According to tradition he was a person of great sagacity and shrewdness. He lived at a period when Highland freebooters made predatory incursions into Kincardine-shire. On one occasion, when these Kateran, as they were called, were hovering in his neighbourhood, he adopted the precaution of concealing his money in the nave of an old cart wheel which lay in the jaw-hole in front of his house. The aperture being plugged up, the robbers entered and left the house without suspecting the existence of the treasure they were treading upon. He married

MARGARET FALCONER: was born 1659 and died December 28, 1749, buried in Glenbervie Churchyard and aged 90 years. She belonged to an old and noble house. Ranulph, son of Walter de Lunkyn, obtained from William the Lion, about the close of the twelfth century, the office of royal Falconer, with several lands in Kincardineshire, which, on account of the owner having charge of the king's hawks, were subsequently designated Halkerton. By the family was assumed the name of Falconer. Sir Alexander Falconer, a zealous adherent of Charles I, was by that monarch appointed a senator of the College of Justice, and was in 1657 raised to the peerage as Lord Falconer of Halkerton. He is now represented by the Earl of Kintore. Had five sons and two daughters:

1. WILLIAM: succeeded his father as tacksman of Brawlinmuir, he married with issue, but his children seem to have died young or unmarried.

2. ELSPETH: married—Gavin, farmer, Drumlithie, in the parish of Fordun.

3. ROBERT: grandfather of the Poet, rented the farm of Clochnahill in the parish of Dunnottar.

4. CHRISTIAN: married—Crabbie, farmer, Craigniston.

5. GEORGE: rented the farm of Elfhill in the parish of Fetteresso.

6. JAMES: born 1690 and died April 3, 1778, aged 88 years. Rented the farm of Hawkhill of Glenbervie, but on the death of his eldest brother William, obtained the lease of Brawlinmuir. He married, first—Christie, by whom he had four sons: James born 1724; Thomas born 1728, baptized 1729, and died 1804; William (first) born 1731; William (second) born 1735; and two daughters, Margaret born 1722; and Catherine born 1726. His second son, Thomas, who was a gardener, learned his trade in the gardens of Dunnottar, having been introduced by his uncle of Clochnahill in the parish of Dunnottar. From Dunnottar gardens it is probable that he was transferred to Inverurie where his Jacobite sympathies got him into trouble. He left for England, where he lived for many years and returned to Glenbervie in a deranged state, where he died. He married Sarah—June 24, 1756.

7. THOMAS: born 1705, died June 8, 1734. His only child, Margaret, died March 24, 1741, aged 8 years.

ROBERT BURNES: grandfather of the Poet, second son of James Burnes and Margaret Falconer, rented the farm of Kinmonth in Glenbervie, from which he removed to the more considerable farm of Clochnahill in Dunnottar. In conjunction with the neighbouring farmers, he built a school at Clochnahill, and aided in supporting a teacher; he married

ISABELLA KEITH: of Criggie, a farm adjoining Clochnahill. Had four sons and six daughters.

1. JAMES: born 1717, died July 17, 1761, aged 44 years. He married in 1745, Margaret Grub (died at Bervie about 1795), by whom he had three sons and three daughters. He was trained to merchandise; in 1732 settled in Montrose, of that Burgh he became a burgess on September 11, 1741, and was elected town councillor on September 26, 1753. Esteemed for his piety and intelligence, he was ordained an elder of the parish church. He became head of that branch of the family which produced Sir Alexander Burnes, linguist, diplomatist and Eastern traveller, who along with his brother Charles was cruelly murdered at Cabool, India, on November 2, 1841; (Sir Alexander Burnes was unmarried and was born May 16, 1805); and also Dr. James Burnes, 1801-1862, born at Montrose, was Physician-General of the Bombay army—likewise distinguished as a diplomatist in connection with the Government in India. He died at Manchester and was buried at Swindon Church, near Cheltenham, Gloucestershire.

2. ROBERT: born 1719, bred a gardener, went to England, returned to Scotland; "Poor Uncle Robert" died in his own house of the "Stane Stair" on January 3, 1789.

3. WILLIAM: the Poet's father, along with his brother Robert, assisted his father on the farm at Clochnahill. But the family were ruined by the terrible winter and spring of 1740, when a general scarcity supervened. In Kincardineshire (the Mearns) many tenant-farmers were reduced to absolute poverty. Several farms in the cold district of Clochnahill were, some years subsequent to 1740, left without cultivation. Robert Burnes and his sons William and Robert, abandoned Clochnahill farm, not, as has been alleged by several of the Poet's biographers, on account of the lease being granted to another, but solely in consequence of the storm in 1740. Mrs. Begg, the Poet's sister, said her father, William Burnes, often alluded to the terrible winter of 1740 as causing the family impoverishment.

4. MARGARET: born 1723, married Archibald Walker at Crawton with issue.

5. ELSPETH: born 1725, married John Caird, farmer in Denside of Dunnottar.

6. JEAN: born 1727, married John Burness, sub-tenant at Bogjorgan, was left a widow, had no family, interred at Fetteresso.

7. GEORGE: born 1729, died young.

8. ISOBEL: born 1730, married William Brand in 1770, dyer Auchenblae, issue, one son, James.

9. MARY: born 1732, died unmarried.

10. A DAUGHTER: whose name is lost and who died young.

WILLIAM BURNES: the father of the Poet and third son of Robert Burnes and Isabella Keith. Born November 11, 1721, at his father's farm, Clochnahill, on the slope of Carmont. Left Clochnahill in the Mearns around 1740 and finally settled in Ayrshire. Died February 13, 1784, aged 63 years. Buried at Kirk Alloway. Married December 15, 1757.

AGNES BROWN: who was born in the Carrick district of Ayrshire, March 17, 1732, and died January 14, 1820, in her son Gilbert's house at Grant's Braes, Haddington, aged 88 years. Her remains were deposited in Bolton Churchyard, near Haddington. Her mother's name was Davidson—NIC DHA'-AIDH of the Clan Chattan. Agnes Brown may have been Celtic on her father's side, and she was certainly Celtic on her mother's. By both parents, therefore, Robert Burns was essentially Highland. It is even possible that there was relationship between Burns and Highland Mary. Had four sons and three daughters,

1. ROBERT BURNS: the Poet of Scotland and Democracy, born January 25, 1759, and died July 21, 1796, aged 37 years. Baptized January 26, 1759, by Mr. William Dalrymple; witnesses, John Tennant and James Young.

2. GILBERT: born September 28, 1760, died 1827. Married June 21, 1791, Jean Breckenridge. Issue, six sons and five daughters.

3. AGNES: died without issue in 1834, interred in Dunkald Churchyard; married William Galt, land-steward to Mr. M. Fortescue, Ireland, who died March 1, 1847.

4. ANNABELLA: died unmarried at Grant's Braes in 1832. Buried in Bolton Churchyard, East Lothian, beside her mother and brother Gilbert.

5. WILLIAM: born July 31, 1767; died in London, unmarried, July 28, 1790.

6. JOHN: died young at Mossgiel.

7. ISABELLA: born 1771, died 1858, aged 87 years. Married December 9, 1793, John Begg, who latterly was factor to Hope Vere, Esq., of Blackwood, Lanarkshire. He met his death by his horse rearing and falling back upon him. Issue, six sons and three daughters. Mrs. Begg's remains were consigned to the grave in Alloway Churchyard, in which, seventy-five years before, her father's dust had been deposited.

The remains of the Poet's father, William Burnes, were deposited in the churchyard of Alloway, where a simple tombstone was erected to his memory by his son, the Poet. When the Poet became famous, visitors to the churchyard struck off and carried away chips from the tombstone until it wholly disappeared. It was substituted by another, reared at the cost of Mr. David Auld, a patriotic gentleman of the neighbourhood. The inscription was composed by the Poet:

THIS STONE WAS ERECTED
TO THE MEMORY OF

WILLIAM BURNESS

LATE FARMER IN LOCHLEA, PARISH OF TARBOLTON,
WHO DIED FEBRUARY 13TH, 1784. AGED 63 YEARS,
AND WAS BURIED HERE.

O YE WHOSE CHEEK THE TEAR OF PITY STAINS,
DRAW NEAR WITH PIOUS REV'RENCE AND ATTEND!
HERE LIE THE LOVING HUSBAND'S DEAR REMAINS,
THE TENDER FATHER, AND THE GEN'ROUS FRIEND;
THE PITYING HEART THAT FELT FOR HUMAN WOE;
THE DAUNTLESS HEART THAT FEARED NO HUMAN PRIDE;
THE FRIEND OF MAN, TO VICE ALONE A FOE;
FOR EV'N HIS FAILINGS LEANED TO VIRTUE'S SIDE.

III

Descendants of Robert Burns and Jean Armour

I N THE YEAR 1804 when Robert Burns II was eighteen years of age he obtained a situation at the Stamp Office, London. He remained at the post for twenty-six years, and during the whole of that time although on the best of terms he never once saw his mother. He was the eldest of a family of nine, as follows:

	BORN	DIED	AGE
ROBERT:	September 3, 1786	May 14, 1857	71
FRANCIS WALLACE:	August 18, 1789	July 9, 1803	14
WILLIAM NICOL:	April 9, 1791	February 21, 1872	81
ELIZABETH RIDDELL:	November 21, 1792	September, 1795	3
JAMES GLENCAIRN:	August 21, 1794	November 18, 1865	71
MAXWELL:	July 26, 1796	April 24, 1799	3

JEAN, a twin with her brother ROBERT, was born on September 3, 1786. She died at the age of fourteen months. Twin daughters, born on March 3, 1788, died soon after birth. MAXWELL, the fifth and youngest son, named after Dr. Maxwell, the physician who attended the Poet in his last illness, was born the day of his father's funeral.

ROBERT II: the Poet's eldest son, on leaving the Grammar School of Dumfries, proceeded to the University of Edinburgh, where he spent two sessions and one at Glasgow University. Appointed, in 1804, to a clerkship in the Stamp Office, London. In 1833 he got his superannuation allowance of £120 or £150 a year, when he visited his mother at Dumfries, whom he had not seen

ROBERT BURNS,
THE ELDEST SON OF THE POET

COL. WILLIAM NICOL BURNS,
THIRD SON OF THE POET

LIEUT.-COL. JAMES GLENCAIRN
BURNS, FOURTH SON OF THE
POET

ANNIE BURNS BURNS,
DAUGHTER OF JAMES GLEN-
CAIRN BURNS (Second Marriage)

GEORGE IAN BURNS GOWRING, only son of VIOLET BURNS GOWRING

MABEL BURNAND HUTCHINSON, wife of ROBERT BURNS HUTCHINSON, 1937

ROBERT BURNS HUTCHINSON and his youngest daughter, JEAN, 1938

ROBERT BURNS HUTCHINSON and his youngest son, BEVERLEY, 1937

ROBERT BURNS HUTCHINSON, great-grandson of BURNS, in his home in Vancouver, British Columbia for twenty-six years. At Dumfries he fixed his residence. He was about ten years old when his father died, he remembered him, but not so as to describe his personal aspects. Into the hands of his son the Bard placed the works of the English poets, and encouraged him to read them, which he did. He did not know that his father was a poet until the neighbours, after his decease, spoke of him as such to his mother. In form of head and facial lineaments Robert strongly resembled his father. With a vigorous intellect, improved by intensive and varied reading, he possessed a memory singularly retentive. In London and Dumfries he added to his finances by giving private lessons in mathematics and in the classics. He excelled in conversation. He died on May 14, 1857, at the age of seventy-one, surviving his wife by about twenty-two years, his remains were conveyed to the vault of his father's mausoleum. He married at London, on March 24, 1809, Anne Sherwood, by whom he had a daughter Eliza, who married on September 27, 1836, Bartholmew James Everitt, assistant-surgeon in the East India Company's service, who died in London on April 20, 1840. The only child of Mr. and Mrs. Everitt was Martha Burns Everitt, who married John Thomas of Martinstown, County Wexford. They had no issue and Mrs. Thomas died in 1909.

ROBERT BURNS II also had a son named Robert and a daughter named Jean Armour. They were brought up in the family in open acknowledgment of their relationship. In every sense of the word but the most technical they were the children of a legitimate Scottish marriage, and legitimacy in its technical sense could have been obtained at any moment by an action of declarator in the Court of Sessions.

JEAN ARMOUR BURNS, the daughter of Robert Burns II, married and had a daughter, Jean Armour Burns Brown.

ROBERT III, the eldest son of Robert II, married Mary Campbell, and taught a private school in Dumfries for over thirty years, until the new School Board obliged him to give it up. He died in 1879 in that town. His eldest son,

ROBERT IV, the last of the dynasty, was born in Dumfries and educated in his father's school. He enlisted in the Household Brigade of the Scots Fusilier Guards, and quartered with his regiment in London for seven years, in Dublin for thirteen months, at Shorncliffe and elsewhere. Three times he volunteered for active service but without success. On leaving the army he eventually obtained the keepership of the city of Edinburgh Gunpowder Magazine at Blackhall on the Queensferry Road. He married Jane Palmer, the daughter of a farmer of Mouswald, near Dumfries.

WILLIAM NICOL: third son of the Poet, was born at Ellisland on April 9, 1791; he was named after his father's friend, William Nicol of Edinburgh. On leaving Dumfries Academy in his sixteenth year, sailed as a midshipman to India, soon afterwards he obtained an Indian cadetship. Proceeding to the Madras Presidency, he there served as an officer of the 7th Native Infantry for thirty-three years. He ultimately commanded his regiment. In 1843 he retired from the army and returning to Britain settled at Cheltenham, with his brother, James Glencairn, then Major Burns. In 1855 he became colonel by brevet. He died at Cheltenham on February 21, 1872, aged 81. His remains were deposited in the vault of the Poet's mausoleum. He married in 1822 Catherine Adelaide Crone, daughter of Richard Crone, of Summer Hill, Dublin, who died without issue, at Killudghee, in India, on June 29, 1841. He enjoyed a substantial pension of £1,000 or £1,100 a year. He resembled the Poet a good deal, and he also seems to have written verses.

JAMES GLENCAIRN: the fourth son of the Poet, named after his father's noble friend, the Earl of Glencairn, was born at Dumfries on August 12, 1794. Was a scholar at Christ's Hospital, London, as well as the Dumfries Grammar School. Obtaining a cadetship, he sailed for India in June, 1811. Arriving in Calcutta, he there joined the 15th Regiment of Bengal Native Infantry. In 1817 he was appointed by the Marquis of Hastings, Governor-General, to an important post in the Commissariat. As Captain Burns, he visited Britain in 1831, returning to India in 1833, when he received from Lord Metcalfe the important office of Judge and Collector of Cachar. In 1839 he finally returned to Britain with the rank of Majór. He resided for several years near London. He acted as Government Commissioner in an inquiry into the conditions of the operatives in paper mills, on which he presented a valuable report. His brother, Lieutenant-Colonel William Nicol Burns, having retired from active service in 1843, he arranged to reside with him in Cheltenham. In 1844 the brothers were celebrated by a festive "Welcome" on the banks of the Doon. James Glencairn Burns obtained the brevet rank of Lieutenant-Colonel in 1855. He died at Cheltenham on November 18, 1865, and his remains interred in the vault of the Poet's mausoleum. Colonel James was an accomplished Oriental scholar; he was occasionally chosen examiner in Hindustanee in Cheltenham College. Possessed of dramatic power, he took part in private theatricals. Abundantly facetious and good-humoured.

COLONEL JAMES GLENCAIRN BURNS married first, in April, 1818, SARAH ROBINSON, daughter of James Robinson, who in 1820 became Postmaster of Sunderland, County Durham, England. Sarah died at Neemuch, in India, on November 7, 1821, at the age of twenty-four. Of their marriage was born a son, Robert Shaw, who died in India, on December 11, 1821, aged eighteen months; also two daughters, of whom one, Jean Elizabeth, died at sea, June 5, 1823, in her fifth year.

SARAH BURNS, the surviving daughter, born November 2, 1821, was married on July 24, 1847, at St. Mary's Church, Cheltenham, England, to Dr. Berkeley Westropp Hutchinson, a native of Balinastoe, Galway, Ireland. Dr. and Mrs. Hutchinson lived in England until 1852, when they proceeded to Australia with their three children: ARABELLA ANN BURNS HUTCHINSON, born May 30, 1848, at Cheltenham; ARTHUR VINCENT BURNS HUTCHINSON, born June 6, 1849, at Cambridge; and ROBERT BURNS HUTCHINSON, born March 8, 1851, at Cambridge. These three children died on board ship on the way to Australia and were buried at sea. To Dr. and Mrs. Hutchinson a son, BERKELEY BURNS HUTCHINSON, was born at Warrnambool, Australia, June 22, 1853, and died nine months after birth. A daughter, ANNIE BURNS VINCENT HUTCHINSON, was born at Warrnambool on July 15, 1854.   On November 10, 1855, another son, ROBERT BURNS HUTCHINSON, was born at Cheltenham, while his mother was on a visit to her father, Colonel James Glencairn Burns, in England.   Mrs. Hutchinson returned to Australia with her son Robert in 1857.   Three other children were afterwards born in Australia: VIOLET BURNS HUTCHINSON, MARGARET CONSTANCE BURNS HUTCHINSON, and MARION BURNS HUTCHINSON.   Marion was born March 4, 1862, at Mossgiel, near Albury, New South Wales, and died ten days after birth.   Dr. Berkeley Westropp Hutchinson died near Melbourne, Australia, February 28, 1889, aged 74 years, and Mrs. Hutchinson, the Poet's grand-daughter, died at Cheltenham, England, in 1908, aged 87 years.

Colonel James Glencairn Burns, married secondly in June, 1828, MARY BECKETT, daughter of Captain Beckett of Enfield; she died at Gravesend, November 13, 1844, aged fifty-two years.   Her only child, ANNIE BURNS BURNS, born September 7, 1830, died at Cheltenham May 20, 1925, unmarried.

ROBERT BURNS HUTCHINSON, only surviving son of Sarah Elizabeth Maitland Tombs Hutchinson and Dr. Berkeley Westropp Hutchinson, in 1891 married MABEL BURNAND, who was born in 1870; of their marriage were born: three sons— ROBERT BURNS HUTCHINSON in 1892; HUGH BURNAND WESTROPP BURNS HUTCHIN- SON in 1899; BERKELEY WESTROPP BURNS HUTCHINSON, September 12, 1908; and three daughters—DOROTHEA BURNS HUTCHINSON, in 1893; ROBINA BURNS HUTCHINSON, in 1897; and JEAN BURNS HUTCHINSON, January 3, 1903.   Their eldest son, Robert, died in infancy.   Dorothea married, in 1916, CLARENCE SABOURIN, who was born in 1893, and they have three sons and one daughter: MARY, born January 15, 1920; ROBERT, born September 6, 1922; and JOHN, born May 6, 1930; and BERKELEY, born April 2, 1934.   Their eldest son, Robert, is training as an airman at Halton R.A.F. Camp, England.   Robina married, in 1920, GEORGE DENNIS, and they have two sons: ROBERT, born December 12, 1922; and PHILIPP, born November, 1926.   Hugh married in 1926 KATHLEEN MORTIMER and they have three daughters: NADINA OLIVE, born October 23, 1928; DOROTHY JEAN, born April 16, 1934; and MAUREEN ANNE, born September 4, 1935.

ROBERT BURNS HUTCHINSON was educated at the Blue Coat School, Christ's Hospital, England, until fifteen years old, then went to Cheltenham College as a day boy.   He went to India as a tea-planter, but after some years returned to England.   Later he proceeded to the United States and worked in Chicago, until he had a very serious encounter with some roughs on his way home from work and was nearly killed.   He afterwards undertook farming in Milner, British Columbia, and eventually poor health compelled him to give it up.   In 1923 he went to Fiji in the South Sea Islands and engaged in the hardwood lumber business for a time. It did not prove profitable, and he returned to Canada.   Eventually he retired and took up residence in Vancouver.   His youngest daughter, Jean, is secretary to an Automobile Club in Los Angeles, California, and his two sons, Hugh and Berkeley, are also in California, the latter with the Union Oil Company, Los Angeles, and the former with the Texas Oil Company in Long Beach.

ANNIE BURNS VINCENT HUTCHINSON, born at Warrnambool, Australia, July 15, 1854, married JAMES SCOTT of Brookside, Adelaide, South Australia. (His father was an English Naval Officer who went to Australia on his retirement, and bought Brookside.) Mr. and Mrs. Scott had no issue, both died in Australia, Mrs. Scott in 1935, aged 81 years.

VIOLET BURNS HUTCHINSON, born July 10, 1859, at Beechworth, Victoria, Australia, married GEORGE HOOD GOWRING, M.A., Hertford College, Oxford, eldest son of the Rev. George Gowring, vicar of White Lackington, Somerset. George Hood Gowring was a master at Berkhamsted Grammar School for some fourteen years, and in 1902 took a preparatory school at St. Bede's, Eastbourne, Sussex; he retired in 1934, to live at Godalming, Surrey, where he died January 31, 1936. Mr. and Mrs. Gowring's only child, GEORGE IAN BURNS GOWRING, born at Berkhamsted, December 27, 1900, married AILEEN MARY ELDER MCCORMICK on May 3, 1930, and they have one son, MICHAEL IAN GOWRING, born July 17, 1937. Mrs. Violet Burns Gowring, great-granddaughter of the Poet, lives at Godalming.

MARGARET CONSTANCE BURNS HUTCHINSON (commonly called Daisy) was born at Mossgiel on the Murray, New South Wales, September 5, 1860. In 1863 she went to England with her mother, Sarah Elizabeth Maitland Tombs Hutchinson, and her sister, Violet Burns Hutchinson, and her brother, Robert Burns Hutchinson. Margaret was educated at the Cheltenham Ladies' College, and lived in Cheltenham until her death, December 8, 1917, and was unmarried.

On a quiet street in Vancouver, not far from Stanley Park, in a house surrounded by trees, an elderly couple are placidly spending their days. The lady, bright and alert, is the niece of the late Sir Francis C. Burnand, late Editor of *Punch*; her husband, who is in his eighty-third year, is ROBERT BURNS HUTCHINSON, a brother of Violet Burns Gowring *nee* Hutchinson, and great-grandson of the Poet, Robert Burns.

In compiling the Descendants of Robert Burns and Jean Armour, the author received the kindest co-operation of his friend, MR. CHARLES STUART BURNESS, a kinsman of Burns, descended from THOMAS BURNESS (1728-1804), second cousin of the Poet's father.

After serving twenty-one years in the London Scottish, Mr. Burness in 1905 came to Canada and joined the 48th Highlanders of Toronto, the 15th Battalion overseas. He went overseas in October, 1914, with the First Canadian Contingent, was disabled in France, and was evacuated to England in October, 1915. He did duty in the Canadian Pay Office until July, 1919, and then returned to Toronto.

Mr. Burness, in 1924, was president of the Burns Literary Society of Toronto.

IV

The Life of Robert Burns

Written by the Poet Himself

To DR. JOHN MOORE (1729-1802) the Poet addressed a letter, after his first visit to Edinburgh, giving a history of his life, up to the period of his writing. In a composition never intended to see the light, elegance or perfect correctness of composition will not be expected. These, however, will be compensated by the opportunity of seeing the Poet, as he gives the incidents of his life, unfold the peculiarities of his character with all the careless vigour and open sincerity of his mind.

TO DR. JOHN MOORE

Sir,—   Mauchline, 22d August, 1787.

For some months past I have been rambling over the country; but I am now confined with some lingering complaints, originating, as I take it, in the stomach. To divert my spirits a little in this miserable fog of ennui, I have taken a whim to give you a history of myself. My name has made some little noise in this country; you have done me the honour of interesting yourself very warmly in my behalf; and I think a faithful account of what character of a man I am, and how I came by that character, may perhaps amuse you in an idle moment. I will give you an honest narrative; though I know it will be often at my own expense;—for I assure you, Sir, I have, like Solomon, whose character, excepting in the trifling affair of wisdom, I sometimes think I resemble,—I have, I say, like him, "turned my eyes to behold madness and folly," and, like him, too, frequently shaken hands

19

with their intoxicating friendship. . . . After you have perused these
pages, should you think them trifling and impertinent, I only beg leave to
tell you, that the poor author wrote them under some twitching qualms of
conscience, arising from a suspicion that he was doing what he ought not
to do; a predicament he has more than once been in before.

I have not the most distant pretensions to assume that character which
the pye-coated guardians of escutcheons call a gentleman. When at
Edinburgh last winter, I got acquainted in the Herald's Office; and, looking
through that granary of honours, I there found almost every name in the
kingdom: but for me,

> My ancient but ignoble blood
> Has crept through scoundrels ever since the flood.

Gules, purpure, argent, &c. quite disowned me.

My father was of the north of Scotland, the son of a farmer, and was
thrown by early misfortunes on the world at large; where, after many
years' wanderings and sojournings, he picked up a pretty large quantity of
observation and experience, to which I am indebted for most of my little
pretensions to wisdom.—I have met with few who understood "men,
their manners, and their ways," equal to him; but stubborn, ungainly
integrity, and headlong ungovernable irascibility, are disqualifying circumstances; consequently, I was born a very poor man's son. For the
first six or seven years of my life, my father was gardener to (Mr. Ferguson
of Doonholm,) a worthy gentleman of small estate in the neighbourhood of
Ayr. Had he continued in that station, I must have marched off to be one
of the little underlings about a farm-house; but it was his dearest wish and
prayer to have it in his power to keep his children under his own eye, till
they could discern between good and evil; so, with the assistance of his
generous master, my father ventured on a small farm on his estate. At
those years, I was by no means a favourite with any body. I was a good
deal noted for a retentive memory, a stubborn, sturdy something in my
disposition, and an enthusiastic idiot piety. I say idiot piety, because I
was then but a child. Though it cost the schoolmaster some thrashings,
I made an excellent English scholar; and by the time I was ten or eleven
years of age, I was a critic in substantives, verbs, and particles. In my
infant and boyish days, too, I owed much to an old woman (Jenny Wilson)
who resided in the family, remarkable for her ignorance, credulity, and
superstition. She had, I suppose, the largest collection in the country of
tales and songs concerning devils, ghosts, fairies, brownies, witches, warlocks, spunkies, kelpies, elf-candles, dead-lights, wraiths, apparitions,
cantraips, giants, enchanted towers, dragons, and other trumpery. This
cultivated the latent seeds of poetry; but had so strong an effect on my

imagination that to this hour, in my nocturnal rambles, I sometimes keep a sharp look-out in suspicious places: and though nobody can be more sceptical than I am in such matters, yet it often takes an effort of philosophy to shake off these idle terrors.   The earliest composition that I recollect taking pleasure in, was "The Vision of Mirza," and a hymn of Addison's, beginning, "How are thy servants blest, O Lord!"   I particularly remember one half-stanza, which was music to my boyish ear:

> For though on dreadful whirls we hung
> High on the broken wave.

I met with these pieces in Mason's *English Collection*, one of my school-books.   The two first books I ever read in private, and which gave me more pleasure than any two books I ever read since, were *The Life of Hannibal*, and *The History of Sir William Wallace*.   Hannibal gave my young ideas such a turn, that I used to strut in raptures up and down after the recruiting drum and bag-pipe, and wish myself tall enough to be a soldier; while the story of Wallace poured a Scottish prejudice into my veins, which will boil along there till the flood-gates of life shut in eternal rest.

Polemical divinity about this time was putting the country half-mad; and I, ambitious of shining in conversation parties on Sundays between sermons, at funerals, &c., used, a few years afterwards, to puzzle Calvinism with so much heat and indiscretion that I raised a hue and cry of heresy against me, which has not ceased to this hour.

My vicinity to Ayr was of some advantage to me.   My social disposition, when not checked by some modifications of spirited pride, was, like our catechism definition of infinitude,—without bounds or limits.   I formed several connexions with other younkers who possessed superior advantages, the youngling actors, who were busy in the rehearsal of parts in which they were shortly to appear on the stage of life, where, alas! I was destined to drudge behind the scenes.   It is not commonly at this green age that our young gentry have a just sense of the immense distance between them and their ragged play-fellows.   It takes a few dashes into the world, to give the young great man that proper, decent, unnoticing disregard for the poor, insignificant, stupid devils, the mechanics and peasantry around him, who were perhaps born in the same village.   My young superiors never insulted the clouterly appearance of my ploughboy carcass, the two extremes of which were often exposed to all the inclemencies of all the seasons.   They would give me stray volumes of books: among them, even then, I could pick up some observations; and one, whose heart I am sure not even the "Munny Begum" scenes have tainted, helped me to a little French.   Parting with these my young friends and benefactors as they occasionally went off for the East or West Indies, was often to me a sore affliction; but I was soon called to more serious evils. My father's generous master died; the farm proved a ruinous bargain; and, to clench the misfortune, we fell into the hands of a factor, who sat for the picture I have drawn of one in my Tale of "The Twa Dogs." My father was advanced in life when he married; I was the eldest of seven children; and he, worn out by early hardships, was unfit for labour. My father's spirit was soon irritated, but not easily broken. There was a freedom in his lease in two years more; and, to weather these two years, we retrenched our expenses. We lived very poorly: I was a dexterous ploughman, for my age; and the next eldest to me was a brother (Gilbert) who could drive the plough very well, and help me to thrash the corn. A novel-writer might perhaps have viewed these scenes with some satisfaction; but so did not I; my indignation yet boils at the recollection of the scoundrel factor's insolent threatening letters, which used to set us all in tears.

This kind of life—the cheerless gloom of a hermit, with the unceasing moil of a galley-slave, brought me to my sixteenth year; a little before which period I first committed the sin of Rhyme. You know our country custom of coupling a man and woman together as partners in the labours of harvest. In my fifteenth autumn my partner was a bewitching creature, a year younger than myself. My scarcity of English denies me the power of doing her justice in that language; but you know the Scottish idiom— she was a bonnie, sweet, sonsie lass. In short, she, altogether unwittingly to herself, initiated me in that delicious passion, which, in spite of acid disappointment, gin-horse prudence, and book-worm philosophy, I hold to be the first of human joys, our dearest blessing here below! How she caught the contagion I cannot tell: you medical people talk much of infection from breathing the same air, the touch, &c.; but I never expressly said I loved her. Indeed, I did not know myself why I liked so much to loiter behind with her, when returning in the evening from our labours; why the tones of her voice made my heart-strings thrill like an Æolian harp; and particularly why my pulse beat such a furious ratan, when I looked and fingered over her little hand to pick out the cruel nettle stings and thistles. Among her other love-inspiring qualities, she sung sweetly; and it was her favourite reel, to which I attempted giving an embodied vehicle in rhyme. I was not so presumptuous as to imagine that I could make verses like printed ones, composed by men who had Greek and Latin; but my girl (Nelly Kilpatrick) sung a song, which was said to be composed by a small country laird's son, on one of his father's maids, with whom he was in love; and I saw no reason why I might not rhyme as well as he; for, excepting that he could smear sheep, and cast peats, his father living in the moorlands, he had no more scholar-craft than myself.

Thus with me began love and poetry: which at times have been my only, and, till within the last twelve months, have been my highest enjoyment. My father struggled on till he reached the freedom in his lease, when he entered on (Lochlea, in Tarbolton parish,) a larger farm, about ten miles farther in the country. The nature of the bargain he made was such as to throw a little ready money into his hands at the commencement of his lease, otherwise the affair would have been impracticable. For four years we lived comfortably here; but a difference commencing between him and his landlord as to terms, after three years' tossing and whirling in the vortex of litigation, my father was just saved from the horrors of a jail by a consumption, which after two years' promises, kindly stepped in, and carried him away, to "where the wicked cease from troubling, and the weary are at rest."

It is during the time that we lived on this farm, that my little story is most eventful. I was, at the beginning of this period, perhaps the most ungainly, awkward boy in the parish—no solitaire was less acquainted with the ways of the world. What I knew of ancient story was gathered from Salmon's and Guthrie's geographical grammars; and the ideas I had formed of modern manners, of literature, and criticism, I got from the *Spectator*. These with Pope's Works, some plays of Shakespeare, Tull and Dickson on Agriculture, *The Pantheon*, Locke's *Essay on the Human Understanding*, Stackhouse's *History of the Bible*, Justice's *British Gardener's Directory*, Boyle's *Lectures*, Allan Ramsay's *Works*, Taylor's *Scripture Doctrine of Original Sin*, *A Select Collection of English Songs*, and Hervey's *Meditations*, had formed the whole of my reading. The collection of Songs was my *vade mecum*. I pored over them driving my cart, or walking to labour, song by song, verse by verse: carefully noting the true, tender, or sublime, from affectation and fustian. I am convinced I owe to this practice much of my critic craft, such as it is.

In my seventeenth year, to give my manners a brush, I went to a country dancing school.—My father had an unaccountable antipathy against these meetings; and my going was, what to this moment I repent, in opposition to his wishes. My father, as I said before, was subject to strong passions; from that instance of disobedience in me, he took a sort of dislike to me, which I believe was one cause of the dissipation which marked my succeeding years. I say dissipation, comparatively with the strictness, and sobriety, and regularity of Presbyterian country life; for though the Will o' Wisp meteors of thoughtless whim were almost the sole lights of my path, yet early ingrained piety and virtue kept me for several years afterwards within the line of innocence. The great misfortune of my life was to want an aim. I had felt early some stirrings of ambition, but they were the blind gropings of Homer's Cyclops round the walls of his cave.

I saw my father's situation entailed on me perpetual labour. The only two openings, by which I could enter the temple of Fortune, was the gate of niggardly economy, or the path of little chicaning bargain-making. The first is so contracted an aperture, I never could squeeze myself unto it;—the last I always hated—there was contamination in the very entrance! Thus abandoned of aim or view in life, with a strong appetite for sociability, as well from native hilarity as from a pride of observation and remark; a constitutional melancholy or hypochondriasm that made me fly solitude; add to these incentives to social life, my reputation for bookish knowledge, a certain wild logical talent, and a strength of thought, something like the rudiments of good sense; and it will not seem surprising that I was generally a welcome guest where I visited, or any great wonder that always, where two or three met together, there was I among them. But far beyond all other impulses of my heart, was *un penchant à l'adorable moitié du genre humain*. My heart was completely tinder, and was eternally lighted up by some goddess or other; and, as in every other warfare in this world, my fortune was various; sometimes I was received with favour, and sometimes I was mortified with a repulse. At the plough, scythe, or reap-hook, I feared no competitor, and thus I set absolute want at defiance; and as I never cared farther for my labours than while I was in actual exercise, I spent the evenings in the way after my own heart. A country lad seldom carries on a love adventure without an assisting confidant. I possessed a curiosity, zeal, and intrepid dexterity, that recommended me as a proper second on these occasions; and, I dare say, I felt as much pleasure in being in the secret of half the loves of the parish of Tarbolton, as ever did statesman in knowing the intrigues of half the courts of Europe.—The very goose feather in my hand seems to know instinctively the well-worn path of my imagination, the favourite theme of my song; and is with difficulty restrained from giving you a couple of paragraphs on the love adventures of my compeers, the humble inmates of the farm house and cottage; but the grave sons of science, ambition, or avarice, baptize these things by the name of Follies. To the sons and daughters of labour and poverty, they are matters of the most serious nature; to them, the ardent hope, the stolen interview, the tender farewell, are the greatest and most delicious parts of their enjoyments.

Another circumstance in my life which made some alteration in my mind and manners, was that I spent my nineteenth summer on a smuggling coast, a good distance from home, at a noted school to learn mensuration, surveying, dialling, &c., in which I made a pretty good progress. But I made a greater progress in the knowledge of mankind. The contraband trade was at that time very successful, and it sometimes happened to me to fall in with those who carried it on. Scenes of swaggering riot, and roaring dissipation were till this time new to me; but I was no enemy to social life. Here, though I learnt to fill my glass, and to mix without fear in a drunken squabble, yet I went on with a high hand with my geometry, till the sun entered Virgo, a month which is always a carnival in my bosom, when a charming filette, who lived next door to the school, overset my trigonometry, and set me off at a tangent from the sphere of my studies. I however, struggled on with my sines and co-sines for a few days more; but, stepping into the garden one charming noon to take the sun's altitude, there I met my angel,

> Like Proserpine gathering flowers,
> Herself a fairer flower.

It was in vain to think of doing any more good at school. The remaining week I staid, I did nothing but craze the faculties of my soul about her, or steal out to meet her; and the two last nights of my stay in the country, had sleep been a mortal sin, the image of this modest and innocent girl had kept me guiltless.

I returned home very considerably improved. My reading was enlarged with the very important addition of Thomson's and Shenstone's Works; I had seen human nature in a new phasis; and I engaged several of my school-fellows to keep up a literary correspondence with me. This improved me in composition. I had met with a collection of letters by the wits of Queen Anne's reign, and I pored over them most devoutly: I kept copies of any of my own letters that pleased me; and a comparison between them and the composition of most of my correspondents flattered my vanity. I carried this whim so far, that, though I had not three farthings' worth of business in the world, yet almost every post brought me as many letters as if I had been a broad plodding son of day-book and ledger.

My life flowed on much in the same course till my twenty-third year. *Vive l'amour, et vive la bagatelle*, were my sole principles of action. The addition of two more authors to my library gave me great pleasure; Sterne and Mackenzie—*Tristram Shandy*, and *The Man of Feeling*—were my bosom favourites. Poesy was still a darling walk for my mind; but it was only indulged in according to the humour of the hour. I had usually half a dozen or more pieces on hand; I took up one or other as it suited the momentary tone of the mind, and dismissed the work as it bordered on fatigue. My passions, when once lighted up, raged like so many devils, till they got vent in rhyme; and then the conning over my verses, like a spell, soothed all into quiet! None of the rhymes of those days are in print, except "Winter, a Dirge," the eldest of my printed pieces, "The Death of Poor Mailie," "John Barleycorn," and songs first, second, and third! Song second was the ebulliton of that passion which ended the forementioned school business.

My twenty-third year was to me an important era. Partly through whim, and partly that I wished to set about doing something in life, I joined a flax-dresser in a neighbouring town (Irvine) to learn his trade. This was an unlucky affair. My * * *; and to finish the whole, as we were giving a welcome carousal to the new year, the shop took fire, and burnt to ashes: and I was left like a true poet,—not worth a sixpence.

I was obliged to give up this scheme; the clouds of misfortune were gathering thick round my father's head; and, what was worst of all, he was visibly far gone in a consumption; and to crown my distresses, a belle fille whom I adored, and who had pledged her soul to meet me in the field of matrimony, jilted me, with peculiar circumstances of mortification. The finishing evil that brought up the rear of this infernal file, was my constitutional melancholy being increased to such a degree, that for three months I was in a state of mind scarcely to be envied by the hopeless wretches who have got their mittimus—

Depart from me, ye accursed!

From this adventure, I learned something of a town life; but the principal thing which gave my mind a turn, was a friendship I formed with a young fellow, (Richard Brown) a very noble character, but a hapless son of misfortune. He was the son of a simple mechanic; but a great man in the neighbourhood, taking him under his patronage, gave him a genteel education, with a view of bettering his situation in life. The patron dying just as he was ready to launch out into the world, the poor fellow, in despair, went to sea; where, after a variety of good and ill fortune, a little before I was acquainted with him, he had been set on shore by an American privateer, on the wild coast of Connaught, stripped of everything. I cannot quit this poor fellow's story without adding, that he is at this time master of a large West-Indiaman belonging to the Thames.

His mind was fraught with independence, magnanimity, and every manly virtue. I loved and admired him to a degree of enthusiasm, and of course strove to imitate him. In some measure I succeeded; I had pride before, but he taught it to flow in proper channels. His knowledge of the world was vastly superior to mine, and I was all attention to learn. He was the only man I ever saw who was a greater fool than myself where woman was the presiding star; but he spoke of illicit love with the levity of a sailor, which hitherto I had regarded with horror. Here his friendship did me a mischief; and the consequence was that, soon after I resumed the plough, I wrote the "Poet's Welcome." My reading only increased, while in this town, by two stray volumes of *Pamela*, and one of *Ferdinand Count Fathom*, which gave me some idea of novels. Rhyme, except some religious pieces that are in print, I had given up; but meeting with *Fergus-*

son's Scottish Poems, I strung anew my wildly-sounding lyre with emulating vigour. When my father died, his all went among the hell-hounds that prowl in the kennel of justice; but we made a shift to collect a little money in the family amongst us, with which, to keep us together, my brother and I took (Mossgiel) a neighbouring farm. My brother wanted my hair-branded imagination, as well as my social and amorous madness; but, in good sense, and every sober qualification, he was far my superior.

I entered on this farm with a full resolution, "Come, go to, I will be wise!" I read farming books; I calculated crops; I attended markets; and, in short, in spite of "the devil, and the world, and the flesh," I believe I should have been a wise man; but the first year, from unfortunately buying bad seed, the second, from the late harvest, we lost half our crops. This overset all my wisdom, and I returned, "like the dog to his vomit, and the sow that was washed to her wallowing in the mire."

I now began to be known in the neighbourhood as a maker of rhymes. The first of my poetic offspring that saw the light, was a burlesque lamentation on a quarrel between two reverend Calvinists, both of them dramatis personae in my "Holy Fair." I had a notion myself, that the piece had some merit; but, to prevent the worst, I gave a copy of it to a friend who was very fond of such things, and told him that I could not guess who was the author of it, but that I thought it pretty clever. With a certain description of the clergy, as well as laity, it met with a roar of applause. "Holy Willie's Prayer" next made its appearance, and alarmed the kirk-session so much, that they held several meetings to look over their spiritual artillery, if haply any of it might be pointed against profane rhymers. Unluckily for me, my wanderings led me on another side, within point-blank shot of their heaviest metal. This is the unfortunate story that gave rise to the printed poem, "The Lament." This was a most melancholy affair, which I cannot yet bear to reflect on, and had very nearly given me one or two of the principal qualifications for a place among those who have lost the chart, and mistaken the reckoning of rationality. I gave up my part of the farm to my brother; in truth, it was only nominally mine; and made what little preparation was in my power for Jamaica. But, before leaving my native country for ever, I resolved to publish my poems. I weighed my productions as impartially as was in my power: I thought they had merit; and it was a delicious idea that I should be called a clever fellow, even though it should never reach my ears—a poor negro driver;—or perhaps a victim to that inhospitable clime, and gone to the world of spirits! I can truly say, that *pauvre inconnu* as I then was, I had pretty nearly as high an idea of myself and of my works as I have at this moment, when the public has decided in their favour. It ever was my opinion, that the mistakes and blunders, both in a rational and religious point of view, of which we see thousands daily guilty, are owing to their ignorance of themselves.—To know myself, had been all along my constant study. I weighed myself alone; I balanced myself with others; I watched every means of information, to see how much ground I occupied as a man and as a poet; I studied assiduously nature's design in my formation—where the lights and shades in my character were intended. I was pretty confident my poems would meet with some applause; but, at the worst, the roar of the Atlantic would deafen the voice of censure, and the novelty of West-Indian scenes make me forget neglect. I threw off six hundred copies, of which I had got subscriptions for about three hundred and fifty.— My vanity was highly gratified by the reception I met with from the public; and, besides, I pocketed, all expenses deducted, nearly twenty pounds. This sum came very seasonably, as I was thinking of indenting myself, for want of money to procure my passage. As soon as I was master of nine guineas, the price of wafting me to the torrid zone, I took a steerage-passage in the first ship that was to sail from the Clyde; for

> Hungry ruin had me in the wind.

I had been for some days skulking from covert to covert, under all the terrors of a jail; as some ill-advised people had uncoupled the merciless pack of the law at my heels. I had taken the last farewell of my few friends; my chest was on the road to Greenock; I had composed the last song I should ever measure in Caledonia, "The gloomy night is gathering fast," when a letter from Dr. Blacklock to a friend of mine, overthrew all my schemes, by opening new prospects to my poetic ambition. The Dr. belonged to a set of critics, for whose applause I had not dared to hope. His opinion, that I would meet with encouragement in Edinburgh for a second edition, fired me so much, that away I posted for that city, without a single acquaintance, or a single letter of introduction. The baneful star which had so long shed its blasting influence in my zenith, for once made a revolution to the nadir; and a kind Providence placed me under the patronage of one of the noblest of men, the Earl of Glencairn. *Oublie moi, Grand Dieu, si jamais je l'oublie!*

I need relate no farther. At Edinburgh I was in a new world; I mingled among many classes of men, but all of them new to me, and I was all attention to catch the characters and manners "living as they rise." Whether I have profited, time will show.

*   *   *   *   *

My most respectful compliments to Miss Williams. Her very elegant and friendly letter I cannot answer at present, as my presence is requisite in Edinburgh, and I set out to-morrow.

V

The Life of Robert Burns

Written by the Poet's Brother, Gilbert

AT THE TIME of Burns' death, his brother Gilbert was unaware that the Poet had written the foregoing narrative of his life while in Ayrshire; and having been appealed to by Mrs. Dunlop for some memoirs of his brother, he complied with her request in a letter, from which the following narrative is chiefly extracted. When Gilbert Burns afterward saw the letter of his brother Robert to Dr. John Moore, he made some annotations upon it, which shall be noticed as we proceed.

Robert Burns was born on January 25, 1759, in a small house about two miles from the town of Ayr, and within a few hundred yards of Alloway Church, which his poem of "Tam o' Shanter" has rendered immortal. The name, which the Poet and his brother modernized into Burns, was originally Burnes, or Burness. Their father, William Burnes, was the son of a farmer in Kincardineshire, and had received the education common in Scotland to persons in his condition of life; he could read and write, and had some knowledge of arithmetic. His family having fallen into reduced circumstances, he was compelled to leave his home in his nineteenth year, and turned his steps toward the south in quest of a livelihood. The same necessity attended his elder brother, Robert.

I have often heard my father, says Gilbert Burns, in his letter to Mrs. Dunlop, describe the anguish of mind he felt when they parted on the top of a hill on the confines of their native place, each going off his several way in search of new adventures, and scarcely knowing whither he went. My father undertook to act as a gardener, and shaped his course to Edinburgh, where he wrought hard when he could get work, passing through a variety of difficulties. Still, however, he endeavoured to spare something for the support of his aged parents: and I recollect hearing him mention his having sent a bank-note for this purpose, when money of that kind was so scarce in Kincardineshire, that they scarcely knew how to employ it when it arrived.

From Edinburgh, William Burnes passed westward into the County of Ayr, where he engaged himself as a gardener to the laird of Fairly, with whom he lived two years; then changing his service for that of Crawford of Doonside. At length, being desirous of settling in life, he took a perpetual lease of seven acres of land from Dr. Campbell, physician in Ayr, with the view to commencing nurseryman and public gardener; and, having built a house upon it with his own hands, married, in December, 1757, Agnes Brown, the mother of our Poet, who still survived. The first fruit of this marriage was Robert, the subject of these memoirs, born on January 25, 1759, as has already been mentioned. Before William Burnes had made such progress in preparing his nursery, he was withdrawn from that undertaking by Mr. Ferguson, who purchased the estate of Doonholm, in the immediate neighbourhood, and engaged him as his gardener and overseer; and this was his situation when our Poet was born. Though in the service of Mr. Ferguson, he lived in his own house, his wife managing her family and her little dairy, which consisted sometimes of two, sometimes of three milch cows; and this state of unambitious content continued till the year 1766. His son Robert was sent by him, in his sixth year, to a school at Alloway-Mill, about a mile distant, taught by a person of the name of Campbell; but this teacher being in a few months appointed master of the workhouse at Ayr, William Burnes, in conjunction with some other heads of families, engaged John Murdoch in his stead. The education of our Poet, and of his brother Gilbert, was in common; and of their proficiency under Mr. Murdoch we have the following account:

With him we learnt to read English tolerably well, and to write a little. He taught us, too, the English grammar. I was too young to profit

THE BIRTHPLACE OF BURNS

Born in a cottage thatched with straw,
He mingled with poor, an' rich an' braw,
He is a credit tae us a',
The rantin', rovin', Robin.

—*Thomas A. Gillen (1869-   )*

THE ROOM IN WHICH BURNS WAS BORN

AGNES BROWN,
THE MOTHER OF BURNS

GILBERT BURNS,
BROTHER OF THE POET

ISABELLA BURNS (MRS. BEGG),
THE POET'S YOUNGEST SISTER

VIOLET BURNS GOWRING,
GREAT-GRANDDAUGHTER OF
BURNS

much from his lessons in grammar; but Robert made some proficiency in it—a circumstance of considerable weight in the unfolding of his genius and character; as he soon became remarkable for the fluency and correctness of his expression, and read the few books that came in his way with much pleasure and improvement; for even then he was a reader when he could get a book.   Murdoch, whose library at that time had no great variety in it, lent him *The Life of Hannibal*, which was the first book he read (the school-books excepted,) and almost the only one he had an opportunity of reading while he was at school: for *The Life of Wallace*, which he classes with it in one of his letters to you, he did not see for some years afterwards, when he borrowed it from the blacksmith who shod our horses.

It appears that William Burnes approved himself greatly in the service of Mr. Ferguson, by his intelligence, industry and integrity. In consequence of this, with a view to promoting his interest, Mr. Ferguson leased him a farm, of which we have the following account:

The farm was upwards of seventy acres, (between eighty and ninety English statute measure,) the rent of which was to be forty pounds annually for the first six years, and afterwards forty-five pounds. My father endeavoured to sell his lease-hold property, for the purpose of stocking this farm, but at that time was unable, and Mr. Ferguson lent him a hundred pounds for that purpose.   He removed to his new situation at Whitsuntide, 1766.   It was, I think, not above two years after this, that Murdoch, our tutor and friend, left this part of the country; and there being no school near us, and our little services being useful on the farm, my father undertook to teach us arithmetic in the winter evenings, by candlelight; and in this way my two eldest sisters got all the education they received.   I remember a circumstance that happened at this time, which, though trifling in itself, is fresh in my memory, and may serve to illustrate the early character of my brother.   Murdoch came to spend a night with us, and to take his leave when he was about to go into Carrick.   He brought us, as a present and memorial of him, a small compendium of English Grammar, and the tragedy of *Titus Andronicus*, and, by way of passing the evening, he began to read the play aloud.   We were all attention for sometime, till presently the whole party was dissolved in tears.   A female in the play (I have but a confused remembrance of it) had her hands chopt off, and her tongue cut out, and then was insultingly desired to call for water to wash her hands.   At this, in an agony of distress, we with one voice desired he would read no more.   My father observed, that if we would not hear it out, it would be needless to leave the play with us.

R.B.—4

Robert replied, that if it was left he would burn it. My father was going to chide him for this ungrateful return to his tutor's kindness; but Murdoch interfered, declaring that he liked to see so much sensibility; and he left *The School for Love*, a comedy, (translated I think from the French,) in its place.

Nothing could be more retired than our general manner of living at Mount Oliphant; we rarely saw anybody but the members of our own family. There were no boys of our own age, or near it, in the neighbourhood. Indeed, the greatest part of the land in the vicinity was at that time possessed by shopkeepers, and people of that stamp, who had retired from business, or who kept their farm in the country, at the same time that they followed business in town. My father was for sometime almost the only companion we had. He conversed familiarly on all subjects with us, as if we had been men; and was at great pains, while we accompanied him in the labours of the farm, to lead the conversation to such subjects as might tend to increase our knowledge, or confirm us in virtuous habits. He borrowed Salmon's *Geographical Grammar* for us, and endeavoured to make us acquainted with the situation and history of the different countries in the world; while, from a book-society in Ayr, he procured for us the reading of Derham's *Physico- and Astro-Theology*, and Ray's *Wisdom of God in the Creation*, to give us some idea of Astronomy and Natural History. Robert read all these books with an avidity and industry scarcely to be equalled. My father had been a subscriber to Stackhouse's *History of the Bible*, then lately published by James Meuross, in Kilmarnock: from this Robert collected a competent knowledge of ancient history; for no book was so voluminous as to slacken his industry, or so antiquated as to damp his researches. A brother of my mother, who had lived with us for sometime, and had learnt some arithmetic by our winter evening's candle, went into a bookseller's shop in Ayr, to purchase *The Ready Reckoner, or Tradesman's Sure Guide*, and a book to teach him to write letters. Luckily, in place of *The Complete Letter-Writer*, he got by mistake a small collection of letters by the most eminent writers, with a few sensible directions for attaining an easy epistolary style. This book was to Robert of the greatest consequence. It inspired him with a strong desire to excel in letter-writing, while it furnished him with models by some of the first writers in our language.

My brother was about thirteen or fourteen, when my father, regretting that we wrote so ill, sent us, week about, during a summer quarter, to the parish school of Dalrymple, which, though between two and three miles distant, was the nearest to us, that we might have an opportunity of remedying this defect. About this time a bookish acquaintance of my father's procured us a reading of two volumes of Richardson's *Pamela*,

which was the first novel we read, and the only part of Richardson's works
my brother was acquainted with till towards the period of his commencing
author. Till that time, too, he remained unacquainted with Fielding,
with Smollett, (two volumes of *Ferdinand Count Fathom*, and two volumes
of *Peregrine Pickle* excepted,) with Hume, with Robertson, and almost
all our authors of eminence of the later times. I recollect, indeed, my
father borrowed a volume of English history from Mr. Hamilton of Bour-
treehill's gardener. It treated of the reign of James I., and his unfortunate
son, Charles, but I do not know who was the author; all that I remember
of it is something of Charles' conversation with his children. About this
time, Murdoch, our former teacher, after having been in different places
in the country; and having taught a school sometime in Dumfries, came
to be the established teacher of the English language in Ayr, a circumstance
of considerable consequence to us. The remembrance of my father's
former friendship, and his attachment to my brother, made him do every
thing in his power for our improvement. He sent us Pope's works, and some
other poetry, the first that we had an opportunity of reading, excepting
what is contained in *The English Collection*, and in the volume of the
Edinburgh Magazine for 1772; excepting also those "excellent new songs"
that are hawked about the country in baskets, or exposed on stalls in
the streets.

The summer after we had been at Dalrymple school, my father sent
Robert to Ayr, to revise his English grammar, with his former teacher.
He had been there only one week, when he was obliged to return, to assist
at the harvest. When the harvest was over, he went back to school, where
he remained two weeks; and this completes the account of his school
education, excepting one summer quarter, some time afterwards, that he
attended the parish school of Kirkoswald, (where he lived with a brother
of my mother's), to learn surveying.

During the two last weeks that he was with Murdoch, he himself was
engaged in learning French, and he communicated the instructions he
received to my brother, who, when he returned, brought home with him a
French dictionary and grammar, and the *Adventures of Telemachus* in the
original. In a little while, by the assistance of these books, he had acquired
such a knowledge of the language, as to read and understand any French
author in prose. This was considered as a sort of prodigy, and through
the medium of Murdoch, procured him the acquaintance of several lads
in Ayr, who were at that time gabbling French, and the notice of some
families, particularly that of Dr. Malcolm, where a knowledge of French
was a recommendation.

Observing the facility with which he had acquired the French language,
Mr. Robinson, the established writing-master in Ayr, and Mr. Murdoch's

particular friend, having himself acquired a considerable knowledge of the Latin language by his own industry, without ever having learnt it at school, advised Robert to make the same attempt, promising him every assistance in his power.   Agreeably to this advice, he purchased *The Rudiments of the Latin Tongue*, but finding this study dry and uninteresting, it was quickly laid aside.   He frequently returned to his *Rudiments* on any little chagrin or disappointment, particularly in his love affairs; but the Latin seldom predominated more than a day or two at a time, or a week at most.   Observing himself the ridicule that would attach to this sort of conduct if it were known, he made two or three humorous stanzas on the subject, which I cannot now recollect, but they all ended,—

> So I'll to my Latin again.

Thus you see Mr. Murdoch was a principal means of my brother's improvement.   Worthy man! though foreign to my present purpose, I cannot take leave of him without tracing his future history.   He continued for some years a respected and useful teacher at Ayr, till one evening that he had been overtaken in liquor, he happened to speak somewhat disrespectfully of Dr. Dalrymple, the parish minister, who had not paid him that attention to which he thought himself entitled.   In Ayr he might as well have spoken blasphemy.   He found it proper to give up his appointment.   He went to London, where he still lives, a private teacher of French. He has been a considerable time married, and keeps a shop of stationery wares.

The father of Dr. Paterson, now physician at Ayr, was, I believe, a native of Aberdeenshire, and was one of the established teachers in Ayr, when my father settled in the neighbourhood.   He early recognized my father as a fellow-native of the north of Scotland, and a certain degree of intimacy subsisted between them during Mr. Paterson's life.   After his death, his widow, who is a very genteel woman, and of great worth, delighted in doing what she thought her husband would have wished to have done, and assiduously kept up her attentions to all his acquaintance.   She kept alive the intimacy with our family, by frequently inviting my father and mother to her house on Sundays, when she met them at church.

When she came to know my brother's passion for books, she kindly offered us the use of her husband's library, and from her we got the *Spectator*, Pope's *Translation of Homer*, and several other books that were of use to us.   Mount Oliphant, the farm my father possessed in the parish of Ayr, is almost the very poorest soil I know of in a state of cultivation. A stronger proof of this I cannot give, than that, notwithstanding the extraordinary rise in the value of lands in Scotland, it was, after a considerable sum laid out in improving it by the proprietor, let a few years ago five pounds per annum lower than the rent paid for it by my father thirty years ago. My father, in consequence of this, soon came into difficulties, which were increased by the loss of several of his cattle by accidents and disease.—To the buffetings of misfortune, we could only oppose hard labour, and the most rigid economy. We lived very sparing. For several years butcher's meat was a stranger in the house, while all the members of the family exerted themselves to the utmost of their strength, and rather beyond it, in the labours of the farm. My brother, at the age of thirteen, assisted in thrashing the crop of corn, and at fifteen was the principal labourer on the farm, for we had no hired servant, male or female. The anguish of mind we felt at our tender years, under these straits and difficulties, was very great. To think of our father growing old (for he was now above fifty), broken down with the long continued fatigues of his life, with a wife and five children, and in a declining state of circumstances— these reflections produced in my brother's mind and mine sensations of the deepest distress. I doubt not but the hard labour and sorrow of this period of his life, was in a great measure the cause of that depression of spirits with which Robert was so often afflicted through his whole life afterwards. At this time he was almost constantly afflicted in the evenings with a dull headache, which at a future period of his life, was exchanged for a palpitation of the heart, and a threatening of fainting and suffocation in his bed in the night-time.

By a stipulation in my father's lease, he had a right to throw it up, if he thought proper, at the end of every sixth year. He attempted to fix himself in a better farm at the end of the first six years, but failing in that attempt, he continued where he was for six years more. He then took the farm of Lochlea, of a hundred and thirty acres, at the rent of twenty shillings an acre, in the parish of Tarbolton, of Mr. . . ., then a merchant in Ayr, and now (1797) a merchant in Liverpool. He removed to this farm at Whitsunday, 1777, and possessed it only seven years. No writing had ever been made out of the conditions of the lease; a misunderstanding took place respecting them; the subjects in dispute were submitted to arbitration, and the decision involved my father's affairs in ruin. He lived to know of this decision, but not to see any execution in consequence of it. He died on the 13th of February, 1784.

The seven years we lived in Tarbolton parish (extending from the seventeenth to the twenty-fourth of my brother's age), were not marked by much literary improvement; but, during this time, the foundation was laid of certain habits in my brother's character, which afterwards became but too prominent, and which malice and envy have taken delight to enlarge on. Though when young he was bashful and awkward in his intercourse with women, yet when he approached manhood, his attachment to their society became very strong, and he was constantly the victim of some fair enslaver. The symptoms of his passion were often such as nearly to equal those of the celebrated Sappho. I never indeed knew that he "fainted, sunk, and died away;" but the agitations of his mind and body exceeded any thing of the kind I ever knew in real life. He had always a particular jealousy of people who were richer than himself, or who had more consequence in life. His love, therefore, rarely settled on persons of this description. When he selected any one out of the sovereignty of his good pleasure, to whom he should pay his particular attention, she was instantly invested with a sufficient stock of charms, out of the plentiful stores of his own imagination; and there was often a great dissimilitude between his fair captivator, as she appeared to others, and as she seemed when invested with the attributes he gave her. One generally reigned paramount in his affections, but as Yorick's affections flowed out toward Madame de L—— at the remise door, while the eternal vows of Eliza were upon him, so Robert was frequently encountering other attractions, which formed so many under-plots in the drama of his love. As these connections were governed by the strictest rules of virtue and modesty (from which he never deviated till he reached his twenty-third year), he became anxious to be in a situation to marry. This was not likely to be soon the case while he remained a farmer, as the stocking of a farm required a sum of money he had no probability of being master of for a great while. He began, therefore, to think of trying some other line of life. He and I had for several years taken land of my father for the purpose of raising flax on our own account. In the course of selling it, Robert began to think of turning flax-dresser, both as being suitable to his grand view of settling in life, and as subservient to the flax raising. He accordingly wrought at the business of a flax-dresser in Irvine for six months, but abandoned it at that period, as neither agreeing with his health nor inclination. In Irvine he had contracted some acquaintance of a freer manner of thinking and living than he had been used to, whose society prepared him for overleaping the bounds of rigid virtue which had hitherto restrained him. Towards the end of the period under review (in his twenty-fourth year), and soon after his father's death, he was furnished with the subject of his Epistle to John Rankin. During this period also he became a freemason, which was his first introduction to the life of a boon companion. Yet, notwithstanding these circumstances, and the praise he has bestowed on Scotch drink (which seems to have misled his historians), I do not recollect, during these seven years, nor till towards the end of his commencing author (when his growing celebrity occasioned his being often in company), to have ever seen him intoxicated; nor was he at all given to drinking. A stronger proof of the general sobriety of his conduct need not be required than what I am about to give. During the whole of the time we lived in the farm of Lochlea with my father, he allowed my brother and me such wages for our labour as he gave to other labourers, as a part of which, every article of our clothing, manufactured in the family, was regularly accounted for. When my father's affairs drew near a crisis, Robert and I took the farm of Mossgiel, consisting of a hundred and eighteen acres, at the rent of ninety pounds per annum (the farm on which I live at present), from Mr. Gavin Hamilton, as an asylum for the family in case of the worst. It was stocked by the property and individual savings of the whole family, and was a joint concern among us. Every member of the family was allowed ordinary wages for the labour he performed on the farm. My brother's allowance and mine was seven pounds per annum each. And during the whole time this family-concern lasted, which was for four years, as well as during the preceding period at Lochlea, his expenses never in any one year exceeded his slender income. As I was intrusted with the keeping of the family accounts, it is not possible that there can be any fallacy in this statement in my brother's favour. His temperance and frugality were every thing that could be wished.

The farm of Mossgiel lies very high, and mostly on a cold, wet bottom. The first four years that we were on the farm were very frosty, and the spring was very late. Our crops in consequence were very unprofitable; and, notwithstanding our utmost diligence and economy, we found ourselves obliged to give up our bargain, with the loss of a considerable part of our original stock. It was during these four years that Robert formed his connection with Jean Armour, afterwards Mrs. Burns. This connection could no longer be concealed, about the time we came to a final determination to quit the farm. Robert durst not engage with his family in his poor unsettled state, but was anxious to shield his partner, by every means in his power, from the consequences of their imprudence. It was agreed therefore between them, that they should make a legal acknowledgment of an irregular and private marriage; that he should go to Jamaica to push his fortune; and that she should remain with her father till it might please Providence to put the means of supporting a family in his power.

Mrs. Burns was a great favourite of her father. The intimation of a marriage was the first suggestion he received of her real situation. He was in the greatest distress, and fainted away. The marriage did not appear to him to make the matter better. A husband in Jamaica appeared to him and his wife little better than none, and an effectual bar to any other prospects of a settlement in life that their daughter might have. They therefore expressed a wish to her, that the written papers which respected the marriage should be cancelled, and thus the marriage rendered void. In her melancholy state, she felt the deepest remorse at having brought such heavy affliction on parents that loved her so tenderly, and submitted to their entreaties. Their wish was mentioned to Robert. He felt the deepest anguish of mind. He offered to stay at home, and provide for his wife and family in the best manner that his daily labours could provide for them; that being the only means in his power. Even this offer they did not approve of; for humble as Miss Armour's station was, and great though her imprudence had been, she still, in the eyes of her partial parents, might look to a better connexion than that with my friendless and unhappy brother, at that time without loss or biding place. Robert at length consented to their wishes; but his feelings on this occasion were of the most distracting nature: and the impression of sorrow was not effaced, till by a regular marriage they were indissolubly united. In the state of mind which this separation produced, he wished to leave the country as soon as possible, and agreed with Dr. Douglas to go out to Jamaica, as an assistant overseer, or, as I believe it is called, a book-keeper, on his estate. As he had not sufficient money to pay his passage, and the vessel in which Dr. Douglas was to procure a passage for him was not expected to sail for some time, Mr. Hamilton advised him to publish his poems in the mean time by subscription, as a likely way of getting a little money, to provide him more liberally in necessaries for Jamaica. Agreeably to this advice, subscription-bills were printed immediately, and the printing was commenced at Kilmarnock, his preparations going on at the same time for his voyage. The reception, however, which his poems met with in the world, and the friends they procured him, made him change his resolution of going to Jamaica, and he was advised to go to Edinburgh to publish a second edition. On his return, in happier circumstances, he renewed his connexion with Mrs. Burns, and rendered it permanent by a union for life.

Thus, Madam, have I endeavoured to give you a simple narrative of the leading circumstances in my brother's early life. The remaining part he spent in Edinburgh, or in Dumfriesshire, and its incidents are as well known to you as to me. His genius having procured him your patronage and friendship this gave rise to the correspondence between you, in which, I believe, his sentiments were delivered with the most respectful, but most unreserved confidence, and which only terminated with the last days of his life.

VI

The Life of Robert Burns

Written by his only Schoolmaster, John Murdoch

O<small>F A FAMILY</small> so interesting as
that which inhabited the cottage of William Burnes, and particularly of the father of the family, the reader will perhaps be
willing to listen to some further account. What follows is given
by one already mentioned with so much honour in the narrative
of Gilbert Burns, Mr. John Murdoch, the preceptor of the Poet,
who in a letter to Joseph Cooper Walker, Esq., of Dublin, author
of the *Historical Memoirs of the Irish Bards*, and the *Historical
Memoirs of the Italian Tragedy*, thus expresses himself:

Sir,—

I was lately favoured with a letter from our worthy friend, the Rev.
Wm. Adair, in which he requested me to communicate to you whatever
particulars I could recollect concerning Robert Burns, the Ayrshire poet.
My business being at present multifarious and harassing, my attention is
consequently so much divided, and I am so little in the habit of expressing
my thoughts on paper, that at this distance of time I can give but a very
imperfect sketch of the early part of the life of that extraordinary genius,
with which alone I am acquainted.

William Burnes, the father of the poet, was born in the shire of Kincardine, and bred a gardener. He had been settled in Ayrshire ten or
twelve years before I knew him, and had been in the service of Mr. Crawford
of Doonside. He was afterwards employed as a gardener and overseer by

Provost Ferguson of Doonholm, in the parish of Alloway, which is now united with that of Ayr. In this parish, on the road side, a Scotch mile and a half from the town of Ayr, and half a mile from the bridge of Doon, William Burnes took a piece of land, consisting of about seven acres; part of which he laid out in garden ground, and part of which he kept to graze a cow, &c., still continuing in the employ of Provost Ferguson. Upon this little farm was erected an humble dwelling, of which William Burnes was the architect. It was, with the exception of a little straw, literally a tabernacle of clay. In this mean cottage, of which I myself was at times an inhabitant, I really believe there dwelt a larger portion of content than in any palace in Europe. The "Cotter's Saturday Night" will give some idea of the temper and manners that prevailed there.

In 1765, about the middle of March, Mr. Wm. Burnes came to Ayr, and sent to the school where I was improving in writing, under my good friend Mr. Robinson, desiring that I would come and speak to him at a certain inn, and bring my writing-book with me. This was immediately complied with. Having examined my writing, he was pleased with it—(you will readily allow he was not difficult,)—and told me that he had received very satisfactory information of Mr. Tennent, the master of the English school, concerning my improvement in English, and in his method of teaching. In the month of May following, I was engaged by Mr. Burnes, and four of his neighbours, to teach, and accordingly began to teach the little school at Alloway, which was situated a few yards from the argillaceous fabric above mentioned. My five employers undertook to board me by turns, and to make up a certain salary at the end of the year, provided my quarterly payments from the different pupils did not amount to that sum.

My pupil, Robert Burns, was then between six or seven years of age; his preceptor about eighteen. Robert, and his younger brother, Gilbert, had been grounded a little in English before they were put under my care. They both made a rapid progress in reading, and a tolerable progress in writing. In reading, dividing words into syllables by rule, spelling without book, parsing sentences, &c., Robert and Gilbert were generally at the upper end of the class, even when ranged with boys by far their seniors. The books most commonly used in the school were the *Spelling Book*, the *New Testament*, the *Bible*, Mason's *Collection of Prose and Verse*, and Fisher's *English Grammar*. They committed to memory the hymns, and other poems of that collection, with uncommon facility. This facility was partly owing to the method pursued by their father and me in instructing them, which was, to make them thoroughly acquainted with the meaning of every word in each sentence that was to be committed to memory. By the bye, this may be easier done, and at an earlier period than is generally thought. As soon as they were capable of it, I taught them to turn verse into its natural prose order; sometimes to substitute synonymous expressions for poetical words, and to supply the ellipses. These, you know, are the means of knowing that the pupil understands his author. These are excellent helps to the arrangement of words in sentences, as well as to a variety of expression.

Gilbert always appeared to me to possess a more lively imagination, and to be more of the wit than Robert. I attempted to teach them a little church music: here they were left far behind by all the rest of the school. Robert's ear, in particular, was remarkably dull, and his voice untuneable. It was long before I could get them to distinguish one tune from another. Robert's countenance was generally grave, and expressive of a serious, contemplative, and thoughtful mind. Gilbert's face said, "Mirth, with thee I mean to live"; and certainly, if any person who knew the two boys, had been asked which of them was the most likely to court the muses, he would surely never have guessed that Robert had a propensity of that kind.

In the year 1769, Mr. Burnes quitted his mud edifice, and took possession of a farm (Mount Oliphant) of his own improving, while in the service of Provost Ferguson. This farm being at a considerable distance from the school, the boys could not attend regularly; and some changes taking place among the other supporters of the school, I left it, having continued to conduct it for nearly two years and a half.

In the year 1772, I was appointed (being one of five candidates who were examined) to teach the English school at Ayr; and in 1773, Robert Burns came to board and lodge with me, for the purpose of revising the English grammar, &c., that he might be better qualified to instruct his brothers and sisters at home. He was now with me day and night, in school, at all meals, and in all my walks. At the end of one week, I told him, that, as he was now pretty much master of the parts of speech, &c., I should like to teach him something of French pronunciation; that when he should meet with the name of a French town, ship, officer, or the like, in the newspapers, he might be able to pronounce it something like a French word. Robert was glad to hear this proposal, and immediately we attacked the French with great courage.

Now there was little else to be heard but the declension of nouns, the conjugation of verbs, &c. When walking together, and even at meals, I was constantly telling him the names of different objects, as they presented themselves, in French, so that he was hourly laying in a stock of words and sometimes little phrases. In short, he took such pleasure in learning, and I in teaching, that it was difficult to say which of the two was most zealous in the business: and about the end of the second week of our study of the French, we began to read a little of the *Adventures of Telemachus*, in Fenelon's own words.

But now the plains of Mount Oliphant began to whiten, and Robert was summoned to relinquish the pleasing scenes that surrounded the grotto of Calypso; and, armed with a sickle, to seek glory by signalizing himself in the fields of Ceres—and so he did; for although but about fifteen, I was told that he performed the work of a man.

Thus was I deprived of my very apt pupil, and consequently agreeable companion, at the end of three weeks, one of which was spent entirely in the study of English, and the other two chiefly in that of French. I did not, however, lose sight of him; but was a frequent visitant at his father's house, when I had my half-holiday; and very often went, accompanied with one or two persons more intelligent than myself, that good William Burnes might enjoy a mental feast. Then the labouring oar was shifted to some other hand. The father and the son sat down with us, when we enjoyed a conversation, wherein solid reasoning, sensible remark, and a moderate seasoning of jocularity, were so nicely blended as to render it palatable to all parties. Robert had a hundred questions to ask me about the French, &c., and the father, who had always rational information in view, had still some question to propose to my more learned friends, upon moral or natural philosophy, or some such interesting subject. Mrs. Burnes, too, was of the party as much as possible;

> But still the house affairs would draw her thence,
> Which ever as she could with haste dispatch,
> She'd come again, and with a greedy ear,
> Devour up their discourse. . . .

and particularly that of her husband. At all times, and in all companies, she listened to him with a more marked attention than to any body else. When under the necessity of being absent, while he was speaking, she seemed to regret as a real loss, that she had missed what the good man had said. This worthy woman, Agnes Brown, had the most thorough esteem for her husband of any woman I ever knew. I can by no means wonder that she highly esteemed him: for I myself have always considered William Burnes as by far the best of the human race that ever I had the pleasure of being acquainted with—and many a worthy character I have known. I can cheerfully join with Robert in the last line of his epitaph (borrowed from Goldsmith),—

> And even his failings lean'd to virtue's side.

He was an excellent husband, if I may judge from his assiduous attention to the ease and comfort of his worthy partner, and from her affectionate

behaviour to him, as well as her unwearied attention to the duties of a
mother.

He was a tender and affectionate father; he took pleasure in leading his
children in the path of virtue; not in driving them as some parents do,
to the performance of duties to which they themselves are averse. He took
care to find fault but very seldom; and therefore, when he did rebuke, he
was listened to with a kind of reverential awe. A look of disapprobation
was felt; a reproof was severely so; and a stripe with the tawz, even on the
skirt of the coat, gave heart-felt pain, produced a loud lamentation, and
brought forth a flood of tears.

He had the art of gaining the esteem and good-will of those that were
labourers under him. I think I never saw him angry but twice, the one
time it was with the foreman of the band, for not reaping the field as he was
desired; and the other time, it was with an old man, for using smutty
inuendoes and double entendres. Were every foul mouthed old man to
receive a seasonable check in this way, it would be to the advantage of the
rising generation. As he was at no time overbearing to inferiors, he was
equally incapable of that passive, pitiful, paltry spirit, that induces some
people to keep booing and booing in the presence of a great man. He
always treated superiors with a becoming respect; but he never gave the
smallest encouragement to aristocratical arrogance. But I must not pre-
tend to give you a description of all the manly qualities, the rational and
Christian virtues, of the venerable William Burnes. Time would fail me.
I shall only add, that he carefully practised every known duty, and avoided
every thing that was criminal; or, in the apostle's words, "Herein did he
exercise himself in living a life void of offence towards God and towards
men." O for a world of men of such dispositions! We should then
have no wars. I have often wished, for the good of mankind, that it were
as customary to honour and perpetuate the memory of those who excel
in moral rectitude, as it is to extol what are called heroic actions: then
would the mausoleum of the friend of my youth overtop and surpass most
of the monuments I see in Westminster Abbey.

Although I cannot do justice to the character of this worthy man, yet you
will perceive, from these few particulars, what kind of person had the
principal hand in the education of our Poet. He spoke the English language with more propriety (both with respect to diction and pronunciation),
than any man I ever knew with no greater advantages. This had a very
good effect on the boys, who began to talk, and reason like men, much
sooner than their neighbours. I do not recollect any of their contemporaries, at my little seminary, who afterwards made any great figure, as
literary characters, except Dr. Tennant, who was chaplain to Colonel

Fullarton's regiment, and who is now in the East Indies.   He is a man of
genius and learning; yet affable, and free from pedantry.

Mr. Burnes, in a short time, found that he had over-rated Mount
Oliphant, and that he could not rear his numerous family upon it.   After
being there some years, he removed to Lochlea, in the parish of Tarbolton,
where, I believe, Robert wrote most of his poems.

But here, Sir, you will permit me to pause.   I can tell you but little
more relative to our Poet.   I shall, however, in my next, send you a copy of
one of his letters to me, about the year 1783.   I received one since, but it is
mislaid.   Please remember me, in the best manner, to my worthy friend
Mr. Adair, when you see him, or write to him.

Hart Street, Bloomsbury Square,
London, Feb. 22d, 1799.

As the narrative of Gilbert Burns was written at a time when he
was ignorant of the existence of the preceding narrative of his
brother, so this letter of Mr. Murdoch was written without his
having any knowledge that either of his pupils had been employed
on the same subject.   The three relations serve, therefore, not
merely to illustrate, but to authenticate each other.   Though the
information they convey might have been presented with a shorter
compass, by reducing the whole into one unbroken narrative, it is
scarcely to be doubted, that the reader will be far more gratified
by a sight of these original documents themselves.

VII

Death and Funeral of Robert Burns

Eᴀʀʟʏ ɪɴ ᴊᴀɴᴜᴀʀʏ, 1796, Robert
Burns contracted the fatal chill which brought on an attack of
fever. On a last effort to recover his health, he went on July 4
to Brow, a sea-bathing hamlet on the Solway. There he was visited
by Maria Riddell, who thought "the stamp of death was imprinted
on his features." He was convinced himself that his illness would
prove fatal, and some time before this he had said to his wife,

> Don't be afraid, I'll be more respected a hundred years after I am dead
> than I am at present.

His earthly career did not terminate until July 21 in the same
year. Early in the morning, he sank into delirium; the children
were brought to see their parent for the last time in life. They
stood round the bed, while calmly and gradually he sank into his
last repose. His last expression was a muttered reference to the
threatening letter he had received from the clothier's law-agent.
On the evening of Sunday, July 24, the Poet's remains were
removed to the Dumfries Town Hall.

The spot of ground in St. Michael's Churchyard, where all that
was mortal of the Bard was deposited on Monday, July 25, 1796,
had been selected by himself in the north-east corner of the
cemetery.

When I am laid in my grave I wish to be stretched at my full length, that
I may occupy every inch of the ground that I have a right to.

[Extract from one of Burns' published letters.]

Allan Cunningham describes the interment of the Poet's mortal
remains in the following words:

The multitude who accompanied Burns to the grave went step by step
with the chief mourners; they might amount to ten or twelve thousand.
Not a word was heard; and, though all could not be near and many would
not see, when the earth closed on their darling poet there was no rude
impatience shown, no fierce disappointment expressed. It was an impressive and mournful sight to see men of all ranks and persuasions and opinions
mingling as brothers and stepping side by side down the streets of Dumfries,
with the remains of him who had sang of their loves, joys, and domestic
endearments, with a truth and tenderness which none, perhaps, have been
equalled.

BORN 25TH JANUARY, 1759

DIED 21ST JULY, 1796

AGED 37 YEARS

The sun that rose over the grave by the churchyard wall in
Dumfries was the sun of immortality.

The widow of Burns placed over the grave a simple slab of
freestone which for several years was the only monument. Eventually, however, the spontaneous action of his ardent admirers,
amongst whom was General Dunlop, son of the Poet's dear and
true friend, Mrs. Dunlop of Dunlop, resulted in the erection of a
mausoleum worthy of his genius. Money flowed in freely for the
scheme—from lowly peasants and mechanics to royalty itself, the
subscriptions including one of fifty guineas from George IV, then
Prince Regent. Sir Walter Scott and other leading literary men
of the day eagerly lent their aid.

There was no room for the structure at the original burial place,
and it was therefore built on a site in the south-east of the old
churchyard. The foundation stone of the mausoleum was laid
on June 6, 1815. On September 19, 1815, the remains of the Poet,
and of his two sons who had been buried by his side, were lifted
and reinterred in the new vault. The mausoleum was fully
completed in 1818.

The mausoleum is in the form of a Greek temple; it is adorned

THE BURNS STATUE, TORONTO

Toronto, Canada, gave to the Dominion its first statue of Robert Burns. It is a fine bronze, the work of the noted sculptor, D. W. Stevenson, R.S.A., of Edinburgh, and stands on a beautiful site in the north-east corner of the Allan Gardens.

The statue was unveiled before a great gathering of lovers of Burns on the afternoon of July 21, 1902. The unveiling ceremony was performed by Mrs. David Walker, wife of the President of the Burns Monument Committee, while Rev. Professor William Clark, D.C.L.,

TOMBSTONES OF THE POET'S ANCESTORS IN GLENBERVIE CHURCHYARD

delivered the oration. Mayor Oliver A. Howland accepted the statue in behalf of the city of Toronto, which undertook the perpetual care of it, the committee having handed over to the city treasury for that purpose a balance of five hundred and fifty dollars left after paying for the monument. Twice each year, on the anniversary of the Poet's birth and death, the Scottish Societies decorate the statue with flowers, while on Decoration Day the school children of the city place flowers around the base. Thus the enthusiastic attention of the rising generation is drawn to Burns and his inspiring works.

THE HOUSE WHERE BURNS DIED
BURNS MAUSOLEUM, DUMFRIES
THE FUNERAL OF BURNS, DUMFRIES, JULY 25, 1796

with a mural sculpture by Peter Turnerelli (a London sculptor born in Belfast, Ireland, of Italian parents), representing the Genius of Scotland finding Burns at the plough, and casting over him her poetic mantle.

Since the completion of the mausoleum, the vault has been opened to receive the remains of Mrs. Burns (the Poet's "Bonnie Jean"), and of three of his sons—Robert, James and William. The tombstone which covered the Poet's original grave now lies within the mausoleum.

The simple record which is described thereon is as follows:

IN MEMORY OF ROBERT BURNS

WHO DIED THE 21st JULY, 1796

IN THE 37th YEAR OF HIS AGE

Under the statuary by Peter Turnerelli is carved the one honoured word—BURNS.

Neither epitaph nor popular inscription is needed by the man whose name and fame are impressed in the hearts of all his countrymen, and admirers throughout the length and breadth of this world.

Henry S. Murray, J.P., of Glenmayne, Galashiels, on Saturday, May 31, 1913, said:

There is more true guidance for life and conduct in the life and poetry of Robert Burns than in all the droning and moral sermons of pedants and musty self-righteous philosophers since the beginning of time. For, what is the essence of Burns' teaching? Freedom in the State, in the individual, courage, independence, manliness, sympathy, with an allowance for human weakness, general benevolence towards all mankind, and gentle treatment of the animal creation. It is quite possible that the teacher himself lapsed on occasion from his high ideals. However that may be, Burns' teaching remains, and the true greatness of our hero is being now realized all the world over, and monuments and memorials are being raised in his honour everywhere.

THE CLOSING YEAR JULY, 1795-JULY, 1796

Three gates of deliverance, it seems to us, were open for Burns: clear poetical activity; madness; or death. The first with longer life, was still possible, but not probable. . . . The second was still less probable, for his mind was ever among the clearest and firmest. So the milder third gate was opened for him: and he passed not softly, yet speedily, into that still country, where the hail-storms, and fire-showers do not reach, and the heaviest-laden wayfarer at length lays down his load.

—Thomas Carlyle.

Burns was a rheumatic from his boyhood. Read carefully the story of his life, and you will find all along the line mention of this congenital malady—from the tub of cold water at his bedside in Mount Oliphant and Mossgiel, to the cold-water cure referred to in Mrs. Dunlop's letters.

—The Editor [Burns Chronicle, January, 1914].

On a winter day in Edinburgh, in the memorable year 1786-1787, Francis Jeffrey on his way home was staring at a man whose appearance had arrested his attention. A person standing at a shop door tapped him on the shoulder and said: "Ay, laddie, ye may well look at that man! That's Robert Burns."

Jeffrey never saw Burns again, but the great critic was to write from Craigcrook, in 1837, to a friend:

In the last week I have read all Burns' life and works—not without many tears, for the life especially. What touches me most is the pitiable poverty in which that gifted being (and his noble-minded father) passed his early days in the painful frugality to which their innocence was doomed, and the thought how small a share of the useless luxuries in which we (such comparatively poor creatures) indulge would have sufficed to shed joy and cheerfulness in their dwellings, and perhaps to have saved that glorious spirit from the trials and temptations under which he fell prematurely. I could lie down in the dirt and cry and grovel there, I think, for a century to save such a soul as Burns from the suffering and contamination and the degradation which the arrangements of the universe imposed upon him.

—Francis, Lord Jeffrey (1773-1850)

When Robert Burns Died, the Following Obituary Appeared in the Edinburgh *Advertiser* of July 26, 1796

On the 21st inst., died at Dumfries, after a lingering illness, the celebrated Robert Burns. His poetical compositions, distinguished equally by the force of native humor, by the warmth and tenderness of passion and by the glowing touches of a descriptive pencil, will remain a lasting monument of the vigor and versatility of a mind guided only by the lights of nature and by the inspiration of genius. The public to whose amusement he has so largely contributed will learn with regret that his extraordinary endowments were accompanied with frailties which rendered them useless to himself and his family. The last months of his short life were spent in sickness and indigence, and his widow, with five children, and in the hourly expectation of a sixth, is now left without any resource but what she may hope from the regard due to the memory of her husband.

The public are respectfully informed that contributions for the wife and family of the late Robert Burns (who are left in circumstances of extreme distress) will be received at the houses of Sir William Forbes' Co., of Messrs. Mansfield, Ramsay & Co., and at the shops of the Edinburgh booksellers.

It is proposed to publish some time hence a posthumous volume of the poetical remains of Robert Burns for the benefit of the author's family; his friends and acquaintances are requested to transmit such poems and letters as may happen to be in their possession to Alexander Cunningham, Writer, George-street, Edinburgh, or to John Syme Esq., Ryedale, Dumfries. It is hoped that, in the meantime, none of his original productions will be communicated to the public through the channels of newspapers or magazines, so as to injure the sale of the intended publication.

VIII

The Mother of Robert Burns

To EVERY SCOT the father of Robert Burns is a figure which shines with unmistaken clearness. We have been told of his austere piety, his love of learning, his Jacobite sympathies, and his deep abiding love for "wife and weans." But of Agnes Brown, the mother of the Poet, the average man in the street is profoundly ignorant.

The eldest of six children, she was born on March 17, 1732, at her father's farm, Craiginton, Kirkoswald. It is not generally recognised that, on his mother's side, Burns had Covenanting blood in his veins. His mother could claim kinship with the John Brown who was butchered on his own doorstep by Claverhouse. His maternal great-grandfather had shed his blood on Airds Moss. When a question of right or wrong was at stake, Agnes Brown herself was as consistently steadfast as any of her martyred ancestors.

HOUSEWIFE AT TEN

As a child she attended a school of a kind, where the village weaver worked at his loom as he instructed his pupils. When she was only ten years old her mother died and the little girl was installed in the home to look after the whole family.

Two years later her father married again, and the twelve-year-old girl was sent to her grandmother, Mrs. Rennie. Illustrating the simple nature of their lives, it is said that, when the old lady was pleased with her grand-daughter's output, she would give her, by way of "kitchen," a piece of white bread.

We next find the girl, who had so early assumed a woman's cares, attending her blind old uncle, William Brown. He it was who used to sit in his armchair by the fire, the tears running down his face, while his niece sang "The Life and Age of Man." It was this old song which first suggested to the Poet, "Man was made to mourn."

She was of a happy disposition, and "she had a never-failing store of old ballads and songs on which her poetical son must have been fed in boyhood." It was from her, too, that he inherited his glowing black eyes.

A BLIGHTED ROMANCE

While still in her teens she was betrothed to a ploughman—an engagement which lasted for seven years. Then she heard that her lover had been guilty of a moral lapse, and she, who was to be the mother of Burns, could not forgive. She might sacrifice her happiness—but not her conscience.

Soon afterwards she met William Burnes at Maybole. The attraction was mutual and immediate, and they were married on December 15, 1757.

In the "auld clay biggin" at Alloway, which William Burnes built with his own hands, her first-born son arrived on January 25, 1759. When the baby was only nine days old, a storm blew off the gable of the cottage, and the mother and child were carried in the night-time to a neighbour's house for shelter. Of her life in the days which followed, a nineteenth-century poet has finely speculated—

> . . . dreamt she ever as she sang to still
> His infant heart in slumber sweet and long,
> That he, who silent lay the while, should fill
> Half the round world with song.

WIFE AND MOTHER

We can picture her busy and bustling about her household duties. There is one tale of how she made her exhausted husband rest while she herself went out to thresh the corn he was too weak to tackle.   The night would come, and, as the children gathered round the table with their books, she would sit down, "to gar auld claes look amaist as weel as new."

Her son's success never turned her head.   Others who had previously shunned him might begin to flatter.   Most characteristically, his mother breathed a prayer that, when rejoicing in his gifts, he would not forget the Giver.   She accepted his fame with the matter-of-fact assurance of one who had always known that it was on the way.   Had she not often listened when William Burness repeated with profound conviction, "Whoever may live to see it, something extraordinary will come from that boy"?

Burns' Debt of Gratitude

She looked after the Poet's first babies with the same care and tenderness she had shown to her own.   When he married Jean Armour she cared for his bride and taught her the duties of a farmer's wife while Robert, down in Dumfriesshire, was building his house.   He, for his part, never forgot what he owed his mother. When he received his long-delayed settlement from Crech, he at once despatched £180 to Mossgiel—an act for which he sensibly refused to accept any credit.

I was conscious (he wrote) that the wrong side of the balance was pretty heavily charged, and I thought that throwing a little filial piety and fraternal affection into the scale in my favour might help to smooth matters at the grand reckoning.

She was sixty-four years old when her first-born died.   Her last years were placidly spent in the house of her son Gilbert at Grant's Braes.   In the year 1820 she passed peacefully away, and was buried in Bolton Churchyard, near Haddington.   In those last years of her life she was recognized as the mother of Scotland's national bard.

> He sleeps among the eternal; nothing mars
> His rest, nor ever pang to him returns;
> Write too her epitaph among the stars;
> Mother of Robert Burns.

IX

The Poet's Brother William

VERY LITTLE is known of the Poet's brother William, but Mr. William Will, author of *Robert Burns as a Volunteer*, and in 1918 president of the Burns Club of London, England, went to considerable pains to find out where he died and was buried, and herewith appended is a full account of his research.

Although Robert Burns, unlike so many of his brother Scots, cast behind him the seductive invitations to make London his home, he had many family and literary associations with the Capital. His brother, William Burnes, the third son of the family, who was born at Alloway on 31st July, 1767, worked as a journeyman saddler in London, coming hence from Newcastle.

Burns displayed a paternal solicitude for this lad, and the letters to his expatriated brother were charming examples of the domestic felicity that characterized the Poet's life.

We find Burns, as early as 1787 on his return from his Highland tour, writing to his brother Gilbert: "I have been trying for a berth for William, but am not likely to be successful."

In the following month Burns wrote again, the burden of his letter being "Courage, brother!"

My dear William,—I am extremely sorry at the misfortune to your legs. I beg you will never let any worldly concern interfere with the more serious matter, the safety of your life and limbs. I have not had time in these hurried days to write you anything more than a mere how d'ye letter. I will only repeat my favourite quotation:

> What proves the hero truly great
> Is never, never to despair.

My house shall be your welcome home; and as I know your prudence (would to God you had resolution equal to prudence!) if anywhere at a distance from friends, you should need money, you know my direction by post.

From Isle on March 25, 1789, Burns wrote to William at Longtown:

I have stolen from my corn sowing this minute to write a line to accompany your shirt and hat, for I can no more. Your sister Nannie arrived yesternight, and begs to be remembered to you. Write me every opportunity—never mind postage.

P.S. If you are not then gone from Longtown I'll write you a long letter by this day se'ennight. If you should not succeed in your tramps, don't be dejected, or take any rash step—return to us in that case, and we will court Fortune's better humour. Remember this I charge you.

We gather from Burns' letters that the young saddler lacked "smeddum."

In a letter to William at Newcastle-on-Tyne, the Poet wrote from Ellisland on Aug. 14, 1789:

My dear William,—I received your letter, and am very happy to hear that you have got settled for the winter. I enclose you the two guinea-notes of the Bank of Scotland, which I hope will serve your need. It is indeed, not quite so convenient for me to spare money as it once was, but I know your situation, and I will say it, in some respects, your worth. I have no time to write at present, but I beg you will endeavour to pluck up a little more of the Man than you used to have. Remember my favourite quotations:

> On reason build resolve,
> That pillar of true majesty in man,

and

> What proves the hero truly great,
> Is never, never to despair!

Your mother and sisters desire their compliments. A Dieu je vous commende.

To his friend and early teacher, John Murdoch, Burns wrote on July 16, 1790, asking Murdoch to send a note to William, who was then working with Mr. William Barber, saddler and harness-maker, 181 Strand (it was really 281), "and the poor fellow will joyfully wait on you, as one of the few surviving friends of the man whose name, and Christian name, too, he has the honour to bear.'' But the invitation arrived too late, for ere the schoolmaster reached Burnes, the young saddler—he was but 23—had passed to his rest.

Where William Burnes resided and died and where he was buried, it is now impossible to say definitely. Charles Rogers in his *Genealogical Memoirs of the Family of Robert Burns* says, that "He died at London, July, 1790, and his remains were deposited in St. Paul's churchyard; the spot of his interment was unmarked and is now unknown.'' But he gives no authority for his statement, and it cannot be borne out by the records of St. Paul's or the registers of the parishes having burial rights in the Churchyard. The Rev. Lewis Gilbertson, the rector of St. Martin's, Ludgate Hill, kindly searched the Register of St. Gregory and St. Mary Magdalene, which parishes had burial rights in the Churchyard, but without success. The Rev. H. C. Dimsdale, rector of St. Augustine and St. Faith's Old Change, obligingly searched the Registers of these two parishes, but again with no success. Mr. Dimsdale informed me that so far as he knew no person who was not a parishioner of St. Faith's was buried in St. Paul's before the fire. Parishioners now have the right to be buried there, and both parishes claimed the Churchyard vaults.

My friend, Mr. H. C. Lyall, a young Scotsman who courageously organised an Information and Research Bureau in London, took up the search with me, and we examined, not only the burial registers of the parishes having burial rights in St. Paul's, but the register of every parish where there was a possibility of William Burnes having been buried, and ultimately found in the register of burials of St. Mary-le-Strand, the entry under date July, 1790, the name "William Burne.'' We have no knowledge of the parish in which Burnes died, but we do know that he worked in the Strand; and it is not unlikely that he was buried in the Church of the parish in which he worked; and the spelling of "Burne" for "Burnes" would not be an unlikely example of the carelessness with which such entries were made in those days.

There is a possible excuse for the erroneous statement that Burnes was buried in St. Paul's, for, as stated by the Rev. Mr. Hillersdon, rector of St. Mary-le-Strand, it was quite usual for a person to have his funeral service taken at his favourite church, and to be buried in the ground of his parish church. Thus if William Burnes had attended St. Paul's, his clergyman would probably have read the service there, but the interment would have taken place at St. Mary-le-Strand if that was his parish church.

There is a small churchyard attached to St. Mary's, and this church had a burial ground in Great Russell Street, which, however, has disappeared.   As Burnes was a man in poor circumstances it was unlikely that a headstone was erected to mark his burial place, so that his last resting place it is now impossible to locate.

We are almost safe in assuming that the William Burne who was buried in St. Mary's, Strand, burying ground on 28th July, 1790, was William Burnes, the brother of the Poet, who worked in the Strand, and who died four days previously.

LETTER FROM JOHN MURDOCH (1765-1824)

TO

ROBERT HARTLEY CROMEK (1770-1812)

This letter was communicated to me, says Robert Hartley Cromek, by a gentleman, to whose liberal advice and information I am much indebted, Mr. John Murdoch, the tutor of the poet, accompanied by the following interesting note:

London, Hart-Street,

Bloomsbury,

December 28th, 1807.

Dear Sir,—

The following letter which I lately found among my papers, I copy for your perusal, partly because it is Burns', partly because it makes honourable mention of my rational Christian friend, his father; and likewise, because it is rather flattering to myself.   I glory in no one thing, so much as an intimacy with good men:—the friendship of others reflects no honour. When I recollect the pleasure (and I hope benefit) I received from the conversation of William Burns, especially when on the Lord's day we walked together for about two miles to the house of prayer, there publicly to adore the Giver of all Good.   I entertain an ardent hope that together we shall "renew the glorious theme in distant worlds," with powers more adequate to the mighty subject—the exuberant beneficence of the Great Creator.   But to the letter:—Here follows the letter to Burns, relative to his brother William;

I promised myself a deal of happiness in the conversation of my dear young friend; but my promises of this nature generally prove fallacious.   Two visits were the utmost that I received.   At one of them however, he repeated a lesson which I had given him about twenty years before, when he was a mere child, concerning the pity and tenderness due to animals.   To that lesson (which it seems was brought to the level of his capacity), he declared himself indebted for almost all the philanthropy and general sympathy he possessed.

Let not parents and teachers imagine that it is needless to talk seriously to children. They are sooner fit to be reasoned with than is generally thought. Strong and indelible impressions are to be made before the mind be agitated and ruffled by the numerous train of distracting cares and unruly passions, whereby it is frequently rendered almost unsusceptible of the principles and precepts of rational religion and sound morality.

But I find myself digressing again. *Poor William!* then in the bloom and vigour of youth, caught a putrid fever, and in a few days, *as real chief mourner, I followed his remains* to the land of forgetfulness.

JOHN MURDOCH

X

The Bachelors' Club

About the end of the year 1780, the Poet, his brother Gilbert and five other young men of the Tarbolton neighbourhood, formed themselves into a society, the declared objects of which were to relax themselves after toil, to promote sociality and friendship, and to improve the mind. The laws and regulations were furnished by Burns. The members were to meet after the labours of the day were over, once a week, in a small public-house in the village, where each should offer his opinion on a given question or subject, supporting it by such arguments as he thought proper. The debate was to be conducted with order and decorum; and after it was finished, the members were to choose a subject for discussion at the ensuing meeting. The sum expended by each member was not to exceed threepence; and, with the humble potation that this could procure, they were to toast their mistresses, and to cultivate friendship with each other. This society continued its meetings regularly for some time. In the autumn of 1782, wishing to preserve some account of their proceedings, they purchased a book into which their laws and regulations were copied, with a preamble, containing a short history of their transactions down to that period. This curious document, which is evidently the work of the poet, has been discovered, and it deserves a place in his memoirs.

HISTORY OF THE RISE, PROCEEDINGS AND REGULATIONS OF THE BACHELORS' CLUB

Of birth or blood we do not boast,
Nor gentry does our club afford,
But ploughmen and mechanics we
In Nature's simple dress record.

—DAVID SILLAR.

As the great end of human society is to become wiser and better, this ought therefore to be the principal view of every man in every station of life. But as experience has taught us, that such studies as inform the head and mend the heart, when long continued, are apt to exhaust the faculties of the mind, it has been found proper to relieve and unbend the mind by some employment or another, that may be agreeable enough to keep its powers in exercise, but at the same time not so serious as to exhaust them. But, superadded to this, by far the greater part of mankind are under the necessity of earning the sustenance of human life by the labour of their bodies, whereby, not only the faculties of the mind, but the nerves and sinews of the body, are so fatigued, that it is absolutely necessary to have recourse to some amusement or diversion, to relieve the wearied man, worn-down with the necessary labours of life.

As the best of things, however, have been perverted to the worst of purposes, so, under the pretence of amusement and diversion, men have plunged into all the madness of riot and dissipation; and, instead of attending to the grand design of human life, they have begun with extravagance and folly, and ended with guilt and wretchedness. Impressed with these considerations, we, the following lads in the parish of Tarbolton, viz. Hugh Reid, Robert Burns, Gilbert Burns, Alexander Brown, Walter Mitchell, Thomas Wright, and William McGavin, resolved, for our mutual entertainment, to unite ourselves into a club or society, under such rules and regulations, that while we should forget our cares and labours in mirth and diversion, we might not transgress the bounds of innocence and decorum; and after agreeing on these, and some other regulations, we held our first meeting at Tarbolton, in the house of John Richard, upon the evening of the 11th of November, 1780, commonly called the Hallowe'en, and after choosing Robert Burns president for the night, we proceeded to debate on this question:

Suppose a young man bred a farmer, but without any fortune, has it in his power to marry either of two women, the one a girl of large fortune, but neither handsome in person, nor agreeable in conversation, but who can manage the household affairs of a farm well enough; the other of them a girl every way agreeable in person, conversation, and behaviour, but without any fortune; which of them shall he choose?

Finding ourselves very happy in our society, we resolved to meet once a month in the same house, in the way and manner proposed, and shortly thereafter we chose Robert Ritchie for another member. In May, 1781, we brought in David Sillar, and in June, Adam Jamaison, as members. About the beginning of the year 1782, we admitted Matthew Patterson, and John Orr, and in June following we chose James Patterson as a proper brother for such a society. The club being thus increased, we resolved to meet at Tarbolton on the race-night, the July following, and have a dance in honour of our society. Accordingly we did meet, each one with a partner, and spent the evening in such innocence and merriment, such cheerfulness and good humour, that every brother will long remember it with pleasure and delight.

Rules and Regulations to be Observed in the Bachelors' Club

1st. The Club shall meet at Tarbolton every fourth Monday night, when a question of any subject shall be proposed, disputed points of religion only excepted, in the manner hereafter directed; which question is to be debated in the club, each member taking whatever side he thinks proper.

2nd. When the club is met, the president, or, he failing, some one of the members, till he come, shall take his seat; then the other members shall seat themselves; those, who are for one side of the question, on the president's right-hand; and those who are for the other side, on his left; which of them shall have the right hand is to be determined by the president. The president and four of the members being present, shall have power to transact any ordinary part of the society's business.

3rd. The club met and seated, the president shall read the question out of the club's book of records, (which book is always to be kept by the president), then the two members nearest to the president shall cast lots who of them shall speak first, and according as the lot shall determine, the member nearest the president on that side shall deliver his opinion, and the member nearest on the other side that spoke first; then the second member on the side that spoke second; and so on to the end of the company; but if there be fewer members on the one side than on the other, when all the members of the least side have spoken according to their places, any of them, as they please among themselves, may reply to the remaining members of the opposite side; when both sides have spoken, the president shall give his opinion, after which they may go over it a second or more times, and so continue the question.

4th. The club shall then proceed to the choice of a question for the subject of next night's meeting. The president shall first propose one, and any other member who chooses may propose more questions; and whatever one of them is most agreeable to the majority of members, shall be the subject of debate next club-night.

5th. The club shall, lastly, elect a new president for the next meeting; the president shall first name one, then any of the club may name another, and whoever of them has the majority of votes shall be duly elected; allowing the president the first vote, and the casting vote upon a par, but none other. Then after a general toast to mistresses of the club, they shall dismiss.

6th. There shall be no private conversations carried on during the time of debate, nor shall any member interrupt another while he is speaking, under the penalty of a reprimand from the president for the first fault, doubling his share for the reckoning for the second, trebling it for the third, and so on in proportion for every other fault; provided always, however, that any member may speak at any time after leave asked, and given by the president. All swearing and profane language, and particularly all obscene and indecent conversation, is strictly prohibited, under the same penalty as aforesaid in the first clause of this article.

7th. No member, on any pretence whatever, shall mention any of the club's affairs to any other person but a brother member, under the pain of being excluded; and particularly if any member shall reveal any of the speeches or affairs of the club, with a view to ridicule or laugh at any of the rest of the members, he shall be for ever excommunicated from the society; and the rest of the members are desired, as much as possible, to avoid, and have no communication with him as a friend or comrade.

8th. Every member shall attend at the meetings, without he can give a proper excuse for not attending; and it is desired that every one who cannot attend, will send his excuse with some other member; and he who shall be absent three meetings without sending such excuse, shall be summoned to the club-night, when, if he fails to appear, or send an excuse, he shall be excluded.

9th. The club shall not consist of more than sixteen members, all bachelors belonging to the parish of Tarbolton; except a brother-member marry, and in that case he may be continued, if the majority of the club think proper. No person shall be admitted a member of this society, without the unanimous consent of the club; and any member may withdraw from the club altogether, by giving a notice to the president in writing of his departure.

10th.   Every man proper for a member of this society, must have a frank, honest, open heart; above anything dirty or mean; and must be a professed lover of one or more of the female sex.   No haughty, self-conceited person, who looks upon himself as superior to the rest of the club, and especially no mean-spirited wordly mortal, whose only wish is to heap up money, shall upon any pretence whatever be admitted.   In short, the proper person for this society is, a cheerful, honest hearted lad, who, if he has a friend that is true, and a mistress that is kind, and as much wealth as genteely to make both ends meet—is just as happy as this world can make him.

The philosophical mind will dwell with interest and pleasure, on an institution that combined so skillfully the means of instruction and of happiness, and if grandeur look down with a smile on these simple annals, let us trust that it will be a smile of benevolence and approbation.   It is with regret that the sequel of the Bachelors' Club of Tarbolton must be told.   It survived several years after the Poet removed from Ayrshire, but, no longer sustained by his talents, or cemented by his social affections, its meetings lost much of their attraction.   At length, in an evil hour, dissension arising amongst its members, the institution was given up, and the records committed to the flames.   Happily the preamble and the regulations were spared; and, as matter of instruction and of example, they are transmitted to posterity.

After the family of the bard removed from Tarbolton to the neighbourhood of Mauchline, he and his brother Gilbert were requested to assist in forming a similar institution there.   The regulations of the club at Mauchline were nearly the same as those of the club at Tarbolton; but one laudable alteration was made. The fines for non-attendance at Tarbolton had been spent in enlarging their scanty potations; at Mauchline it was resolved, that the money thus collected, should be set apart for the purchase of books.

Though the records of the society at Tarbolton are lost, and those of the society at Mauchline have not been transmitted, yet we may safely affirm, that Burns was a distinguished member of both these associations, which were well calculated to excite and to develop the powers of his mind.

ROBERT BURNS, DEPUTE MASTER
By W. Stewart Watson

TARBOLTON HOUSE, IN WHICH BURNS WAS MADE A FREEMASON

TARBOLTON PROCESSION OF ST. JAMES' LODGE

XI

Robert Burns and Freemasonry

In 1736 several Edinburgh lodges met and formed the Grand Lodge of Scotland, the governing and regulating authority of Scottish freemasonry. The bicentenary of that event was celebrated in November, 1936, with befitting pomp and ceremony.

Previous to the foundation of Grand Lodge, the Lodge of Kilwinning (now described as Mother Kilwinning, and No. 0 on the roll of the Grand Lodge), was the governing body in Freemasonry, and issued charters for the formation of new lodges throughout the country. It was by Mother Kilwinning that a charter was issued, in 1771, to Tarbolton (locally, Tarbouton), and a lodge was formed taking the name of Tarbolton Kilwinning. Two years later dissensions arose, and certain of the brethren applied to the Grand Lodge, still somewhat insecure on its throne. These twenty brethren, led by Sir Thomas Wallace, obtained a charter dated February 26, 1773, and this new lodge received the title of Lodge St. David, No. 174 on the roll of the Grand Lodge. The Earl of Dumfries was Grand Master Mason that year. Those who had remained in Lodge Tarbolton Kilwinning apparently thought it well to be under the ægis of Grand Lodge, and a year later, on May 27th, they also petitioned for and received a charter from Grand Lodge, their number on the roll being 178, and their designation St. James Tarbolton Kilwinning. The Duke of Athol was Grand Master this year, but did not sign the charter as the Earl of Dumfries had signed the other.

It is not known how the two lodges fared during the next few years, but probably financial difficulties weighed heavily upon them. At any rate, on June 25, 1781, the two lodges united. We learn from the Minutes of Lodge St. David, that in the previous December proposals for union had been made, and it is recorded that in June, "having considered on our offers to St. James's Lodge respecting a junchen, also their answer, finds by majority of votes that both lodges may unite on terms offered and exchanged this day." It was agreed that this United Lodge should bear the name of St. David, the name doubtless being chosen because St. David held the older charter. Apparently Mother Kilwinning had no voice in the arrangements, and her original warrant of 1771 was set aside.

Some confusion has been created by the fact that shortly before, and again after Burns became a Freemason, there existed two lodges in Tarbolton; but at the time of his initiation they were united under the name of Lodge St. David, which is therefore the name of his mother lodge. Subsequently a secession occurred, and Lodge St. James resumed its independence under Captain James Montgomerie as Grand Master. Burns associated himself with this seceding body, and it was in St. James Lodge that his active Masonic life was spent.

The Lodges had effected a "junchen" in the midsummer of 1781, and on July 4th of that year, at the age of twenty-two and a half years, "Robert Burness in Lochly was entered an Apprentice." The Minute is signed, "Joph. Norman M." The entry money was twelve shillings and sixpence, and was paid on the same day. Tradition says he was introduced by a tailor in Tarbolton, Alexander Wood by name: others maintain that his sponsor was John Rankine, the farmer, to whom he had addressed epistles.

Apparently Burns left home immediately after being made a Freemason for his unlucky venture in Irvine, and so did not receive his second and third degrees until October. On the first of that month he was passed and raised. Thenceforward the name of Burns is found only in the books of St. James Lodge.

Four years after his initiation he became Depute-Master, an office which was then elective and practically as important as that of Worshipful Master today. At that time the office of Worshipful Master was really honorary, the Master not attending and not being expected to attend the Lodge except, perhaps, for the annual and other ceremonious and important meetings.

Burns occupied the chair for three years, and twenty-nine of the Minutes are signed by him as Depute-Master, and three of them are in his own handwriting. Sitting in the East for the first time on June 29, 1785, the last Minute signed by him as Depute-Master was May 23, 1788.

The rules of the Lodge are interesting reading. One is as follows:

Whereas always a Lodge means a company of men, worthy and circumspect, gathered together in order to promote charity, friendship, civility, and good neighbourhood; it is enacted that no member shall speak slightingly, detractingly or calumniously of any of his brethren behind their backs, so as to damage them in their professions or reputation, without any certain grounds; and any member committing such an offence must humble himself by asking "on his knees the pardon of such person or persons as his folly or malice hath agrieved." Obstinate refusal to comply with the finding of the brethren assembled shall be met by expulsion from the Lodge, with every mark of ignominy and disgrace that is consistent with justice and Freemasonry.

The St. James Tarbolton Lodge met in a public house known as the "Cross Keys" which was run by James Manson. The house is now in ruins, scarcely anything but the bare walls standing. It is at the end of the village on the road to Willie's Mill, the house of William Muir, the great friend of the Burns father and son. Burns never forgot the kindness shown by William Muir to his wife, Jean Armour (Bonnie Jean), when she was turned out by her father. It was with the Muirs she found shelter until Burns secured a house in Mauchline. When Mr. Muir died, Burns wrote an Epitaph in 1793:

To My Friend and Father's Friend
William Muir, Tarbolton

An honest man here lies at rest;
As e'er God with his image blest,
The friend of man, the friend of truth
The friend of age, and guide of youth,
Few hearts like his with virtue warmed;
Few heads with knowledge so informed
If there's another world, he lives in bliss
If there is none, he made the best of this.

It was here also that Burns met John Wilson, so graphically
described in his poem "Death and Dr. Hornbook." He was
schoolmaster in Tarbolton, Session Clerk in the Parish Kirk, also
kept a small store in which he sold simple drugs. His advertise-
ment ran as follows: "Advice given gratis, in common disorders
at his shop." This tickled Burns' fancy, and brought forth the
poem "Death and Dr. Hornbook," which Burns composed on his
way home from a Masonic meeting, when, as he admits,

> The *clachan yill* had made me *canty*   *village ale, lively*
> I *wasna fou*, but just had plenty;   *was not full*
> I *stachered whyles*, but yet took *tent* aye   *staggered sometimes, heed*
> To free the ditches;
> *An'* hillocks, stones an' bushes *kent* aye   *and, knew*
> *Frae ghaists* an' witches.   *from ghosts*

John Wilson, a Past Depute-Master of St. James Lodge, was
Secretary during the time that Burns was Depute-Master. He
afterwards left Tarbolton, taught school in Glasgow, and was
Session Clerk in the Gorbels Parish Church.

It was during Burns' tenure of office that Professor Dugald
Stewart, a summer visitor to Ayrshire, was made an honorary
member of the Lodge, and thus began a friendship of great value
to the Poet during his visit to the capital. Burns describes him as
"the most perfect character I ever saw." Their early morning
walks on the Braid Hills were a delight to both. Writing of his
visit to the Ayrshire Lodge, Stewart says:

He (Burns) had occasion to make some short unpremeditated compliments to different individuals from whom he had no reason to expect a
visit, and everything he said was happily conceived, and forcibly as well
as fluently expressed. . . . His manner of speaking in public had
evidently the marks of some practice in extempore elocution.

It may be of interest to add that another honorary member of
this period was Claude Alexander, of Ballochmyle, brother of the
lady who was the theme of Burns' beautiful song, "The Bonnie
Lass of Ballochmyle."

Burns signs the Minute relating to the visit of Professor Dugald
Stewart to the Lodge, who at that time was tenant of Catrine
House. The record is as follows:

A deputation of the Lodge met at Mauchline on 25th July, 1787, and entered Brother Alexander Allison of Barmuir, an apprentice. Likewise admitted Brothers Professor Stewart of Catrine, and Claude Alexander, Esq. of Ballochmyle; Claud Nelson, Esq., Paisley; John Farquhar Gray, Esq., of Gilmilnscroft; and Dr. George Grierson, Glasgow, honorary members of the Lodge.

ROBT. BURNS, D.M.

The Poet's attendances as Depute-Master of St. James Tarbolton Lodge were, 1785: June 29th, July 30th; August 2nd and 18th; September 7th and 15th; October 26th; November 19th; December 1st and 7th; in 1786: January 7th; March 1st; June 7th, 15th, 25th; July 29th; August 18th; October 5th; (Sorn) November 10th.

At the March 1st meeting his brother Gilbert was Passed and Raised, and both he and the Poet signed Burns instead of Burness, as they had done formerly. Chambers says that his first notable deviation from Burness was in the poem "Mossgiel," probably to suit the necessities of rhyme, and that he made the final change to Burns on April 14, 1786. The last letter to which Burns seems to have subscribed his name Burness was dated April 3, 1786, from Mossgiel to Mr. Robert Aiken. His next recorded letter, dated April 17, 1786, from Mossgiel to Mr. McWhinnie, Ayr, is signed Burns.

We now come to the great year, 1786, when Burns published the Kilmarnock edition of his poems and suddenly leapt into fame. During the eighteen months of 1785-1786 his Muse was prolific, pouring forth satire, epistle, song and narrative in rapid profusion. He might have doubled the Kilmarnock edition, so much had he ready then.

On March 27, 1786, Burns was introduced by Gavin Hamilton to Lodge Loudon Kilwinning, Newmilns, No. 51, and admitted as a joining member. The Minute of his admission reads:

Much to the satisfaction of the Lodge, Mr. Robert Burns, Mossgiel, Mauchline, introduced by the Right Worshipful, was admitted as a member of this Lodge. John Norton, merchant, in Newmilns, is answerable for Robert Burns admission money.

This was the first Lodge out of Tarbolton that Burns joined. Purely Kilwinning in its origin, and holding its warrant, dated

February 13, 1747, direct from Mother Kilwinning, it did not come within the jurisdiction of the Grand Lodge of Scotland until 1818.

Burns must have been the life and soul of the St. James Lodge in more ways than one. The Minutes show that there were more meetings when he was an office-bearer than at any other period. There are three short Minutes written in full by the Poet. The first is dated "Tarbolton, 1st September, 1784," but is unsigned, a circumstance not uncommon amongst the records of that time. This Minute bears marks of literary conceit at any rate, the antithesis being worthy of note. It is almost ludicrous to find the world-famed Poet writing this:

This night—the Lodge met and ordered four pounds of candles, and one quire of eightpence paper for the use of the Lodge which money was laid out by the Treasurer, and the candles and paper laid in accordingly.

The other Minutes, written fully in the Poet's hand, are as follows:

Tarbolton, June 23, 1786.—This night the Lodge met, and Robert Andrew, a brother of St. David's Tarbolton, was admitted by unanimous vote, gratis; likewise James Good, having been duly recommended was entered an apprentice. R. Burns, D.M.

Tarbolton, August 18th (no year, but from the dates immediately below, sure to be 1786).—This night the Lodge met, and James Tennent, from Ochiltree, having been recommended was admitted accordingly. Robt. Burns, D.M.

Major William Parker, of Assloss, Master of Lodge St. John, No. 22, Kilmarnock, a banker, became one of Burns' principal friends and a subscriber for thirty-five copies of the first edition of the poems. In 1802, he succeeded to the estate of Assloss, about two miles out of Kilmarnock. He is "Willie" in the song "Ye Sons of Old Killie"—a contraction for Kilmarnock. It is said to have been composed by Burns on the occasion of his admission as an honorary member of the Lodge.

> Ye sons of old Killie, assembled by Willie,
> To follow the noble vocation;
> Your thrifty old mother has scarce such another
> To sit in that honoured station.

I've little to say but only to pray,
As praying's the ton of your fashion;
A prayer from the Muse you well may excuse,
Tis seldom her favourite passion.

Ye powers who preside o'er the wind and the tide,
Who marked each element's border;
Who form'd this frame with beneficent aim,
Whose sovereign statute is order.

Within this dear mansion may wayward contention,
Or withere'd envy ne'er enter;
May secrecy round be the mystical bound,
And brotherly love be the centre.

The original of the song has the following note attached to it:

This song, wrote by Mr. Burns was sung by him in the Kilmarnock Kil-winning Lodge in 1786, and given by him to Major Parker, who was Master of the Lodge.

Burns had many Masonic brethren in "Auld Killie," notably his publisher, John Wilson, and it was not unfitting that here he should receive his first honorary membership.

On October 26, 1786, Burns was made an honorary member of Lodge St. John, No. 22, Kilmarnock. This Lodge received its charter from Mother Kilwinning on November 14, 1734, its principal petitioner being William, fourth Earl of Kilmarnock, afterwards beheaded on Tower Hill for the part he took in the attempted restoration of the House of Stewart, when all the honours attached to his name were attainted. Originally the Lodge was entirely operative. The Minute of the Lodge on the date of Burns' affiliation to it concludes:

Robert Burns, poet, from Mauchline, a member of St. James, Tarbolton, was made an honorary member of the Lodge.

(Signed) WILL PARKER.

This was the first Lodge to designate Burns as "poet," and to accord him the distinction of honorary membership.

When Robert Burns arrived in Edinburgh on Tuesday, November 28, 1786, Masonry was in great vogue. Eleven or twelve

Lodges there held monthly meetings, and the officials of Grand Lodge were in the habit of visiting each Lodge once in the year. Among these officials were the Duke of Atholl, the Earl of Balcarras, Lord Haddo, Sir William Forbes, the Hon. Col. James Murray, Sir James Hunter-Blair, the Earl of Buchan, Thomas Hay of Hayston, Mr. Campbell of Shawfield, Mr. Grant of Monnymusk, Dr. Nathaniel Spens, Francis Lord Napier, Lord Binning, J. Stewart of Allanbank, James Wolfe Murray (Lord Cringletic), the Earl of Morton, John Clark of Eldin (Lord Eldin).

Burns regularly attended the Masonic meetings in Edinburgh, but these were restricted to reasonable evening hours. His bedfellow, John Richmond (then a law-student and clerk from Mauchline) says:

> Burns, though frequently out into company, usually returned at good hours and went soberly to bed, where he could prevail from his companion, by little bribes, to read to him till he fell asleep.

On January 14, 1787, Burns writes to John Ballantyne from Edinburgh:

> I went to a Mason Lodge yesternight where the Most Worshipful Grand Master Charteris and all the Grand Lodge of Scotland visited. The meeting was most numerous and elegant; all the different Lodges about town were present in all their pomp. The Grand Master who presided with great solemnity, and honour to himself as a gentleman, and Mason, among other general toasts gave, "Caledonia and Caledonia's Bard brother B——; which rung through the whole assembly with multiplied honours and acclamations. As I had no idea such a thing would happen I was downright thunderstruck, and trembling in every nerve made the best return in my power. Just as I had finished some of the Grand Officers said, so loud as I could hear, with a most comforting accent, "very well indeed" which set me something to rights again.

The Lodge in which this incident took place was St. Andrews, No. 49, at the time quite a renowned Masonic centre in Edinburgh.

Thursday, February 1, 1787, Burns attended a meeting of the Canongate Kilwinning Lodge, No. 2, Alexander Ferguson, Esq., of Craigdarroch, Right Worshipful Master, in the chair.

> The R. W. Master having observed that Brother Burns was at present in the Lodge—who is well known as a great poetic writer, and for a late

publication of his works, which have been universally commended—submitted that he should be assumed a member of the Lodge, which was unanimously agreed to, and he was assumed accordingly.   (Lodge Minutes)

The Lodge welcomed Burns with whole-hearted enthusiasm, which found tangible expression, not only at meetings, but also in supporting and assisting the preparation of the first Edinburgh edition of his works.   Many famous men have passed through the portals of the Lodge.   The roll of members includes the names of men famous in history, literature, law, medicine, and other spheres. The bi-centenary memorial epitomizes Lodge Canongate Kilwinning, No. 2, in these words:

To her ranks has come such a phalanx of the great and good in every field of human activity, as might well make her the envy of the proudest sister in the land.   Her brightest names are not hers alone, but Scotland's and among them are many that posterity will not willingly let die.

St. John's Chapel is of great antiquarian interest as the home of Lodge Canongate Kilwinning, and is probably the oldest Masonic Chapel in the world.

The traditions of Canongate Kilwinning, as an operative body, begin with the building of Holyrood Abbey and Palace, when, by Royal Warrant, skilled builders and craftsmen were brought from all parts of the country to assist in the work.   The Abbey was founded by King David I, in 1128, for the Canons Regular of St. Augustine, and dedicated to the Holy Rood or Cross brought to Scotland by his mother, the pious Margaret.   The Cross was called the Black Rood of Scotland.   The Lodge was practically identified with the religious foundation of the Abbey, till the growing Burgh of Canongate outside the walls of Edinburgh became of sufficient importance, amid the religious struggles of the sixteenth and seventeenth centuries, to confer rights of free trade apart from the protection of the Church.   The trade societies of the Burgh never owed any allegiance to Edinburgh, and the somewhat arrogant attempts made by the trades of the latter to exercise control in the Canongate invariably led to indignant repudiation.

The Canongate Masons, however, while dating their corporate privileges from King David's charter to the Canons of Holyrood and the constitution of the Burgh of Canongate, and being entirely separate from and independent of Edinburgh, identified themselves with the general body of Freemasons in Scotland in 1677, five years after the Parish Church was transferred from the Abbey. In that year they accepted a warrant from Mother Kilwinning, which—as the Head, though in influence only the second Lodge in the Kingdom—was at the time exercising the functions of Grand Lodge. Mother Kilwinning had a traditional connection, similar to that of Canongate, with the skilled ecclesiastical builders and architects of the time.

Like several other Lodges in England and Scotland, and owing to the incompleteness or absence of documentary evidence of earlier existence, precedence thus runs conventionally from a much later date, 1677, than the real inception of the Lodge warrants. In respect of its constitution at so early a date as a purely speculative Lodge, independent of and uncontrolled by any trade organization or incorporation, it takes rank as one of the very oldest of existing Lodges. It is one of the few which cannot, and does not, produce to candidates or any one else any "charter or warrant of constitution from the Grand Lodge of Scotland." Indeed, the initiative in forming Grand Lodge was taken by Lodge Canongate Kilwinning, and one of its members, William St. Clair of Rosslyn, became first Grand Master of Scotland.

The Lodge holds its Annual Festival on St. John the Baptist's Day, corresponding with the Summer Solstice; its bright red clothing and apt motto both pointedly refer to the dawn of day in the East and to ancient Sun Worship. As the Sun never sets but to rise again, so, according to the oldest forms at every Communication, the work is closed, but the Lodge is never closed—only adjourned.

The Lodge preserves the ancient Scottish arrangement of the interior, having the Master's and Wardens' Chairs at the three points of a triangle, the Master's Chair forming the apex. This is the correct and most ancient arrangement of a Scottish Lodge, corresponding with the so-called Higher Degrees, and also with the Continental Masonic systems, but differing from the English and American systems.

During recent years the Lodge premises have been greatly enlarged and improved, increasing the size of the Refectory, as well as adding a large museum between the Chapel itself and the new

St. John Street frontage, designed to harmonize with the older part of the building. Subsequent extensions have included the old theatre on the east side of Old Playhouse Close, and the town house of the Earls of Wemyss in St. John Street. The old entrance to the Lodge by St. John's Close can now be used at any time. It gives access to the Refectory Kitchen and to an arched vault in the basement. On the middle flat, to which access is obtained by a turreted staircase, is the Old Kitchen of the Tenandries. The pillars on either side of the door between the Old Kitchen and the Secretary's room are from the Old Council Chambers in Leith. The fireplace now disclosed was formerly covered by masonry and partitions. The Lodge possesses an interesting Museum, containing many unique articles connected with the Craft. The organ in the Chapel is probably the oldest in use in Scotland, and the only existing one on which the songs of Burns were played in his presence.

Recent honorary members include Field Marshal Earl Haig, Lord Ampthill, Earl of Donghmore, Lord Newlands, General Sir Francis Davies, Sir Arthur Conan Doyle, Field Marshal Lord Kitchener, Field Marshal Earl Roberts. There are also the records of honorary membership having been extended to H.R.H. King Oscar II of Sweden and Norway, and H.R.H. the Crown Prince Frederick of Denmark.

When a Right Worshipful Master is elected to the Chair of this Lodge, it is with the feeling that he has a responsibility to uphold great traditions. The Lodge has had a wonderful list of famous Right Worshipful Masters, and Alexander Ferguson (a grandson of Annie Laurie) perhaps little knew what honour he was bringing to himself when, as Master, he signed the Minute on February 1, 1787, admitting Burns a member of the Lodge.

There is no further reference in the Minutes to Burns' later visits, but a well-authenticated tradition assigns the monthly meeting of March 1, 1787, as the date on which, if not elected and regularly installed in the modern fashion, he was proclaimed and acknowledged as Poet-Laureate of the Lodge. It has to be remembered that while only statutory meetings of the Lodge are recorded in the Minutes, the Lodge held many other meetings in the course of the session. As early as 1802 a Minute records the purchase of an engraving dated 1798, two years after his death, on which he is designated Poet-Laureate of Canongate Kilwinning. On February 9, 1815, the Minute records:

The R. W. Master stated that he had observed a public subscription had been commenced for the purpose of erecting a Mausoleum to the memory of Robert Burns, who was a member and Poet-Laureate of this Lodge. . . . He then submitted to the meeting the propriety of the Lodge commencing a Subscription . . . being the only manner in which they can testify their respect for the memory of a public character so immediately connected with them, and who on many occasions contributed so generally to the harmony of the Masonic order, and to that of this Lodge, Canongate Kilwinning, in particular.

On 8th June a sum of twenty guineas was voted, and acknowledgment by Dr. Duncan, Dumfries, in these terms: "This tribute of respect to the memory of your Laureate is not only most interesting in itself, but must be highly gratifying to all the admirers of the Bard."

Some time ago the Grand Lodge finally and judicially established, after an elaborate and exhaustive inquiry, that the "Inauguration of Burns as Poet-Laureate" actually occurred. The late Peter Ross, in his book, *Scotland and the Scots*, published in 1889, states:

On March 1st, 1787, an unusually brilliant meeting of Canongate Kilwinning Lodge was held, and at an early period in the evening the master, Ferguson of Craigdarroch, conferred on Burns the title of Poet-Laureate of the Lodge, and he was crowned with a wreath of evergreen. Hence came to be fulfilled the vision he had so well described, in which the Scottish Muse crowned his brow with laurel:

> "And wear thou this" she solemn said
> And bound the holly round my head;
> The polish'd leaves and berries red
> Did rustling play,
> And like a passing thought she fled
> In light away.

That night was probably, in Burns' own judgment, the climax of his career. Honoured by his brother-Masons as no Mason of his time had been honoured, publicly acknowledged as "Caledonia's Bard" and Poet-Laureate of his Lodge, his new volume passing rapidly through the press with the most brilliant prospects of success, and petted and caressed on every side, it was a grand position for a man to reach unaided by gentle birth or princely fortune; and that Burns retained his native modesty amid it all is, as has often been said, the most wonderful feature of the glowing story.

W. Stewart Watson, a well-known Edinburgh artist and a member of the Canongate Kilwinning Lodge, painted a very fine picture of this impressive incident. In a notice in the *Freemason's Quarterly Review* of December 31, 1845, the artist is reported as being engaged on a painting of the poet Burns in the act of being received into membership with the Canongate Kilwinning Lodge. When the picture was finished it was reviewed in the *Scotsman* on March 25, 1846, under the heading, "The Inauguration of Burns."

This historic painting was presented to the Grand Lodge of Scotland, in 1863, by the family of the late Dr. James Burnes (1801-1862), the distinguished Indian traveller and administrator, whose father, Provost James Burnes (1780-1852), was a cousin of Burns.   Attached to the picture is the inscription: "The Inauguration of Robert Burns as Poet-Laureate, of Lodge Canongate Kilwinning, 1st March, 1787."

It is to the interpretation of this picture that we owe the interesting little book, *A Winter with Robert Burns*, in which the notabilities assembled in the canvas are introduced to us in a brief biographical survey.

Some sixty persons are shown in the picture, including Burns himself, and the following:

Alexander Ferguson of Craighdarroch, Master......................................(-1796)
Hon. Francis Charteris, Lord Elcho, Grand Master.............................(1749-1808)
James Sandilands, ninth Earl of Torpichen.......................................(1759-1815)
Archibald, eleventh Earl of Eglinton..(1733-1796)
James Cunningham, fourteenth Earl of Glencairn (Burns' earliest and
    best friend and patron in Edinburgh)..(1749-1791)
David, Earl of Buchan...(1742-1829)
Charles More, of the Royal Bank, Depute Master...............................(   )
Patrick Miller of Dalswinton..(1731-1815)
James Dalrymple of Orangefield...(-1795)
Sir John Whitefoord...(-1803)
Sir William Forbes of Pitsligo, Bart...(1739-1806)
John Mercer, writer, Secretary...(   )
William Mason, Grand Secretary...(   )
James Burnet—Lord Monboddo, the eccentric and learned...................(1714-1779)
The Hon. Henry Erskine..(1746-1817)
George Spankie, Treasurer..(   )

Baron Norton..(-1820)
Henry MacKenzie, author of *The Man of Feeling*.................................(1745-1831)
The Hon. William Gordon, Lord Kenmure...(1763-1840)
Alexander Cunningham, Jeweller..(1763-1812)
William Dunbar, W.S. Senior Warden..(-1807)
Kenneth Love, tailor, Serving Brother...( )
William Nicol, Teacher of Latin, Edinburgh High School......................(1744-1797)
William Cruickshank, Teacher...(-1793)
Louis Cauvin, French Teacher...(1754-1825)
Allan Masterton, Writing Master and Composer of Music...................(-1789)
Signor Stabilini, a celebrated player on the violin.................................( )
James Tytler, Apothecary, an out-and-out Bohemian...........................(-1798)
Thomas Neil, undertaker...(1730-1800)
James Dhu, Corporal of the Town Guard, Grand Tyler........................( )
Alexander Campbell, organist, etc..(1764-1824)
John Campbell, undertaker and teacher of music................................(1750-1795)
Samuel Clark, Organist of Cowgate Chapel.......................................( )
Georgie Cranstoun, Vocalist...(-1820)
J. G. C. Schetky, Music Teacher..( )
Professor Dugald Stewart, Philosopher...(1753-1828)
William Creech, the Bookseller...(1745-1815)
Peter Williamson, a man of "Curious Adventures"..............................(1735-1799)
William Smellie, Printer..(1740-1795)
Peter Hill, Bookseller (Creech's Business Manager).............................( )
Sir James Hunter-Blair, Grand Treasurer..(1741-1787)
Francis, seventh Earl Napier..(1758-1823)
James Boswell of Auchenleck, Esq., Advocate....................................(1740-1795)
Alexander Nasmyth, Limner...(1759-1840)
James Johnston, Engraver...(-1811)
Francis Grose, Esq., F.S.A. London and Perth....................................(1743-1791)
James Gregory, M.D..(1753-1824)
Alexander Wood, Surgeon...(1725-1807)
David Ramsay of the *Edinburgh Evening Courant*.............................(-1813)
John Gray, W.S. City Clerk...( )
John Miller, Advocate, Junior Warden..( )
Captain Fr. Baillet of Milton House...( )
Robert Ainslie, W.S...(1766-1838)
William Woods, Tragedian...(1750-1802)

This canvas, by W. Stewart Watson (1800-1870), hangs in the Freemason's Hall, Edinburgh, and is exceptionally valuable as a gallery of authentic portraits of the Poet's friends. A daguerreotype of the original painting was presented to Joseph Michael Smith (1809-1888), ship owner of Monkwearmouth, Sunderland, and is now in the possession of his son, Grant F. O. Smith.

1787 Robert Burns (Caledonia's Bard)
1835 James Hogg (The Ettrick Shepherd)
1836 William Hay (The Lintie o' Moray)
1842 E. W. Lane, M.D.
1846 Francis Nicoll
1850 James Marshall
1851 N. J. Mansabins
1853 William Pringle
1860 Anthony O'Neal Haye (Author of *Poemate*, and Editor of the *Scottish Freemason Magazine*)
1872 Captain Lawrence Archer
1879 Bryan Charles Waller, M.D. of Masongill
1880 Andrew Stevenson, M.A. (Author of *The Laureate Wreath*, etc.)
1887 Charles H. Mackay
1890 Wallace Bruce (Author of *The Old Organ*, etc.)
1897 Charles Martin Hardie, R.S.A.
1899 Alexander Anderson (Surfaceman)
1902 F. N. Hepburn (Gabriel Setoun)
1905 Rudyard Kipling
1909 Stewart Home
1918 Joseph Inglis, W.S., P.M.
1920 T. S. Muir, M.A., P.M.
1922 Allan M'Neil, M.A., P.M.
1923 John B. Peden, P.M.
1926 Dr. J. C. Stewart

The atmosphere Burns discovered in Masonry made an immediate and irresistible appeal to his deep love of human nature, as well as to the appreciation of God's created works which is every Poet's heritage. From the time of his initiation onwards we find Masonry continually peeping forth in his productions. Could any man deaf to the real aims of the Craft have penned these world-famous lines?

> Then let us pray that come it may—
> As come it will for a' that—
> That sense and worth, o'er a' the earth,
> May bear the gree and a' that,
> For a' that, and a' that,
> It's comin' yet for a' that,
> That man to man, the world o'er
> Shall brothers be for a' that.

There, in a stanza, is expressed the whole ideal of Freemasonry. And here is another Masonic verse from Burns' hand:

> A ye whom social pleasure charms,
> Whose heart the tide of kindness warms
> Wha hold your being on the terms,
> Each aid the others,
> Come to my bowl, come to my arms
> My friends, my brothers.

From the second edition of his *Poems*, published by Creech early in March, 1787, Burns acquired a sum of money (to the credit of his countrymen they were not slow in subscribing). Upwards of fifteen hundred names, and among them the highest and most distinguished in Scotland, appear on the list. Many of the subscribers took more than one copy, and paid more than the shop price, six shillings. Since Burns had stipulated for the profit on the subscription copies, besides the payment of one hundred pounds, his gain was considerable. Nearly three thousand copies were soon dispersed over the country. Many of them went to England, some to Valladolid; Donay, Paris, and Ratisbon appear in the list of subscribers. East, west, north and south flew the effusions of "Coila's Bard," and everywhere were they received with the same warm and affectionate welcome that enabled him not only to partake of the pleasures of Edinburgh, but to gratify a desire he had long entertained of visiting those parts of his native country, most attractive by their beauty or their grandeur, a desire which the return of summer naturally revived. The scenery on the banks of the Tweed, and of its tributary streams, strongly interested him; and accordingly he left Edinburgh, May 6, 1787, on a tour through a country celebrated in the rural songs of Scotland. Wherever he went his fame marched before him. Indeed, it had by now arrived at a pitch when there was no arresting its growth, and the Poet seems to have been a little frightened by his popularity. To one of his early Ayrshire patrons he wrote from Edinburgh: "I tremble lest I should be dragged too suddenly into the glare of polite and learned observation."

He travelled on horseback, and was accompanied during some parts of the journey by Robert Ainslie, a gentleman who enjoyed much of his friendship and of his confidence. One of the towns

ST. JOHN'S LODGE, THE HOME OF LODGE CANONGATE KILWINNING
No. 2, EDINBURGH. BUILT IN 1735.

(Looking south-east.)

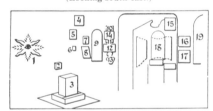

1. The All-Seeing Eye, Mural painting behind R.W.M.'s chair.
2. The perfect Ashlar.
3. The Altar on the tessilated carpet.
4. Another of the four emblematic banners.
5. Etching of the fine portrait of Robert Burns after Skirving.
6. Silhouette of Robert Burns, by Mefers, 1787.
7. Engraving of Burns after Taylor.
8. Engraved portrait of Robert Burns, by Walter after Nasmyth.
9. Mural painting of Robert Burns as the lyric muse.
10. Subscription list of Canongate Kilwinning Brothers for Mausoleum erected in Greyfriars Church-yard, Dumfries, in memory of Robert Burns, who was affiliated on February 1, 1787, and crowned Poet-Laureate on March 1, 1787
11. Letter of acknowledgment to No. 10.
12. Deed of Election of Brother William St. Clair of Rosslyn as Grand Master and of other office-bearers of Grand Lodge, November 30, 1736. Presented by Professor W. E. Aytoun.
13. The Poet-Laureate's seat in the Lodge is under a fine half-life-size bust of Robert Burns, its first recorded Poet-Laureate.
14 and 15. Pair of finely emblazoned armorial bearings of Lodge Canongate Kilwinning carried in Masonic processions.
16. Oil painting of Thomas MacKenzie, H.M. Solicitor-General.
17. Engraving of Henry Lord Brougham, assumed member of the Lodge, June 24, 1800.
18. The organ bought from Mr. Snetzlear, London, in 1754, erected in an apse especially built for it in the west of the Lodge in 1756. It is valued for its fine mellow tone. The keyboard is black with white ivory accidentals. It was placed in its present position, in the south of the Lodge, at a later date.
19. Portion of the Mural painting depicting Shakespeare as the Tragic Muse. Outside the margin of the photo is the J.W.'s Chair, forming the south-west angle of the triangle, the apex of which is the R.W.M.'s Chair on the dais. This working evades the necessity of anyone in the Lodge turning his back to the W.R.M.

ST. JOHN'S LODGE, THE HOME OF LODGE CANONGATE KILWINNING
No. 2, EDINBURGH. BUILT IN 1735.

(Looking north-east.)

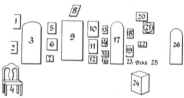

1. Portrait of W. N. Fraser of Tornaveen. R. W. M. 1853-1855, and 1865-1866. Painted by Brother Stewart Watson.
2. Engraved portrait of James Gregory, M.D., 1753-1821. Initiated 1789. Professor of Physics, Edinburgh University.
3. Mural painting of Alexander Pope, representing Epic Poetry.
4. Senior Warden's chair. Lodge Canongate Kilwinning works on the equilateral triangle in remembrance of its origin as an operative lodge by Mother Kilwinning, Ayrshire, in 1677.
5. Portrait of A. L. Robertson, W.S. R.W.M. 1815-1830, and 1860-1861. Painted by Brother Stewart Watson.
6. Portrait of Robert Jack in his robes as Bailie of Canongate. Died 1754. Early painting possibly by Alan Ramsay, Jr.
7. Memorial tablet to memory of Brethren who fell in the Great War, 1914-1918.
8. Masonic sundial of Lodge Canongate Kilwinning, from which the J.W. takes his time.
9. Full-length portrait of the M.W.G.M., William St. Clair of Rosslyn (believed to be the work of Alan Ramsay, Jr., the son of the Poet, who was made a mason in 1736). St. Clair was initiated in Lodge Canongate Kilwinning, May 18, 1736, and raised, November 22nd, and occupied the chair the same evening. On November 24, 1736, his Deed of Demition (written by Brother David Maull, W.S. Secretary of Lodge Canongate Kilwinning) was presented by him on behalf of himself and his heirs as Hereditary Grand Masters. This permitted Grand Lodge being formed in Mary's Chapel on St. Andrew's Day, Nov 30, 1736.
10. Portrait in oils of Alexander McNeill, Advocate R.W.M. 1830-1838. Painted by Charles Samoski, and presented by Prince Czartorski and other Polish patriots admitted to the Lodge membership in 1835.
11. Mrs. Jack's portrait, which by the Deed of Gift in 1880 was to hang along with that of No. 6 (Bailie Robert Jack). It is a companion picture by the same painter.
12. Portrait of Sir Joshua Reynolds by himself in oils. Possibly a copy.
13. Engraving of King George IV, then Prince Regent and M.W.G.M. of England.
14. Engraving of Lord Provost George Drummond, M.W.G.M. R.W.M. 1764.
15. "The Knight," painted by W. Etty, R.A.
16. Engraving of Alexander Adam, LL.D., initiated 1771. Rector of the High School.
17. Mural painting of Sir Walter Scott as the romantic muse, c. 1830.
18. Engraving of Alexander Nasmyth, initiated 1771. Nasmyth painted the most widely known portrait of Robert Burns.
19. Photogravure of King Edward VII as M.W.G.M. of England.
20. One of the four symbolic old banners hung in the Lodge.
21. James Hogg, the Ettrick Shepherd, initiated and crowned Poet-Laureate of the Lodge at Innerleithen in 1835. Medallion.
22. Coloured etching, "Dr. Syntax at Freemason's Hall," by Rowlandson.
23. The old ballot box of the Lodge, still used.
24. The Altar.
25. The unpolished Ashlar.
26. The R.W.M.'s chair, the history of which would fill a volume.
27. Old-style fireplace, still in use.

visited by Burns and his friend Robert Ainslie was Eyemouth. Burns' diary reads:

Saturday—spend the day at Mr. Grieve's—made a royal arch mason at St. Abb's Lodge. Mr. William Grieve, the eldest brother, a joyous, warm-hearted jolly clever fellow—takes a hearty glass, and sings a good song. Mr. Robert, his brother, and partner in trade, a good fellow, but says little. Take a sail after dinner. Fishing of all kinds pay tythes at Eyemouth.

The entry made on this occasion in the Lodge books is as follows:

Eyemouth, 19th May, 1787.

At a general encampment held this day, the following brethren were made Royal Arch Masons, viz.—Robert Burns, from the Lodge of St. James' Tarbolton, Ayrshire, and Robert Ainslie, from the Lodge of St. Luke's, Edinburgh, by James Carmichael, William Grieve, Daniel Dow, John Clay, Robert Grieve, etc. etc., Robert Ainslie paid one guinea admission dues; but on account of R. Burns' remarkable poetical genius, the encampment unanimously agreed to admit him gratis; and considered themselves honoured by having a man of such shining abilities for one of their companions.

Burns, having spent about three weeks in exploring the south of Scotland, crossed the Tweed over the Coldstream bridge into Northumberland. He knelt down on the English side and poured forth uncovered, and with strong emotion, the prayer for Scotland contained in the last two stanzas of the "Cotter's Saturday Night." Mr. Ker and Mr. Hood, two gentlemen with whom he had become acquainted in the course of his tour, accompanied him. On his way to Newcastle, Burns stopped at Alnwick and Warkworth. Respecting both these places a few brief entries were made in his diary. Thus he records that "Mr. Wilkin, the agent of the Duke of Northumberland, 'a discreet, sensible, ingenious man,' showed him the curiosities and treasures of Alnwick Castle." Hexham and Morpeth were both visited. The following entries were made in his diary:

Monday, 28th May 1787. Slept at Morpeth—a pleasant enough little town—and on next day to Newcastle. Met with a very agreeable, sensible fellow—a Mr. Chattox, who shows us a great many civilities and dines and sups with us.

Newcastle was the farthest away Burns ever got from Scotland.

R.B.—7

Wednesday, 30th—Leave Newcastle early in the morning and ride over a fine country to Hexham to breakfast.

He then proceeded to Wardrue, the celebrated Spa, to Long-town (where he parted with his friends, Messrs. Hood and Ker), and Carlisle. After spending a few days at Carlisle with his friend Mr. Mitchell, he returned to Scotland, and at Annan his journal terminates abruptly. From Annan, Burns proceeded to Dumfries, and then through Sanquhar to Mossgiel, near Mauchline, in Ayrshire, where he arrived about June 8, 1787. It will easily be conceived with what pleasure and pride he was received by his mother, his brothers and sisters. He had left them poor and comparatively friendless; he returned to them high in public estimation, and easy in his circumstances. He returned to them unchanged in his ardent affections, and ready to share with them to the uttermost farthing the pittance that fortune had bestowed.

Having remained with them a few days, he proceeded again to Edinburgh and immediately set out on a journey to the Highlands. Of this tour no particulars have been found among his manuscripts. From this journey Burns returned to his friends in Ayrshire, with whom he spent the month of July, renewing his friendships, and extending his acquaintance throughout the country, where he was now very generally known and admired.

In the possession of the St. James' Lodge, Tarbolton, there is a letter of much interest. It was written by Burns and, needless to say, is much prized by its members. It has to do with the non-payment of dues, and on this occasion, Decree was got out against some flagrant offenders, and a Warrant procured. However, it was never enforced, but in many cases Charity was dispensed, and debts cancelled when the debtor seemed in poor circumstances. Leniency was ever urged by Burns towards the poor debtor, of this we have in the following letter:

Edinburgh, August 27th, 1787.

The Right Worshipful Master,
St. James' Lodge Tarbolton,
c-o James Manson, Innkeeper,
Tarbolton.

Men and Brethern:

I am sorry it is not in my power to be with you at your quarterly meeting. If I am absent in body, believe me I shall be with you in spirit. I suppose those who owe us monies by bill or otherwise will appear—I mean those we summoned. If you please, I wish you would delay prosecuting defaulters till I come home. The court is up, and I shall be home before it sits down again. In the meantime take a note of who appear and who do not, of our faulty debtors, will be in my humble opinion right; and those who confess debt, and crave days; I think we should spare them.

Farewell.

R. BURNS.

This letter is framed with a glass case, and is always carried by the youngest Apprentice Mason when the Lodge turns out for any Masonic function or procession.

A gentleman, desirous of an introduction to Burns, applied to Dr. James Mackenzie of Mauchline, by whom he was introduced at an accidental roadside interview, during which Burns stated that he was that same evening to be in the Masonic Lodge.

In the evening Mackenzie and his friend proceeded to the Lodge, but arriving rather late, the meeting was already constituted and pretty far advanced in jollity. After sitting for sometime the stranger whispered in the doctor's ear "What has become of Burns?" "Become of him!" said Mackenzie. "Don't you see him in the Chair?" "No," said his friend, "that is certainly not the man we saw in the forenoon." It was the Poet, nevertheless, under new circumstances.

The annual meeting of Lodge St. James was always held on St. John the Baptist's Day, June 24th, and the anxiety of Burns to have it properly attended is evinced by a verified note which he sent, to this same friend, Mr. John Mackenzie (surgeon, and author of the *Origin of Morals*), who had some time before expressed a fear lest his duty to his patients should prevent his being present.

> Friday first's the day appointed
> By the Right Worshipful anointed,
> To hold our grand procession;
> To get a blad o' Johnie's morals
> And taste a swatch o' Manson's barrels
> I' the way of our profession.
>
> The Master and the Brotherhood
> Would a' be glad to see you;
> For me I would be mair than proud
> To share the mercies wi' you.

If Death, then, wi *skaith*, then	*hurt*
Some mortal heart is *hechtin*	*threatening*
Inform him and storm him	
That Saturday you'll *fecht* him.	*fight*

This anniversary was always borne in mind by Burns, and, on one occassion, when in a despondent mood, he wrote:

Tarbolton, twenty-fourth of June,
You'll find me in a better tune.

About the beginning of September he again set out for Edinburgh on an extended tour of the Highlands, accompanied by his friend William Nicol.   We find a reference to him in the well-known poem, "Willie Brewed a Peck o' Maut" which is really a Masonic song.   The meeting which it celebrates took place between the Poet, William Nicol, of the High School, Edinburgh, and Allan Masterton, another schoolmaster, and musical amateur; the three were members at the time of Lodge Canongate Kilwinning,   Nicol had bought a small farm named Laggan, in the parish of Dunscore, Dumfriesshire, where he spent the autumn vacations.   Allan Masterton and the Poet went on a visit to the "Illustrious Lord of Laggan's many hills."   Nicol, as in duty bound, produced his best. Tradition asserts, that day dawned long ere the guests rose to depart.   "The air is Masterton's," says Burns, "the song is mine. We had such a joyous meeting, that Mr. Masterton and I agreed, each in his own way, to celebrate the business."

O' Willie brew'd a peck o' *maut*	*of malt*
And Rob and Allan cam' to *pree;*	*taste*
Three blither hearts, that lee-lang night,	
Ye wadna find in Christendie.	
We are *na fou*, we're no that fou	*not full*
But just a drappie in our *ee;*	*eye*
The cock may craw, the day may daw,	
An' aye we'll taste the barley *bree*	*brew*
Here are we met, three merry boys,	
Three merry boys, I trow, are we;	
And mony a night we've merry been,	
And *mony mae* we hope to be!	**many** *more*

It is the moon,—I *ken* her horn   *know*
That's blinking in the *lift sae hie*,   *heavens so high*
She shines sae bright to *wile* us hame,   *guide*
But, by my sooth! she'll wait a wee.

What first shall rise to gang awa'
A cuckold, coward loon is he.
Wha last beside his *chan* shall fa'   *chair*
He is the King among us three!

Lockhart has pronounced this "the best of all Burns' bacchanalian pieces."

When Burns left Mossgiel for Ellisland, in 1788, he at once affiliated with Lodge St. Andrew in Dumfries. His affiliation fee was ten shillings. Among other by-laws of this Lodge we read, that a brother in good standing for three years shall receive three shillings a week, if he falls into distress, and that a brother who appears "disguised in liquor" may be severely punished. The latter regulation is interesting in view of the Dumfries gossip and slander of a later day. Burns filled the office of Senior Warden and attended with regularity. (1791: December 27th; 1792: February 26th; May 14th, June 5th; November 22nd, 30th; 1793: November 29th; 1796: January 28th, April 14th.) On January 28, 1796, Burns attended the Lodge to recommend James Georgeson, merchant, as an apprentice. The last recorded occasion was in April, 1796, three months before his death, when Captain Adam Gordon was initiated.

It has been stated that Burns' connection with Freemasonry led him at times into excesses. That there is some truth in this cannot be denied, but it was not to the extent that one or two writers suggest. It was a hard-drinking age, such as we fortunately have been spared. Masonic gatherings, we have been told, were convivial meetings of jolly good fellows, which might often be without wit but never could be without drink. The conditions of farm life were all but intolerable, and early broke the Poet's health. Opportunities for education and social intercourse were limited in country districts, and his soul craved for society in that dry, individualistic age. Masonry provided such an atmosphere and gave an outlet for his high spirits. However much he may have indulged the practices of his time, as we all do in various ways, there was always the ideal of sociability, brotherly love, good companionship in the foreground. We must not overlook the fact, that it was the same intensity of feeling that made him a poet which also broke down the restraints that curb men of colder passion. True, he writes verses like these:

> Then fill up a bumper and make it o'er-flow,
> And honours Masonic prepare for to throw.
> May every true brother of the compass and square
> Have a big-bellied bottle when harassed with care.

But here is the nobler man and Mason:

> For thus the royal mandate ran
> When first the human race began,
> The social friendly, honest man
> Whate'er he be,
> 'Tis he fulfils great Nature's plan
> And none but he.

And again he writes:

God knows I am no saint: I have a whole lot of sins and follies to answer for: but if I could, and I believe I do as far as I can, I would wipe away all tears from all eyes.

This is the very core of Burns' spirit—"brotherly love at the centre"; and surely it is also the very core of our Masonic faith and brotherhood, however far we may fall short of realizing the ideal. It does not mean a silly, unintelligent dispensing of charity to all and sundry, but only to a "worthy" brother in distress. Burns has pointed out that our feelings are not to be gauged by money payments at all:

> A man may tak a neibour's part,
> Yet hae nae cash to spare him.

Here he gives voice to his deepest feelings:

> Nae treasures nor pleasures
> Could make us happy lang,
> The heart ay's the part ay
> That makes us right or wrang.

Or again:

> The heart benevolent and kind
> The most resembles God.

This is the true Burns, the Burns who from his earliest years, when he was being trained by his God-fearing father, was ever filled with veneration of holy things. He had not studied the V. S. L. in vain. Passing from material charity to the spiritual "charity which suffereth long and is kind, and thinks no evil," we find Burns again expressing our highest thoughts in these words:

> Then gently scan your brother man
> Still gentler sister woman:
> Tho' they may gang a kennin' wrang,
> To step aside is human.

Such charity has for long been denied the Poet himself. Yet Burns was discriminating in his brotherly love; he was a cannie Scot, a prudent man, and counselled the "Young Friend":

> Ay free, *aff han'*, your story tell   *off hand*
> When *wi'* a bosom cronie,   *with*
> But still keep something to yersel'
> Ye scarcely tell to *onie*.   *any*

In a letter addressed to Sir John Whitefoord, Grand Master, Burns says:

We look on our Masonic Lodge to be a serious matter, both with respect to the character of Masonry itself and likewise as it is a charitable society.

Gilbert Burns tells us that when Burns became a Freemason it was his first introduction to the life of a boon companion.

Yet not these circumstances and the praise he had bestowed on Scotch drink (which seems to have misled his historians), I do not recollect these seven years nor till the end of his commencing author (when his growing celebrity occasioned him often being in company), to have ever seen him intoxicated, nor was he at all given to drink.

The friends Burns acquired in Edinburgh circles, highest in Masonic rank, were: Francis Charteris, Lord Elcho, the Grand

Master; Lord Torpichen, a name which is associated with the history of Masonry from the very first period; Archibald Montgomerie, Earl of Eglinton; James Cunningham, Earl of Glencairn, through whose influence the Caledonian Hunt became the patrons of the second edition of the *Poems;* Patrick Miller of Dalswinton, who will ever be remembered in connection with the early history of steam navigation; Dalrymple of Orangefield; Sir William Forbes, of Pitsligo, a famous Edinburgh banker, who would have been Lord Pitsligo had his forebears attended to their own business instead of marching out with Prince Charlie in the rebellion of 1745; James Burnet, Lord Monboddo, one of the Lords of Session, a zealous believer in what is now known as the Darwin Theory long before Darwin was born, and one of the most curious characters which that cabinet of curiosities—the Edinburgh Court of Sessions—has furnished to the world; Professor Dugald Stewart, the greatest of Scottish philosophers, who was Chaplain of Kilwinning Lodge; Frances Napier, Lord Napier, an officer who figures in the war of the American Revolution under General Burgoyne; William St. Clair, Earl of Roslin, in whose family the Grand Mastership of Scotland was long hereditary. There were hundreds of lesser degree, including very many advocates and writers, such as Alexander Cunningham and William Dundas, also William Nicol, one of the masters of the High School. With such friends is it a wonder that in the most fashionable parlours he was received with the honours usually awarded to distinguished strangers? But the wonder is that he, so recently a petty farmer in a remote county, could at once take his place in such circles and hold his own against all comers.

Burns was contemplating emigration to Jamaica, and bade farewell to his Masonic brethren in St. James in these well-known moving lines:

> Adieu! a heart warm, fond adieu!
> Dear brothers of the mystic tie!
> Ye favour'd, ye enlighten'd few
> Companions of my social joy!
> Tho' I to foreign lands must hie,
> Pursuing Fortune's slidd'ry ba',
> With melting heart, and brimful eye,
> I'll mind you still, tho' far awa'.

Oft have I met your social band,
And spent the cheerful festive night;
Oft' honour'd with supreme command,
Presided o'er the sons of light;
And by that hieroglyphic bright,
Which none but craftsmen ever saw!
Strong memory on my heart shall write
Those happy scenes when far awa'.

May freedom harmony and love,
Unite far in the grand design,
Beneath th' omniscient eye above,
The glorious Architect divine!
That you may keep th' unerring line,
Still rising by the plummet's law,
Till order bright completely shine
Shall be my pray'r when far awa'.

And you, farewell! whose merits claim,
Justly, that highest badge to wear![1]
Heav'n bless your honour'd noble name,
To Masonry and Scotia dear!
A last request permit me here,
When yearly ye assemble a'
One round I ask it with a tear,
To him the Bard that's far awa'.

In these words Burns bade farewell to his Masonic Brethren. The concluding verse, it is said, affected them deeply. They knew that "hungry ruin had him in the wind"—that his evil fortune was forcing him to a strange land and an inhospitable clime; they knew that his prospects were dark at home, and they were not free from the presentiment which haunted his mind, that they were darker abroad.

To so fervent a patriot as Burns this contemplated exile must have been all but intolerable, for the Almighty had implanted in his breast a sacred and indissoluble attachment towards that country whence he had derived his birth and infant nurture. In his earliest years he tells us:

[1] Sir John Whitefoord, the Grand Master.

> Even then a wish, I min' its power,
> A wish that to my latest hour
> Shall strongly heave my breast—
> That I for puir auld Scotland's sake
> Some usefu' plan or beuk could make
> Or sing a song at least.

But another Mason, Dr. Blacklock, intervened and changed the Poet's career.

The noble Farewell of Burns to the Brethren of St. James Tarbolton is sung or recited by the oldest Past Master present at the yearly meeting, now held in honour of the Poet on the nearest Friday to his birthday. It is a religious duty never to be omitted, and the "Immortal Memory" is given with full "Masonic Honours."

Lodge St. James Tarbolton is the Mecca toward which the feet of many Burns students and Masonic brothers turn, for it still possesses many interesting relics of the Poet. Besides the old Minute Book of the Lodge there is the chair in which he sat as the Depute-Master; the mallet which he used in ruling his Lodge; the Jewel and Apron he wore; and, last but not least, the Volume of the Sacred Law, which he himself presented to the Lodge.

Robert Burns was a real and enthusiastic Mason. His presence among his Masonic brethren brought life and mirth and happiness: he breathed the very spirit of brotherly love into his fellow-men because it was so deeply-seated and all-pervading in his own nature, and he has left us such a heritage of glorious song that our harmony board may never lack enjoyment. From the time he entered Masonry, in 1781, till his death in 1796, his interest never flagged, as is shown by his attendances at, and identifying himself with Lodges wherever he happened to be for a time—Ayr, Kilmarnock, Newmilns, Edinburgh, Eyemouth, Dumfries. He honoured and exemplified the Tenets and Principles of Freemasonry to the end of his short but wonderful career.

One of his noblest lyrics is penned in gratitude over the bier of his patron, James, Earl of Glencairn, after whom he names one of his sons, and a good Mason in his day:

> The bridegroom may forget the bride
> Was made his wedded wife yestreen:
> The monarch may forget the crown
> That on his head an hour has been;
> The mother may forget the child
> That smiles sae sweetly on her knee;
> But I'll remember thee, Glencairn,
> And a' that thou hast done for me.

Truly a great object lesson to one and all.

Yet he did not confine his sympathy to his fellowmen; the whole realm of nature claimed a place in his heart. He loved the wimplin burn, the flowery dell, wood and glen and moor, bird and beast, as well as man. His heart bled for the wounded hare and the uprooted daisy: even a louse had his sympathy in a modified and distant degree, and his pet eweie when she "warsl't ower in the ditch" made the saut tears trickle down his nose. She bequeathed her blether to puir Hughoc, and to us all this bit of excellent advice:

> An' when ye think *upo'* your mither   *about*
> Mind to be kind to *yin* anither.   *one*

What a perfect understanding had grown up between the farmer and his auld mare! Here Burns is at his very best, as he rehearses the great ploys man and horse had had together, and how at the end, when twenty-nine years' work was done:

> An' think na, ma auld trusty servan'
> That now perhaps thou's less deservin'
> And thy auld days may end in starvin'.

Burns was the first to give expression to this affection for the beasts that toil for man. How keenly he could imagine the minds of "The Twa Dogs" and see what went on inside their heads. How sublimely he pities the mouse when he sees the irreparable disaster he has unwittingly brought down on its defenceless head. With what unerring instinct he pictures it "wi monie a weary nibble" build up its frail house against the winter's sleety drizzle and cranreugh cauld, only to be dashed to pieces by his plough, like the best-laid schemes o' men. How humiliating for us to be coupled with this destructive vermin, till the Poet reminds us, that we are poor earth-born companions and fellow-mortals; that the same Potter has moulded mice and men alike in one clay, and foreordained them to the same doom—"unto dust thou shalt return."

Mr. A. Baine Irvine, in his oration delivered at the Scots Lodge of Freemasons, No. 2319, on Burns' Nicht held at the Holborn Restaurant, London, January 24, 1929, said:

His piercing vision enabled him to see at once and in startling clearness that equity, fairness, to say nothing of humanity, must, indeed, all be but sickly plants in an atmosphere of repression where one class lords it over another, and, in general, "Man's inhumanity to man makes countless thousands mourn."

> He taught us how to shape our life into nobler ends;
> He wrought to make men Brothers, Builders, Friends.

NOTE: Several quotations in this chapter are from the lecture given at Edinburgh, January 21, 1938, by W. King Gillies, M.A., LL.D., P.M., Lodge Canongate Kilwinning, No. 2, to the Masters and Past Masters Association of the Metropolitan District, the Lothians and Berwickshire.

XII

The Correspondents of Robert Burns

MANY of Scotland's most distinguished sons and daughters, as well as hard working folk who earned their bread by the sweat of their brow, were Burns' correspondents.

MISS ELIZABETH BURNETT...1765-1790
THE DUCHESS OF GORDON...1746-1812
THE COUNTESS OF GLENCAIRN...
MISS MARGARET (PEGGY) CHALMERS.. -1843
JAMES CUNNINGHAM, EARL OF GLENCAIRN.....................................1749-1791
REV. DR. THOMAS BLACKLOCK..1721-1791
DR. JOHN MOORE..1729-1802
DR. HUGH BLAIR..1718-1800
REV. JOHN SKINNER..1721-1807
WILLIAM TYTLER OF WOODHOUSELEE...1711-1792
MRS. DUNLOP OF DUNLOP...1731-1815
WILLIAM SMELLIE..1740-1795
MRS. BRUCE OF CLACKMANNAN...1696-1791
GEORGE THOMSON...1757-1851
JAMES BURNETT, LORD MONBODDO..1714-1799
CAPTAIN FRANCIS GROSE...1730-1791
HON. HENRY ERSKINE...1746-1817
JAMES DALRYMPLE OF ORANGEFIELD... -1795
DR. JAMES GREGORY...1753-1824
HENRY MACKENZIE...1745-1831
PROFESSOR DUGALD STEWART...1753-1828
DR. ADAM FERGUSON...1723-1816
ROBERT AINSLIE..1766-1838
JOHN BEUGO..1759-1841
JOHN MURDOCH...1747-1824
WILLIAM NICOL..1744-1797
JOHN SYME..1754-1831
SIR JOHN WHITEFOORD.. -1803
ROBERT HERON...1764-1807
CLARINDA, MRS. AGNES M'LEHOSE..1759-1841
JOHN M'MURDO... -1803
ROBERT HARTLEY CROMEK...1770-1812
RICHARD BROWN...

WILLIAM CRUICKSHANK.. -1793
ALEXANDER CUNNINGHAM... 1763-1812
ROBERT MUIR.. 1758-1788
WILLIAM MUIR... 1745-1793
SIR WILLIAM FORBES OF PITSLIGO, BART... 1739-1806
ARCHIBALD SKIRVING.. 1749-1819
WILLIAM CREECH.. 1745-1815
WILLIAM BURNESS.. 1721-1784
ALEXANDER NASMYTH... 1757-1840
DR. JAMES CURRIE... 1756-1805
DR. JOHN MACKENZIE.. -1837
JOHN BALLANTINE... 1743-1812
GAVIN HAMILTON... 1751-1805
DAVID SILLAR.. 1760-1830
JAMES JOHNSON.. -1811
ROBERT AIKEN.. 1739-1807

MISS ELIZABETH BURNETT [1765-1790]

Elizabeth Burnett was the youngest daughter of the elegant and eccentric Lord Monboddo. She is alluded to in the Poet's address to Edinburgh. She was a lady of exquisite beauty and grace, and her pleasing personality delighted everyone. Burns was a frequent visitor to Lord Monboddo's home during 1786-1787. Asked by Father Geddes if he admired the young lady, he replied, "I admire God Almighty more than ever; Miss Burnett is the most heavenly of all His Works." She was greatly attached to her father, and after her mother's death she kept home for him till she died.

I had the honour, says the Poet to Mrs. Dunlop, of being pretty well acquainted with her, and have seldom felt so much at the loss of an acquaintance, as when I heard that so amiable and accomplished piece of God's work was no more.

This may be contrasted with his opinion of her, expressed shortly after his first introduction:

There has not been anything nearly like her in all the combinations of beauty, grace and goodness the great Creator has formed, since Milton's Eve, on the first day of her existance.

Her life was of short duration. She died of consumption on June 17, 1790. Burns wrote the following Elegy late in 1790:

> Life ne'er exulted in so rich a prize
> As Burnett, lovely from her native skies;
> Nor envious death so triumph'd in a blow,
> As that which laid th' accomplish'd Burnett low.

Thy form and mind, sweet maid, can I forget?
In richest ore the brightest jewel set!
In thee high Heaven above was truest shown,
And by his noblest work the Godhead best is known.

In vain ye flaunt in summer's pride, ye groves;
Thou crystal streamlet with thy flowery shore,
Ye woodland choir that chant your idle loves,
Ye cease to charm—Eliza is no more!

Ye heathy wastes, inmix'd with reedy fens;
Ye mossy streams, with sedge and rushes stor'd;
Ye rugged cliffs o'erhanging dreary glens,
To you I fly, ye with my soul accord.

Princes, whose cumbrous pride was all their worth,—
Shall venal lays their pompous exit hail?
And thou sweet excellence! forsake our earth,
And not a Muse in honest grief bewail?

We saw thee shine in youth and beauty's pride,
And virtue's light, that beams beyond the spheres;
But like the sun eclips'd at morning tide,
Thou left'st us darkling in a world of tears.

The parent's heart that nestled fond in thee,
That heart how sunk, a prey to grief and care;
So deckt the woodbine sweet yon aged tree,
So from it ravish'd, leaves it bleak and bare.

THE DUCHESS OF GORDON [1746-1812]

Born at Edinburgh, in 1746, the Duchess was the second daughter of Sir William Maxwell of Monteith. Married October 28, 1767, to Alexander, fourth Duke of Gordon, she at once became the recognized queen of Edinburgh society. Besides being possessed of considerable beauty, she was also noted for her wit and gaiety of temperament. Burns attended several of her drawing-room parties. Her Grace acknowledged that Burns was the only man she ever met whose conversation carried her off her feet, while others wondered and were unable to comprehend how an unlettered ploughman, as he was called, could move them to tears or laughter without any seemingly great effort on his part. Her Grace was particularly charmed with the Poet and his writings, and frequently asked him to recite one or more of his poems before her guests. She subscribed liberally for the Edinburgh edition of the *Poems*, and there is no doubt she appreciated the genius and worth of Burns to a much greater extent than many of the people with whom he associated. In her later years the Duchess lived apart from her husband.

The subject of a celebrated painting by Charles Martin Hardie, A.R.S.A., is taken from an incident in the life of Burns while at the height of his popularity in Edinburgh. It represents a meeting of the "literati" and other notables assembled in the drawing-room of the Edinburgh residence of the Duchess of Gordon. The Poet is seen, attired in the prevailing costume of the time (blue coat with brass buttons, yellow striped vest, buckskin breeches and top boots), standing before the group in the act of reciting his poem "A Winter Night." Opposite Burns, and fronting him, is his hostess, the Duchess of Gordon, seated resplendent in rose-coloured drapery and gown of rich brocade, posed somewhat as she appears in Reynolds' half-length, her cheek propped by her hand, intently listening. She died at London, April 11, 1812, at the age of sixty-six.

THE COUNTESS OF GLENCAIRN

The Countess resided at Coates House, near Edinburgh, and Burns was introduced to her on his first visit to the Scottish Capital. She was the mother of his patron and friend, James Cunningham, fourteenth Earl of Glencairn. According to Robert Chambers, "by her origin, the Countess was a somewhat remarkable person among the nobility, being the daughter of a village musician who was raised to unexpected wealth by the bequest of a fortunate relative. In a letter from the Poet to the Countess (Ellisland, 1789) occurs the famous passage:

I would much rather have it said, that my profession borrowed credit from me, than that I borrowed credit from my profession.

BURNS RECITING "A WINTER NIGHT" IN THE HOME OF
THE DUCHESS OF GORDON

Henry Erskine   William Tytler   Henry Mackenzie
Dr. Adam Ferguson   William Creech
Countess of Glencairn   Robert Burns   Alexander Nasmyth
Earl of Glencairn
Lord Monboddo
Miss Burnett
Peggy Chalmers
Duchess of Gordon
Dr. James Gregory
(of Gregory's Mixture fame)

DUMFRIES MARKETPLACE

PORTRAIT OF
THOMAS BLACKLOCK, D.D.

PORTRAIT OF ELIZABETH
BURNETT OF MONBODDO

PORTRAIT OF MRS. DUNLOP
OF DUNLOP.

PORTRAIT OF CAPTAIN
FRANCIS GROSE, F.S.A.

MISS MARGARET (PEGGY) CHALMERS [-1843]

Miss Margaret Chalmers was the heroine of the two lyrics, "Where Braving Angry Winter's Storms" and "My Peggy's Charms," and the supposed heroine of the Poet's last song, "Fairest Maid on Devon Banks," written July 12, 1796, nine days before he died. She was the youngest daughter of John Chalmers of Fingland in Dumfriesshire. Having sold his estate, he removed to Mauchline, and here Margaret was brought up. She was a cousin of Charlotte Hamilton. Burns was introduced to her at the house of Dr. Blacklock in Edinburgh, and afterward renewed the acquaintance while she was staying at the home of her uncle, Mr. Tait of Harveston. There is no doubt her personal elegance and accomplished mind made a deep impression on the Poet, and she became one of his most cherished friends and correspondents. "Indeed," says Mr. Lockhart, "with the exception of his letters to Mrs. Dunlop, there is no part of his correspondence which may be quoted so uniformly to his honour"; while Dr. Blacklock said: "Her gentleness and vivacity had a favourable influence on the manners of Burns, who always appeared to advantage in her presence."

Miss Chalmers was married December 9, 1788, to Mr. Lewis Hay, of Forbes & Co.'s bank. He died at Edinburgh, February 28, 1800. Mrs. Hay died at Pau in Berne in the spring of 1843.

JAMES CUNNINGHAM, EARL OF GLENCAIRN [1749-1791]

Born in 1749, James Cunningham succeeded to the title in 1775. In 1778 he was appointed Captain to a company in Lord Frederick Campbell's Regiment of Fencibles. He married Lady Isabella Erskine, in 1785, but there was no issue to the marriage and the title became extinct.

The Earl interested himself in the fortunes of the Poet. He carried the Kilmarnock edition of his *Poems* to Edinburgh and introduced it as a literary curiosity, besides desiring his factor, Mr. Alexander Dalzell, to convey to the Poet his high opinion of its merits, and his wish to befriend him. It was, moreover, through his influence that the Caledonian Hunt subscribed so liberally for the Edinburgh edition of Burns' *Poems*. The exertions of His Lordship did not end here; he did much, and he promised more, but "death the tyrant fell and woodie," stepped in and put an end to the Poet's hopes. Till his death, Burns retained a high sense of his obligations to Lord Glencairn.

As to forgetting the family of Glencairn (he thus writes to Her Ladyship), Heaven is my witness, with what sincerity I could use these old verses, which please me more in their rude simplicity than the most elegant lines I ever saw:

> If thee, Jerusalem, I forget
> Skill part from my right hand.
>
> My tongue to my mouth's roof let cleave,
> If I do thee forget,
> Jerusalem, and thee above
> My chief joy do not set.

Shortly after His Lordship's death, in 1791, Burns thus expressed himself to Lady E. Cunningham:

As all the world knows my obligations to the late Earl of Glencairn, I would wish to show as openly as possible that my heart glows, and shall ever glow, with the most grateful sense and rememberance of his Lordship's goodness. The sables that I did myself the honour to wear to his Lordship's memory were not the "mocking of woe." Nor shall my gratitude perish with me! If among my children I shall have a son that has a heart, he shall hand it down to his child as a family honour, and a family debt, that my dearest existence I owe to the noble house of Glencairn.

On account of ill health His Lordship went to Lisbon, in 1790, intending to pass the winter months there, but finding that he derived no benefit, left for home. He died at Falmouth, January 30, 1791, and was buried there.

REV. THOMAS BLACKLOCK, D.D. [1721-1791]
BY PETER ROSS [1847-1902]

One of the most touching and beautiful lives which the literary history of Scotland brings under our notice is that of Reverend Thomas Blacklock, the discoverer of Robert Burns. It was he whose verdict, upon reading a copy of the first edition of Burns' *Poems*, caused that genius to abandon his projected voyage to Jamaica and enter upon his brilliant season in Edinburgh. Probably but for this service Blacklock would long since have been forgotten, or, at best, be remembered only by a few literary students. As it is, his memory is preserved by the kindly, important, although brief, part he played in the terribly real drama of Burns' life, and so long as the great Scottish bard is honoured, so long will the memory of the kindly, blind poet be kept green.

The life of Thomas Blacklock deserves more than a passing degree of study for the example it furnishes us of sweet content and patient, hopeful, Christian resignation and joy. Even his poetry merits a better fate than the utter neglect which has overtaken it, for his verses contain many beautiful fancies, graceful word pictures, a deep religious sentiment, and a manly, honest, straightforward tone which cannot fail to entertain, refresh, and strengthen the reader. Blacklock was born in the royal burgh of Annan, Dumfriesshire, November 10, 1721. His father was a bricklayer, and poor. When about six months old the future poet was seized with smallpox, the most dangerous and vindictive disease of those days, and although the baby "warstled" through and recovered, it destroyed his eyesight for ever. So far as any impression of nature from actual observation was concerned, he might as well have been born blind. Still it is curious, in reading his poetry, to find how correctly his landscapes are drawn, how true his ideas of form and colour, and how discriminating his notions of beauty of plants and flowers. Only on one subject did his "darkness" lead him astray, and concerning that I shall speak further on. Being thus by his infirmity incapable of indulging in the usual frolics of childhood, Blacklock early manifested a delight in intellectual exercises. He loved to have books of all sorts read to him, and managed somehow to pick up a little Latin. Poetry was his delight. He never tired of listening to the words of the great masters of English song, and, as was natural under the circumstances, soon began to weave verses himself. These created quite an impression in Annan, and an eminent physician of the time kindly took the lad to Edinburgh, and defrayed the cost of his studies at the university there, with the view of his qualifying for the ministry. The publication of a volume of his verses also assisted the blind poet very materially, and in 1759 he was regularly licensed as a preacher.

At that time the only way to secure an appointment to a church in Scotland, at least in the "kirk by law established," was to obtain the favourable notice of such of the gentry as had the right of "presentation." In Blacklock's case the patron was not long wanting. The Earl of Selkirk appointed him minister of Kirkcudbright, and the poet doubtless felt that his future happiness and comfort were as fully assured as humanity could make them. But both the Earl and the minister had forgotten the existence of a stronger power than either of them—the people. The parishioners flatly refused to acquiesce in the arrangement. They declined to allow a blind man to act as their spiritual guide, and broke into open rebellion. They denounced the Earl for throwing the burden of maintaining his protégé upon them, derided the Poet for imagining that he could be a faithful and efficient minister in spite of his affliction, and impugned the law itself for permitting such an important matter as the selection of a caretaker for hundreds of souls to be at the whim or caprice of any one man. Blacklock was by no means fitted for carrying on his share in such a conflict as this, and gladly accepted a small annuity from the church in return for abandoning all claim to the active pastorate. Thus secured from all chance of actual want, Blacklock settled in Edinburgh with his wife. There she added to their income by keeping a few boarders, while he earned a little by his literary labours.

His home was a happy one, probably one of the happiest to be found in the capital of Scotland during that drunken, sceptical era. It ranked as one of the literary centres of the city, and its society was always refined, intellectual and pure. Sometimes the poet felt a sadness of heart, a great depression of soul, as he thought of the darkness to which he was doomed, but on such occasions he would take his lute and play his favourite religious and secular airs until the fit had passed. He was devoted to his wife, and believed her to be one of the most beautiful women in the world. He never wearied of extolling her beauty to his guests, and often caused them much embarrassment by the extravagance of his eulogies. She was, in reality, a good woman and a loyal and kind helpmate, but her features were of the homeliest type. This was the greatest delusion under which he ever laboured, yet he derived so much pleasure from it that none of his friends had the heart to tell him the truth. Her great and constant kindness to him were sufficient to sustain the idea, and his life was all the happier because of the belief.

The days and years in the little homestead passed on like a song. Religion, true, deep, practical, earnest religion, entered into all the doings of the inmates, and made their happiness real and abiding. The only extravagances of the poet were the little supper parties at which he entertained his literary friends. His house, too, was ever open, and the visitor to Edinburgh was always certain of a hearty welcome.

To the *Encyclopædia Britannica* Blacklock contributed a long and interesting article on "Blindness," and among his other prose works is one on *The Consolations of Religion*. On both these themes he was well qualified to write from personal experience. Blindness had no terrors and but few regrets for him, for the consolations of religion not only fully upheld him, but inspired him with a degree of cheerfulness which gratified and delighted all who knew and loved him. He wrote many sermons and religious works, but these appear to have long since spent their usefulness, and are now forgotten.

While religion was the star of Blacklock's life and prose composition its task, poetry was its pastime and delight. His muse was ever fresh, joyous and innocent. In his descriptive pieces and songs his style was somewhat affected, as was the fashion of his time. In his religious verses, however, Blacklock appears at his best. All his stiffness and artificiality seem to disappear, and the theme makes him rise into the truest elements of song—simplicity, sweetness, earnestness and truth. The Sixteenth Paraphrase gives us an example of his religious muse, which is familiar enough to Scottish readers, although not generally known on the other side of the Atlantic:

> In life's gay morn, when sprightly youth
>   With vital ardour glows,
> And shines in all the fairest charms
>   Which beauty can disclose,—
> Deep on thy soul, before its powers
>   Are yet by vice enslaved,
> Be thy Creator's glorious name
>   And character engraved.
>
> For soon the shades of grief shall cloud
>   The sunshine of thy days;
> And cares and toils in endless round
>   Encompass all thy ways.
> Soon shall thy heart the woes of age
>   In mournful groans deplore;
> And sadly muse on former joys
>   That now return no more.

Here is another of his hymns, a veritable song of triumph:

> Come, O my soul! in sacred lays
> Attempt thy great Creator's praise;
> But oh, what tongue can speak his fame?
> What mortal verse can reach the theme?
>
> Enthroned amid the radiant spheres
> He glory, like a garment, wears;
> To form a robe of light divine,
> Ten thousand suns around him shine.
>
> In all our Maker's grand designs,
> Almighty power with wisdom shines;
> His works through all this wondrous frame,
> Declare the glory of his name.
>
> Raised on devotion's lofty wing,
> Do thou, my soul, his glories sing.
> And let his praise employ thy tongue,
> Till listening worlds shall join the song.

Dr. Blacklock died July 7, 1791, at Edinburgh. His fame rests secure, not upon his poetry, beautiful as much of it is, or upon his theological and other writings, but upon the good which he accomplished during his own beautiful life. In a scoffing, doubting, rebellious age this man, poor in worldly goods, and deprived of one of the grandest of the human faculties, passed on during his appointed years with a heart overflowing with song, and a prayer of trust and resignation constantly on his lips. His home was as a haven of content, hope and faith in a troubled era in the history of old Edinburgh, and his kindly, winning words lifted many besides Robert Burns out of a slough of despond. May the sod grow green, the daisies spring luxuriantly, and the sun cast a golden halo on the grave in Buccleuch street kirkyard in which rest, "in the full assurance of a glorious resurrection," the earthly remains of good old Dr. Blacklock.

Dr. Blacklock sent the following letter to Burns:

> Dear Burns, thou brother of my heart,
> Both for thy virtues and thy art:
> If art it may be called in thee,
> Which nature's bounty, large and free,
> With pleasure on thy breast diffuses,
> And warms thy soul with all the Muses.
> Whether to laugh with easy grace,
> Thy numbers move the sage's face,
> Or bid the softer passion rise,
> And ruthless souls with grief surprise,
> Tis nature's voice distinctly felt,
> Through thee her organ, thus to melt.
>
> Most anxiously I wish to know,
> With thee of late how matters go;
> How keeps thy much-loved Jean her health?
> What promises thy farm of wealth?
> Whether the muse persists to smile,
> And all thy anxious cares beguile?
> Whether bright fancy keeps alive?
> And how thy darling infants thrive?
>
> 'Fore me, with grief and sickness spent,
> Since I my journey homeward bent,
> Spirits depress'd no more I mourn,
> But vigour, life, and health return.
> No more to gloomy thoughts a prey,
> I sleep at night, and live all day;

By turns my book and friend enjoy,
And thus my circling hours employ!
Happy while yet these hours remain,
If Burns could join the cheerful train,
With wonted zeal, sincere and fervent,
Salute once more his humble servant.

Thomas Blacklock.

Burns answered with the following:

To Dr. Blacklock, Ellisland, 21 Oct. 1789

Wow, but your letter made me *vauntie!*	*proud*
And are ye hale, and weel, and *cantie?*	*cheerful*
I kenn'd it still your *wee bit jauntie*	*little jaunt*
Wad *bring ye to:*	*restore you*
Lord send you aye as weel's I want ye,	
And then ye'll do.	

The ill-thief blaw the Heron[1] south!	
And never drink be near his drouth!	
He tauld mysel' by word o' mouth	
He'd tak' my letter;	
I *lippen'd* to the *chiel* in trouth,	*trusted, fellow*
And *bade* nae better.	*asked*

But *aiblins* honest Master Heron	*perhaps*
Had at the time some dainty fair one,	
To *ware* his theologic care on,	*spend*
And holy study;	
And tir'd o' sauls to waste his *lear* on,	*learning*
E'en tried the body.	

But what d'ye think, my trusty *fier,*	*friend*
I'm turned a gauger—Peace be here!	
Parnassian *queens,* I fear, I fear	*nymphs*
Ye'll now disdain me,	
And then my fifty pounds a year	
Will little gain me.	

Ye *glaikit,* gleesome, daintie *damies,*	*giddy; dames*
Wha by Castalia's *wimplin'* streamies,	*purling*
Lowp, sing, and lave your pretty limbies,	*leap*
Ye ken, ye ken,	
That strang necessity supreme is	
'Mang sons o' men.	

[1] Robert Heron.

I ha'e a wife and twa wee *laddies*,   *boys*
They *maun ha'e* brose and *brats o' duddies;*   *must have; rags of clothing*
Ye ken yoursels my heart right proud is,
            I need na vaunt,   ⎧ *cut off; twist ropes made of*
But I'll *sned* besoms—*thraw saugh woodies*,   ⎨   *willow withes*
            Before they want.   ⎩

Lord help me thro' this world o' care!
I'm weary sick o't late and air!
Not but I ha'e a richer share
            Than many ithers;
But why should ae man better fare,
            And a' men brithers?

Come, Firm Resolve, take thou the van,
Thou stalk o' carl-hemp[1] in man!
And let us mind, faint heart ne'er wan
            A lady fair;
Wha does the utmost that he can,
            Will *whyles* do mair.   *sometimes*

But to conclude my silly rhyme,
(I'm scant o' verse, and scant o' time)
To make a happy fireside clime
            To *weans* and wife,   *children*
That's the true pathos and sublime
            Of human life.

My compliments to sister Beckie;
And eke the same to honesty Lucky,
I wat she is a dainty *chuckie*,   *good wife or matron*
            As e'er tread clay!
And gratefully, my guid auld cockie,
            I'm yours for aye.

DR. JOHN MOORE [1729-1802]

One of the first men of established literary reputation who befriended Burns was the son of the Rev. Charles Moore, minister of the gospel at Stirling, where he was born, in 1729.

At Glasgow, Dr. Moore received both his elementary and academical education. So precocious were his talents, that in 1747, when only seventeen years of age, he was honoured with the

[1] "You have a stalk of carl-hemp in you," a Scotch expression meaning you have manly strength of character.

especial patronage of Colonel Campbell, of the 54th Regiment, afterwards the fifth Duke of Argyll, by whom he was introduced to the hospitals connected with the British army in Flanders, and brought under the notice of various distinguished officers, as a young man likely to be an ornament to the medical profession. At the conclusion of the war, he was for some time an attache to the British Embassy of Lord Albermarle, in Paris. He afterwards settled in practice in Glasgow, as the partner of Mr. Hamilton, the university professor of anatomy.

Dr. Moore married and was the father of several children. Early in 1769, he agreed to take the charge of the young Duke of Hamilton, step-son of the first patron, a youth of fourteen, possessed of the most excellent dispositions, but whose health was such as to require the constant attendance of a physician. With this gay nobleman, Dr. Moore made one short excursion on the continent. But the connection was abruptly dissolved in July by the death of the Duke, upon whose tomb his affectionate attendant inscribed a poetical epitaph, testifying to the promise which was thus early blighted.

In the following year, Dr. Moore was selected to attend the next brother and heir of the deceased Duke—the noted Douglas, Duke of Hamilton, now a sickly boy, and as yet innocent of the vices that ultimately clouded a career which talent and generosity had combined with almost princely rank and fortune to render illustrious. Dr. Moore and this young nobleman spent five years in continental travel, finally returning in 1778 when His Grace had attained his majority. In that year Dr. Moore removed his family to London, with the design of prosecuting his profession in a higher sphere than could be commanded in Glasgow. As yet, though advanced to middle life, he had given the world no decided proof of his literary talents; but this he now did (1779) by the publication of his *View of Society and Manners in France, Switzerland, and Germany*, a work of so much vivacity and intelligence that it instantly attained a great popularity in the author's own country, and was translated into French, German, and Italian.

In 1785, he produced a volume entitled *Medical Sketches*, which treats in a popular rather than a scientific manner several important topics relative to health and disease, not without an intermixture of pleasant stories and humorous sarcasm. It was at the close of

the ensuing year that his attention was drawn to the poetry of
Burns. Some expression of admiration which he had employed
regarding it, in a letter to Mrs. Dunlop, and which that lady
transmitted to Burns, led to a correspondence between the learned
physician and the comparatively unlettered bard, in which the one
party appears kind without the least affectation of superiority,
and the other respectful with as little display of servility. To
Dr. Moore, the Poet, in the ensuing August (1787), addressed a
sketch of his own life, which was published in the front of Dr.
Currie's memoir, and has effectually associated the names of those
very opposite men in our literary history.

Dr. Moore, when on the verge of sixty (1789), appeared for the
first time as a writer of fiction. His novel, *Zeluco*, which was then
published, assumed, and has ever since maintained, a respectable
place amongst works of that class, on account of the powerful
moral painting which forms the most conspicuous feature of its
composition. His subsequent novels, *Edward* and *Mordaunt*,
respectively published in 1796 and 1800, were less esteemed.

He was consequently enabled to gratify the curiosity of the
British public by a work under the title of *A Journal During a
Residence in France*. A subsequent work, under the title of
A View of the Causes and Progress of the French Revolution, closes
the list of Dr. Moore's publications.

After several years spent in ease and retirement, at Richmond,
he died at his house at Clifford St., London, February 29, 1802.
He left five sons, the eldest of whom was the gallant and lamented
General Sir John Moore.

REV. DR. HUGH BLAIR [1718-1800]

Born at Edinburgh, April 7, 1718, Dr. Blair corresponded with
Burns and appears on the list of subscribers for the 1787 edition of
the *Poems*. He was educated at Edinburgh, and became Minister
of Canongate Church in 1743, and of Lady Yester's in 1754. He
published a number of volumes of sermons in addition to a few
other works chiefly of a religious character.

It is not easy forming an exact judging judgement of any one; but, in
my opinion, Dr. Blair is merely an astonishing proof of what industry and
application can do. Natural parts like his are frequently to be met with

—his vanity is proverbially known among his acquaintances—but he is justly at the head of what may be called fine writing; and a critic of the first—the very first in prose: even in poesy, a good bard of Nature's making can only take the pas of him. He has a heart, not of the finest water, but far from being an ordinary one. (Burns.)

Dr. Blair died at Edinburgh, December 27, 1800, aged eighty-two.

Burns wrote to Dr. Blair from Edinburgh, May 3, 1787.

Reverend and Much Respected Sir:

I leave Edinburgh tomorrow morning, but could not go without troubling you with half a line, sincerely to thank you for the kindness, patronage and friendship you have shown me. I often felt the embarrassment of my singular situation; drawn forth from the veriest shades of life to the glare of remark; and honoured by the notice of those illustrious names of my country, whose works, while they are applauded to the end of time, will ever instruct and mend the heart.   However the meteor-like novelty of my appearance in the world might attract notice, and honour me with the acquaintance of the permanent lights of genius and literature, those who are truly benefactors of the immortal nature of man, I know very well that my utmost merit was far unequal to the task of preserving that character when once the novelty was over; I have made up my mind that abuse, or almost even neglect, will not surprise me in my quarters.

I have sent you a proof impression of Beugo's work for me, done on Indian paper, as a trifling but sincere testimony with what heart-warm gratitude I am, &c.

ROBERT BURNS.

Dr. Blair responded to Burns' epistle in these terms:

Dear Sir:—I was favoured this forenoon with your very obliging letter, together with an impression of your portrait, for which I return you my best thanks.   The success you have met with I do not think was beyond your merits; and if I have had any small hand in contributing to it, it gives me great pleasure.   I know no way in which literary persons who are advanced in years can do more service to the world, than in forwarding the efforts of rising genius, or bringing forth unknown merit from obscurity. I was the first person who brought out notice to the world of Ossian; first, by the *Fragments of Ancient Poetry*, which I published, and afterwards, by my setting on foot the undertaking for collecting and publishing the *Works of Ossian;* and I have always considered this as a meritorious action of my life.

Your situation as you say, was indeed very singular; and is being brought out, all at once, from the shades of deepest privacy to so great a share of public notice, and observation, you had to stand a severe trial. I am happy that you have stood it so well; and as far as I have known or heard, though in the midst of many temptations, without reproach to your character or behaviour.

You are now, I presume, to retire to a more private walk of life; and I trust will conduct yourself there with industry, prudence, and honour. You have laid the foundation for just public esteem. In the midst of those employments which your situation will render proper, you will not, I hope, neglect to promote that esteem, by cultivating your genius, and attending to such productions of it as may raise your character still higher. At the same time, be not in too great a haste to come forward. Take time and leisure to improve your talents. For on any second production you give the world, your fate, as a poet, will very much depend. There is no doubt a gloss of novelty which time wears off. And as you very properly hint yourself, you are not to be surprised, if in your rural retreat you do not find yourself surrounded with that glare of notice and applause which here shone upon you. No man can be a good poet without being somewhat of a philosopher. He must lay his account, that any one, who expresses himself to public observation, will occasionally meet with the attacks of illiberal censure, which it is always best to overlook and despise. He will be inclined sometimes to court retreat, and disappear from public view. He will not affect to shine always; that he may at proper seasons come forth with more advantage and energy. He will not think himself neglected if he be not always praised. I have taken the liberty, you see, of an old man to give advice and make reflections, which your own good sense will, I daresay, render unnecessary.

As you mention you being just about to leave town, you are going, I should suppose, to Dumfriesshire, to look at some of Mr. Miller's farms. I heartily wish the offers to be made you there will answer; as I am persuaded you will not easily find a more generous and better hearted proprietor to live under than Mr. Miller. When you return, if you come this way, I will be happy to see you, and to know concerning your future plans of life. You will find me by the 22nd of this month, not in my house in Argyle-Square but at a country house at Restalrig, about a mile east from Edinburgh, near the Musselburgh road.

Wishing you all success and prosperity, I am, with real regard and esteem,

> Dear Sir,
>> Yours sincerely,
>>> HUGH BLAIR.

REV. JOHN SKINNER [1721-1807]

John Skinner was born at Balfour, near Aberdeen, October 3, 1721, where, under his father, schoolmaster of the parish of Birse, at a very early period he displayed an uncommon genius, particularly for acquiring the knowledge of the Latin language. Having finished his academical courses at Marischal College, Aberdeen, he soon after became assistant to the schoolmaster of Monymusk. Here it was that, enjoying in the house of Monymusk every advantage for prosecuting his studies and improving his mind in the attainment of useful learning, together with the benefit of reading under the direction of a worthy Episcopal clergyman in that neighbourhood, he became a convert to the principles of Episcopacy, and united himself to the venerable remains of the old established Church of Scotland. In 1740, when nineteen years of age, he went to Shetland to act as preceptor in the family of Mr. Sinclair of Houss and Scalloway, where he remained about two years. Already he had commenced acquaintance with the muses, and on the death of his employer, in 1741, he embalmed his memory in an elegy, at the same time composing for him a Latin epitaph of such elegance and purity as to command the admiration of the learned Ruddiman. The only Episcopal clergyman in this remote region was a Mr. Hunter, a venerable and modest man, of whose condition we acquire some idea from his memorandum-book, still preserved at Scalloway, in which he mentions, year after year, the receipt of about five pounds as the "encouragement" (the word was used in no ironical sense) which was extended towards him by his poor and scattered flock. Mr. Skinner married the daughter of this truly primitive apostle and, in 1742, on his return to Aberdeen, entered into holy orders, and became the pastor of Longside.

For the ensuing sixty-five years, Mr. Skinner spent a laborious life in the pastoral charge of a numerous congregation, answering, almost literally, to Goldsmith's description of the village preacher.

> A man he was to all the country dear,
> And passing rich with forty pounds a year;
> Remote from towns he ran his godly race,
> Nor e'er had chang'd—nor wish'd to change his place.

The early part of Mr. Skinner's career was chequered by misfortune. Although he was not personally a friend of the house of Stewart, he could not help being involved in the persecution which the unhappy insurrection of 1745-1746 brought upon the Scottish episcopal communion. A military party came to his house when his wife was on child-bed, turned his family to the door, took away everything that was valuable, or which could be conveniently carried, and demolished the little chapel in which he officiated. On one occasion he was seized and imprisoned in the jail of Aberdeen, for no other offence than that of preaching to more than four persons. During this residence in a common jail, and suffering all the hardships of a close confinement, next to a humble trust in the Divine goodness, his chief resource lay in the conversation of a few worthy friends, at the hours when they were allowed to visit him, and in the liberal supply of books which they had the means of procuring for him. These were his constant companions when all others were excluded; and he has been often heard to say, that no six months of his life ever passed away with so little interruption to his studies as the term of his legal imprisonment. The activity of his mind seemed to increase in proportion to his want of bodily exercise; and though he amused himself now and then with some lighter productions of a poetical turn; yet the general bent of his thoughts lay towards more grave and serious subjects, and he even employed himself with philosophic tranquillity in writing a treatise on the Hebrew Shechinah. For many years, in consequence of the severity of the statutes against Episcopacy in Scotland, he was obliged either to officiate to his congregation in fours, or to take four within doors, and allow the rest to overhear him, as they best might, through the open doors and windows.

The day before the close of his own professional career, his eldest son had become the bishop of his diocese, and a son of that gentleman had also taken holy orders. On one occasion, the three —grandfather, father and son—officiated together in the chapel at Longside. Mr. Skinner lost his wife in 1799, and when his son some years after met a similar misfortune, it was proposed that the old man should withdraw from the scene of his duties, and spend the remainder of his days with his son at Aberdeen. Accordingly, in June, 1807, he bade a tearful adieu to a flock over which he had presided for the greater part of a century, and which did not contain one individual whom he had not baptized. But the term of his life was approaching, and on the sixteenth of the same month he gently expired in his chair, after dining happily with three generations of his descendants. He was buried at Longside, where a handsome monument has been erected to him.

Mr. Skinner wrote a poetical epistle to Burns, and a postscript to the letter reads:

> This auld Scots muse I've courted lang,
> And spar'd nae pains to win her;
> Dowff tho' I be in rustic sang,
> I'm no a late beginner.
> But now auld age taks dowie turns,
> Yet troth, as i'm a sinner,
> I'll aye be fond of Robie Burns,
> While I can sign—
>
> John Skinner.

Linshart, Sept. 25th, 1787.

WILLIAM TYTLER OF WOODHOUSELEE [1711-1792]

The celebrated antiquary, whose *Dissertation on Scottish Song and Music* was long the standard authority on the subject, was born October 12, 1711. He was the author of *An Enquiry, Historical and Critical, into the Evidence against Mary Queen of Scots*, besides numerous essays on various antiquarian and other subjects. He also edited *The Poetical Remains of James I of Scotland*. Johnson was greatly indebted to him for assistance in the preparation of the first volume of the *Museum*. He was a warm friend of Burns and one of his advisors and patrons. He died September 12, 1792.

Burns addressed the fine poem, "Revered Defender of Beauteous Stuart," to William Tytler, Esq., of Woodhouselee, and enclosed his picture:

> Revered defender of beauteous Stuart,
> Of Stuart, a name once respected,
> A name which to love was the mark of a true heart,
> But now 'tis despis'd and neglected.

Tho' something like moisture conglobes in my eye,
    Let no one misdeem me disloyal;
A poor friendless wand'rer may well claim a sigh,
    Still more if that wand'rer were royal.

My fathers that name have rever'd on a throne;
    My fathers have fallen to right it;
Those fathers would spurn their degenerate son,
    That name should he scoffingly slight it.

Still in prayers for King George I most heartily join,
    The Queen, and the rest of the gentry;
Be they wise, be they foolish, is nothing of mine;
    Their title's avow'd by my country.

But why of this epocha make such a fuss,
    That gave us the Hanover stem?
If bringing them over was lucky for us,
    I'm sure 'twas as lucky for them.

But, loyalty, truce! we're on dangerous ground;
    Who knows how the fashions may alter?
The doctrine to-day that is loyalty sound.
    To-morrow may bring us a halter.

I send you a trifle, a head of a bard,
    A trifle scarce worthy your care;
But accept it, good Sir, as a mark of regard,
    Sincere as a saint's dying prayer.

Now life's chilly evening dim shades in your eye,
    And ushers the long dreary night;
But you, like the star that athwart gilds the sky,
    Your course to the latest is bright.

MRS. DUNLOP [1731-1815]

Frances Wallace, the only daughter and ultimately the heiress
of Sir Thomas Wallace, Baronet, of Craigie, in Ayrshire, was
born about the year 1731, and at the age of seventeen became the
wife of John Dunlop, Esquire, of Dunlop, in the same county.
The family of Dunlop is traced back to the year 1260, as the

possessors of the estate in Cunningham, from which they take their name.

Although Mrs. Dunlop brought into her husband's family a very large fortune, together with the mansion of Craigie, beautifully situated on the Ayr, she was content to spend the whole of her married and dowager life, with the exception of occasional visits, in retirement at Dunlop. She there became the mother of five sons and five daughters, all of whom, except one, survived her. Her eldest son succeeded, under the name of Sir Thomas Wallace, to her paternal estate of Craigie.

Mr. Dunlop settled his own estate upon the second son, James Dunlop, a Lieutenant-General in the army, and at one time representative of the Stewartry of Kirkcudbright in parliament, whose son, John Dunlop of Dunlop, was in 1838 member for Ayrshire.

Mrs. Dunlop died, May 24, 1815, at the ripe old age of eighty-four.

Mrs. Dunlop possessed the qualities of mind suited to her high lineage. Preserving, in the decline of life, the generous affections of youth, her admiration of the Poet was converted into a sincere admiration of the man, which pursued him in after life through good and evil report, in poverty, in sickness, and in sorrow, and which continued to his infant family, when deprived of their parent.

Gilbert Burns, in a letter to Dr. Currie, said:

Of all the friendships which Robert acquired in Ayrshire or elsewhere, none seemed more agreeable to him than that of Mrs. Dunlop of Dunlop. . . . He was on the point of setting out for Edinburgh, before Mrs. Dunlop had heard of him. About the time of his publishing in Kilmarnock, she had been afflicted with a long and severe illness, which had reduced her mind to the most distressing state of depression.

In this situation, a copy of the poems was laid on her table by a friend, and, happening to open in the "Cotter's Saturday Night," she read it over with the greatest pleasure and surprise; the Poet's description of the simple cottagers, operated on her mind like the charm of a powerful exorcist, expelling the demon ennui, and restoring her to her wonted inward harmony and satisfaction.

Mrs. Dunlop sent off an express to Mossgiel, distant fifteen or sixteen miles, with a very obliging letter to my brother, desiring him to send half a dozen copies of his poems, if he had them to spare, and begging he would do her the pleasure of calling at Dunlop House as soon as convenient. This was the beginning of a correspondence which ended only with the Poet's life. One of the last uses he made of his pen was a short letter written from Brow, dated 12th July, 1796, to this lady.

The Poet's first letter to Mrs. Dunlop was as follows:

Ayrshire July 1786

Madam:—I am truly sorry I was not at home yesterday, when I was so much honoured with your order for my copies, and incomparably more by the handsome compliments you are pleased to pay my poetic abilities. I am fully persuaded that there is not any class of mankind so feelingly alive to the titillations of applause as the sons of Parnassus: nor is it easy to conceive how the heart of the poor bard dances with rapture, when those, whose character in life gives them a right to be polite judges, honour him with their approbation. Had you been thoroughly acquainted with me, Madam, you could not have touched my darling heart-chord more sweetly than by noticing my attempts to celebrate your illustrious ancestor, the saviour of his country.

"Great patriot here! ill-requited chief! ill-requited chief!" The first book I met with in my early years, which I perused with pleasure, was *The Life of Hannibal;* the next was, *The History of Sir William Wallace;* for several of my earlier years I had few other authors; and many a solitary hour have I stole out, after the laborious vocations of the day, to shed a tear over their glorious but unfortunate stories. In these boyish days I remember, in particular, being struck with that part of Wallace's story where these lines occur,

> Syne to the Legion wood, when it was late,
> To make a silent and a safe retreat.

I chose a fine summer Sunday, the only day of life allowed, and walked half a dozen of miles to pay my respects to the Legion wood, with as much devout enthusiasm as ever pilgrim did to Loretto; and as I explored every den and dell where I could suppose my heroic countryman to have lodged, I recollect (for even then I was a rhymer) that my heart plowed with a wish to be able to make a song on him in some measure equal to his merits.

ROBERT BURNS.

Burns to Mrs. Dunlop, March 4, 1789

But for the consolation of a few solid guineas, I could almost lament the time that a momentary acquaintance with wealth and splendour put me so much out of conceit with the sworn companions of my road through life— insignificance and poverty! . . . Often, as I have glided with humble stealth through the pomp of Princes Street, it has suggested itself to me, as an improvement on the present human figure, that a man, in proportion to his own conceit of his consequence in the world, should have power to push out the longitude of his common size, as a snail pushes out his horns, or as we draw out a prospect glass.

Burns to Mrs. Dunlop, January 2, 1793

Occasional hard drinking is the devil to me: against this I have again and again set my resolution, and have greatly succeeded. Taverns I have totally abandoned; it is the private parties in the family way, among the hard-drinking gentlemen of this country, that do me the mischief; but even this, I have more than half given over.

Burns to Mrs. Dunlop, New Year's Day, 1795

This is the season of wishes, and mine are most fervently offered up for you! What a transient business is life! Very lately I was a boy,—but t'other day I was a young man,—and I already begin to feel the rigid fibre and stiffening joints of old age coming fast o'er my frame!

WILLIAM SMELLIE [1740-1795]

A short time before Burns' introduction to Edinburgh society, William Smellie, Lord Newton, Charles Hay, and a few more wits of the Parliament House had founded a convivial club called "The Crochallan Fencibles" (a mock allusion to the Bonaparte Volunteer movement), which met in a tavern kept by a genial old Highlandman named "Dannie Douglas," whose favourite song, "Cro Chalien," suggested the dual designation of the club. Smellie was "drill hangman" of the corps and introduced Burns as a member in January, 1787, and it was his duty to drill Burns as a recruit. Cleghorn also appears to have been on the muster-roll of this rollicking regiment, which supplies a key to much of Burns' correspondence with him. How the revelry of the boon companions was stimulated and diversified may be as easily imagined as described. Smellie was a native of Edinburgh, educated at Duddington and the High School. At an early age he was apprenticed to the printing trade, and while thus engaged applied himself diligently and with great success to a study of the Ancient Classics. He also completed a full medical course. In 1765 he became partner with John Balfour in a printing business, and the firm ultimately became Printers to the University. On the dissolution of the firm, Smellie took in William Creech as a partner, engaging himself with other literary projects. He was jointly connected with Creech in printing and publishing the Edinburgh edition of Burns' *Poems*, and he had much to do in revising the proof sheets, so that he and the Poet for a time were constant associates. He was born 1740, and died June 24, 1795.

Burns wrote of William Smellie:

> His uncomb'd hoary locks, wild staring, thatch'd
> A head for thought profound and clear, unmatch'd,
> Yet tho' his coustic wit was biting-rude,
> His heart was warm, benevolent, and good.
>
> R. B.

MRS. BRUCE OF CLACKMANNAN [1696-1791]

Mrs. Bruce was born in 1696. On the death of her husband, Henry Bruce of Clackmannan, July 8, 1772, without surviving issue, the main line of the family became extinct. Mrs. Bruce continued to reside in the massive old tower of the family, situated on a hill at the west end of the town of Clackmannan, where she kept the sword and helmet said to have been worn by King Robert the Bruce at the Battle of Bannochburn.

Mrs. Bruce conferred on Burns and Dr. James McKittrick Adair the honour of knighthood, remarking that she had a better right to confer that title than some people. Great vigour of body and enthusiasm of mind she retained in old age, although latterly she was almost deprived of speech by a paralytic affliction, and preserved her hospitality and urbanity. She survived to November 4, 1791, when she had reached the grand old age of ninety-five. The sword and helmet then passed by her will to the Earl of Elgin at his seat of Broomhall, whom she had regarded as the chief of the family since her husband's death. The tower where the family flourished so long, and where Burns was entertained, has, since the death of Mrs. Bruce, fallen into ruin.

GEORGE THOMSON [1757-1851]

In 1792, Mr. George Thomson, Clerk of the Honourable Board of Trustees in Edinburgh, and distinguished as a musical amateur, projected a work entitled *A Select Collection of Original Scottish Airs for the Voice:* to which are added, introductory and concluding symphonies and accompaniments for the Piano Forte and Violin, by Plezel and Koseluck, with select and Characteristic Verses by the most admired Scottish Poets. (Mr. Thomson's work was completed in six volumes—one edition being in folio and another in octavo. Only one half-volume was published during the life of Burns.) Although personally unacquainted with Burns, Mr. Thomson's thoughts naturally turned to the great living master of Scottish song, and he applied to him, by letter, explaining the nature of his publication, and begging to know if he could furnish him with "twenty or twenty-five songs" suited to "particular melodies," and otherwise assist in improving the words usually appended to many favourite Scottish airs.   "Profit," Mr. Thomson avowed, to be "quite a secondary consideration" in his projected work, but he was willing to pay the Poet "any reasonable price" he should "please to demand."   Burns, although contributing at the time to Johnson's *Musical Museum*, entered with promptitude, and even enthusiasm, into Mr. Thomson's views; and from the above period till within a week of his death, he continued a zealous correspondent of the musician's, furnishing him with one hundred and twenty songs, more than one-half of which were wholly original, and the rest improvements on old verses or verses of his own which had previously appeared in the *Museum*.

As to any remuneration (said the Poet in his first letter), you may think my songs either above or below price; for they shall absolutely be either one or the other. In the honest enthusiasm with which I embark in your undertaking, to talk of money, wages, fee, hire, &c., would be "downright prostitution of soul."

Mr. Thomson was born at Limekilns, Fifeshire, March 4, 1757, where his father taught school.   When twenty-five years of age he married Miss Miller, whose father was a Lieutenant in the 50th Regiment, and her mother the daughter of George Peter, Esq., of Chapel in Berwickshire.   Mr. Thomson had six daughters and two sons, the elder was a Lieutenant-Colonel of Engineers, and the other an Assistant-Commissary General.

Mr. Thomson, in a letter to Robert Chambers dated March 29, 1838, wrote:

Upon my publishing the first 25 melodies, with Plezel's symphonies and accompaniments, and songs by different authors, six of Burns' songs being

of that number, (and those six were all I published in his lifetime) I, of
course sent a copy of this half volume to the Poet; and, as a mark of my
gratitude for his excessive kindness, I ventured, with all possible delicacy,
to send him a small pecuniary present, notwithstanding what he had said
on this subject. He retained it after much hesitation, but wrote me that
if I presumed to repeat it, he would, on the least motion of it, indignantly
spurn what was past, and commence entire stranger to me.

Mr. Thomson died at Leith, February 18, 1851, and was buried
in Kensal Green Cemetery.

JAMES BURNETT, LORD MONBODDO [1714-1799]

The eccentric and learned author of the *Origin and Progress of
Language* and *Ancient Metaphysics* was born, in 1714, at Monboddo,
Kincardineshire, and educated at Aberdeen, where he studied for
the Bar. He passed as Advocate in February, 1737, and was
appointed a Lord of Session in 1767. He became prominent in
Masonic circles, and it was at one of these meetings in Edinburgh
that Burns was introduced to him. Before the latter had been
four weeks in the city he writes (December 27th) that he had
had the honour to be entertained more than once at Monboddo's
house. Elizabeth Burnett, the youngest daughter of Lord Monboddo, is the subject of the Poet's beautiful elegy, "On the Death
of the Late Miss Burnett." Lord Monboddo died May 26, 1799,
at the age of eighty-five.

James Edgar, the celebrated artist, painted a very fine picture of Burns
and several others being entertained at Lord Monboddo's house. Some
nineteen persons are shown in the picture, including Burns, Miss Burnett,
the Duchess of Gordon, the Earl of Glencairn, Dr. Blacklock, Dr. John
Moore, Dr. Hugh Blair, Rev. John Skinner, William Tytler of Woodhouselee, Mrs. Bruce of Clackmannan, Mrs. Dunlop of Dunlop, William Smellie,
George Thomson, Esq., President Dundas, Lord Monboddo, Captain Grose,
Dugald Stewart, Dr. Adam Ferguson and Principal Robertson.

CAPTAIN FRANCIS GROSE [1730-1791]

Francis Grose was the son of a jeweller, and was born in 1730 at
Greenford, Middlesex. A good education, respectable talents,
and an independency left to him by his father, enabled him to
enter life with the happiest prospects; but these were soon overcast
by the consequences of a too easy and self-indulgent disposition.

Having become Captain and Paymaster of the Surrey militia, he is said to have kept no other accounts but his two pockets, receiving into the one, and paying from the other; at the same time he had all the habits of a *bon-vivant*, as that style of life was practised at the period—the consequences of which were, that he became a poor man, and an extremely fat one, much about the same time, and while still only about thirty years of age.

To the poverty of Grose, however, was owing the subsequent celebrity of his name. Under the strong compulsion of poverty, he began a career as an artist and antiquary, for which his hitherto dormant talents were eminently fitted. Between the years 1773 and 1788, he had produced his *Antiquities of England and Wales* in eight volumes quarto, consisting of nearly six hundred views drawn by himself, and a large amount of letter-press; his *Treatise on Ancient Armour and Weapons*, and his *Military Antiquities* (a history of the English Army, from the Conquest to the Present Time), together with several works of a light and whimsical nature, inclusive of his well-known *Slang Dictionary*.

It was in 1789, while travelling to Scotland for the purpose of drawing and chronicling the antiquities of that country, that he met with Burns at the hospitable table of Mr. Riddel, in the mansion of Friar's Carse. The figure of the man, which was justly said to be the very title-page to a joke—his numberless droll remarks and stories—and, in perhaps a less degree, his great learning and shrewd penetrating sense, made a great impression on the Poet; and, to use the words quoted on the occasion by Mr. Gilbert Burns, the two became "unco pack and thick thegither."

The intimacy was a memorable one for the admirers of Burns, for it led, as is well known, to the composition of "Tam O'Shanter," which first appeared in *The Antiquities of Scotland*, published next year. The verses in which Burns sketches off the figure, character, and habits of the antiquary, were great favourites with Sir Walter Scott. Grose died suddenly of apoplexy, in Dublin, May 12, 1791, while on an antiquarian tour in Ireland.

HON. HENRY ERSKINE [1746-1817]

Born at Edinburgh, November 1, 1746, Henry Erskine studied for the Bar at St. Andrews, Glasgow and Edinburgh, and was admitted Advocate in 1765. He became Dean of the Faculty of

Advocates, and twice held the office of Lord Advocate for Scotland. He was a friend and patron of Burns as well as a brother Mason. On the same night that Burns visited Lodge Canongate Kilwinning, December 7, 1786, he wrote to his friend, Gavin Hamilton:

My Lord Glencairn and the Dean of Faculty, Mr. H. Erskine, have taken me under their wing; and, by all probability, I shall soon be the tenth worthy and the eighth wise man of the world. I have met in Mr. Dalrymple of Orangefield what Solomon emphatically calls a "friend that sticketh closer than a brother."

Henry Erskine also deserves the last appellation, for he did much to further the interests of the Poet, who wrote concerning him:

> Collected Harry stood awee,
> Then open'd out his arm, man;
> His lordship sat wi' ruefu' e'e,
> And ey'd the gathering storm, man;
> Like wind-driv'n hail, it did assail,
> Or torrents owre a linn, man;
> The Bench sae wise, lift up their eyes,
> Half-wauken'd wi' the din, man.

Henry Erskine was kind and generous and it was once said of him: "There's nae a puir man in Scotland need want a friend or fear a foe while Henry Erskine lives." The ballad of Burns, entitled "The Dean of Faculty," was written after Erskine had been defeated for the office of "Dean" by Robert Dundas of Arniston.

He died at his home, Avondale, West Lothian, October 8, 1817, aged seventy-one.

JAMES DALRYMPLE [-1795]

James Dalrymple of Orangefield, near Ayr, on succeeding to his father's estate, became famous as a leader in convivial society, presiding at public dinners, singing exquisite songs in Mason lodges, etc. He was one always required to complete a jolly circle, and always to be had. From these circumstances, Burns became known to him before the visit to Edinburgh; and this gentleman was the first to take the Poet by the hand and lead him into every variety of life in Edinburgh.—*A Winter with Robert Burns.*

Burns certainly valued his friendship very highly. In a letter to Gavin Hamilton dated from Edinburgh, December 7, 1786, he says: "I have met in Mr. Dalrymple of Orangefield 'a friend that sticketh closer than a brother'"; and in a letter to Robert Aiken, Edinburgh, December 16, 1786, he says: "Mr. Dalrymple of Orangefield I shall ever remember."

Dalrymple died March 6, 1795.

DR. JAMES GREGORY [1753-1824]

James Gregory was born in 1753; and died April 2, 1824. Educated at Edinburgh and Aberdeen, he became Professor of Medicine in the University of Edinburgh, succeeding his father, Dr. John Gregory, to that office. He was the author of *Philosophical and Literary Essays, A Guide for Gentlemen Studying Medicine, First Lines of the Practice of Physic*, and one or two other works. Burns was introduced to him at a party in the home of Lord Monboddo, and afterwards met him frequently in Canongate Kilwinning Lodge. The two men became warm friends, although a criticism which the doctor made on the poem, "On Seeing a Wounded Hare Limp By," was not altogether to the Poet's liking.

Doctor Gregory was noted as a Latin scholar, and is kindly referred to by Burns in his "Lament for the Absence of William Creech, Publisher," as "Worthy Greg'ry's Latin Face."

On April 6, 1787, Doctor Gregory presented Burns with a copy of an English translation of Cicero's *Select Orations*, and in this the Poet made the following inscription:

Edin. 23rd April, 1787. This book, a present from the truly worthy and learned Dr. Gregory, I shall preserve to my latest-hour, as a mark of the gratitude, esteem, and veneration I bear the Donor. So help me God!
—Robert Burns.

HENRY MACKENZIE [1745-1831]

The author of *The Man of Feeling, The Man of the World, Julia de Roubigne, Life of Dr. Blacklock*, besides several other works, tragedies and comedies, was born in Edinburgh on August 19, 1745. He was the son of a well-known physician, and received a careful and classical education. He later studied law and went to London to obtain a knowledge of the modes of English exchequer practice. Shortly after returning to his native city he was appointed attorney for the Crown in the Exchequer Court.

He became editor at one time of a weekly paper called *The Lounger*, and in this paper on December 9, 1786, he published the first critique which had appeared on the *Poems* of Burns—a critique which awarded the poet a great deal of praise and served to introduce his poems to the fashionable and higher ranks of society throughout Scotland and England.

Mackenzie was well known in Masonic circles, and he and the Poet met frequently, especially while the latter was in Edinburgh. It was to him that Sir Walter Scott dedicated *Waverley*. Having been introduced to Mr. Pitt, Mackenzie was later indebted to him for the appointment of Comptroller of Taxes for Scotland, an office which he held till the time of his death, January 14, 1831.

PROFESSOR DUGALD STEWART [1753-1828]

The greatest of Scottish philosophers was born at Edinburgh, November 22, 1753, son of Matthew Stewart the Metaphysician. He was educated at Glasgow, and appointed Professor of Moral Philosophy at Glasgow in 1786. He was the author of various philosophical works, an edition of which, consisting of eleven volumes, was published in 1854-1858, edited by Sir William Hamilton.

He resided at a villa at Catrine. The town of Catrine stands on the banks of the Ayr, about two miles from Mauchline and a few miles from the Poet's farm. Burns was introduced to the Professor in October, 1786, and each learned in time to place a high value on the other's genius. Burns dined with the Professor and Lord Daer (son of the Earl of Selkirk) at Catrine House, shortly after the publication of the Kilmarnock edition of the *Poems*, and they met each other frequently afterwards in Edinburgh.

Gilbert Burns said of Catrine House:

A sweet little place on the banks of the Ayr, belonging to Professor Dugald Stewart, where he used to reside during the interval of his labours in the University (as his father had done before him) till banished from it by the erection of a Cotton-Mill Village, immediately adjoining.

Professor Stewart died at Edinburgh, June 11, 1828, at the age of seventy-five.

In a letter dated May 3, 1788, from Mauchline, Burns wrote to Professor Stewart:

Sir,—I inclose you one or two of my bagatelles. If the fervent wishes of honest gratitude have any influence with the great, unknown Being who frames the chain of causes and events, prosperity and happiness will attend your visit to the continent, and return you safe to your native shore.

Wherever I am, allow me, Sir, to claim it as my privilege to acquaint you with my progress in my trade of rhymes; as I am sure I could say it with truth, that, next to little fame, and the having it in my power to make life more comfortable to those whom nature has made dear to me, I shall ever regard your countenance, your patronage, your friendly good offices, as the most valued consequence of my late success in life.

                                             ROBERT BURNS.

In a letter to Francis Grose from Dumfries, dated 1792, Burns writes:

I believe among all our Scots literati you have not met with Professor Dugald Stewart, who fills the moral philosophy chair in the University of Edinburgh. To say that he is a man of the first parts, and, what is more, a man of the first worth, to a gentleman of your general acquaintance, and who so much enjoys the luxury of unencumbered freedom and undisturbed privacy, is not perhaps recommendation enough:—but when I inform you Mr. Stewart's principal characteristic is your favourite feature; that sterling independence of mind, which, though every man's right, so few men have the courage to claim, and fewer still the magnanimity to support:—When I tell you, that unseduced by splendour, and undisgusted by wretchedness, he appreciates the merits of the various actors in the great drama of life, merely as they perform their parts—in short, he is a man after your own heart, and I comply with his earnest request in letting you know that he wishes above all things to meet with you. His house, Catrine, is within less than a mile of Sorn Castle, which you proposed visiting; or if you could transmit him the inclosed, he would with the greatest pleasure meet you any where in the neighbourhood. I write to Ayrshire to inform Mr. Stewart that I have acquitted myself of my promise. Should your time and spirits permit your meeting with Mr. Stewart, 'tis well; if not, I hope you will forgive this liberty, and I have at least an opportunity of assuring you with what truth and respect,

                      I am, Sir,
                          Your great admirer
                          And very humble servant,
                                             ROBERT BURNS.

DR. ADAM FERGUSON [1723-1816]

Born at Logierait, Perthshire, June 20, 1723, Adam Ferguson died February 22, 1816. He was educated at Edinburgh and Perth until he was sixteen years of age, then studied at St. Andrews, and took his M.A. degree, July 4, 1742. He became Professor of Natural Philosophy in the Edinburgh University in 1759, and of Moral Philosophy in 1764.

It was at Professor Ferguson's house that Sir Walter Scott met Burns and Dugald Stewart and several others of literary reputation. A celebrated painting by Charles Martin Hardie, A.R.S.A., commemorates the meeting between Sir Walter Scott and the Poet, when the former was in his fifteenth year. The painting is a masterly work of art, and the scene is in the house of Professor Adam Ferguson at Edinburgh.

ROBERT AINSLIE [1766-1838]

Born at Berrywell, near Duns, January 13, 1766, Robert Ainslie was educated for the Bar, and became a Writer of the Signet in 1789. He was introduced to Burns at a Masonic meeting in Edinburgh, and grew so intimate with him that he became his companion, part of the way, on his first Border tour. He was introduced to Clarinda, and is frequently mentioned in the correspondence connected with that interesting episode in the Poet's career. He is the hero of the song "Robin Shure in Hairst." On account of his intimacy with the Poet he was welcomed into many of the leading literary circles of the day in Edinburgh. In 1798 Ainslie married Miss Jane Cunningham, daughter of Lieutenant-Colonel Cunningham of the Scottish Brigade. Later he became an Elder in the Church of Scotland. He was the author of two small religious works, *A Father's Gift to His Children* and *Reasons for the Hope that Is Within Us*. Ainslie died April 11, 1838, aged seventy-two. Some time before his death he presented Sir Walter Scott with a manuscript copy of "Tam O' Shanter" which he had received from Burns.

JOHN BEUGO [1759-1841]

John Beugo was the engraver of the Poet's portrait that formed the frontispiece to the Edinburgh edition of the *Poems*, 1787. He was born in 1759, and died December 13, 1841.

Burns to John Ballantine, February 24, 1787

I am getting my phiz done by an eminent engraver (John Beugo, Princes Street), and if it can be ready in time, I shall appear in my book, looking, like other fools, to my title-page.

Burns to Dr. Hugh Blair, Edinburgh, May 3, 1787

. . . I have sent you a proof impression of Beugo's work for me, done on India paper as a trifling but sincere testimony with what heart-warm gratitude I am, &c.

ROBERT BURNS.

Burns to Mr. Beugo, Engraver, Edinburgh, from Ellisland,
September 9, 1788

My dear Sir: . . . Could you conveniently do me one thing?— whenever you finish any head, I should like to have a proof copy of it. I might tell you a long story about your fine genius; but, as what every body knows cannot have escaped you, I shall not say one syllable about it.

ROBERT BURNS.

An engraver named Beugo, much cleverer in his art than any man residing in Edinburgh, transferred the likeness (from Nasmyth's painting) to copper. He took the greatest possible pains with the face, having the Poet to sit himself before it was finished, and the result was a likeness which, notwithstanding a criticism on it by Sir Walter Scott, must undoubtedly be regarded as that on which the friends of Burns have set their stamp of approbation.

ROBERT CHAMBERS.

JOHN MURDOCH [1747-1824]

John Murdoch, the Poet's only schoolmaster, was an Ayrshire man, born in 1747, and had received a liberal education. He was in all respects a very competent teacher. He conducted the little school at Alloway for two and a half years, and during the time the Burns family had removed to Mount Oliphant and the attendance of the two boys, Robert and Gilbert, became very irregular. On leaving Alloway, Murdoch went to Dumfries, where he taught for some time. In 1773 he was appointed to the school at Ayr, and here the Poet spent three weeks with him studying English and French. He ultimately married and removed to London, where he set up as a teacher of the French language, and it was from him that the Poet received intelligence of the death of his brother William in that city in 1790. While in London Murdoch published some educational works. He died April 20, 1824, at Lisson Grove, North West London, then a country district, and now small shops.

In his latter days (says Robert Chambers) illness had reduced Murdoch to the brink of destitution, and an appeal was made to the friends and admirers of his illustrious pupil in his behalf. Some money was thus raised and applied to the relief of his necessities.

WILLIAM NICOL [1744-1797]

Born at Dumbretton, in the parish of Annan, in 1744, William Nicol was educated at the Annan Academy and the University of Edinburgh. On completing his studies at the latter place he engaged in teaching, and in 1774 was appointed a teacher in the High School, Edinburgh. Burns became acquainted with him during his first visit to the Scottish capital, and the two men became warm friends and continued so all through life. "Kind-hearted Willie," Burns terms him in a letter written shortly after leaving Edinburgh the first time.

Nicol accompanied the Poet on his second Border tour, and caused considerable trouble and annoyance by becoming quarrelsome and impatient while Burns paid his respects to the Duke and Duchess of Gordon at Gordon Castle. It was the visit by the Poet and Allan Masterton to Nicol at Moffat that brought into existence the famous bacchanalian song, "O, Willie Brew'd a Peck o' Maut."

In 1795 Nicol had a disagreement with the Rector of the High School, resigned his position and opened a school on his own account. Late hours and intemperate habits, however, it is said, had so impaired his constitution that he was unable to attend to the duties of the school, and the experiment was abandoned within two years. Nicol died April 21, 1797.

Nicol was a man of ability, but ill-tempered, narrow-minded, pedantic, and harsh or even brutal with his pupils. He was a great admirer of Burns, and proud to associate with him in the way of conviviality and otherwise, though apparently he had little genuine wit or humour in his own compositions. He was the "Willie" of Burns' grand drinking song, and for this if for nothing else, he deserves to be held in remembrance—though he also gave Burns good advice on occasions. Lockhart (whose father-in-law, Sir Walter Scott, was a pupil at the High School in Nicol's time) considered him "a most dangerous associate" for the poet, since "with a warm heart the man united a fierce, irascible temper, a scorn of many of the decencies of life, a noisy contempt of religion, at least of the religious institutions of his country, and a violent propensity for the bottle." (*The Afton Burns.*)

Sir Walter Scott says Burns has left a curious testimony of his skill in a letter to Mr. Nicol, "an attempt to read a sentence of which would break the teeth of most modern Scotchmen":

To Mr. W. Nichol,
Master of the High School, Edinburgh,

Carlisle, June 1, 1787.

Kind Honest-Hearted Willie,

I'm sitten down here, after seven and forty miles ridin', e'en as forjesket and forniaw'd as a forfoughten cock, to g'e you some notion o' my land-lowper-like stravaguin sin' the sorrowfu' hour that I sheuk hands and parted wi' auld Reekie.

My auld, ga'd gleyde o' a meere has huckyall'd up hill and down brae, in Scotland and England, as teuch and birnie as a very devil wi' me. It's true, she's as poor's a sangmaker and as hard's a kirk, and tipper-taipers when she taks the gate, first like a lady's gentlewoman in a minuwae, or a hen on a het girdle; but she's a yauld, poutherie Girran for a' that, and has a stomach like Willie Stalker's meere that wad ha'e digeested tumbler wheels, for she'll whip me aff her five stimparts o' the best aits at a down-sittin' and ne'er fask her thumb. When once her ringbanes and spavies, her crucks and cramps, are fairly soupl'd, she beets to, beets to, and aye the hindmost hour the tightest. I could wager her price to a thretty pennies, that for taw or three wooks ridin' at fifty miles a-day, the de'il sticket o' five gallophers acqueesh Clyde and Whithorn could east saut on her tail.

I ha'e dander'd owere a' the kintra frae Dumbar to Selcraig, and ha'e forgather'd wi' mony a guid fellow, and mony a weelfar'd hizzie. I met wi' taw dink guines in particular, ane o' them a sonsie fine, fodgel lass, baith braw and bonnie; the tither was a clean-shankit, straight, tight, weel-far'd winch, as blythe's a lintwhite on a flowerie thorn, and as sweet and modest's a new blawn plumrose in a hazie shaw. They were baith bred to mainers by the benk and onie ane o' them had as muckle smeddum and rumblegumtion as the half o' some presbytries that you and I baith ken. They play'd me sic a deevil o' a shavie that I daur say if my harigals were turned out, ye wad see twa nicks i' the heart o' me like the mark o' a kail-whittle in a custock.

I was gaun to write you a lang pystle, but, Gude forgi'e me, I gat mysel' sae noutouriously bitchify'd the day after kail-time that I can hardly stoiter but and ben.

My best respecks to the guidwife and a' our common friens, especiall Mr. & Mrs. Cruickshank, and the honest guidman o' Jock's Lodge.

I'll be in Dumfries the morn, gif the beast be to the fore, and the branks bide hale.

Gude be wi' you, Willie!   Amen.

ROBERT BURNS.

JOHN SYME [1754-1831]

This man was one of Burns' most intimate friends during his residence in Dumfries, and one of his executors after his decease. He was a man of lively talents, social and benevolent character, and a style of manners that forcibly recalled the gentleman of a former age.   His father was a Writer to the Signet, in extensive practice, and the proprietor of the estate of Barncailzie in the Stewartry of Kirkcudbright.   Though Mr. Syme in early life studied enough of the law to be afterwards an expert master of all common forms, he preferred the military profession, and about the year 1773 entered the 72nd Regiment with the commission of ensign.   Soon after, abandoning this pursuit, he retired to his father's estate, and devoted himself to the life of a gentleman farmer, improving with all possible zeal, and spending much of his leisure time in field sports.   But the disaster of the Ayr Bank, in whose ruin his father was involved, ultimately proved the means of depriving him of his home at Barncailzie, and in 1791 he removed to Dumfries, to fulfil the duties of a lucrative appointment which he had in the meantime obtained, that of Distributor of Stamps for the district.

The apartments which he occupied in this capacity formed the ground floor of a house of no fine appearance in what was then called the Friar Vennel, but now Bank Street, a few yards from the walk along the Nith.   When Burns, at the close of 1791, removed from Ellisland to Dumfries, he became the tenant of the floor immediately above Mr. Syme's office; and ere long a friendship of the warmest nature took place between these two individuals.

THE MEETING OF BURNS AND SCOTT

In 1786, in Sciennes House, Edinburgh, the residence of Professor Adam Ferguson:
Adam Ferguson, Burns, Ferguson Jr., Scott, Joseph Black, M.D., John Moore,
Dugald Stewart, Adam Smith, Dr. James Hutton (geologist).

BURNS AT LORD MONBODDO'S HOUSE

Earl of Glencairn	Dr. Hugh Blair	George Thomson, Esq.
Duchess of Gordon	Rev. John Skinner	President Dundas
Miss Burnett	William Tytler of Woodhouselee	Lord Monboddo
Dr. Blacklock	Mrs. Bruce of Clackmanan	Captain Grose
Dr. John Moore	Mrs. Dunlop of Dunlop	Dugald Stewart
Burns	William Smellie	Dr. Adam Ferguson
		Principal Robertson

PORTRAIT OF BURNS
By Sir Henry Raeburn

PORTRAIT OF BURNS
After Nasmyth

PORTRAIT OF BURNS
After Skirving

Mr. Syme, who was Burns' senior by a very few years, was enabled, by his gentlemanly connection in the district, to introduce the Poet to many eminent persons.   In July, 1793, they had a ride together through Galloway, in the course of which the Distributor took the bard to the residence of the Glendownynes of Parton, Mr. Gordon of Kenmure (afterwards Viscount Kenmure), and the Earl of Selkirk.   A letter by Mr. Syme, descriptive of this little tour, is published in the memoir of the Poet.   Mr. Syme then, and during his whole life, kept a most hospitable table, to which men of all grades of rank, provided they possessed estimable qualities, were welcome; and here accordingly the strangest associations some-times took place, a landed gentleman of princely fortune perhaps sitting beside his neighbour's head gardener, or a party of majors and captains beside some sharp-witted Dumfries tradesman. The scene of these hospitalities was a stone-paved room in the villa of Eyedale, on the west side of the Nith.   The wit of the host was as lively as his welcome was kind.   Burns was a frequent guest at Eyedale, and we have his own words attesting the esteem in which he held Mr. Syme as a host:

> Who is proof to thy personal converse and wit,
> Is proof of all other temptation.

Such is the language of an impromptu note written in December, 1795.   After the death of Burns, Mr. Syme became the most conspicuous resident friend of the family, whose claims on the public he was indefatigable in urging.   It was also at his pressing request, joined to that of Mr. Gilbert Burns and Mrs. Dunlop of Dunlop, that Dr. Currie undertook the task of publishing the Poet's works, and writing the requisite biographical memoir.   Along with Gilbert Burns, Mr. Syme proceeded to Liverpool, and spent three weeks in Dr. Currie's house, for the purpose of giving information respecting the Poet and explaining whatever was obscure with respect to dates and allusions in his writings.   So in November, 1829, he was able to write the following vivid description of the personal demeanour and aspect of Burns, in a letter to Mr. Henry Constable of Edinburgh, who had requested his opinion of a portrait of the Poet, painted by a Mr. Taylor.

The Poet's expression (says Mr. Syme) varied perpetually, according to the idea which predominated in his mind; and it was beautiful to mark how well the play of his lips indicated the sentiment he was about to utter. His eyes and lips, the first remarkable for fire, and the second for flexibility, formed at all times an index to his mind, and as sunshine or shade predominated you might have told a priori, whether the company was to be favoured with a scintillation of wit, or a sentiment of benevolence, or a burst of fiery indignation. I cordially concur with what Sir Walter Scott says of the Poet's eyes. In his animated moments, and particularly when his anger was aroused by instances of tergiversation, meanness, or tyranny, they were actually like coals of living fire.

Mr. Syme died at Dumfries, on November 24, 1831, in the seventy-seventh year of his age.

SIR JOHN WHITEFOORD [-1803]

Sir John was one of the early patrons of Burns, and, what was more, a generous defender of his character. Sir John was an enthusiastic Mason, and was held in high esteem by all who knew him. He was proprietor of the estates of Whitefoord and Ballochmyle in Ayrshire, but, through the mismanagement of his predecessor (who is said to have furnished Scott with the groundwork of his character of Sir Arthur Wardour in the *Antiquary*), and the failure of the Douglas and Heron Bank, he was obliged to dispose of these, and take up his residence at Whitefoord House in the Canongate of Edinburgh. His manners were affable and gentlemanly. Burns was ever a welcome guest at his home in the Scottish capital. Sir John died at Edinburgh, April 8, 1803.

It may interest the lovers of English literature to know that the Whitefoord celebrated by Goldsmith, in his poem of Retaliation, was Sir John.

> Merry Whitefoord farewell! For thy sake, I admit
> That a Scot may have humour—I had almost said wit
> This debt to thy memory I cannot refuse,
> The best natur'd man with the worst humour'd muse.

ROBERT HERON [1764-1807]

A writer distinguished for the eccentricity of his genius was born at New Galloway, November 6, 1764. He was the son of a poor weaver, who from the remarkable love of learning and assiduity in pursuits of knowledge displayed by his son, with the characteristic ambition of the Scottish peasantry, early designed him for the Church. From necessity he early devoted himself to literary pursuits, and such was the versatility of his talents, that he wrote on all subjects—history, biography, science, criticism—with rare talent and power. He was unfortunately distinguished by habits of extravagance, and was frequently at the mercy of his creditors. Nearly the whole of the first volume of the *History of Scotland* was written while confined in jail for debt. He went to London, in 1799, and contributed largely to the periodicals of the day. For some time he derived a good income from this source, but unfortunately his evil habits again beset him; he was thrown into Newgate, where he remained many months in the greatest distress. Being seized with a lingering illness, he was removed to St. Pancras Hospital, where he died, April 13, 1807, a melancholy example of the insufficiency of genius, of however high an order, to secure happiness, without the accompaniments of religion and of virtue.

Heron was the author of a *Life of Burns*, containing a very eloquent estimate of his genius. He visited Burns at Ellisland in 1789, and carried a letter for the Poet to Dr. Blacklock at Edinburgh which he failed to deliver.

CLARINDA [1759-1841]

Clarinda was the assumed name of a lady in Edinburgh, of superior personal attractions and much sensibility, with whom Burns became acquainted towards the close of the year 1787. He had only seen her once (in the house of his friend, Miss Nimmo, on which occasion Clarinda invited him to tea, as referred to in his first letter to her), and when his leg was severely bruised by a hackney coach, which confined him to his lodgings for several weeks, a large correspondence ensued, he adopting the name of Sylvander, and the lady that of Clarinda. On his recovery from the accident, he was often in the company of the lady till his departure from Edinburgh, one or two months afterward. He only saw her once again, in December, 1791, but they corresponded occasionally till near the period of his death.

Clarinda was the daughter of a highly respectable surgeon in Glasgow, and her maiden name, Agnes Craig. When only seventeen years of age (in July, 1776), she was married to a Mr.

M'Lehose, a law agent in the same city; but the union proved an unhappy one, from dissimilarity of temper and sentiment, and ended in a separation, after Mrs. M'Lehose had given birth to four children, all of whom died young except one. She lived in comparatively comfortable circumstances on the proceeds of an annuity judiciously invested on her behalf by her father before he died.

She survived Burns nearly half a century, although she was of his own age, having been born in the same year. Her death took place at a house which she had long occupied on the Calton Hill, Edinburgh, in October, 1841.

JOHN M'MURDO [-1803]

Son of Robert M'Murdo of Drumlaurig, he became Chamberlin to the Duke of Queensberry and had his residence at Dumfries Castle. Burns entertained a warm regard for him and his family, and was a frequent and welcome guest at his home, especially after 1793, when they had settled in a house near Dumfries.

The "Lines on John M'Murdo, Esq.," were sent to him accompanied by some of the Poet's poems. Seven letters addressed to M'Murdo are recorded in the Poet's correspondence. M'Murdo is supposed to have been one of the witnesses present at the famous Whistle Contest. Some critics credit him with being the "Factor John" in "The Kirk's Alarm." He died at Bath, December 4, 1803.

ROBERT HARTLEY CROMEK [1770-1812]

A native of Hull, England, Cromek was born in 1770. He was educated for the legal profession, but gradually acquired a preference for literary pursuits. At an early age he proceeded to London, where he took up the study of engraving. In 1808 he visited Scotland for the express purpose of collecting information about Burns. In the same year he published his *Reliques of Robert Burns*. This was followed, in 1810, by *Select Scottish Songs, Ancient and Modern*. About this time he met Allan Cunningham, who furnished him with a quantity of fictitious song lore which he published in his *Remains of Nithdale and Galloway Song*. Cromek died March 14, 1812.

RICHARD BROWN

My twenty-third year (writes Burns) was to me an important era. Partly through whim, and partly that I wished to set about doing something in life, I joined a flaxdresser in a neighbouring town (Irvine), to learn the trade. . . . From this adventure I learned something of a town life; but the principal thing that gave my mind a turn was a friendship I found with a young fellow, a very noble character but a hopeless son of misfortune. . . . His knowledge of the world was vastly superior to mine, and I was all attention to learn.

Brown became master of a West Indiaman belonging to the Thames. Seven letters to Brown appear in the Poet's correspondence.

Written as they were (says Professor Walker) at a period when the Poet was in the meridian of his reputation, they show that he was at no time dazzled with success so as to forget the friends who had anticipated the public by discovering his merit.

Burns to Richard Brown, December 30, 1787

Do you recollect a Sunday we spent together in Eglinton Woods? You told me, on my repeating some verses to you, that you wondered I could resist the temptation of sending verses of such merit to a magazine. It was from this remark I derived that idea of my own power which encouraged me to endeavour at the character of a poet.

WILLIAM CRUICKSHANK [-1793]

Cruickshank was a teacher in the Canongate Hill School, Edinburgh, and later was appointed to a classical mastership in the Edinburgh High School. He is said to have been a man of "irreproachable character, amiable, and gentle to a degree."

> His faults they a' in Latin lay
> In English nane e'er kent them.

He was an active member of St. Luke's Masonic Lodge, Edinburgh, and it is possible he and the Poet were introduced to each other at one of the meetings there. They became warm friends, and Burns resided at Cruickshank's house for some time while in Edinburgh. Miss Jenny Cruickshank, the only daughter, was a great favourite of the Poet, and she inspired the two beautiful

lyrics, "A Rose-bud by My Early Walk" and "Beautiful Rose-bud
Young and Gay."

William Cruickshank died March 8, 1793.

ALEXANDER CUNNINGHAM [1763-1812]

Burns was introduced to this gentleman while in Edinburgh
during the winter of 1786-1787, and the two men founded a
friendship which continued through life. In the Poet's correspondence fourteen letters are recorded addressed to Alexander
Cunningham, the last one being dated from Brow, July 7, 1796.

Cunningham, a nephew of Dr. William Robertson, the historian,
was a well-known lawyer practising in Edinburgh. He was also a
prominent member of St. David's Lodge, F. & A.M., and one of the
"Crochallan Fencibles." At one period of his life he had anticipated being married to Miss Anna Stewart, daughter of John
Stewart of East Craigs, but after paying his addresses for some
months to the young lady, she jilted him and married Dr. Forrest
Dewar, who later became one of the Bailies of Edinburgh.

Cunningham's love affairs form the subject of a number of the
Poet's compositions, notably "To Alexander Cunningham,
Writer," "Song, Anna Thy Charms," "She's Fair and Fause,"
and "Had I a Cave." Cunningham was married, April 10, 1793,
to Miss Agnes Moir, youngest daughter of the Rev. Henry Moir,
who at one time officiated as minister at Auchtertoul. Later in
life he formed a partnership with a goldsmith. After the Poet's
death, he was very active, along with John Syme and Dr. William
Maxwell, in raising a subscription for the stricken family. He
also advocated the publishing at once of a collected edition of the
Poet's works. Cunningham was born in Edinburgh, 1763, and
died January 27, 1812.

Burns to Alexander Cunningham, February 24, 1794

For these two months, I have not been able to lift a pen. My constitution and frame-work, ab origine, blasted with a deep, incurable taint of
hypochondria, which poisons my existence. I have exhausted, in reflection,
every topic of comfort: a heart at ease might have been charmed with my
reasonings; but as to myself, I was like Judas Iscariot preaching the gospel:
he might melt and mould the hearts around him, but his own kept its
native incorrigibility.

Robert Burns to Alexander Cunningham, Brow, July 7, 1796

Alas, my friend, I fear the voice of the bard will soon be heard among you no more. For these eight or ten months, I have been sometimes bedfast, and sometimes not; but these three months, I have been tortured by an excruciating rheumatism, which has reduced me to nearly the last stage. You actually would not know me if you saw me. Pale, emaciated, and so feeble as occasionally to need help from my chair, my spirits fled—fled!—but I can no more on this subject. The deuce of the matter is this: when an exciseman is off duty, his salary is reduced to £25, instead of £50. What way, in the name of thrift, shall I maintain myself, and keep a horse in country quarters, with a wife and five children at home, on £50?

WILLIAM MUIR [1745-1793]

A miller at Tarbolton, Muir was an early and intimate friend of the Burns family, and a neighbour while the latter resided at Lochlea.

"My own friend, and my father's friend," says Burns in his Epitaph—"On a Friend." "Willie's Mill" is the scene of "Death and Dr. Hornbook." Mrs. Muir gave shelter to Jean Armour at the time she was expelled from her father's home, a kindness never forgotten by the Poet. Muir died in 1793.

ROBERT MUIR [1758-1788]

Robert Muir, born 1758, was for many years in business as a wine merchant in Kilmarnock. An early and lifelong friend of the Poet, he was a subscriber for seventy-two copies of the Kilmarnock edition and forty copies of the first Edinburgh edition. Some of the Poet's most interesting letters were addressed to Robert Muir. He died April 22, 1788.

Muir, thy weaknesses were the abberations of human nature, but thy heart glowed with everything generous, manly and noble; and if ever emanations from the all-good Being animated a human form, it was thine. (Robert Burns.)

SIR WILLIAM FORBES OF PITSLIGO, Bart. [1739-1806]

Sir William was born at Edinburgh, April 5, 1739, and died November 12, 1806. He was descended of the younger branch of the ancient family of Monymusk, on Donside, Aberdeenshire, and, by his paternal grandmother, from the still older family of the Lords Pitsligo of that county.   His father, a barrister, died when he was four years of age, and he was educated in Aberdeen, under the care of his mother.   He was, in 1754, apprenticed to Messrs. Couts, bankers, Edinburgh, who afterwards admitted him as a partner.   On the death of one of the Messrs. Couts, in 1763, a new company was formed, consisting of Sir William, Sir James Hunter Blair, and Sir R. Herries, the last of whom retired in 1773, on which the firm was changed to Forbes, Hunter & Co.   In 1770 he married Miss Elizabeth, daughter of Sir James Haig.   He took an active interest in the promotion of the leading public charitable, educational, literary and commercial institutions of Edinburgh, and maintained an intimacy with the distinguished personages of the day, both in London and Scotland.   He published a life of Dr. Beattie.   Sir William was of a social character; he commanded a fund of anecdote, and had great conversational powers.   He was initiated into Masonry on November 16, 1759, and at subsequent periods served as presiding Master, and in other offices both in that and the Grand Lodge.   At the Masonic meetings he had the opportunity of knowing Burns personally, and subscribed for forty copies of the second edition.

This is a passage from Sir William's address to the Grand Lodge on St. Clair of Roslin's death:

The uncertainty of life is of all reflections the most obvious; yet though the most important, it is unhappily too often the most neglected.   What a damp would come over our spirits, what agitations would be raised even in this assembly, were the book of fate to be unrolled to our view.   If Providence should permit us to penetrate this moment into futurity, and to foresee the fate of ourselves and others only to the end of the present year, some of us, who, perhaps, suppose death to be at a great distance, would see him already at the very door.   Some who, in full security are dreaming of a long course of years yet to come, would find that they have already entered on their last; and that, before it come to a close, they, like our departed brother, shall be mingled with the dust.   A great part of this assembly, by the course of nature, will probably survive a little longer; but it is morally certain that some of us, before the sun has made another annual revolution, will be removed hence to that unchangeable state, where our doom will be fixed for ever.   And although Heaven has wrapped in impenetrable darkness who they are that shall pass through the vale of the shadow of death, during that short period, in order that we may all live in a state of habitual preparation, yet who can have the presumption to say that he himself shall not be the first to visit

> That undiscover'd country
> From whose bourne no traveller returns.

ARCHIBALD SKIRVING [1749-1819]

Son of Adam Skirving, author of "Hey, Johnnie Cope," was born near Haddington in 1749. He displayed a decided talent for drawing in early life, and was sent to study art at London and later at Rome. He afterwards settled in Edinburgh, where he soon attracted wide attention by his portraits in chalk and crayon. Burns and Skirving were frequently seen together. His best-known work is his bust portrait of Robert Burns. The portrait is very popular. It is now in the Scottish National Portrait Gallery. Skirving died suddenly at Inveresk, May 19, 1819.

WILLIAM CREECH [1745-1815]

Son of the minister of Newbattle, in Midlothian, born April 21, 1745. Educated at Dalkeith and Edinburgh, he became one of the Bailies of Edinburgh in 1788, and served as Lord Provost from 1811 to 1813. He conducted for many years an extensive publishing and printing business, making his shop in Edinburgh the centre of Scottish literary gossip. He was the original publisher of the works of Beattie, Campbell, Mackenzie, Stewart, Adam and others, and from his establishment, in 1787, came the first Edinburgh edition of the *Poems* of Burns. Mr. Creech died January 14, 1815. Burns wrote a poem on William Creech, "Lament for the Absence of William Creech, Publisher."

WILLIAM BURNESS [1721-1784]

Burns, when he was twenty-two years of age, wrote the following letter to his father:

To William Burness.

Honoured Sir,   Irvine, December 27th, 1781.

I have purposely delayed writing in the hope that I should have the pleasure of seeing you on New-Year's-day; but work comes so hard upon us, that I do not choose to be absent on that account, as well as for some other little reasons, which I shall tell you at meeting.　My health is nearly the same as when you were here, only my sleep is a little sounder, and on the whole I am rather better than otherwise, though I mend by very slow degrees.　The weakness of my nerves has so debilitated my mind, that I dare neither review past wants, nor look forward into futurity; for the least anxiety of perturbation in my breast produces most unhappy effects on my whole frame.　Sometimes, indeed, when for an hour or two my spirits are a little lightened, I glimmer a little into futurity; but my principal, and indeed my only pleasurable, employment, is looking backwards and forwards in a moral and religious way; I am quite transported at the thought, that ere long, perhaps very soon, I shall bid an eternal adieu to all the pains, and uneasiness, and disquietudes of this weary life; for I assure you I am heartily tired of it; and if I do not very much deceive myself, I could contentedly and gladly resign it.

> The soul, uneasy, and confined at home,
> Rests and expatiates in a life to come.

It is for this reason I am more pleased with the 15th, 16th, and 17th verses of the 7th Chapter of Revelation, than with any ten times as many verses in the whole Bible, and would not exchange the noble enthusiasm with which they inspire me for all that this world has to offer.　As for this world, I despair of ever making a figure in it.　I am not formed for the bustle of the busy, nor the flutter of the gay.　I shall never again be capable of entering into such scenes.　Indeed, I am altogether unconcerned at the thoughts of this life.　I forsee that poverty and obscurity probably await me, and I am, in some measure, prepared, and daily preparing to meet them.　I have but just time and paper to return you my grateful thanks for the lessons of virtue and piety you have given me, which were too much neglected at the time of giving them, but which I hope have been remembered ere it is yet too late.　Present my dutiful respects to my mother, and my compliments to Mr. & Mrs. Muir; and with wishing you a merry New-Year's-day, I shall conclude.　I am, honoured Sir, your dutiful son,

ROBERT BURNESS.

P.S.　My meal is nearly out, but I am going to borrow till I get more.

One of the most striking letters in the Collection (Cromek's *Reliques of Burns*), and, to us, one of the most interesting, is the earliest of the whole series, being addressed to his father in 1781, six or seven years before his name had been heard out of his own family.　The author was then a common flax-dresser and his father a poor peasant;—yet there is not one trait of vulgarity, either in the thought or expression, but, on the contrary, a dignity and elevation of sentiment, which must have been considered as of good omen in a youth of much higher condition.   (Jeffrey.)

This letter written several years before the publication of his poems, when his name was as obscure as his condition was humble, displays the philosophic melancholy which so generally forms the poetical temperament, and that buoyant and ambitious spirit, which indicates a mind conscious of its strength.   At Irvine, Burns at this time possessed a single room for his lodgings, rented perhaps at the rate of a shilling a week.   He passed his days in constant labour, as a flaxdresser, and his food consisted chiefly of oatmeal, sent to him from his father's family.   The store of this humble though wholesome nutriment, it appears was nearly exhausted, and he was about to borrow until he could obtain a supply.   Yet even in this situation his active imagination had formed to itself pictures of eminence and distinction.   His despair of making a figure in the world shows how ardently he wished for honourable fame; and his contempt of life, founded on this despair, is the genuine expression of a youthful and generous mind. In such a state of reflection and of suffering, the imagination of Burns naturally passed the dark boundries of our earthly horizon, and rested on those beautiful creations of a better world, where there is neither thirst, nor hunger, nor sorrow, and where happiness shall be in proportion to the capacity of happiness.   (Currie.)

Burns to James Burness, Montrose, Lochlea, February 17, 1784

Dear Cousin—On the 13th current, I lost the best of fathers.   Though, to be sure, we have had long warning of the impending stroke, still the feelings of nature claim their part; and I cannot recollect the tender endearments and parental lessons of the best of friends and ablest of instructors, without feeling what perhaps the calmer dictates of reason would partly condemn.

ALEXANDER NASMYTH [1757-1840]

A native of Edinburgh, Alexander Nasmyth was born in 1757. After finishing his education, he proceeded to London, where he became a pupil of Allan Ramsay, portrait painter, son of the celebrated Scottish poet.   A few years later he went to Rome, where he studied historical landscape and portraiture painting. On his return to Scotland he established himself as an artist, and amongst his earlier productions was the only authentic portrait of Burns, which was painted to be engraved by John Beugo for the first Edinburgh edition of the *Poems*.   This portrait is now in the National Gallery of Scotland, and a replica of it is in the National

Portrait Gallery, London.   It is a full-length portrait and was not painted from sittings, but from a pencil sketch taken by the artist while in the company of the Poet.

Mr. Nasmyth also prepared, for *Constable's Miscellany*, a sketch of the poet at full-length, as he appeared in Edinburgh in the first hie-day of his reputation; dressed in light jockey boots, and very tight buckskin breeches, according to the fashion of the day, and in what was considered as the Fox-livery, viz; a blue coat, and buff waist-coat, with broad blue stripes. The surviving friends of Burns who have seen the "vignette" are unanimous in pronouncing it to furnish a very lively representation of the bard as he first attracted public notice on the streets of Edinburgh.   The scenery of the background is very nearly that of Burns' native spot—The Kirk of Alloway, and the Bridge of Doon.   (Lockhart.)

Mr. Nasmyth was a member of the Original Society of Scottish Artists, and an Associate of the Royal Institution.   In 1822 he published sixteen views of places described in the Waverley Novels.   He died at Edinburgh, April 10, 1840.

DR. JAMES CURRIE [1756-1805]

James Currie was born at Kirkpatrick-Fleming, Dumfriesshire, May 31, 1756.   His father was the minister of that parish, but later removed to Middlebie.   He was educated first at the parochial school of Middlebie and afterwards at the seminary of Dr. Chapman of Dumfries.   On completing his studies, he entered the service of a company of American merchants, and from 1771 to 1776 he filled a clerical position with a mercantile firm at Cabin Point, Virginia, U.S.A.   On his return home, he resolved to take up the study of medicine and attended the medical classes of Edinburgh and Glasgow, receiving in due time his degree of M.D. from the latter.   In 1780, on the advice of several of his friends, he settled at Liverpool, where in a few years he became a well-known and successful practising physician.   He also became a member of the Medical Society of London, and contributed many important essays and papers to the prominent Medical Journals of the time. In 1783, he married Miss Lucy Wallace, the daughter of a prosperous Liverpool merchant.   A few years later he began to suffer from a pulmonary affection, and was compelled to retire from his practice for some time.   He was advised to travel, and set out on a journey to Bristol, from which, however, he received no material benefit. He then removed to Matlock in the hope that the dry climate there, along with the hot baths, would prove beneficial in his case, but again he was disappointed. He next undertook a journey through Scotland, and while travelling in Dumfriesshire he was introduced to Burns and at once became one of his most enthusiastic admirers. His health also began to improve rapidly, and a few months later he was able to return to Liverpool and again resume his work.

Shortly after the death of Burns, in 1796, a demand arose all over the country for a complete edition of his writings. Various names were suggested for this important undertaking, but ultimately the choice fell to Dr. Currie, who in 1800 published on behalf of the Poet's family "*The Works of Robert Burns*, and an account of his life, and criticisms on his writings; to which are prefixed some observations on the Character and Condition of the Scottish peasantry." Dr. Currie died at Sidmouth, August 31, 1805.

DR. JOHN MACKENZIE [-1837]

The doctor had attended the Poet's father in a professional capacity in the early spring of 1783, and this is how Burns and he first met. He afterwards gave his impression of the Poet on that occasion in a letter to Professor Walker, written in 1810, in which he said:

The poet seemed distant, suspicious and without any wish to interest or please. He kept himself very silent in a dark corner of the room; and, before he took any part in the conversation, I frequently detected him scrutinizing me during my conversation with his father and brother. But, afterwards, when the conversation, which was on a medical subject, had taken the turn he wished, he began to engage in it, displaying a dexterity of reasoning, an ingenuity of reflexion and a familiarity with topics apparently beyond his reach, by which his visitor was no less gratified than astonished.

From the period of which I speak, I took a lively interest in Robert Burns and, before I was acquainted with his poetical powers, I perceived that he possessed very great mental abilities, an uncommonly fertile and lively imagination, a thorough acquaintance with many of our Scottish poets and an enthusiastic admiration of Ramsay and Fergusson. Even within the subjects with which he was acquainted, his conversation was rich in well-chosen figures, animated and energetic. Indeed, I have always thought that no person could have a just idea of the extent of Burns' talents who had not had an opportunity of hearing him converse. His discrimination of character was great beyond that of any person I ever knew and I have often observed to him that it seemed to be intuitive. I seldom ever knew him to make a false estimate of character, when he formed an opinion from his own observation and not from the representation of persons to whom he was partial.

Dr. John Mackenzie was a man of excellent character, broad sympathies and good social position. He was one of those friends possessing literary taste to whom Burns submitted his poems and whose discerning appreciation of their genius was of the highest encouragement to the Poet, as well as of eminent service in developing his muse and making it known to the world. He, himself, had written pamphlets on some of the religious controversies of the time, under the pseudonym of "Common Sense," and one on the *Origin of Morals*—hence the reference in the lines of Burns:

> To get a blaud of Johnnie's Morals,
> And taste a swatch of Manson's Barrels.

JOHN BALLANTINE [1743-1812]

An important Masonic and social friendship was formed between Burns and John Ballantine of Castlehill, Provost of Ayr, to whom Burns inscribed "The Brigs of Ayr." Ballantine became the friend and confidant of Sir Walter Scott in the production of the Waverley Novels. He was himself the author of a novel entitled *The Widow's Lodgings*. Scott gave him the nickname of "Rigdum-funidos."

In 1801, Ballantine instituted the Allowa' Club, with the view of celebrating regularly the anniversary of the Poet's birth, and it was he who asked the Rev. Hamilton Paul to furnish an annual ode in honour of the Poet, which he did for nineteen consecutive years.

GAVIN HAMILTON [1751-1805]

Burns made the acquaintance of Gavin Hamilton in Lodge St. James, when the latter suggested that the Poet should collect and publish an edition of his poems, advice which was also tendered by Aiken, Goldie and Ballantine. Burns acted on the advice, as is well known, and the edition, published in 1780, was dedicated to Gavin Hamilton.

Gavin Hamilton died on February 5, 1805, at the age of fifty-four. No tombstone marks his grave in the Auld Kirkyard, the reason for the omission being, according to local tradition, at his own request. A marble tablet, bearing a suitable inscription, was, however, erected by the Patrick Burns Club on April 12, 1919.

> The poor man's friend in need,
> The gentleman in word and deed.
>
> ROBERT BURNS.

DAVID SILLAR [1760-1830]

"A Brother Poet," born in 1760 at Spittalside, near Tarbolton, where his father occupied a farm, in early life he became an intimate friend of the Burns family. Burns writes:

I was introduced by Gilbert, not only to his brother but to the whole of that family, where in a short time I became a frequent and, I believe, not unwelcome visitor. After the commencement of my acquaintance with the bard, we frequently met upon Sundays at Church, when between sermons, instead of going with our friends or lassies to the inn, we often took a walk in the fields.

David Sillar became a teacher in the parish school at Tarbolton, and afterwards opened a school of his own at Commonside. In 1873 he began business as a grocer in Irvine, but this not proving successful, he went to Edinburgh with the intention of engaging in literary work. Failing also in this, he returned to Irvine, and again resumed the work of teaching. Ultimately he drifted into local politics, and became a Town Councillor and Magistrate. In 1789 he published a volume of his poems, for which Burns, then at Ellisland, assisted in obtaining subscribers. In 1811 he wrote a letter for Josiah Walker's edition of Burns, giving his recollections of the Poet, and the same year he fell heir to a large legacy from a brother, after which he gradually withdrew into private life. He died May 2, 1830. Burns' two "Epistles to Davie" are among his very best.

JAMES JOHNSON [-1811]

Johnson was an engraver and music-seller in Edinburgh, when Burns made his acquaintance. A native of Ettrick, he is described by the Poet as "a good, worthy, honest fellow." He published *The Scots Musical Museum* in six volumes (1787-1803), to which Burns contributed at least one hundred and fifty pieces. Johnson is credited with being the first person to use pewter plates for engraving music. He died in indigent circumstances, February 26, 1811.

ROBERT AIKEN [1739-1807]

One of Burns' earliest friends and patrons, Robert Aiken spoke of his poetry in high terms wherever he went, and subscribed for one hundred and five copies of the Kilmarnock edition. Burns writes: "My chief patron, who is pleased to express great approbation of my works." Gilbert Burns writes: "A man of worth and taste, of warm affections, and connected with a most respectable circle of friends and relations." He was a great orator in addition to being a lawyer of high standing. He successfully defended Gavin Hamilton before the Presbytery of Ayr on charges preferred against him by the Kirk Session of Mauchline regarding his neglect of certain church duties. He was for many years Surveyor of Taxes in Ayr. "The Cotter's Saturday Night" is dedicated to "R. Aiken, Esq."

> My lov'd, my honour'd much respected friend,
> No mercenary bard his homage pays;
> With honest pride I scorn each selfish end,
> My dearest need a friend's esteem and praise.

He is the "glib-tongued Aiken" of "Holy Willie's Prayer," the "Orator Bob" of "The Kirk's Alarm," and the "Aiken dear" of "The Farewell." Robert Aiken was born August 23, 1739, and died May 24, 1807.

THE SOLDIER'S RETURN
The Hero and the Heroine

ROBERT BURNS IN THE FOX LIVERY
After Nasmyth

BURNS AND BONNIE JEAN
(Married)

Dear Brother

It will be no very pleasing news to you to be told that I am dangerously ill, & not likely to get better. — An inveterate rheumatism has reduced me to such a state of debility, & my appetite is totally gone, so that I can scarce stand on my legs. — I have been a week at sea-bathing, & I will continue there or in a friend's house in the country all the summer. — God help my wife & children, if I am taken from their head! — They will be poor indeed. — I have contracted one or two serious debts, partly from my illness these many months & partly from too much thoughtlessness as to expense when I came to town that will cut in too much on the little I leave them in your hands. — Remember me to my Mother. yours

July 10th 1796.   R BURNS

LETTER OF ROBERT BURNS TO HIS BROTHER, GILBERT

XIII
Religion

ROBERT BURNS looked into the running streams of his day.   Listening to Nature's voice, he heard the eternal beating of the heart of God.

A Prayer in the Prospect of Death
(1781)

Where with intention I have err'd,
No other plea I have,
   But Thou art good; and Goodness still
   Delighteth to forgive.
                    —ROBERT BURNS.

To Mrs. Dunlop
(New-Year-Day-Morning 1789)

I am a very sincere believer in the Bible, but I am drawn to it by the conviction of a man, not by the halter of an ass.   .   .   .

We know nothing, or next to nothing, of the substance or structure of our souls, so cannot account for those seeming caprices in them that one should be particularly pleased with this thing, or struck with that, which, on minds of a different cast, makes no extraordinary impression.   I have some favourite flowers in Spring, among which are the mountain daisy, the harebell, the foxglove, the wild briar-rose, the budding birch, and the hoary hawthorn, that I view and hang over with particular delight.   I never hear the loud, solitary whistle of the curlew in a Summer noon, or the wild mixing cadence of a troup of gray plovers in an Autumnal morning without feeling an elevation of soul like the enthusiasm of devotion of poetry. Tell me, my dear friend, to what can this be owing? Are we a piece of machinery which like the Æolian harp, passive, takes the impression of the passing accident? Or do these workings argue something within as above the trodden clod? I own myself partial to such proofs of those awful and important realities—A God that made all things—man's immaterial and immortal nature—and a world of weal or woe beyond death and the grave.

—ROBERT BURNS.

Common Place Book
(August, 1784)

The grand end of human life is to cultivate an intercourse with that Being to Whom we owe life, with every enjoyment that renders life delightful; and to maintain an integritive conduct towards our fellow-creatures.

—ROBERT BURNS.

Address to the Unco Guid
(1786)

Who made the heart, 'tis He alone
    Decidedly can try us;
    He knows each chord—its various tone,
Each spring—its various bias;
Then at the balance let's be mute,
We never can adjust it,
What's done we partly may compute
But know not what's resisted.

—ROBERT BURNS.

Introduction to "A Winter Night"
(1786)

Winter raises the mind to a serious sublimity favourable to everything great and noble. There is scarcely any earthly object gives me more pleasure but something which exalts me—something which enraptures me—than to walk in the sheltered side of a wood, or high plantation in a cloudy winter day, and hear the stormy wind howling among the trees and raving over the plain. It is my best season for devotion; my mind is wrapt up in a kind of enthusiasm to Him, Who, in the pompous language of the Hebrew bard, "Walks on the wings of the wind."

—ROBERT BURNS.

To Clarinda
(1787)

My definition of worth is short; truth and humanity respecting our fellow-creatures; reverence and humility in the presence of that Being, my Creator and Preserver, and Who, I have every reason to believe, will one day be my Judge.

—ROBERT BURNS.

To Miss Chalmers
(Edinburgh, 12th December, 1787)

I have taken tooth and nail to the Bible, and am got through the five books of Moses and half way in Joshua. It is really a glorious book. I sent for my book-binder to-day and ordered him to get me an octavo Bible in sheets, the best paper and print in town, and bind it with all the elegance of his craft.

—ROBERT BURNS.

To Mrs. Dunlop

The voice of Nature loudly cries
And many a message from the skies
That something in us never dies.

—ROBERT BURNS.

To Clarinda
(8th January, 1788)

He who is our Author and Preserver, and will one day be our Judge, must be—not for His sake in the way of duty, but from the native impulse of our hearts—the object of our reverential awe and grateful adoration.

He is almighty and all-bounteous; we are weak and dependent; hence prayer and every other sort of devotion. He is not willing that any should perish, but that all should come to everlasting life; consequently, it must be in every-one's power to embrace this offer of everlasting life; otherwise He could not in justice condemn those who did not. A mind pervaded, actuated, and governed by purity, truth and charity, though it does not merit Heaven, yet it is an absolutely necessary requisite, without which Heaven can neither be obtained nor enjoyed; and, by Divine promise, such a mind shall never fail of attaining "everlasting life"; hence the impure, the deceiving, the uncharitable, exclude themselves from eternal bliss by their unfitness for enjoying it.

The Supreme Being has put the immediate administration of all this—for wise and good ends known to Himself—into the hands of Jesus Christ, a great Personage, whose relation to us is a Guide and Saviour, and Who, except for our own obstinacy and misconduct, will bring us all, through various ways, and by various means to bliss at last.

These are my tenets, my lovely friend, and which I think cannot well be disputed.

My creed is pretty nearly expressed in the last clause of Jamie Dean's grace, an honest weaver in Ayrshire: "Lord, grant that we may lead a gude life, for a gude life makes a gude end—at least it helps weel."

—ROBERT BURNS.

To Mr. Muir

Mossgiel, 7th March, 1788.

I trust the Spring will renew your shattered frame, and make your friends happy. You and I have often agreed that life is no great blessing on the whole. The close of life, indeed to a reasoning age, is,—

> Dark as was chaos, ere the infant sun
> Was roll'd together, or had try'd his beams
> Athwart the gloom profound.

But an honest man has nothing to fear. If we lie down in the grave, the whole man a piece of broken machinery, to moulder with the clods of the valley, be it so; at least there is an end of pain, care, woes and wants: if that part of us called mind does survive the apparent destruction of the man—away with old-wife prejudices and tales! Every age and every nation has had a different set of stories; and as the many are always weak of consequence, they have often, perhaps always been deceived: A man conscious as having acted an honest part among his fellow creatures—even granting he may have been the sport at times of passions and instincts—he goes to a great unknown Being, who could have no other end in giving him existance but to make him happy, who gave him those passions and instincts, and well knows their force.

These my worthy friend, are my ideas, and I think they are not far different from yours. It becomes a man of sense to think for himself, particularly in a case when all men are equally interested, and where, indeed, all men are equally in the dark.

Adieu my dear Sir; God send us a cheerful meeting!

—ROBERT BURNS.

One of the Last Letters to Clarinda
(1788)

Nothing astonishes me more, when a little sickness clogs the wheels of life, than the thoughtless career we run in the hour of health. "None saith, Where is God, my maker, that giveth songs in the night: who teacheth us more knowledge than the beasts of the field and more understanding than the fowls of the air. . . ."

The dignified and dignifying consciousness of an honest man, and the well grounded trust in approving Heaven, are two most substantial sources of happiness.

—ROBERT BURNS.

To Mrs. Dunlop
(13th December, 1789)

If there is another world, it must only be for the just, the benevolent, the amiable, and the humane; what a flattering idea, then, is a world to come! Would to God I as firmly believed it as I ardently wish it! There I should meet an aged parent, now at rest from the many buffetings of an evil world, against which he so long and so bravely struggled.

—ROBERT BURNS.

Isabella (Mrs. Begg), the Poet's Sister

He (Robert) was a father to me, and my knowledge of the Scriptures I had in my youth, I derived from his teaching.

XIV
Highland Mary
MARY CAMPBELL, 1763-1786

MARY CAMPBELL was born, in 1763, at Auchanmore, near Dunoon, the eldest of a family of six children. Her parents were Archibald and Agnes Campbell, who were married June 19, 1762. Little is known of her early years. While still a girl she appears to have spent some time with an uncle, the Rev. David Campbell of Loch Ranza, in Arran, and on leaving his home became a servant at Montgomery Castle; here, it is supposed, she first became acquainted with the Poet. Later she became a nurse-maid in the family of Gavin Hamilton at Mauchline, and while there renewed her acquaintance with Robert Burns. About this time Burns had quarrelled with the Armour family, and the story goes that his affections became centred on Mary Campbell. He is said to have offered himself in marriage to her, and to have been accepted, although it was agreed between them that the marriage was not to take place for some time. Meanwhile Mary gave up her situation and prepared to visit her parents in Campbeltown. Before leaving for her home, the lovers had a final meeting, and as tokens of fidelity exchanged Bibles with each other.

Mary passed the summer and autumn in Campbeltown, and on her way back to Ayrshire was offered and accepted a situation in the family of Colonel MacIvor in Glasgow. Her brother Robert, who lived in Greenock with a ship carpenter named Peter Mac-Pherson (a relative of Mary's mother), had agreed to become a bound apprentice as a carpenter to his employer, and to honour the occasion had invited his family to a social party which was to be held in the MacPherson house.   Mary and her father were present at this social gathering, and nothing unusual seems to have occurred until the next day, when Robert became alarmingly ill and was found to be stricken with typhus fever.   Mary nursed him zealously until he was convalescent, and then was stricken down herself.   We do not know how long she suffered, but her illness terminated fatally about the end of the year 1786, and her remains were buried in the Old West Kirk burying grounds in a plot of ground which Peter MacPherson had but recently purchased. Her grave remained unmarked as far as her name was concerned for fifty-eight years, or until 1842, when a number of admirers of the Poet subscribed towards the erection of a small but appropriate monument to mark her resting-place.   In person Mary is said to have been about the medium height, with a wealth of reddish hair. Her eyes were dark blue, and her nature inclined to be vivacious and playful.   Her mother used to speak of her as a paragon of gentleness, amiability and sincerity.   In the words of her famous admirer, "My Highland Lassie was a warm-hearted, charming young creature as ever blessed a man with generous love."

A beautiful life-size statue of Highland Mary, erected at Dunoon, was unveiled on August 1, 1896.

On account of the extension of the works of Messrs. Harland & Wolff, Greenock, this company purchased the property of the Old West Church, and the remains of Mary Campbell were reverently removed and transferred on November 13, 1920, to the Greenock Cemetery.

Mary Campbell was the inspirer of some of the most beautiful lyrics in our language, indeed in any language.   "To Mary in Heaven," "Highland Mary," "Highland Lassie" and "Will Ye Go to the Indies, My Mary?" are lyrics that will endure for all time.   And as Mr. Colin Rae Brown has said: "While the universal fame of Burns lives enrolled upon the annals of everlasting memory, Highland Mary can never die—can never be forgotten.   Side by side with that of Scotland's Ploughman Poet, her name will stand emblazoned upon the time-stained scroll of immortality." And why not?   Had there been no Highland Mary, would not the grand heart-utterings, the sweet-soul-moving sentiments, which she alone inspired, have remained unwritten?   Should we ever have read that perhaps most beautiful of odes addressed to "Highland Mary"—have ever been moved to tears by those nobly passionate lines, "To Mary in Heaven" which fall upon you like the wailing of the saddened soul from which they were wrung? Love is the grand-parent of Genius. Love begets inspiration; inspiration begets Genius. We can never begrudge, then, the honour, the fame, and the immortality which belongs by right to those by whom the great are inspired.

—JOHN D. ROSS (1927).

Among the relics in the Monument at Alloway is the Bible in two volumes given by Burns to Highland Mary. On the fly-leaf of the first volume is written in the Poet's hand-writing: "And ye shall not swear by my name falsely, neither shalt thou profane the name of thy God: I am the Lord." *Leviticus, XIX: 12.* In the second volume: "Thou shalt not forswear thyself, but shall perform unto the Lord thine oaths." *St. Matthew, V: 33.* In both volumes is written "Robert Burns, Mossgiel," with his Masonic mark appended. In one of the volumes is preserved a lock of Highland Mary's hair.

These volumes came into possession of Mary's mother and were kept in the family. William Anderson, Mason, who lived at Benton, near Dunbarton, a grandson, took them with him to Canada, in 1834. Circumstances forced him to part with them, after being assured they would be carefully treasured beyond the risk of loss or destruction. A party of gentlemen in Montreal bought them for £25, and sent them to the Provost of Ayr for presentation to the Monument. On Thursday, December 24, 1840, they were formally presented to Provost Limond, at a dinner in honour of the occasion; and on the Poet's birthday, January 25, 1841, were delivered to the Custodian of the Monument at a public meeting and dinner, in the Burns Arms Inn, Alloway.

In 1930 and 1932 books on the life of Robert Burns were published containing a story, that "Highland Mary" shortly before her death gave birth to a premature infant. This belief, no doubt, is founded upon the finding of portions of a child's coffin in the grave of Mary Campbell at Greenock. No evidence has been forthcoming to confirm the supposition that this must have been a child of Mary Campbell. The story caused much discussion, and has been utterly refuted by students and lovers of Burns everywhere.

The Right Rev. Lauchlan MacLean Watt, Minister of Glasgow Cathedral from 1923 to 1934, and Moderator of the Church of Scotland in 1933, took the matter up from all angles, and wrote a note to the *Burns Chronicle*, 1933, as follows:

I recently wrote a letter to the *Times Literary Supplement* (London) in connection with statements regarding "Highland Mary." That letter brought first-hand information which I communicated to the same journal; and I am certain it will be interesting to readers of the *Burns Chronicle* to bring these together.

In the *Life of Burns*, by Mr. F. B. Snyder, mention is made of a part of a child's coffin having been found in "Highland Mary's" grave at Greenock; and the question is raised as to whether this is proof that "Highland Mary" died in child-bed, her baby being buried in the same grave.

I have been for thirty-five years a parish minister in Scotland—in urban and rural parishes—and it was the universal custom in the case of a mother dying in travail, and her child dying with her, that both were buried together in the same coffin. I have never known it to be otherwise. The infant was laid on the mother's breast. There was no separate coffin.

If, as it is suggested, Mary Campbell died in child-bed, and her babe with her, it is within her own coffin that the evidence should have been looked for.

I have enquired at our largest funeral undertaker in this city, and what I have said is confirmed by him. The remains of a child's coffin would prove that some child—probably of a relative or friend—was buried there, but it is no proof whatever that it was Mary Campbell's.

A few weeks later I was able to write, in supplement to the above:

The following facts have been brought to my notice and they illuminate the whole case clearly.

Agnes Hendry, born on January 4th, died on February 27th, 1827, at Greenock—forty-one years after "Highland Mary." The baby's father, Captain Duncan Hendry, had come from Campbeltown just before the birth of the child; and Peter MacPherson, his friend and neighbour, gave him permission to bury her in the family burying-place, in "Highland Mary's" grave. Miss J. Hendry, 2 Margaret Street, Greenock, often heard her father speak of this, and members of other branches of the Hendry family have heard their parents relate that their baby aunt was buried in "Highland Mary's" grave. They are all emphatically clear as to what they were told by their respective parents in regard to the matter; and in a family tree of Mr. Duncan Hendry, Jeweller, Hamilton Street, Greenock, the fact is recorded. Mr. Hendry anticipated that when the grave would be opened in November, 1920, a child's coffin would be found, and knew whose it was.

Had Mary Campbell borne an illegitimate child to anybody—but especially to Burns—it could not have been kept secret, for Greenock was a small place then, and gossip would have found in this a real tit-bit.

The narrative of Mary Campbell's death as in Mrs. Carswell's book is entirely imaginary. She speaks of Mary's "little golden-haired sister" sitting by the death-bed. But Mary Campbell's sister, Anne Campbell, was at the time a married woman and the mother of a family—her son being James Anderson, who as a lad attended the funeral, and passed on the memory of it to his family and friends.

The following letter from Bailie Carmichael on the subject seems to me to make these facts clear, and to confirm them:

76 Finnart Street,
Greenock, October 4th, 1932.

Rev. and Dear Sir,

I was convener of the Cemetery and Parks Committee of the Corporation of Greenock when, owing to the Harland and Wolff scheme, the three lairs in the Old West Church burying-ground, in one of which "Highland Mary" was buried, were opened, and all that was found therein transferred to the new cemetery. I was present when the lairs were opened, and saw everything that was taken out of them. The lairs were only four feet deep when the old shore was exposed. On the bottom of the North lair, in the north-west corner, was found the bottom board of an infant's coffin. It was perfect in shape, but sodden with water. I told my friend Mr. Hendry of this, when he told me that in all probability the bottom board belonged to the coffin which had contained the body of Captain Duncan Hendry's child, buried in 1827.

Yours faithfully
(Signed) W. HILLHOUSE CARMICHAEL, J.P.

I think these facts make it clear that an unkind and ungenerous libel has been set adrift to haunt the memory of the dead.

—LAUCHLAN MACLEAN WATT.

The Cathedral,
Glasgow.

XV

Poems and Epistles, 1773-1796

THE GENIUS Burns—wielding with unrivalled power what Ruskin characterizes as "the sweetest, richest, subtlest, most musical of all the living dialects of Europe" —is a writer whose every word is deserving of study. No poet, except Shakespeare, is more quoted than Burns.

	PAGE
Epitaph on William Muir	65
Ye Sons of Old Killie	68
Note to John Mackenzie	81
Willie Brew'd a Peck o' Maut	82
Noble Farewell to the Brethren of St. James' Tarbolton Lodge	86
Elegy on Miss Burnett	92
To Dr. Blacklock	101
Revered Defender of Beauteous Stuart	109
O, Once I Loved a Bonnie Lass	155
My Father was a Farmer	156
The Toast	157
The Death and Dying Words of Poor Mailie	158
Man was Made to Mourn	160
Holy Willie's Prayer	163
Epistle to Davie	166
War Song	170
Death and Doctor Hornbook	171
Rantin', Rovin', Robin	176
To a Mouse	177

PAOE

The Cotter's Saturday Night 179
Address to the Deil 185
The Jolly Beggars 189
The Auld Farmer's New-Year Morning Salutation to his Auld Mare
　　Maggie 198
The Twa Dogs 201
Address to the Unco Guid 208
To a Louse 210
The Holy Fair 211
To a Mountain Daisy 218
Despondency 220
A Bard's Epitaph 222
Epistle to a Young Friend 223
The Bonnie Lass of Ballochmyle 226
Nature's Law 227
The Brigs of Ayr 228
A Winter Night 235
Address to Edinburgh 238
Address to a Haggis 240
Tam Samson's Elegy 242
Epistle to the Guidwife of Wauchope House 245
Inscription on the Tombstone 248
The First Kiss at Parting 248
Peggy's Charms 249
Up in the Morning Early 249
I Love my Jean 250
Auld Lang Syne 250
John Anderson, my Jo 251
To Mary in Heaven 252
The Wounded Hare 254
Lines Written in a Wrapper Enclosing a Letter to Captain Grose . 255
Reply to a Gentleman who asked Burns if he would not like to be a
　　Soldier 256
Thanksgiving for Victory 256
Tam o' Shanter 257
Lament for James, Earl of Glencairn 264
Sweet Afton 266
The Soldier's Return 267
Lines Written Extempore in a Lady's Pocketbook 269
Wandering Willie 270
Scots Wha Hae 270

PAGE

Sonnet 272
Does Haughty Gaul Invasion Threat 272
Ye Banks and Braes of Bonnie Doon 274
A Man's a Man For a' that 274
The Red Red Rose 276
Fairest Maid on Devon Banks 277
Youth, an Unpublished Poem 277
Poem by Robert Burns, Hitherto Unpublished 278
To an Artist 304
Epigram on Bad Roads 304
The Henpecked Husband 304
Epigram on Captain Francis Grose 304
Extempore in the Court of Sessions 305
On Commissary Goldie's Brains 305
On Burns' Horse being Impounded 305
Katherine Jaffray 306
Written to a Gentleman who had sent the Poet a Newspaper . . 307

O, ONCE I LOVED A BONNIE LASS [1773]

Composed at Mount Oliphant, in the Autumn of 1773

The following composition was the first of my performances, and done at an early period of life, when my heart glowed with honest warm simplicity; unacquainted and incorrupted with the ways of a wicked world. The performance is, indeed, very purile and silly; but I am always pleased with it, as it recalls to my mind those happy days when my heart was yet honest, and my tongue was sincere.   The subject of it was a young girl (Nelly Kilpatrick) who really deserved all the praises I have bestowed on her.   I not only had this opinion of her then—but I actually think so still, now that the spell is long since broken, and the enchantment at an end. [*Robert Burns.*]

> O once, I lov'd a bonnie lass
> Aye, and I love her still;
> And whilst that virtue warms my breast,
> I'll love my handsome Nell.
>
> As bonnie lasses I hae seen,
> And mony full as *braw;*   *gaily dressed*
> But, for a modest gracefu' mien,
> The like I never saw.

A bonnie lass, I will confess,
Is pleasant to the *e'e;*   *eye*
But, without some better qualities,
She's no a lass for me.

But Nelly's looks are blythe and sweet,
And what is best of a',
Her reputation is complete,
And fair without a flaw.

She dresses ay sae clean and neat,
Both decent and genteel;
And then there's something in her gait
Gars ony dress look weel.   *makes*

A gaudy dress and *gentle* air   *well-born*
May slightly touch the heart;
But it's innocence and modesty
That polishes the dart.

'Tis this in Nelly pleases me,
'Tis this enchants my soul;
For absolutely in my breast
She reigns without control.

MY FATHER WAS A FARMER [1782]

The following song is a wild rhapsody, miserably deficient in versification;
but as the sentiments are the genuine feelings of my heart, for that reason
I have a particular pleasure in conning over it.   [*Robert Burns.*]

My father was a farmer upon the Carrick border,
And carefully he bred me in decency and order;
He bade me act a manly part, though I had ne'er a farthing;
For without an honest manly heart, no man was worth regarding.

Then out into the world my course I did determine;
Tho' to be rich was not my wish, yet to be great was charming:
My talents they were not the worst, nor yet my education:
Resolv'd was I, at least to try, to mend my situation.

In many a way, and vain essay, I courted Fortune's favour;
Some cause unseen still stept between, to frustrate each endeavour;
Sometimes by foes I was o'erpower'd, sometimes by friends forsaken;
And when my hope was at the top, I still was worst mistaken.

Then sore harass'd, and tir'd at last, with Fortune's vain delusion,
I dropt my schemes, like idle dreams, and came to this conclusion:
The past was bad, and the future hid, its good or will untried;
But the present hour was in my pow'r, and so I would enjoy it.

No help, nor hope, nor view had I, nor person to befriend me;
So I must toil, and sweat, and broil, and labour to sustain me;
To plough and sow, to reap and mow, my father bred me early;
For one, he said, to labour bred, was a match for Fortune fairly.

Thus all obscure, unknown, and poor, thro' life I'm doom'd to wander,
Till down my weary bones I lay in everlasting slumber;
No view nor care, but shun whate'er might breed me pain or sorrow;
I live to-day as well's I may, regardless of to-morrow.

But cheerful still, I am as well as a monarch in his palace,
Tho' Fortune's frown still hunts me down, with all her wonted malice:
I make indeed my daily bread, but ne'er can make it farther:
But as daily bread is all I need, I do not much regard her.

When sometimes by my labour, I earn a little money,
Some unforeseen misfortune comes gen'rally upon me;
Mischance, mistake, or by neglect, or my goodnatur'd folly:
But come what will, I've sworn it still, I'll ne'er be melancholy.

All you who follow wealth and power with unremitting ardour,
The more in this you look for bliss, you leave your view the farther:
Had you the wealth Potosi boasts, or nations to adore you,
A cheerful, honest-hearted clown I will prefer before you.

THE TOAST [1782]

At a dinner given by the Dumfries volunteers, for the purpose of commemorating the anniversary of Rodney's victory of April 12, 1782, Burns was called on for a song. He replied by reciting the following:

Instead of a song, boys, I'll give you a toast,
Here's the memory of those on the twelfth that we lost;
That we lost, did I say? nay, by heaven, that we found!
For their fame it shall last while the world goes round.
The next in succession, I'll give you the King,
Who'er would betray him, on high may he swing;
And here's the grand fabric, our free Constitution,
As built on the base of the great Revolution;
And longer with politics, not to be cramm'd,
Be anarchy curs'd, and be tyranny damn'd;
And who would to Liberty e'er prove disloyal,
May his son be a hangman, an he his first trial.

THE DEATH AND DYING WORDS OF POOR MAILIE [1782]

The Author's Only Pet Yowe,
An Unco Mournfu' Tale

The circumstances of the poor sheep were pretty much as the poet has described them. He had, partly by way of frolic, bought a ewe and two lambs from a neighbour, and she was tethered in a field adjoining the field at Lochlea. He and I were going out with our teams, and our two younger brothers to drive for us at mid-day, when Hugh Wilson, a curious looking awkward boy, clad in plaiding, came to us with much anxiety in his face, with the information that the ewe had entangled herself in the tether and was lying in the ditch. Robert was much tickled with Hughoc's appearance and postures on the occasion. Poor Mailie was set to rights, and when we returned from the plough in the evening, he repeated to me her Death and Dying Words, pretty much in the way they now stand. [*Gilbert Burns.*]

As Mailie, an' her lambs thegither
Was ae day nibblin' on the tether,
Upon her *cloot* she *coost* a hitch,   *hoof; cast*
An' owre she *warsl'd* in the ditch: *tumbled struggling*
There, groanin, dying, she did lie,
When Hughoc he cam *doytin* by.   *walking stupidly*

Wi' *glowrin een*, and lifted han's   *staring eyes*
Poor Hughoc like a statue stan's;
He saw her days were near-hand ended,
But, *wae's* my heart he could na mend it! *sorrowful is*
He gaped wide, but naething *spak*,   *spoke*
At length poor Mailie silence *brak*.   *broke*

"O thou, whase lamentable face
Appears to mourn my wofu' case!
My dying words attentive hear,
An' bear them to my Master dear.

"Tell him, if e'er again he keep
As *muckle gear* as buy a sheep—   *much cash*
O, bid him never tie them *mair*,   *more*
Wi' wicked strings o' hemp or hair!
But *ca'* them out to park or hill,   *lead*
An' let them wander at their will:
So may his flock increase, an' grow
To scores o' lambs, and packs o' *woo'!* *wool*

"Tell him, he was a Master *kin'*   *kind*
An' aye was guid to me an' mine;
An' now my dying charge I *gie* him,   *give*
My helpless lambs, I trust them wi' him.

"O, bid him save their harmless lives,
Frae dogs, an' *tods*, an' butcher's knives! *foxes*
But gie them guid cow-milk their fill,
Till they be fit to *fend* themsel;   *provide for*
An' *tent* them duly, e'en an' morn,   *attend to*
Wi' *taets* o' hay an' *ripps* o' corn.   *bits; handfuls*

"An' may they never learn the *gaets*,   *ways*
Of ither vile, *wanrestfu'* pets—   *unrestful*
To slink thro' *slaps*, an' *reave* an' steal, *gaps; rob*
At stacks o' pease, or stocks o' *kail!*   *colewort*
So may they, like their great forbears,
For monie a year come thro' the sheers:
So wives will gie them bits o' bread,
An' bairns *greet* for them when they're dead. *weep*

"My poor *toop-lamb*, my son an' heir,   *tup-lamb*
O, bid him breed him up wi' care!
An' if he live to be a beast,
To put some *havins* in his breast!   *manners*

"An' warn him—what I *winna* name   *will not*
To stay content wi' *yowes* at hame;   *ewes*
An' no to *rin* an' wear his *cloots*,   *run; hoofs*
Like *ither menseless*, graceless brutes. *other unmannerly*

"An' *niest*, my *yowie*, silly thing,   *next; little ewe*
Gude keep thee frae a tether string!
O, may thou ne'er forgather up,
Wi' ony *blastit*, moorland toop;   *worthless*
But ay keep mind to *moop an' mell*,   *associate*
Wi' sheep o' credit like thysel!

"And now, my bairns, wi' my last breath,
I *lea'e* my blessin wi' you *baith:*   *leave; both*
An' when you think upo' your mither,
Mind to be kind to ane anither.

R.B.—12

"Now, honest Hughoc, dinna fail,
To tell my master a' my tale;
An' bid him burn this cursed tether,
An' for thy pains thou'se get my *blather*."   bladder

This said, poor Mailie turn'd her head,
An' clos'd her een amang the dead!

MAN WAS MADE TO MOURN [1784]

Gilbert Burns said the Author used to remark to him that he could not well conceive a more mortifying picture of human life than a man seeking work. Casting about in his mind how this sentiment might be expressed, he composed "Man Was Made to Mourn."

The Poet wrote the dirge—for so he calls it—in his twenty-seventh year (1784).

I had an old grand-uncle with whom my mother lived awhile in her girlish years. The good old man (for so he was) was long blind ere he died, during which time his enjoyment was to sit down and cry, while my mother would sing the simple old song "The Life and Age of Man." It opens thus:

"Upon the sixteenth hundred year
Of God and fifty-three,
Frae Christ was born, that bought us dear,
As writings testifee';
On January the sixteenth day,
As I did ly alone,
With many a sigh and sob did say,
Ah! man is made to moan."

It is this way of thinking, it is these melancholy truths, that makes religion so precious to the poor miserable children of men. (*Robert Burns.*)

When chill November's surly blast
Made fields and forests bare,
One ev'ning, as I wander'd forth
Along the banks of Ayr,
I spied a man, whose aged step
Seem'd weary, worn with care;
His face was furrow'd o'er with years,
And hoary was his hair.

"Young stranger, whither wand'rest thou?"
  Began the rev'rend sage;
"Does thirst of wealth thy step constrain,
  Or youthful pleasure's rage?
Or haply, prest with cares and woes,
  Too soon thou hast began
To wander forth, with me to mourn
  The miseries of man.

"The sun that overhangs yon moors,
  Out-spreading far and wide,
Where hundreds labour to support
  A haughty lordling's pride;—
I've seen yon weary winter-sun
  Twice forty times return;
And ev'ry time has added proofs,
  That man was made to mourn.

"O man! while in thy early years,
  How prodigal of time!
Mis-spending all thy precious hours—
  Thy glorious, youthful prime!
Alternate follies take the sway;
  Licentious passions burn;
Which tenfold force gives Nature's law,
  That man was made to mourn.

"Look not alone on youthful prime,
  Or manhood's active might;
Man then is useful to his kind,
  Supported is his right:
But see him on the edge of life,
  With cares and sorrows worn;
Then Age and Want—oh! ill-match'd pair—
  Shew man was made to mourn.

"A few seem favourites of fate,
  In pleasure's lap carest;
Yet think not all the rich and great
  Are likewise truly blest:
But oh! what crowds in ev'ry land,
  All wretched and forlorn,
Thro' weary life this lesson learn,
  That man was made to mourn!

"Many and sharp the num'rous ills
   Inwoven with our frame!
More pointed still we make ourselves,
   Regret, remorse, and shame;
And man, whose heav'n-erected face
   The smiles of love adorn,—
Man's inhumanity to man
   Makes countless thousands mourn!

"See yonder poor, o'erlabour'd wight,
   So abject, mean, and vile,
Who begs a brother of the earth
   To give him leave to toil;
And see his lordly fellow-worm
   The poor petition spurn,
Unmindful, tho' a weeping wife
   And helpless offspring mourn.

"If I'm design'd yon lordling's slave—
   By Nature's law design'd—
Why was an independent wish
   E'er planted in my mind?
If not, why am I subject to
   His cruelty or scorn?
Or why has man the will and pow'r
   To make his fellow mourn?

"Yet, let not this too much, my son,
   Disturb thy youthful breast:
This partial view of human-kind
   Is surely not the best!
The poor, oppressèd, honest man
   Had never, sure, been born,
Had there not been some recompense
   To comfort those that mourn!

"O Death! the poor man's dearest friend,
   The kindest and the best!
Welcome the hour my aged limbs
   Are laid with thee at rest!
The great, the wealthy fear thy blow,
   From pomp and pleasure torn;
But, oh! a blest relief for those
   That weary-laden mourn!"

HOLY WILLIE'S PRAYER [1785]

Burns' own "argument" to this daring poem is as follows:

"Holy Willie was a rather oldish bachelor elder in the parish of Mauchline, and much and justly famed for that polemical chattering which ends in tippling orthodoxy, and for that spiritualized bawdry which refines to lingering devotion.

"In a sessional process (begun August, 1784) with a gentleman in Mauchline—a Mr. Gavin Hamilton (writer)—Holy Willie (William Fisher) and his priest, Father Auld, after full hearing in the presbytery of Ayr, came off but second best; owing partly to the oratorical powers of Mr. Robert Aiken, Mr. Hamilton's counsel, but chiefly to Mr. Hamilton's being one of the most irreproachable and truly respectable characters in the country. On losing his process, the Muse overheard him at his devotions. Mr. Hamilton was accused of 'habitual neglect of church ordinances,' and was threatened with excommunication; he appealed for protection to the presbytery of Ayr, and (January, 1785) was successful in his appeal.'"

O Thou, who in the heavens does dwell,
Who, as it pleases best Thysel,
Sends ane to heaven an' ten to hell,
　　A' for Thy glory,
And no for *ony* gude or ill   *any*
　　They've done *afore* Thee!   *before*

I bless and praise Thy matchless might,
When thousands Thou hast left in night,
That I am here afore Thy sight,
　　For gifts an' grace
A burning and a shining light
　　To a' this place.

What was I, or my generation,
That I should get *sic* exaltation,   *such*
I *wha* deserve most just damnation   *who*
　　For broken laws,
Five thousand years 'fore my creation,
　　Thro' Adam's cause.

When *frae* my mither's womb I fell,   *from*
Thou might hae plungèd me in hell,
To gnash my gums, to weep and wail,
　　In burnin' lakes,
Where damnèd devils roar and yell,
　　Chain'd to their stakes.

Yet I am here a chosen sample,
To show Thy grace is great and ample;
I'm here a pillar o' Thy temple,
        Strong as a rock,
A guide, a buckler, and example,
        To a' thy flock.

O L—d, Thou *kens* what zeal I bear,   *knowest*
When drinkers drink, an' swearers swear,
An' singin' there, an' dancin' here,
        Wi' great and sma';
For I am keepit by Thy fear
        Free frae them a'.

But yet, O L—d! confess I must,
At times I'm *fash'd* wi' fleshly lust: *troubled*
An' sometimes, too, in *wardly* trust,   *wordly*
        Vile self gets in;
But Thou remembers we are dust,
        Defil'd wi' sin.

O L—d, *yestreen*, Thou kens, wi' Meg—   *yester-even*
Thy pardon I sincerely beg,
O' may't ne'er be a livin plague
        To my dishonour,
An' I'll ne'er lift a lawless leg
        Again upon her.

Besides, I farther *maun* allow,   *must*
Wi' Leezie's lass, three times I trow—
But L—d, that Friday I was *fou*,   *full*
        When I came near her;
Or else, Thou kens, Thy servant true
        Wad never *steer* her.   *disturb*

Maybe Thou lets this fleshly thorn
Buffet Thy servant e'en and morn,
Lest he *owre* proud and high shou'd turn,   *too*
        That he's sae gifted:
If sae, Thy han' maun e'en be borne,
        Until Thou lift it.

L—d, bless Thy chosen in this place,
For here Thou hast a chosen race:

But G—d confound their stubborn face,
    An' blast their name,
Wha bring Thy elders to disgrace
    An' public shame.

L—d, mind *Gaw'n* Hamilton's deserts: *Gavin*
He drinks, an' swears, an' plays at *cartes*,   *cards*
Yet has sae mony takin arts,
    Wi' great and sma',
Frae G—d's ain priest the people's hearts
    He steals awa.

An' when we chasten'd him therefor,
Thou kens how he bred sic a *splore*,   *outburst of ridicule*
As set the warld in a roar
    O' laughing at us;—
Curse Thou his basket and his store,
    Kail an' potatoes.

L—d, hear my earnest cry and pray'r,
Against that Presbyt'ry o' Ayr;
Thy strong right hand, L—d, make it bare
    Upo' their heads;
L—d visit them, an' dinna spare,
    For their misdeeds.

O L—d, my G—d, that glib-tong'd Aiken
My vera heart and flesh are quakin,
To think how we stood sweatin, shakin,
    An' p—'d wi' dread,
While he, wi' hingin lip an' *snakin*   *sneering*
    Held up his head.

L—d, in Thy day o' vengeance try him,
L—d, visit them wha did employ him,
And pass not in Thy mercy by them,
    Nor hear their pray'r,
But for Thy people's sake destroy them,
    An' dinna spare.

But, L—d, remember me an' mine
Wi' mercies temporal an' divine,
That I for grace an' *gear* may shine,   *wealth*
    Excell'd by *nane*,   *none*
And a' the glory shall be thine,
    Amen, Amen!

EPISTLE TO DAVIE [1785]

David Siller, to whom this epistle is addressed, was a native of Tarbolton, a poet and scholar. He published a volume of poems in the Scottish dialect.

Gilbert Burns said with reference to this epistle: "Among the earliest of his poems was the Epistle to Davie. Robert often composed without any regular plan. When anything made a strong impression on his mind, so as to rouse it to any poetic exertion, he gave way to the impulse and embodied the thought in rhyme. If he hit on two or three stanzas to please him, he would then think of proper introductory, connecting, and concluding stanzas; hence the middle of a poem was often first produced. It was, I think, in the summer of 1784, when in the interest of larder labour, Robert and I were weeding in the garden, that he repeated to me the principal part of this epistle.

"I believe the first idea of Robert's becoming an author was started on this occasion.

"I was much pleased with this epistle, and said to him I was of opinion it would bear being printed, and that it would be well received by people of taste; that I thought it at least equal, if not superior, to many of Allan Ramsay's epistles, and that the merit of these, and much other Scottish poetry, seemed to consist principally in the knack of the expression; but here was a strain of interesting sentiment, and the Scotticism of the language scarcely seemed affected, but appeared to be the natural language of the poet; that, besides, there was certainly some novelty in a poet pointing out the consolation that were in store for him when he should go a-begging.

"Robert seemed well pleased with my criticism." [*Gilbert Burns.*]

While winds frae off Ben-Lomond blaw,
An' bar the doors wi' drivin' snaw,
An' *hing us owre the ingle*,   *make us gather round the fire*
I set me down to pass the time,
An' spin a verse or twa o' rhyme,
In hamely, *westlin* jingle: *west country*
While frosty winds blaw in the drift,
Ben to the *chimla lug*,   *into; chimney corner*
I grudge a *wee* the great-folk's gift,   *little*
That live *sae bien* an' snug: *so cosy*
    I *tent* less, and want less   *care*
    Their roomy fire-side;
    But *hanker, and canker*,   *envy and grudge*
    To see their cursed pride.

It's hardly in a body's pow'r,
To keep, at times, frae being sour,
To see how things are shar'd;
How best a' *chiels* are *whyles* in want,   *good fellows; sometimes*
While *coofs* on countless thousands *rant,*   *blockheads; splurge*
Ane *ken na* how to *ware't;*   *know not; spend it*
But Davie, lad, ne'er *fash* your head,   *trouble*
Tho' we hae little *gear;*   *wealth*
We're fit to win our daily bread,
As lang's we're *hale and fier:*   *whole and sound*
"*Mair spier na,* nor fear na,"   *more ask not*
    Auld age ne'er mind a *feg;*   *fig*
The last o' it, the warst o' it,
    Is only but to beg.

To lye in kilns and barns at e'en,
When *banes* are craz'd, and *bluid* is thin,   *bones; blood*
Is, doubtless, great distress!
Yet then content could make us blest;
Ev'n then, sometimes, we'd snatch a taste
Of truest happiness.
The honest heart that's free frae a'
Intended fraud or guile,
However Fortune kick the *ba',*   *ball*
Has ay some cause to smile;
    An' mind still, you'll find still,
    A comfort this nae *sma';*   *small*
    Nae mair then, we'll care then,
    Nae farther we can fa'.   *cannot fall lower*

What tho', like commoners of air,
We wander out, we know not where,
But either house or hal',   *without*
Yet nature's charms, the hills and woods,
The sweeping vales, an' foaming floods,
Are free alike to all.
In days when daisies deck the ground,
And blackbirds whistle clear,
With honest joy our hearts will bound,
To see the coming year:
    On braes when we please then,
    We'll sit an' *sowth* a tune;   *whistle softly*
    Syne rhyme *till't,* we'll time till't,   *afterwards; to it*
    An' sing't when we hae done.

It's no in titles nor in rank;
It's no in wealth like Lon'on bank,
To purchase peace and rest:
It's no in makin *muckle, mair;*   *much into more*
It's no in books, it's no in *lear,*   *learning*
To make us truly blest:
If happiness hae not her seat
An' centre in the breast,
We may be wise, or rich, or great,
But never can be blest;
   Nae treasures nor pleasures
   Could make us happy lang;
   The heart ay's the part ay
   That makes us right or wrang.

Think ye, that *sic* as you and I,   *such*
Wha drudge an' drive thro' wet and dry,
Wi' never ceasing toil;
Think ye, are we less blest than they,
Wha scarcely *tent* us in their way,   *notice*
As hardly worth their while?
Alas! how oft in haughty mood,
God's creatures they oppress!
Or else, neglecting a' that's good,
They riot in excess!
   Baith careless and fearless
   Of either heaven or hell;
   Esteeming, and deeming
   It a' an idle tale!

Then let us cheerfu' acquiesce,
Nor make our scanty pleasures less,
By pining at our state:
And, even should misfortunes come,
I, here wha sit, hae met wi' some—
An's thankfu' for them yet,   *and am*
They *gie* the wit of age to youth;   *give*
They let us *ken oursel;*   *know ourselves*
They make us see the naked truth—
The real guid and ill:
   Tho' losses an' crosses
   Be lessons right severe,
   There's wit there, ye'll get there,
   Ye'll find nae other where.

But *tent me*, Davie, ace o' hearts!   *attend to me*
(To say aught less wad wrang the *cartes*,   *cards*
And flatt'ry I detest)
This life has joys for you and I;
An' joys that riches ne'er could buy,
An' joys the very best.
There's a' the pleasures o' the heart,
The lover an' the frien';
Ye hae your Meg, your dearest part,
And I my darling Jean!
　　It warms me, it charms me,
　　To mention but her name:
　　It heats me, it *beets* me,   *kindles*
　　An' sets me a' on flame!

O all ye Pow'rs who rule above!
O Thou whose very self art love!
Thou know'st my words sincere!
The life-blood streaming thro' my heart,
Or my more dear immortal part,
Is not more fondly dear!
When heart-corroding care and grief
Deprive my soul of rest,
Her dear idea brings relief,
And solace to my breast.
　　Thou Being, All-seeing,
　　O hear my fervent pray'r;
　　Still take her, and make her
　　Thy most peculiar care!

All hail; ye tender feelings dear!
The smile of love, the friendly tear,
The sympathetic glow!
Long since, this world's thorny ways
Had number'd out my weary days,
Had it not been for you!
Fate still has blest me with a friend,
In ev'ry care and ill;
And oft a more endearing band—
A tie more tender still.
　　It lightens, it brightens
　　The tenebrific scene,
　　To meet with, an' greet with
　　My Davie, or my Jean!

O how that Name inspires my style!
The words come *skelpin*, rank an' file,   *rushing*
Amaist before I ken!   *almost*
The ready measure rins as fine,
As Phoebus an' the famous Nine
Were *glowrin* owre my pen.   *staring*
My *spavet* Pegasus will limp,   *spavined*
Till ance he's fairly *het;*   *hot*
And then he'll *hilch,* and *stilt,* an' *jimp,*   *hobble; halt; jump*
And *rin an unco fit;*   *ran uncommon fast*

    But least then the beast then
    Should rue this hasty ride,
    I'll light now, and *dight* now   *wipe down*
    His sweaty, wizen'd hide.

WAR SONG [1791]

(When Burns composed this noble lyric, he wrote on the 17th of December, 1791, to Mrs. Dunlop:

"I have just finished the following song, which, to a lady, the descendant of Wallace—and many heroes of his truly illustrious line—and herself the mother of several soldiers, needs neither preface nor apology."

Of this song, Currie says it is worthy of the Grecian muse—when Greece was most distinguished for genius and valour. Burns wished to print the lyric by itself, and give it to his country: unluckily someone advised him against it, and the Poet lived to be sorry that he yielded to his entreaty.)

SCENE—*A field of battle. Time of the day, evening. The wounded and dying of the victorious army are supposed to join in the following song:*

    1. Farewell, thou fair day, thou green earth, and ye skies,
       Now gay with the broad setting sun!
       Farewell loves and friendships, ye dear tender ties!
       Our race of existence is run!

    2. Thou grim king of terrors, thou life's gloomy foe!
       Go, frighten the coward and slave!
       Go teach them to tremble, fell tyrant! but know,
       No terrors hast thou to the brave!

    3. Thou strik'st the dull peasant,—he sinks in the dark,
       Nor saves e'en the wreck of a name;—
       Thou strik'st the young hero—a glorious mark!
       He falls in the blaze of his fame!

4. In the field of proud honour—our swords in our hands,
   Our king and our country to save—
   While victory shines on life's last ebbing sands
   Oh! who would not die with the brave!

DEATH AND DOCTOR HORNBOOK [1785]
A True Story

John Wilson, parish schoolmaster, Tarbolton, was the hero immortalized by Burns in this poem.

"The schoolmaster of Tarbolton parish, to eke out the scanty subsistence allowed to that useful class of men, had set up a shop of grocery goods. Having accidentally fallen in with some medical books, and become most hobby-horsically attached to the study of medicine, he had added the sale of a few medicines to his little trade. He had got a shop-bill printed, at the bottom of which, overlooking his own incapacity, he had advertised that advice would be given in 'Common disorders at the shop gratis.'

"Robert was at a Mason meeting in Tarbolton, when the dominie made too ostentatious a display of his medical skill. As he parted in the evening from this mixture of pedantry and physic, at the place where he describes his meeting with Death, one of those floating ideas of apparition he mentions in his letter to Dr. Moore, crossed his mind; this set him to work for the rest of his way home." [*Gilbert Burns.*]

Some books are lies frae end to end,	
And some great lies were never penn'd:	
Ev'n ministers they hae been *kenn'd*,	*known*
In holy rapture,	
A rousing *whid* at times to vend,	*fib*
And *nail't* wi' Scripture.	*confirm it*
But this that I am *gaun* to tell,	*going*
Which lately on a night befel,	
Is just as true's the Deil's in hell,	
Or Dublin city:	
That e'er he nearer comes *oursel*	*to ourselves*
'S a *muckle* pity.	*great*
The *clachan yill* had made me *canty*,	*village-ale; merry*
I was na fou, but just had plenty;	
I *stacher'd whyles*, but yet took *tent* ay	*staggered a bit; care*
To *free* the ditches;	*avoid*
An' hillocks, stanes, an' bushes, *kenn'd* ay	*knew*
Frae *ghaists* an' witches.	*ghosts*

The rising moon began to glowre
The distant Cummock hills *out-owre:*   *out over*
To count her horns, wi' a' my pow'r,
    I set mysel;
But whether she had three or four,
    I cou'd na tell.

I was come round about the hill,
An' *todlin* down on Willie's mill,   *tottering*
Setting my staff wi' a' my skill,
    To keep me *sicker;*   *steady*
Tho' leeward *whyles,* against my will,   *now and then*
    I took a *bicker.*   *lurch*

I there wi' Something did forgather,
That pat me in an *eerie swither;*   *fright*
An' awfu' scythe, out-owre ae *shouther,*   *shoulder*
    Clear-dangling, hang;
A three-tae'd *leister* on the ither   *salmon-spear*
    Lay, large an' lang.

Its stature seem'd lang Scotch ells twa,
The queerest shape that e'er I saw,
For fient a *wame* it had *ava;*   *belly; at all*
    And then its shanks,
They were as thin, as sharp an' sma'
    As cheeks o' *branks.*   *wooden bridle*

"*Guid-een,*" quo' I; "Friend! hae ye been *mawin',*   *good evening; mowing*
When ither folk are busy *sawin!*"   *sowing*
It seem'd to mak a kind o' stan',
    But naething spak;
At length, says I, "Friend! whare ye gaun?
    Will ye go back?"

It spak right *howe*—"My name is Death,   *hollow*
But be na' *fley'd.*" Quoth I, "Guid faith,   *alarmed*
Ye're maybe come to stap my breath;
    But *tent* me, *billie;*   *attend; friend*
I *rede* ye weel, tak care o' *skaith,*   *counsel; harm*
    See, there's a *gully!*"   *clasp-knife*

"Gudeman," quo' he, "put up your *whittle*,   *knife*
  I'm no design'd to try its mettle;
But if I did, I wad be *kittle*   *difficult*
    To be *mislear'd;*   *opposed*
I wadna mind it, no that spittle
    Out-owre my beard."

"Weel, weel!" says I, "a bargain be't;
  Come, gie's your hand, an' sae we're *gree't;*   *agreed*
We'll ease our shanks an' tak a seat—
    Come, gies your news;
This while ye hae been *mony a gate*,   *many a road*
    At mony a house."

"Ay, ay!" quo' he, an' shook his head,
"It's e'en a lang, lang time indeed
  Sin' I began to *nick* the thread,   *cut*
    An' choke the breath:
Folk *maun* do something for their bread,   *must*
    An' *sae* maun Death.   *so*

"Sax thousand years are near-hand fled
Sin' I was to the *butching* bred,   *since; butchering*
An' mony a scheme in vain's been laid
    To *stap* or *scar* me;   *stop; scare*
Till ane Hornbook's ta'en up the trade,
    And faith he'll *waur* me.   *beat*

"Ye ken Jock Hornbook i' the *clachan*—   *village*
Deil *mak* his *kings-hood* in a *spleuchan!*—   *put; arrogance; tobacco pouch*
He's grown sae weel acquaint wi' Buchan[1]
    And ither chaps,
The *weans haud* out their fingers laughin',   *children hold*
    An' *pouk* my hips.   *poke*

"See, here's a scythe, an' there's a dart,
They hae pierc'd mony a gallant heart;
But Doctor Hornbook wi' his art
    An' cursed skill,
Has made them baith no worth a fa—t,
    D—n'd haet they'll kill!

---

[1] Buchan's *Domestic Medicine.*

"'Twas but *yestreen*, nae farther *gane*,   *yesterday; past*
I threw a noble throw at ane;
Wi' less, I'm sure, I've hundreds slain;
    But deil-ma-care,
It just *play'd dirl* on the bane,   *quivered*
    But did nae mair.

"Hornbook was by, wi' ready art,
An' had sae fortify'd the part,
That when I looked to my dart,
    It was sae blunt,
Fient haet o't wad hae pierced the heart   *Deuce a bit of it*
    Of a *kail runt*.   *kale-stalk*

"I drew my scythe in sic a fury,
I *near hand cowpit* wi' my hurry,   *nearly tumbled*
But yet the bauld Apothecary
    Withstood the shock;
I might as weel hae try'd a quarry
    O' hard whin rock.

"Ev'n them he *canna* get attended,   *cannot*
Altho' their face he ne'er had *kend* it,   *known*
Just —— in a kail-blade, an' send it,
    As soon's he smells 't,
Baith their disease, and what will mend it,
    At once he tells 't.

"And then a' doctor's saws an' *whittles*,   *knives*
Of a' dimensions, shapes, an' mettles,
A' kinds o' boxes, mugs, an' bottles,
    He's sure to hae;
Their Latin names as fast he rattles
    As A B C.

"Calces o' fossils, earths, and trees;
True sal-marinum o' the seas;
The farina of beans an' pease,
    He has't in plenty;
Aqua-fontis, what you please,
    He can content ye.

DEATH AND DR. HORNBOOK,
1785

TAM O' SHANTER INN,
1938

PORTRAIT OF JEAN ARMOUR
AND HER GREAT-GRANDDAUGHTER,
SARAH ELIZABETH MAITLAND TOMBS

These intended to be written below a noble Earl's picture

Whose is that noble, dauntless brow?
    And whose that eye of fire?
And whose that generous, princely man,
    Ev'n rooted Foes admire?

Stranger, to justly show that brow,
    And mark that eye of fire,
Would take His hand, whose vernal tints,
    His other Works admire.

Bright as a cloudless Summer-sun,
    With stately port he moves;
His guardian Seraph eyes with awe
    The noble Ward he loves.

Among th' illustrious Scottish Sons
    That Chief thou may'st discern,
Mark Scotia's fond, returning eye,
    It dwells upon GLENCAIRN.

FACSIMILE OF BURNS' HANDWRITING
PORTRAIT OF JAMES CUNNINGHAM, EARL OF GLENCAIRN
KILMARNOCK, MARKET-CROSS

"*Forbye* some new, uncommon weapons,   *besides*
Urinus spiritus of capons;
Or mite-horn shavings, filings, scrapings,
    Distilled per se;
Sal-alkali o' midge-tail clippings,
    And mony *mae.*"   *more*

"*Waes* me for Johnie Ged's[1] hole now,"   *woe is*
Quo' I; "If that *thae* news be true!   *these*
His braw calf-ward whare *gowans* grew,   *daisies*
    Sae white and bonie,
Nae doubt they'll *rive it wi' the plew;*   *plough it up*
    They'll ruin Johnie!"

The creature *grain'd* an *eldritch* laugh,   *groaned; ghastly*
And says, "Ye needna yoke the *pleugh,*   *plough*
Kirkyards will soon be till'd eneugh,
    Tak ye nae fear:
They'll a' be trench'd wi mony a *sheugh,*   *furrow*
    In twa-three year.

"Whare I kill'd ane, a fair strae death,
By loss o' blood or want o' breath,
This night I'm free to tak my *aith,*   *oath*
    That Hornbook's skill
Has clad a score i' their last *claith,*   *clothes*
    By drap an' pill.

"An honest *wabster* to his trade,   *weaver*
Whase wife's twa *nieves* were scarce weel-bred,   *fists*
Gat *tippence*-worth to mend her head,   *twopence*
    When it was *sair;*   *sore*
The wife *slade cannie* to her bed,   *slid quietly*
    But ne'er spak *mair.*   *more*

"A country laird had ta'en the *batts,*   *botts*
Or some *curmurring* in his guts,   *disturbance*
His only son for Hornbook sets,
    An' pays him well:
The lad, for twa guid *gimmer-pets,*   *ewes*
    Was laird himsel.

---

[1] The grave-digger.

R.B.—13

"A bonie lass—ye kend her name—
Some ill-brewn drink had *hov'd* her *wame;*   *swelled; belly*
She trusts hersel, to hide the shame,
    In Hornbook's care;
Horn sent her aff to her lang hame,
    To hide it there.

"That's just a *swatch* o' Hornbook's way;   *sample*
Thus goes he on from day to day,
Thus does he poison, kill, an' slay,
    An's weel paid for't;
Yet stops me o' my lawfu' prey
    Wi' his d—n'd dirt:

"But, hark! I'll tell you of a plot,
Tho' dinna ye be speakin o't;
I'll nail the self-conceited sot,
    As dead's a herrin';
Niest time we meet, I'll *wad* a groat,   *next; wager*
    He gets his *fairin'!*"   *reward*

But just as he began to tell,
The auld kirk-hammer strak the bell
Some wee short hour *ayont* the *twal,*   *beyond; twelve*
    Which rais'd us *baith:*   *both*
I took the way that pleas'd mysel',
    And sae did Death.

RANTIN' ROVIN' ROBIN [1785]

There are few of Burns' songs more popular than this, which is sung in every quarter of the globe, on each recurrence of the day referred to in the second stanza. Currie took notice of the tradition recorded in the same verse, that on the night of the Poet's birth a portion of the auld clay biggin, erected by William Burns with his own hands, was blown in by "a blast of Jan'war' win'." It has been often noticed that hurricanes are frequent in this country about the season of Burns' anniversary. Kyle is the central division of Ayrshire.

There was a lad was born in Kyle,
But whatna day o' whatna style,
I doubt it's hardly worth the while
To be sae nice wi' Robin.
    Robin was a rovin' boy,
    Rantin', rovin', rantin', rovin';   *noisy*
    Robin was a rovin' boy,
    Rantin' rovin' Robin!

Our monarch's hindmost year but *ane*   *one*
Was five-and-twenty days begun,
'Twas then a blast o' Janwar' win'
Blew hansel in on Robin.
   Robin was, etc.

The gossip *keekit* in his *loof*,   *peered; palm*
Quo' *scho*, "Wha lives will see the proof,   *she*
This *waly* boy will be nae *coof*:   *goodly; blockhead*
I think we'll ca' him Robin."
   Robin was, etc.

"He'll hae misfortunes great an' sma',
But *ay* a heart *aboon* them a',   *ever; above*
He'll be a credit *till* us a',—   *to*
We'll a' be proud o' Robin."
   Robin was, etc.

"But sure as three times three mak nine,
I see by *ilka* score and line,   *every*
This chap will dearly like our kin',
So *leeze* me on thee, Robin."   *blessings*
   Robin was, etc.

"Guid faith," quo' scho, "I doubt you, sir,
Ye *gar* the lasses lie aspar   *make*
But twenty *fauts* ye may hae *waur*   *faults; worse*
So blessins on thee, Robin!"
   Robin was, etc.

TO A MOUSE [1785]

On turning her up in her nest with the plough, November, 1785

"John Blane, a farm servant at Mossgiel in 1785, and at present (1841) living at Kilmarnock, remembers pursuing a mouse across the field, with the pattle or plough-cleaning utensil, while Burns was ploughing. Burns told him to let the poor creature alone; and was observed to be very thoughtful all day. In the evening, he awoke Blane, for they slept together, and repeated to him his poem on the mouse, the most tender-hearted, perhaps, of all his productions."

Wee, sleekit, cow'rin', tim'rous beastie,
O, what a panic's in thy breastie!
Thou need na start awa sae hasty,
    Wi' *bickerin brattle!*   *hasty scamper*
I wad be *laith* to rin an' chase thee,   *loath*
    Wi' murderin' pattle!

I'm truly sorry man's dominion,
Has broken nature's social union,
An' justifies that ill opinion,
　　　Which makes thee startle
At me, thy poor earth-born companion,
　　　An' fellow-mortal!

I doubt na, *whyles*, but thou may thieve;　*on occasions*
What then? poor beastie, thou *maun* live!　*must*
A *daimen icker* in a *thrave*　*one ear in twenty-four sheaves*
　　　'S a *sma'* request;　*small*
I'll get a blessin' wi' the *lave*,　*rest*
　　　An' never miss't!

Thy wee bit housie, too, in ruin!
Its *silly wa's* the win's are strewin'!　*weak walls*
An' naething now to *big* a new ane,　*build*
　　　O' *foggage* green!　*soft grass*
An' bleak December's winds ensuin',
　　Baith *snell* an' keen!　*biting*

Thou saw the fields laid bare an' waste,
An' weary winter comin fast,
An' cozie here, beneath the blast,
　　　Thou thought to dwell—
Till crash! the cruel *coulter* past　*ploughshare*
　　　Out thro' thy cell.

That wee bit heap o' leaves an' *stibble*,　*stubble*
Has cost thee mony a weary nibble!
Now thou's turn'd out, for a' thy trouble,
　　　But house or *hald*,　*without; hold*
To *thole* the winter's sleety dribble,　*endure*
　　　And *cranreuch cauld!*　*hoar-frost; cold*

But, Mousie, thou art no *thy lane*,　*alone*
In proving foresight may be vain;
The best-laid schemes o' mice an' men
　　　Gang aft agley,　*oft miscarry*
An' *lea'e* us nought but grief and pain,　*leave*
　　　For promised joy!

Still thou art blest, compar'd wi' me!
The present only toucheth thee:
But och! I backward cast my e'e,
      On prospects drear!
An' forward, tho' I canna see,
      I guess an' fear!

THE COTTER'S SATURDAY NIGHT [1785]

To Robert Aiken, Esq.

Gilbert Burns gives the following account of the origin of this poem, which was written in November, 1785, in Mossgiel.

Robert had frequently remarked to me that he thought there was something peculiarly venerable in the phrase, "Let us worship God!" used by a decent, sober head of a family, introducing family worship. To this sentiment of the Author, the world is indebted for "The Cotter's Saturday Night."

When Robert had not some pleasure in view in which I was not thought fit to participate, we used frequently to walk together, when the weather was favourable, on the Sunday afternoons—those precious breathing times to the labouring part of the community—and enjoyed such Sundays as would make one regret to see their number abridged. It was in one of these walks that I first had the pleasure of hearing the Author repeat "The Cotter's Saturday Night." I do not recollect to have read or heard anything by which I was more highly electrified. The fifth and sixth stanzas and the eighteenth thrilled with peculiar ecstacy through my soul. The cotter, in the "Saturday Night," is an exact copy of my father in his manners, his family devotion, and exhortations; yet the other parts of the description do not apply to our family. None of us were "at service out among the farmers roun'." Instead of our depositing our "sair-won penny-fee" with our parents, my father laboured hard, and lived with the most rigid economy, that he might be able to keep his children at home, thereby having an opportunity of watching the progress of our young minds, and forming in them early habits of piety and virtue; and from this motive alone did he engage in farming, the source of all his difficulties and distresses. (*Gilbert Burns.*)

The affectionate reverence with which William Burnes' children ever regarded him, is attended by all who have described him as he appeared in his domestic circle; but there needs no evidence beside that of the Poet himself, who has painted in colours that will never fade "the saint, the father, and the husband" of the "Cotter's Saturday Night." (*John Gibson Lockhart.*)

"The Cotter's Saturday Night" is a noble and pathetic picture of human manners, mingled with a fine religious awe. It comes over the mind like a slow and solemn strain of music. The soul of the poet aspires from the scene of low-thoughted care, and reposes on "the bosom of its Father and its God. (*William Hazlitt.*)

Who is not happy to turn to the noblest poem that genius ever dedicated to domestic devotion—"The Cotter's Saturday Night"? (*Professor John Wilson.*)

After a tiresome day at my office, it refreshes me to have an hour with Burns. (*Sir Wilfrid Laurier.*)

My lov'd, my honour'd, much respected friend!
No mercenary bard his homage pays;
With honest pride, I scorn each selfish end;
My dearest meed, a friend's esteem and praise.
To you I sing, in simple Scottish lays,
The lowly train in life's sequester'd scene;
The native feelings strong, the guileless ways;
What Aiken in a cottage would have been;
Ah! tho' his worth unknown, far happier there I ween!

November chill blaws loud wi' angry *sugh;*	sound
The short'ning winter-day is near a close;	
The miry beasts retreating frae the *pleugh;*	plough
The black'ning trains o' *craws* to their repose:	crows
The toil-worn Cotter frae his labour goes,	
This night his weekly moil is at an end,	
Collects his spades, his mattocks, and his hoes,	
Hoping the morn in ease and rest to spend,	
And weary, o'er the moor, his course does hameward bend.	

At length his lonely cot appears in view,	
Beneath the shelter of an aged tree:	
Th' expectant wee-things, *toddlin'*, *stacher* through	tottering; st.
To meet their dad, wi' *flichterin'* noise and glee.	fluttering
His wee bit *ingle*, blinkin' bonilie,	fire
His clean hearth-stane, his thrifty wifie's smile,	
The lisping infant, prattling on his knee,	
Does a' his weary *kiaugh* and care beguile,	anxiety
And makes him quite forget his labour and his toil.	

Belyve, the elder bairns come drapping in,	by-and-by
At service out, amang the farmers roun';	
Some ca' the pleugh, some herd, some *tentie* rin	attentively
A *cannie* errand to a neibor town:	easy

Their eldest hope, their Jenny, woman-grown,
In youthfu' bloom—love sparkling in her e'e
Comes hame; perhaps, to shew a *braw* new gown,   *fine*
Or deposit her *sair*-won *penny-fee*,   *hard; wages*
To help her parents dear, if they in hardship be.

With joy unfeign'd, brothers and sisters meet,
And each for other's welfare kindly *spiers:*   *enquires*
The social hours, swift-winged, unnotic'd fleet;
Each tells the *uncos* that he sees or hears.   *news*
The parents, partia', eye their hopeful years;
Anticipation forward points the view;
The mother, wi' her needle and her sheers,
Gars auld claes look *amaist* as weel's the new;   *makes; almost*
The father mixes a' wi' admonition due.

Their master's and their mistress's command,
The *younkers* a' are warnèd to obey;   *youngsters*
And mind their labours wi' an *eydent* hand,   *diligent*
And ne'er, tho' out o' sight, to *jauk* or play;   *loaf*
"And O! be sure to fear the Lord alway,
And mind your duty, duly, morn and night;
Lest in temptation's path ye gang astray,
Implore His counsel and assisting might:
They never sought in vain that sought the Lord aright."

But hark! a rap comes gently to the door;
Jenny, wha kens the meaning o' the same,
Tells how a neibour lad came o'er the moor,
To do some errands, and convoy her hame.
The wily mother sees the conscious flame
Sparkle in Jenny's e'e, and flush her cheek;
With heart-struck anxious care, enquires his name,
While Jenny *hafflins* is afraid to speak;   *half*
Weel-pleas'd the mother hears, it's nae wild, worthless rake.

Wi' kindly welcome, Jenny brings him *ben*,   *in*
A strappin' youth, he takes the mother's eye;
Blythe Jenny sees the visit's no ill ta'en;
The father *cracks* of horses, pleughs, and *kye.*   *chats; cows*
The youngster's artless heart o'erflows wi' joy,
But *blate* an' *laithfu'*, scarce can weel behave;   *bashful; timid*
The mother, wi' a woman's wiles, can spy
What makes the youth sae bashfu' and sae grave;
Weel-pleas'd to think her bairn's respected like *the lave.*   *other women*

O happy love! where love like this is found:
O heart-felt raptures! bliss beyond compare!
I've pacèd much this weary, mortal round,
And sage experience bids me this declare,—
"If Heaven a draught of heavenly pleasure spare—
One cordial in this melancholy vale,
'Tis when a youthful, loving, modest pair
In other's arms, breathe out the tender tale,
Beneath the milk-white thorn that scents the evening gale."

Is there, in human form, that bears a heart,
A wretch! a villain! lost to love and truth!
That can, with studied, sly, ensnaring art,
Betray sweet Jenny's unsuspecting youth?
Curse on his perjur'd arts! dissembling, smooth!
Are honour, virtue, conscience, all exil'd?
Is there no pity, no relenting ruth,
Points to the parents fondling o'er their child?
Then paints the ruin'd maid, and their distraction wild?

But now the supper crowns their simple board,
The *halesome parritch*, chief of Scotia's food;   *wholesome porridge*
The soupe their only *hawkie* does afford,   *cow*
That *'yont* the *hallan* snugly chows her *cood;*   *beyond; partition; cud*
The dame brings forth, in complimental mood,
To grace the lad, her *weel-hain'd kebbuck fell;*   *well kept pungent cheese*
And aft he's prest, and aft he ca's it guid:
The frugal wifie, garrulous, will tell
How 'twas a *towmond auld*, sin' lint was i' the *bell.*   *year old; in flower*

The cheerfu' supper done, wi' serious face,
They, round the *ingle*, form a circle wide: *fireside*
The sire turns o'er wi' patriarchal grace,
The big ha'-Bible, ance his father's pride:
His bonnet rev'rently is laid aside,
His *lyart haffets* wearing thin and bare;   *gray temples*
Those strains that once did sweet in Zion glide,
He *wales* a portion with judicious care;   *selects*
And "Let us worship God!" he says, with solemn air.

They chant their artless notes in simple guise,
They tune their hearts, by far the noblest aim;
Perhaps "Dundee's" wild-warbling measures rise,
Or plaintive "Martyrs," worthy of the name;

Or noble "Elgin" *beets* the heaven-ward flame,   *fans*
The sweetest far of Scotia's holy lays:
Compar'd with these, Italian trills are tame;
The tickl'd ears no heartfelt raptures raise;
Nae unison hae they, with our Creator's praise.

The priest-like father reads the sacred page,
How Abram was the friend of God on high;
Or Moses bade eternal warfare wage
With Amalek's ungracious progeny;
Or how the royal bard did groaning lie
Beneath the stroke of Heaven's avenging ire;
Or Job's pathetic plaint, and wailing cry;
Or rapt Isaiah's wild, seraphic fire;
Or other holy seers that tune the sacred lyre.

Perhaps the Christian volume is the theme,
How guiltless blood for guilty man was shed;
How He, who bore in Heaven the second name,
Had not on earth whereon to lay his head:
How His first followers and servants sped;
The precepts sage they wrote to many a land:
How he, who lone in Patmos banished,
Saw in the sun a mighty angel stand;
And heard great Bab'lon's doom pronounc'd by Heaven's command.

Then kneeling down to Heaven's Eternal King,
The saint, the father, and the husband prays:
Hope "springs exulting on triumphant wing,"
That thus they all shall meet in future days,
There, ever bask in uncreated rays,
No more to sigh, or shed the bitter tear,
Together hymning their Creator's praise,
In such society, yet still more dear;
While circling Time moves round in an eternal sphere.

Compar'd with this, how poor Religion's pride,
In all the pomp of method, and of art;
When men display to congregations wide
Devotion's every grace, except the heart!
The Power, incens'd, the pageant will desert,
The pompous strain, the sacerdotal stole;
But haply, in some cottage far apart,
May hear, well-pleas'd, the language of the soul;
And in His Book of Life the inmates poor enroll.

Then homeward all take off their sev'ral way;
The youngling cottagers retire to rest:
The parent-pair their secret homage pay,
And proffer up to Heaven the warm request,
That he who stills the raven's clam'rous nest,
And decks the lily fair in flow'ry pride,
Would, in the way His wisdom sees the best,
For them and for their little ones provide;
But chiefly in their hearts with grace divine preside.

From scenes like these, old Scotia's grandeur springs,
That makes her lov'd at home, rever'd abroad:
Princes and lords are but the breath of kings,
"An honest man's the noblest work of God";
And certes, in fair virtue's heavenly road,
The cottage leaves the palace far behind;
What is a lordling's pomp? a cumbrous load,
Disguising oft the wretch of human kind,
Studied in arts of hell, in wickedness refined!

O Scotia! my dear, my native soil!
For whom my warmest wish to Heaven is sent,
Long may thy hardy sons of rustic toil
Be blest with health, and peace, and sweet content!
And O! may Heaven their simple lives prevent
From luxury's contagion, weak and vile!
Then, howe'er crowns and coronets be rent,
A virtuous populace may rise the while,
And stand a wall of fire around their much-lov'd isle.

O Thou! who pour'd the patriotic tide,
That stream'd thro' Wallace's undaunted heart,
Who dar'd to, nobly, stem tyrannic pride,
Or nobly die, the second glorious part:
(The patriot's God, peculiarly thou art,
His friend, inspirer, guardian, and reward!)
O never, never Scotia's realm desert;
But still the patriot, and the patriot-bard
In bright succession raise, her ornament and guard!

When Burns was first invited to dine at Dunlop-house, a westland dame, who acted as housekeeper, appeared to doubt the propriety of her mistress entertaining a mere ploughman who made rhymes, as if he were a gentleman of old descent. By way of convincing Mrs. M'Guistan, for that was her name, of the Bard's right to such distinction, Mrs. Dunlop gave her "The Cotter's Saturday Night" to read. This was soon done: she returned the volume with a strong shaking of the head, saying, "Nae doubt gentlemen and ladies think mickle o' this, but for me it's naething but what I saw in my father's house every day, and I dinna see how he could hae tauld it ony other way."

ADDRESS TO THE DEIL [1785]

No poet of any age or nation is more graphic than Burns; the characteristic features disclose themselves to him at a glance; three lines from his hand and we have a likeness. And in that rough dialect—in that rude, often awkward metre, so clear and definite a likeness! It seems a draughtsman working with a burnt stick; and yet the burin of a Retsch is not more expressive or exact. (*Thomas Carlyle.*)

Though the greater part of the piece be merely ludicrous and picturesque, there are traits of a delicate and tender feeling, indicating that unaffected softness of heart which is always so enchanting. Every Scottish reader must have felt the effect of this relenting nature, in the stanzas, beginning "Lang-Syne in Eden's bonnie yard"—"Then you, ye auld snec-drawing dog," and "But fare you weel, auld Nickie-ben." (*Lord Jeffrey.*)

O Thou! whatever title suit thee—	
Auld "Hornie," "Satan," "Nick," or "Clootie,"	
Wha in yon cavern grim an' sootie,	
Clos'd under hatches,	
Spairges about the brunstane cootie,	*scatters*
To *scaud* poor wretches!	*scald*
Hear me, auld "*Hangie*," for a wee,	*hangman*
An' let poor damnèd bodies be;	
I'm sure sma' pleasure it can gie,	
Ev'n to a deil,	
To *skelp* an' scaud poor dogs like me,	*spank*
An' hear us squeel!	
Great is thy pow'r an' great thy fame;	
Far *kenn'd* an' noted is thy name;	*known*
An' tho' yon *lowin heugh's* thy hame,	*blazing pit's*
Thou travels far;	
An' faith! thou's neither *lag* nor lame,	*laggard*
Nor *blate* nor *scaur*.	*bashful; easily scared*

Whyles, ranging like a roarin' lion,   *at times*
For prey, a' holes an' corners tryin';
Whyles, on the strong-wing'd tempest flyin',
  Tirlin the kirks;   *unroofing*
Whyles, in the human bosom pryin',
  Unseen thou lurks.

I've heard my rev'rend grannie say,
In lanely glens ye like to stray;
Or where auld ruin'd castles grey
  Nod to the moon,
Ye fright the nightly wand'rer's way,
  Wi' *eldritch croon*.   *ghastly moan*

When twilight did my grannie summon,
To say her pray'rs *douce*, honest woman!   *grave*
Aft' yont the *dyke* she's heard you *bummin'*,   *fence; buzzing*
  Wi' eerie drone;
Or, rustlin', thro' the *boortrees* comin',   *elder-trees*
  Wi' heavy groan.

Ae dreary, windy, winter night,
The stars shot down wi' *sklentin'* slight,   *slanting*
Wi' you, mysel, I gat a fright
  Ayont the loch;   *beyond*
Ye, like a *rash-bush*, stood in sight,   *rush-bush*
  Wi' *waving sough*.   *sighing sound*

The cudgel in my *nieve* did shake,   *fist*
Each bristl'd hair stood like a stake,
When wi' an eldritch, *stoor* "Quaick, quaick,"   *hoarse*
  Amang the springs,
Awa ye *squatter'd* like a drake,   *fluttered*
  On whistling wings.

Let *warlocks* grim, an' wither'd hags,   *male witches*
Tell how wi' you, on ragweed nags,
They skim the muirs an' dizzy crags,
  Wi' wicked speed;
And in kirk-yards renew their leagues,
  Owre howket dead.   *over dug up*

Thence countra wives, wi' toil an' pain,
May plunge an' plunge the *kirn* in vain;   *churn*
For oh! the yellow treasure's *taen*   *taken away*
      By witchin' skill;
An' *dawtit*, twal-pint Hawkie's *gane*   *petted; gone*
      As *yell's* the *bill.*   *dry; bull*

Thence, mystic knots make great abuse
On young *guidmen*, fond, keen an' *croose;*   *husbands; confident*
When the best wark-lume i' the house,
      By *cantraip wit,*   *magic slight*
Is instant made no worth a louse,
      Just at the bit.

When *thowes* dissolve the snawy *hoord,*   *thaws; wreaths*
An' float the jinglin' icy boord,
Then, water-kelpies haunt the foord,
      By your direction;
And 'nighted trav'llers are allur'd
      To their destruction.

And aft your moss-traversin "*Spunkies*"   *will o' the wisps*
Decoy the wight that late an' drunk is:
The *bleezin'*, curst, mischievous monkies   *blazing*
      Delude his eyes,
Till in some miry slough he sunk is,
      Ne'er mair to rise.

When mason's mystic word an' grip
In storms an' tempests raise you up,
Some cock or cat your rage *maun* stop,   *must*
      Or, strange to tell!
The youngest "brither" ye wad *whip*   *carry*
      Aff *straught* to hell.   *straight*

Lang syne in Eden's bonie yard,   *long ago*
When youthfu' lovers first were pair'd,
An' all the soul of love they shar'd,
      The raptur'd hour,
Sweet on the fragrant flow'ry *swaird,*   *sward*
      In shady bow'r;

Then you, ye auld, *snick-drawin'* dog!   *slippery*
Ye came to Paradise incog,
An' play'd on man a cursed *brogue*,   *trick*
    (Black be your *fa'!*)   *doom*
An' *gied* the infant warld a *shog*,   *gave; shock*
    'Maist ruin'd a'.   *almost*

D'ye mind that day when in a *bizz*   *bustle*
Wi' *reekit* duds, an' *reestit gizz*,   *smokey; parched hair*
Ye did present your *smootie* phiz   *sooty*
    'Mang better folk,
An' *sklented* on the man of Uzz   *squinted*
    Your spitefu' joke?

An' how ye gat him i' your thrall,
An' brak him out o' house an' hall,
While scabs an' blotches did him gall,
    Wi' bitter *claw;*   *scratching*
An' *lows'd* his ill-tongu'd, wicked *scaul*,   *loosed; scolding wife*
    Was *warst ava?*   *worst of all*

But a' your doings to rehearse,
Your wily snares an' *fechtin'* fierce,   *fighting*
Sin' that day Michael did you pierce,
    Down to this time,
Wad *ding* a *Lallan* tongue, or *Erse*,   *surpass; Lowland; Gaelic*
    In prose or rhyme.

An' now, auld "Cloots," I ken ye're thinkin',
A certain bardie's rantin', drinkin',
Some luckless hour will send him *linkin'*,   *hopping*
    To your black pit;
But, faith! he'll turn a corner *jinkin'*,   *slyly*
    An' cheat you yet.

But fare-you-weel, auld "Nickie-ben!"
O wad ye tak a thought and men'!
Ye *aiblins* might—I dinna ken—   *perhaps*
    Still hae a stake
I'm wae to think upo' yon den,   *I'm sad*
    Ev'n for your sake!

THE JOLLY BEGGARS [1785]

A Cantata

This famous piece appears to have been composed while the author was at Mossgiel, in November, 1785.

"The Jolly Beggars," for humorous description, and nice discrimination of character, is inferior to no poem of the same length in the whole range of English poetry. The scene indeed is laid in the very lowest department of low life, the actors being a set of strolling vagrants, met to carouse, and barter their rags and plunder for liquor in a hedge ale-house. Yet even in describing the movements of such a group the native taste of the Poet has never suffered his pen to slide into anything coarse or disgusting. The extravagant glee, and outrageous frolic of the beggars, are ridiculously contrasted with their maimed limbs, rags and crutches—the sordid and squalid circumstances of their appearances are judiciously thrown into the shade. Nor is the art of the Poet less conspicuous in the individual figures than in the general mass. The festive vagrants are distinguished from each other by personal appearance and character, as much as any fortuitous assembly in the higher order of life. . . . The most prominent persons are a maimed soldier and his female companion, a hackneyed follower of the camp, a stroller late the consort of a Highland ketteran or sturdy beggar, "but weary fa' the waefu' woodie!" Being now at liberty, she becomes an object of rivalry between "a pigmy scraper with his fiddle" and a strolling tinker. The latter a desperate bandit, like most of his profession, terrifies the musician out of the field, and is preferred by the damsel of course. A wandering ballad singer with a brace of doxies, is last introduced upon the stage. Each of these mendicants sings a song in character, and such a collection of humorous lyrics, connected by vivid poetical description, is not, perhaps, to be paralleled in the English language.

The manuscript was given by Burns himself to Mr. David Woodburn, at that time factor to Mr. M'Adam, of Craigengillan.

When *lyart* leaves bestrow the *yird*,	*withered; earth*
Or wavering like the bauckie-bird,[1]	
Bedim cauld Boreas' blast;	
When hailstanes drive wi' bitter *skyte*,	*stroke*
And infant frosts begin to bite,	
In hoary *cranreuch* drest;	*hoar-frost*
Ae night at e'en a merry *core*	*party*
O' *randie, gangrel bodies*,	*reckless vagrant folks*
In Poosie-Nansie's held the *splore*,	*carousal*
To drink their *orra duddies:*	*superfluous rags*

[1] The old Scotch name for the bat.

Wi' quaffing and laughing,
They ranted an' they sang,
Wi' jumping an' thumping,
The vera girdle [1] rang.

First, *niest* the fire, in auld red rags,   *next*
Ane sat, weel brac'd wi' mealy bags,
And knapsack a' in order;
His *doxy* lay within his arm;   *mistress*
Wi' *usquebae* an' blankets warm   *whiskey*
She *blinket* on her sodger: *gazed amorously*
An' ay he gies the *tozie* drab   *fuddled*
The *tither skelpin* kiss,   *other noisy*
While she held up her greedy *gab*,   *mouth*
Just like an aumous dish [2]
Ilk smack still did crack still,
Just like a cadger's [3] whip;
Then staggering an' swaggering,
He roar'd this ditty up,—

I am a son of Mars who have been in many wars,
And show my cuts and scars wherever I come;
This here was for a wench, and that other in a trench,
When welcoming the French at the sound of the drum.

My prenticeship I past where my leader breath'd his last,
When the bloody die was cast on the heights of Abram [4];
And I served out my trade when the gallant game was play'd,
And the Moro [5] low was laid at the sound of the drum.

I lastly was with Curtis among the floating batt'ries [6],
And there I left for witness an arm and a limb;
Yet let my country need me, with Eliott [7] to head me,
I'd clatter on my stumps at the sound of a drum.

---

[1] Griddle used in Scotland for baking oatmeal cakes and "scones." over the fire.

[2] Alms-dish: the Scottish beggars used to carry a large wooden dish for the reception of such alms as they received in the form of cooked food.

[3] The cadger was a hawker, who travelled the country with a horse or ass, carrying two panniers loaded with merchandise. The term came to be applied to any one who drove a cart regularly for hire, as, a coal-cadger.

[4] The battle-ground in front of Quebec, where Wolfe victoriously fell, 1759.

[5] El Moro was the castle that defended the harbour of Santiago, a small island near the southern coast of Cuba. It was taken by the British, in 1762, after which Havana surrendered.

[6] The destruction of the famous Spanish floating batteries, during the famous siege in 1782, on which occasion Captain Curtis signalized himself.

[7] G. A. Eliott (Lord Heathfield), who defended Gibraltar during a siege of four years.

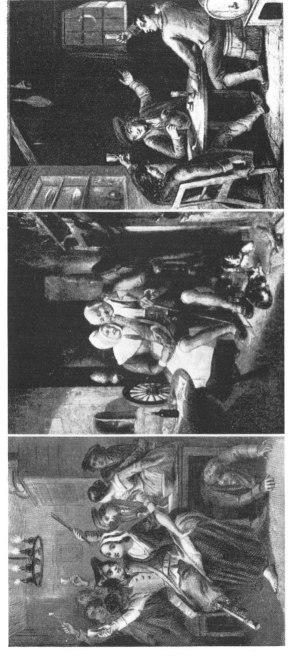

THE JOLLY BEGGARS

I lastly was with Curtis among the floating batt'ries,
And there I left for witness an arm and a limb;
Yet let my country need me, with Eliott to head me,
I'd clatter on my stumps at the sound of a drum.

JOHN ANDERSON, MY JO

But now your brow is beld, John,
Your locks are like the snaw.

WILLIE BREW'D A PECK O' MAUT

It is the moon, —I ken her horn.

In 1775 Britain became involved in hostilities with Spain and General George Augustus Eliott (1717-1790) was sent out
to Gibraltar. His heroic defence, during the famous four years' siege, from June, 1779, to February, 1783, ranks as one
of the most remarkable achievements of British arms. Gibraltar was secured to Britain by the peace of 1783. General
Eliott was, in 1787, created Lord Heathfield, Baron of Gibraltar, by King George III. Captain Roger Curtis, R.N. (1746-
1816), afterwards Admiral Sir Roger Curtis, Bart., G.C.B., destroyed the Spanish floating batteries in 1782.

THE COTTER'S SATURDAY NIGHT
And "Let us worship God!" he says, with solemn air.

BURNS' FIRST LOVE, NELLY KILPATRICK

And now tho' I must beg, with a wooden arm and leg,
And many a tatter'd rag hanging over my bum,
I'm as happy with my wallet, my bottle and my *callet*,   *trull*
As when I used in scarlet to follow a drum.

What tho', with hoary locks, I must stand the winter shocks,
Beneath the woods and rocks, oftentimes for a home,
When the tother bag I sell [1], and the tother bottle tell,
I could meet a troop of hell, at the sound of a drum.

He ended; and the *kebars sheuk*,   *rafters shook*
Aboon the chorus roar;   *above*
While frighted *rattons* backward *leuk*,   *rats; look*
An' seek the *benmost bore:*   *innermost hole*
A fairy fiddler frae the *neuk*,   *nook*
He skirl'd out, encore!
But up arose the martial *chuck*,   *hen*
An' laid the loud uproar.

I once was a maid, tho' I cannot tell when,
And still my delight is in proper young men:
Some one of a troop of dragoons was my daddie,
No wonder I'm fond of a sodger laddie.

The first of my loves was a swaggering blade.
To rattle the thundering drum was his trade:
His leg was so tight, and his cheek was so ruddy,
Transported I was with my sodger laddie.

But the godly old chaplain left him in the lurch;
The sword I forsook for the sake of the church:
He ventur'd the soul, and I *risket* the body,   *risked*
'Twas then I prov'd false to my sodger laddie.

Full soon I grew sick of my sanctified sot,
The regiment at large for a husband I got;
From the gilded spontoon to the fife I was ready,
I asked no more but a sodger laddie.

But the peace it reduc'd me to beg in despair,
Till I met my old boy in a Cunningham [2] fair;
His rags regimental they flutter'd so gaudy,
My heart it rejoic'd at a sodger laddie.

[1] Bag of oatmeal collected by begging and sold for whiskey.
[2] Cunningham fair was held at Stewarton, near Kilmarnock.

And now I have liv'd—I know not how long,
And still I can join in a cup and a song;
But whilst with both hands I can hold the glass steady,
Here's to thee, my hero, my sodger laddie.

Poor Merry-Andrew, in the *neuk*,   *corner*
Sat guzzling wi' a *tinker-hizzie;*   *tinker-wench*
They mind't na wha the chorus *teuk*   *took*
Between themselves they were sae busy:
At length, wi' drink an' courtin dizzy,
He *stoiter'd* up an' made a face;   *staggered*
Then turn'd, an' laid a *smack* on Grizzie,   *kiss*
Syne tun'd his pipes wi' grave grimace.

Sir Wisdom's a fool when he's *fou;*   *full*
Sir Knave is a fool in a session[1],
He's there but a prentice I trow,
But I am a fool by profession.

My grannie she bought me a beuk,
An' I held awa to the school;
I fear I my talent misteuk,
But what will ye *hae* of a fool?   *have*

For drink I would venture my neck;
A *hizzie's* the half of my craft;   *wench*
But what could ye other expect,
Of ane that's avowedly daft?

I ance was tyed up like a *stirk*[2],   *yearling steer*
For civilly swearing and quaffing;
I ance was abus'd i' the kirk,
For *touzling* a lass i' my *daffin.*   *rumpling; frolic*

Poor Andrew that tumbles for sport,
Let naebody name wi' a jeer;
There's even, I'm *tauld*, i' the Court   *told*
A tumbler ca'd the Premier.

Observ'd ye yon reverend lad
Mak faces to tickle the mob;
He rails at our mountebank squad,—
It's rivalship just i' the job.

[1] Apparently, when being tried for some offence.
[2] This refers to the punishment of the "Jougs," an iron collar padlocked round a culprit's neck in a public thoroughfare.

And now my conclusion I'll tell,
For faith I'm confoundedly dry;
The chiel that's a fool for himsel,
Guid L—d! he's far dafter than I.

Then niest outspak a *raucle carlin*   *stout beldam*
Wha kent fu' weel to *cleek* the sterlin;   *steal*
For mony a pursie she had hooked,
An' had in mony a well been *douked:*   *ducked*
Her love had been a Highland laddie,
But weary fa' the waefu' *woodie;*   *gibbet-halter*
Wi' saighs an' sobs she thus began
To wail her *braw* John Highlandman.   *brave*

A Highland lad my love was born,
The *lalland* laws he held in scorn;   *lowland*
But he still was faithfu' to his clan,
My gallant, braw John Highlandman.

Chorus.

   Sing hey my braw John Highlandman!
   Sing ho my braw John Highlandman!
   There's not a lad in a' the lan'
   Was match for my John Highlandman!

With his *philibeg* an' tartan plaid,   *kilt*
An' guid claymore down by his side,
The ladies' hearts he did trepan,
My gallant, braw John Highlandman.

We ranged a' from Tweed to Spey[1],
An' liv'd like lords an' ladies gay;
For a lalland face he feared none,—
My gallant, braw John Highlandman.

They banish'd him beyond the sea,
But ere the bud was on the tree,
Adown my cheeks the pearls ran,
Embracing my John Highlandman.

But och! they catch'd him at the last,
And bound him in a dungeon fast:
My curse upon them every one,
They've hanged my braw John Highlandman!

[1] Tweed separates Scotland from England: Spey is a river in Inverness-shire.   The phrase
means from South to North of Scotland.

And now a widow I must mourn
The pleasures that will ne'er return;
No comfort but a hearty can,
When I think on John Highlandman.

A pigmy scraper wi' his fiddle,
Wha us'd at *trystes* an' fairs to *driddle*,   *cattle markets; play*
Her strappin limb and *gausy* middle   *buxom*
      (He reach'd nae higher)
Had holed his heartie like a riddle,
      An' *blawn't* on fire.   *blown it*

Wi' hand on *hainch*, and upward e'e,   *haunch*
He croon'd his gamut, one, two, three,
Then in an arioso key,
      The wee Apollo
Set off wi' allegretto glee
      His giga solo.

Let me *ryke* up to *dight* that tear   *reach, wipe*
An' go wi' me an' be my dear;
An' then your every care an' fear
May whistle owre the *lave o't*.[1]   *rest of it*

Chorus.

    I am a fiddler to my trade,
    An' a' the tunes that e'er I play'd,
    The sweetest still to wife or maid,
    Was whistle owre the lave o't.

At *kirns* an' weddins *we'se* be there   *harvest-homes; we shall*
An' O sae nicely's we will fare!
We'll *bowse* about till Daddie Care   *carouse*
Sing whistle owre the lave o't.

Sae merrily's the *banes* we'll *pyke*,   *bones; pick*
An' sun oursells about the *dyke;*   *stone fence*
An' at our leisure, when ye like,
We'll whistle owre the lave o't.

But bless me wi' your heav'n o' charms,
An' while I kittle hair on thairms,[2]
Hunger, *cauld*, an' a sic harms,   *cold*
May whistle owre the lave o't.

---

[1] A popular Scotch air. His meaning is: grant my prayer, and then you can regard all else with indifference.

[2] Tickle the horse-hair of the bow on catgut.

Her charms had struck a sturdy caird[1],
As weel as poor gut-scraper;
He taks the fiddler by the beard,
An' draws a roosty rapier—
He swoor by a' was swearing worth,
To speet him like a *pliver*,   plover
Unless he would from that time forth
Relinquish her for ever.

Wi' ghastly *e'e*, poor tweedle-dee   eye
Upon his *hunkers* bended   haunches
An' pray'd for grace wi' ruefu' face,
An' so the quarrel ended.
But tho' his little heart did grieve
When round the tinkler prest her,
He feign'd to *snirtle* in his sleeve,   snigger
When thus the caird address'd her:

My bonie lass, I work in brass,
A tinkler is my station;
I've travel'd round all Christian ground
In this my occupation;
I've *taen* the gold, an' been enrolled   taken
In many a noble squadron[2];
But vain they search'd when off I march'd
To go an' *clout* the cauldron.   patch

Despise that shrimp, that wither'd imp.
With a' his noise an' cap'rin;
An' take a share with those that bear
The *budget* and the apron!   tool-bag
And by that *stowp!* my faith an' *houp*   flagon; hope
And by that dear Kilbagie[3],
If e'er ye want, or meet wi' scant,
May I ne'er weet my *craigie*.   throat

The caird prevail'd—th' unblushing fair
In his embraces sunk;
Partly wi' love o'er come *sae sair*,   so sore
An' partly she was drunk:

[1] Cairds were travelling tinkers or horn spoon-makers, and generally gipsies and thieves.
[2] He was a bounty-jumper.
[3] A peculiar sort of whiskey so called, a great favourite with Poosie Nansie's clubs. So named from Kilbagie distillery, in Clackmannan-shire.

Sir Violino, with an air
That show'd a man o' *spunk*,   *mettle*
Wish'd unison between the pair,
An' made the bottle clunk[1]
      To their health that night.

But *hurchin* Cupid shot a shaft,   *urchin*
That play'd a dame a *shavie*—   *trick*
The fiddler rak'd her, fore and aft,
Behint the chicken *cavie*.   *coop*
Her lord, a wight of Homer's craft[2],
Tho' limpin wi' the *spavie*,   *spavin*
He *hirpl'd* up, an' lap *like daft*   *limped; as if crazy*
And shor'd them Dainty Davie[3]
      O' boot that night.   *to boot*

He was a care-defying blade
As ever Bacchus listed!
Tho' Fortune sair upon him laid
His heart, she ever miss'd it.
He had no wish but—to be glad,
Nor want but—when he thirsted;
He hated nought but—to be sad,
An' thus the muse suggested
      His sang that night.

I am a Bard of no regard,
Wi' gentle folks an' a' that;
But Homer-like, the *glowrin byke*,   *staring throng*
Frae town to town I draw that.

Chorus.

  For a' that an' a' that,
  An' twice as *muckle*'s a' that;   *much*
  I've lost but ane, I've twa behin',
  I've wife eneugh for a' that.

I never drank the Muses' *stank*,   *fountain*
Castalia's burn, an' a' that:
But there it streams an' richly reams,
My Helicon I ca' that.[4]

---

[1] Onomatopoetic, for the gurgling sound made in pouring out liquor.
[2] Homer is allowed to be the oldest ballad-singer on record.
[3] A popular Scotch air and song.
[4] We must here imagine the singer to pour out his beer with jovial abandon.

Great love I bear to a' the fair,
Their humble slave an' a' that;
But lordly will, I hold it still
A mortal sin to *thraw* that.   *thwart*

In raptures sweet, this hour we meet,
Wi' mutual love an' a' that;
But for how lang the *flie may stang*   *fancy may last*
Let inclination law that.

Their tricks an' craft hae put me daft,
They've *taen* me in, an' a' that;   *taken*
But clear your decks, an' here's the Sex!
I like the *jads* for a' that.   *jades*

Chorus.
   For a' that an' a' that,
   An' twice as muckle's a' that;
   My dearest bluid, to do them guid,
   They're welcome till't for a' that.

So sung the bard—and Nansies *wa's*   *walls*
Shook with a thunder of applause,
Re'echo'd from each mouth!
They toom'd their pocks[1], they pawn'd their duds
They scarcely left to *coor* their *fuds,*   *cover; hips*
To quench their *lowin* drouth: *flaming*
Then owre again, the jovial thrang
The poet did request
To *lowse* his pack an' *wale* a sang;   *loose; choose*
A ballad o' the best:
He rising, rejoicing,
Between his twa Deborahs,
Looks round him, an' found them
Impatient for the chorus.

See the smoking bowl before us,
Mark our jovial, ragged ring!
Round and round take up the chorus,
And in raptures let us sing—

Chorus.
   A fig for those by law protected!
   Liberty's a glorious feast!
   Courts for cowards were erected,
   Churches built to please the priest.

[1] Emptied their meal-bags for drink.

What is title, what is treasure,
What is reputation's care?
If we lead a life of pleasure,
'Tis no matter how or where!

With the ready trick and fable,
Round we wander all the day;
And at night, in barn or stable,
Hug our *doxies* on the hay.   *sweethearts*

Does the train-attended carriage
Thro' the country lighter rove?
Does the sober bed of marriage
Witness brighter scenes of love?

Life is all a variorum,
We regard not how it goes;
Let them cant about decorum,
Who have character to lose.

Here's to budgets, bags and wallets!
Here's to all the wandering train,
Here's our ragged *brats* and *callets*,   *children; trulls*
One and all cry out, Amen!

Chorus.
   A fig for those by law protected!
   Liberty's a glorious feast!
   Courts for cowards were erected,
   Churches built to please the priest.

THE AULD FARMER'S NEW-YEAR MORNING SALUTATION
TO HIS AULD MARE, MAGGIE [1786]

On giving her the accustomed ripp of corn to hansel in the New-Year

What a delightful piece of autobiography the good old man recites to his auld mare, as he gives her the usual New-Year-Morning hansel! The whole poem is in the Author's best manner, in its happy combination of humour and tenderness.

A guid New-year, I wish thee Maggie!
Hae, there's a *ripp* to thy auld *baggie:*   *handful; stomach*
Tho' thou's *howe-backit* now, an' *knaggie*   *hollow-backed; bony*
      I've seen the day
Thou could hae gaen like ony *staggie,*   *colt*
      Out-owre the *lay*.   *pasture*

Tho' now thou's *dowie*, stiff an' crazy,	*spiritless*
An' thy auld hide's as white's a daisie,	
I've seen thee dappl't, sleek an' *glaizie*,	*glossy*
A bonie gray:	
He should been *ticht* that daur't to *raize* thee,	*fit; rouse*
Ance in a day.	*once on a time*

Thou ance was i' the foremost rank,	
A filly *buirdly*, *steeve* an' *swank;*	*stately; firm; frisky*
An' set weel down a shapely shank,	
As e'er tread *yird;*	*earth*
An' could hae flown out-owre a *stank*,	*ditch*
Like ony bird.	

It's now some nine-an'-twenty year,	
Sin' thou was my guid-father's *meere;*	*mare*
He gied me thee, o' *tocher* clear,	*of dowry*
An' fifty mark;	
Tho' it was sma', 'twas weel-won *gear*,	*money*
An' thou was *stark*.	*strong*

When first I gaed to woo my Jenny,	
Ye then was trottin wi' your *minnie:*	*dam*
Tho' ye was trickie, *slee*, an' funnie,	*sly*
Ye ne'er was *donsie;*	*nervous*
But hamely, *tawie*, quiet, an' *cannie*,	*tractable; gentle*
An' *unco sonsie*.	*very attractive*

That day, ye pranc'd wi' *muckle* pride,	*much*
When ye *bure* hame my bonie bride:	*bore*
An' sweet an' gracefu' she did ride,	
Wi' maiden air!	
Kyle Stewart I could bragget wide,	
For *sic* a pair.	*such*

Tho' now ye *dow* but *hoyte* and hobble	*can; limp*
An' *wintle* like a *saumont-coble*,	*rock; salmon-boat*
That day, ye was a *jinker* noble,	*runner*
For *heels an' win'!*	*speed and wind*
An' ran them till they a' did wauble,	
Far, far behin'!	

When thou an' I were young an' *skiegh*,	*frisky*
An' stable-meals at fairs were *driegh*,	*flat*
How thou wad prance, an' snore, an' *skriegh*,	*neigh*
An' tak the road!	
Town's bodies ran, an' stood *abiegh*,	*aside*
An' *ca't* thee mad.	*called*

When thou was corn't, an' I was mellow,
We took the road aye like a swallow:
At *brooses* thou had ne'er a fellow   *cross-country races*
  For pith an' speed;
But ev'ry tail thou *pay't* them hollow,   *beat*
    Where'er thou *gaed.*   *went*

The sma' droop-rumpl't, hunter cattle,
Might *aiblins waur't* thee for a *brattle;*   *perhaps; beat; dash*
But sax Scotch miles, thou try't their mettle,
    An' *gar't* them *whaizle:*   *made; wheeze*
Nae whip nor spur, but just a *wattle*   *wand*
    O' *saugh* or hazle.   *willow*

Thou was a noble *fittie-lan',*   *right plough horse*
As e'er in *tug* or *tow* was drawn!   *trace; rope*
Aft thee an' I, in *aught* hours' *gaun,*   *eight; going (in plough)*
    On guid March weather,
Hae *turn'd sax rood beside our han',*   *ploughed six roods*
    For days *thegither.*   *together*

Thou never *braing't,* an' *fetch't,* an' *fliskit;*   *plunged; shied, fretted*
But thy auld tail thou wad hae *whisket,*   *whisked*
An' spread *abreed* thy weel-fill'd *brisket,*   *abroad; breast*
    Wi' pith an' power;
Till sprittie knowes wad rair't an' risket,
    An' slypet owre. [1]

When frosts lay lang an' snaws were deep,
An' threaten'd labour back to keep,
I gied thy *cog* a wee bit heap   *feed-box*
    Aboon the *timmer:*   *edge*
I ken'd my Maggie wad na sleep
    For that, or *simmer.*   *before summer*

In cart or car thou never *reestet;*   *baulked*
The *steyest brae* thou wad hae fac't it;   *steepest hill*
Thou never *lap,* an' *stenned,* an' *breasted,*   *leapt; strained, plunged*
    Then stood to *blaw;*   *breathe*
But just thy step a wee thing hastit,
    Thou *snoov't awa.*   *went quietly on*

[1] Until grassy hummocks would be ripped and sheared and turned over.

My pleugh is now thy bairn-time a',
Four gallant brutes as e'er did draw;
Forbye *sax mae* I've *sell't awa*,   *six more; sold off*
    That thou hast nurst:
They drew me *thretteen pund an' twa*,   *fifteen pounds*
    The vera *warst*.   *worst*

Mony a *sair daurk* we twa hae wrought,   *hard day's work*
An' wi' the weary *warl'* fought!   *world*
An' monie an anxious day, I thought,
    We wad be beat!
Yet here to crazy age we're brought,
    Wi' something yet.

An' think na', my auld trusty servan',
That now perhaps thou's less deservin',
An' thy auld days may end in starvin';
    For my last *fow*,   *bit of corn*
A heapet *stimpart*, I'll reserve ane   *gallon*
    Laid by for you.

We've worn to crazy years thegither;
We'll *toyte* about wi' ane anither;   *totter*
Wi' *tentie* care I'll *flit* thy tether   *watchful; move*
    To some *hain'd rig*,   *reserved ridge*
Whare ye may nobly *rax* your leather,   *stretch*
    Wi' sma' fatigue.

THE TWA DOGS [1786]

A Tale

The Tale of the Twa Dogs was composed after the resolution of publishing was nearly taken. Robert had a dog which he called Luath, that was a great favourite. The dog had been killed by the wanton cruelty of some person the night before my father's death. Robert said to me that he should like to confer such immortality as he could upon his old friend Luath, and that he had a great mind to introduce something into the book, under the title of "Stanzas to the Memory of a Quadruped Friend"; but this plan was given up for the Tale as it now stands. Caesar was merely the creature of the Poet's imagination, created for the purpose of holding chat with his favourite Luath. (*Gilbert Burns.*)

The factor who stood for his portrait here was the same of whom he writes to Dr. Moore, in 1787: "My indignation yet boils at the scoundrel

factor's insolent threatening letters which used to set us all in tears."
All who have been bred in country districts will have no difficulty in finding
parallels to factor of the poem.

'Twas in that place o' Scotland's Isle,
That bears the name o' auld King Coil,
Upon a bonie day in June,
When wearing thro' the afternoon,
Twa dogs, that were na *thrang* at hame,   *busy*
Forgather'd *ance* upon a time.   *once*

The first I'll name, they ca'd him Caesar,
Was keepit for his Honor's pleasure:
His hair, his size, his mouth, his lugs,
Shew'd he was nane o' Scotland's dogs;
But *whalpit* some place far abroad,   *whelped*
Whare sailors gang to fish for cod.

His lockèd, letter'd, braw brass collar
Shew'd him the gentleman an' scholar;
But though he was o' high degree,
The fient a pride, nae pride had he;   *deuce a bit of*
But wad hae spent an hour caressin',
Ev'n wi' a tinkler-gipsey's *messan:*   *cur*
At kirk or market, mill or *smiddie*,   *smithy*
Nae *tawted tyke*, tho' e'er sae *duddie*,   *rough cur; ragged*
But he wad stand, as glad to see him,
An' *stroan'd* on stanes an' hillocks wi' him.   *urinated*

The tither was a ploughman's collie—
A rhyming, ranting, roving *billie*,   *fellow*
Wha for his friend an' comrade had him,
And in his freaks had Luath *ca'd* him,   *named*
After some dog[1] in Highland sang,
Was made lang syne—Lord knows how lang.

He was a *gash* an' faithfu' tyke,   *sagacious*
As ever lap a *sheugh* or dyke.   *ditch*
His honest, *sonsie, baws'nt* face   *happy; striped*
Ay gat him friends in ilka place;
His breast was white, his *tousie* back   *shaggy*
Weel clad wi' coat o' glossy black;
His *gawsie* tail, wi' upward curl,   *stately*
Hung owre his *hurdies* wi' a swirl.   *hips*

[1] Cuchullin's dog in Ossian's Fingal.   (R.B. 1786)

Nae doubt but they were *fain o' ither,*	*fond of each other*
And unco *pack an' thick* thegither;	*friendly and intimate*
Wi' social nose *whyles snuff'd an' snowket;*	*sometimes smelled and poked*
Whyles mice an' *moudieworts* they *howket;*	*moles; dug up*
Whyles scour'd awa' in lang excursion	
An' worry'd *ither* in diversion;	*each other*
Till tir'd at last wi' monie a farce,	
They set them down upon their arse,	
An' there began a lang digression	
About the lords o' the creation.	

CAESAR.

I've aften wonder'd, honest Luath,	
What sort o' life poor dogs like you have;	
An' when the gentry's life I saw,	
What way poor bodies liv'd *ava.*	*at all*

Our laird gets in his racked rents	
His coals, his kane, an' a' his *stents*	*assessments*
He rises when he likes himsel;	
His flunkies answer at the bell;	
He ca's his coach; he ca's his horse;	
He draws a bonnie silken purse	
As lang's my tail, whare, thro' the *steeks,*	*stitches*
The yellow letter'd *Geordie keeks.*	*guinea peeps*
Frae morn to e'en it's nought but toiling,	
At baking, roasting, frying, boiling;	
An' tho' the gentry first are *stechin,*	*puffing from gorging*
Yet ev'n the *ha' folk* fill their *pechan*	*servants; stomach*
Wi' sauce, ragouts, an' sic like trashtrie,	
That's little short o' downright *wastrie.*	*waste*
Our whipper-in, *wee blastit wonner,*	*blasted little sinner*
Poor worthless elf, it eats a dinner	
Better than ony tenant-man	
His Honor has in a' the lan':	
An' what poor cot-folk *pit* their *painch* in,	*put, paunch*
I own it's past my comprehension.	

LUATH.

Trowth, Caesar, whyles, they're *fash't* eneugh:	*perplexed*
A cotter *howkin* in a *sheugh,*	*digging; ditch*
Wi dirty stanes *biggin' a dyke,*	*building a fence*
Baring a quarry, and sic like;	
Himsel, a wife, he thus sustains,	
A *smytrie* o' wee *duddie weans,*	*tribe; ragged children*
An' nought but his *han'-daurg,* to keep	*hand's work*
Them right an' tight in *thack an' rape.*	*thatch and rope*

An when they meet wi' sair disasters,
Like loss o' health or want o' masters,
Ye *maist wad* think, a wee touch langer　　　*almost would*
An' they maun starve o' cauld and hunger:
But how it comes, I never *kent* yet,　　　*knew*
They're maistly wonderfu' contented;
An' *buirdly chiels*, an' clever *hizzies*,　　　*hardy fellows; girls*
Are bred in sic a way as this is.

CAESAR.

But then to see how ye're negleckit,
How huff'd, an' cuff'd, an' disrespeckit!
L—d, man, our gentry care as little
For delvers, ditchers, an' sic cattle;
They gang as saucy by poor folk,
As I wad by a stinking *brock*.　　　*badger*

I've notic'd on our laird's *court-day*,　　　*rent-day*
An' mony a time my heart's been *wae*,　　　*sad*
Poor tenant bodies, scant o' cash,
How they maun *thole* a factor's *snash:*　　　*bear; insolence*
He'll stamp an' threaten, curse an' swear,
He'll apprehend them, *poind* their *gear;*　　　*attach; property*
While they maun stan', wi' aspect humble,
An' hear it a', an' fear an' tremble!
I see how folk live that hae riches;
But surely poor-folk maun be wretches!

LUATH.

They're no sae wretched's ane wad think,
Tho' constantly on *poortith's* brink;　　　*poverty's*
They're sae accustom'd wi' the sight,
The view o't gies them little fright.
Then chance and fortune are sae guided,
They're ay in less or mair provided;
An' tho' fatigu'd wi' close employment,
A blink o' rest's a sweet enjoyment.

The dearest comfort o' their lives,
Their *grushie weans* an' faithfu' wives;　　　*thriving children*
The prattling things are just their pride,
That sweetens a' their fire-side.
An' whyles twalpennie worth o' *nappy*　　　*ale*
Can mak' the bodies *unco* happy:　　　*very*
They lay aside their private cares,
To mind the Kirk and State affairs;

They'll talk o' patronage an' priests,
Wi' kindling fury i' their breasts,
Or tell what new taxation's comin',
An' *ferlie* at the folk in Lon'on.   *marvel*

As bleak-fac'd *Hallowmass* returns,   *All Saints' Day*
They get the jovial, rantin *kirns*,   *harvest homes*
When rural life o' ev'ry station
Unite in common recreation;
Love blinks, Wit slaps, an' social Mirth
Forgets there's Care upo' the earth.

That merry day the year begins,
They bar the door on frosty *win's;*   *winds*
The *nappy reeks* wi' mantling *ream*,   *ale; creamy froth*
An' sheds a heart-inspiring steam;
The *luntin* pipe, an' *sneeshin-mill*,   *glowing; snuff-mull*
Are handed round wi' right guid will;
The *cantie* auld folks *crackin' crouse*,   *cheery; talking gaily*
The young anes ranting thro' the house—
My heart has been sae *fain* to see them,   *glad*
That I for joy hae barkit wi' them.

Still it's *owre* true that ye hae said,   *too*
Sic game is now owre aften play'd.   *such*
There's monie a creditable stock
O' decent, honest, *fawsont* folk   *seemly*
Are riven out baith root an' branch,
Some rascal's pridefu' greed to quench,
Wha thinks to knit himsel the faster
In favor wi' some gentle master,
Wha, *aiblins thrang* a parliamentin',   *perhaps busy*
For Britain's guid his saul indentin'—

CAESAR.

   Haith, lad, ye little ken about it: *faith*
For Britain's guid! guid faith! I doubt it.
Say rather, *gaun* as Premiers lead him: *going*
Ay' saying aye or no 's they bid him:
At operas an' plays parading,
Mortgaging, gambling, masquerading,
Or maybe, in a frolic *daft*,   *foolish*
To Hague or Calais takes a waft,
To mak a tour an' tak a whirl,
To learn *bon ton*, an' see the worl'.

There, at Vienna or Versailles,
He *rives* his father's auld entails;   *tears up*
Or by Madrid he takes the rout
To thrum guitars an' *fecht wi' nowt;*   *fight with bulls*
Or down Italian vista startles,
Whore-hunting amang groves o' myrtles:
Then *bowses drumlie* German water,   *swills muddy*
To mak himsel look fair an' fatter,
An' clear the consequential sorrows,
Love-gifts of Carnival signoras.
For Britain's guid!—for her destruction!
Wi' dissipation, feud an' faction.

LUATH.

Hech man! dear sirs! is that the *gate*   *alas; way*
They waste sae mony a *braw* estate!   *fine*
Are we *sae foughten* an' harass'd   *so tired*
For *gear* to *gang* that gate at last?   *money; go*

O would they stay aback *frae* courts,   *from*
An' please themsels wi' country sports,
It wad for ev'ry ane be better,
The *laird*, the tenant, an' the cotter!   *land-owner*
For *thae* frank, rantin', ramblin' *billies*,   *these; fellows*
Fient haet o' them's ill-hearted fellows;   *not a whit of*
Except for breakin' o' their timmer,
Or speakin' lightly o' their *limmer*,   *mistress*
Or shootin' of a hare or moor-cock,
The ne'er-a-bit they're ill to poor folk.

But will ye tell me, master Caesar,
Sure great folk's life's a life o' pleasure?
Nae cauld nor hunger e'er can *steer* them,   *molest*
The vera thought o't need na fear them.

CAESAR.

L—d, man, were ye but *whyles* whare I am,   *sometimes*
The gentles ye wad ne'er envy them!
It's true, they need na starve or sweat,
Thro' winter's cauld, or simmer's heat;
They've nae *sair-wark* to *craze* their banes.   *hard work; wear out*
An' fill auld-age wi' grips an' *granes:*   *groans*
But human bodies are *sic* fools,   *such*
For a' their colleges an' schools,

That when nae real ills perplex them,
They mak enow themsels to vex them;
An' ay the less they hae to *sturt* them,   *distress*
In like proportion less will hurt them.

A country fellow at the pleugh,
His acre's till'd, he's right eneugh;
A country girl at her wheel,
Her *dizzen's* done, she's *unco weel:*   *dozen; all right*
But gentlemen, an' ladies *warst,*   *worst*
Wi' ev'n-down want o' wark are curst.
They loiter, lounging, lank an' lazy;
Tho' *deil-haet* ails them, yet uneasy: *devil a bit*
Their days insipid, dull and tasteles;
Their nights unquiet, lang an' restless.

An' ev'n their sports, their balls an' races,
Their galloping through public places,
There's sic parade, sic pomp an' art,
The joy can scarcely reach the heart.

The men *cast out* in party matches,   *quarrel*
Then *sowther* a' in deep debauches.   *solder*
Ae night they're mad wi' drink an' whoring,   *one*
Niest day their life is past enduring.   *next*

The ladies arm-in-arm in clusters,
As great an' gracious a' as sisters;
But hear their absent thoughts o' *ither,*   *of each other*
They're a' run deils an' *jads thegither.*   *jades together*
Whyles, owre the wee bit cup an' platie,
They sip the scandal-potion pretty;
Or *lee-lang nights,* wi' crabbet *leuks*   *all night long; looks*
Pore owre the devil's pictur'd *beuks;*   *playing-cards*
Stake on a chance a farmer's stackyard,
An' cheat like ony unhang'd blackguard.

There's some exceptions, man an' woman;
But this is gentry's life in common.

By this, the sun was out o' sight,
An' darker *gloaming* brought the night;   *twilight*
The *bum-clock* humm'd wi' lazy drone;   *night-beetle*
The *kye* stood *rowtin'* in' the *loan;*   *cows; lowing; lane*
When up they gat, an' shook their lugs,
Rejoic'd they were na man, but dogs;
An' each took aff his several way,
Resolv'd to meet some ither day.

R.B.—15

ADDRESS TO THE UNCO GUID
or
THE RIGIDLY RIGHTEOUS

My son, these maxims make a rule,	
And lump them aye *thegither;*	*together*
The Rigid Righteous is a fool,	
The Rigid Wise anither;	
The cleanest corn that e'er was *dight*	*winnowed*
May ha'e some *pyles* o' *caff* in;	*grains; chaff*
So ne'er a fellow-creature slight	
For random fits o' *daffin'.*	*merriment*

Solomon—Eccles. VII. 16.

The first stanza has been quoted by one who wrote an estimate of
Burns' writings in the spirit of generous criticism, as an instance of the
strength and clearness of his conceptions, and the consequent progress in
the correctness and congruity of his use of similes.

Of the last stanza of this remarkable poem Wordsworth says:

"The momentous truth of this passage could not possibly have been conveyed
with such pathetic force by any poet that ever lived, speaking in his own voice;
unless it were felt that, like Burns, he was a man who preached from the text of his
own errors; and whose wisdom, beautiful as a flower, that might have risen from
seed sown from above, was in fact a scion from the root of personal suffering."

O ye wha are sae *guid* yoursel',	*good*
Sae pious and sae holy,	
Ye've nought to do but mark and tell	
Your neibours' *fauts* and folly!	*faults*
Whase life is like a *weel-gaun* mill,	*well-going*
Supplied wi' store o' water;	
The heapèt happer's ebbing still,	
An' still the clap plays clatter.	

Hear me, ye venerable *core,*	*company*
As counsel for poor mortals	
That frequent pass *douce* Wisdom's door	*solemn*
For *glaikit* Folly's portals:	*giddy*
I, for their thoughtless, careless sakes,	
Would here *propone* defences—	*state*
Their *donsie* tricks, their black mistakes	*unfortunate*
Their failings and mischances.	

Ye see your state wi' theirs compared,
And shudder at the *niffer;*   *difference*
But cast a moment's fair regard,
What maks the mighty differ?
Discount what scant occasion gave,
That purity ye pride in;
And (what's *aft mair* than *a' the lave*)   *oft more; all the rest*
Your better art o' hidin'.

Think, when your castigated pulse
Gies now and then a *wallop!*   *gives; leap*
What ragings must his veins convulse,
That still eternal gallop!
Wi' wind and tide fair i' your tail,
Right on ye scud your sea-way;
But in the teeth o' *baith* to sail,   *both*
It makes an *unco* lee-way.   *very great*

See Social Life and Glee sit down,
All joyous and unthinking,
Till, quite *transmugrify'd*, they're grown   *changed*
Debauchery and Drinking;
O would they stay to calculate
Th' eternal consequences;
Or your more dreaded hell to state,
Damnation of expenses!

Ye high, exalted, virtuous dames,
Tied up in godly laces,
Before ye *gie* poor Frailty names,   *call*
Suppose a change o' cases;
A dear-lov'd lad, convenience snug,
A treach'rous inclination;
But, let me whisper i' your *lug*,   *ear*
Ye're *aiblins nae* temptation.   *perhaps no*

Then gently scan your brother man,
Still gentler sister woman;
Tho' they may gang a *kennin* wrang,   *slightly*
To step aside is human:
One point must still be greatly dark,
The moving Why they do it;
And just as lamely can ye mark,
How far perhaps they rue it.

Who made the heart, 'tis He alone
Decidedly can try us;
He knows each chord, its various tone,
Each spring, its various bias:
Then at the balance let's be mute,
We never can adjust it;
What's done we partly may compute,
But know not what's resisted.

TO A LOUSE [1786]

On seeing one on a Lady's Bonnet at Church

"Lunardi," that Burns alludes to in the sixth stanza, is a bonnet named after Vincent Lunardi, a balloonist, who made several ascensions in Scotland in 1785. In compliment to him, the Scottish ladies wore what they called "Lunardi bonnets." They were made of gauze, or thin muslin, extended on wire, the upper part representing the balloon, and were for some time universally fashionable. Lunardi died at Lisbon in 1806.

Ha! whaur ye *gaun*, ye crawlin *ferlie!*	*going; wonder*
Your impudence protects you *sairlie;*	*wonderfully*
I *canna* say but ye *strunt* rarely,	*cannot; strut*
Owre gauze and lace;	*over*
Tho' faith! I fear ye dine but sparely	
On *sic* a place.	*such*
Ye ugly, creepin', *blasted wonner,*	*blasted imp*
Detested, shunn'd by *saunt* an' sinner,	*saint*
How *daur* ye set your *fit* upon her—	*dare; foot*
Sae fine a lady?	
Gae somewhere else, and seek your dinner	*go*
On some poor body.	
Swith! in some beggar's *haffet squattle,*	*Away! whiskers settle*
Wi' ither kindred, jumping cattle;	*with other*
There ye may creep, an sprawl, and *sprattle*	*scramble*
In shoals and nations;	
Whaur horn nor bane ne'er *daur* unsettle	*where; dare*
Your thick plantations.	

Now *haud* you there, ye're out o' sight,	*stay*
Below the *fatt'rels* snug an tight;	*puckers*
Na, faith ye yet! ye'll no be right,	*no, hang you!*
Till ye've got on it—	
The vera tapmost, tow'rin height	
O' Miss's bonnet.	

My sooth! right *bauld* ye set your nose out,	*bold*
As plump an' grey as ony *groset:*	*goose-berry*
O for some rank, mercurial *rozet,*	*ointment*
Or *fell,* red *smeddum,*	*deadly; powder*
I'd *gie* you *sic* a hearty dose o't,	*give; such*
Wad dress your *droddum!*	*breech*

I wad nae been surpris'd to spy	
You on an auld wife's *flannen toy;*	*flannel cap*
Or *aiblins* some bit *duddie* boy,	*perhaps; ragged*
On's *wyliecoat;*	*under-vest*
But Miss's fine Lunardi! fye!	
How daur ye do't?	

O Jeany, *dinna* toss your head,	*do not*
An' set your beauties a' *abreid!*	*abroad*
Ye little *ken* what cursed speed	*know*
The *blastie's* makin':	*little imp*
Thae winks an' finger-ends, I dread,	*those*
Are notice takin'!	

O *wad* some Power the *giftie* gie us,	*would; gift*
To see oursels as ithers see us!	
It *wad frae mony* a blunder free us,	*would from many*
An' foolish notion:	
What airs in dress an' gait wad *lea'e* us,	*leave*
An' ev'n devotion!	

THE HOLY FAIR [1786]

"Holy Fair" is a common phrase in the West of Scotland for a Sacramental occasion.

The devotion of the common people on the usual days of worship is as much to be commended as their conduct at the sacrament is to be censured. It is celebrated but once a year, when there are in some places three thousand communicants, and as many idle spectators. Of the first, as many as possible crowd each side of a long table, and the elements are rudely shoven from one to another, and in some places before the day is at an end, fights and other indecencies ensue. It is often made a season of debauchery. (Pennant's *Tom in Scotland*, 1769.)

Scenes such as the Poet described had become a scandal and a disgrace to the Church. The poem was met by a storm of abuse from his old enemies; but amid all their railings, they did not fail to lay it to heart, and from that time onward there was a manifest improvement in the bearing of ministers and people on such occasions. This is not the least of its merits in the eyes of his countrymen of the present day. Notwithstanding the daring levity of some of its allusions and incidents, the Poet has strictly confined himself to the sayings and doings of the assembled multitude—the sacred rite itself is never once mentioned.

Upon a simmer Sunday morn,
When Nature's face is fair,
I walkèd forth to view the corn,
An' snuff the *caller* air.   *fresh cool*
The rising sun owre Galston muirs
Wi' glorious light was *glintin';*   *glancing*
The hares were *hirplin'* down the *furrs,*   *limping; furrows*
The *lav'rocks* they were chantin'   *larks*
     Fu' sweet that day.   *full*

As lightsomely I *glowr'd* abroad   *stared*
To see a scene sae gay,
Three *hizzies,* early at the road,   *wenches*
Cam *skelpin* up the way.   *walking rapidly*
Twa had *manteeles* o' dolefu' black,   *mantles*
But *ane wi' lyart* lining;   *one with gray*
The third, that *gaed a wee* a-back,   *walked a little*
Was in the fashion shining,
     Fu' gay that day.

The twa appear'd like sisters twin,
In feature, form, an' *claes;*   *clothes*
Their visage wither'd, lang an' thin,
An' sour as ony *slaes:*   *sloes*
The third cam up, *hap-stap-an'-lowp,*   *hop-step-and-jump*
As light as *ony lambie,*   *any lambkin*
An' wi' a *curchie* low did stoop,   *curtsey*
As soon as e'er she saw me,
     Fu' kind that day.

Wi' bonnet *aff,* quoth I, "Sweet Lass,   *off*
I think ye seem to ken me,
I'm sure I've seen that bonie face,
But yet I *canna* name ye."   *cannot*

Quo' she, an' laughin as she spak,
An' taks me by the hands,
"Ye, for my sake, hae *gien* the *feck*   *given; most*
Of a' the ten commands
   A *screed* some day."   *rent*

"My name is Fun—your *cronie* dear, *comrade*
The nearest friend ye hae;
An' this is Superstition here,
An' that's Hypocrisy.
I'm *gaun* to Mauchline 'holy fair,' *going*
Gin ye'll go there, yon *runkl'd* pair, *if; wrinkled*
We will get famous laughin
   At them this day."

Quoth I, "Wi' a' my heart, I'll do't;
I'll get my Sunday's *sark* on,   *shirt*
An' meet you on the holy spot;
Faith, we'se hae fine remarkin!"
Then I *gaed* hame at *crowdie*-time, *went; breakfast*
An' soon I made me ready;
For roads were clad, frae side to side,
Wi' mony a *wearie* body,   *toiling*
   In droves that day.

Here farmers *gash*, in ridin' *graith*, *solemn; attire*
Gaed hoddin' by their *cotters;* *went jogging; cottagers*
There swankies young, in braw braid-claith,
Are springing *owre* the gutters. *over*
The lasses, skelpin' barefit, thrang,
In silks an' scarlets glitter;
Wi' sweet-milk cheese, in mony a *whang* *great slice*
An' *farls*, bak'd wi' butter,   *oatmeal cakes*
   Fu' *crump* that day.   *crisp*

When by the "plate" we set our nose,
Weel heapèd up wi' ha'pence,
A greedy *glowr* "black-bonnet[1]" throws, *stare*
An' we *maun* draw our *tippence.* *must; twopence*
Then in we go to see the show:
On ev'ry side they're gath'rin';
Some carryin' *dails*, some chairs an' stools, *planks*
An' some are busy *bleth'rin'* *talking loosely*
   Right loud that day.

[1]A cant name for the elder who stood at "the plate" on which the offerings were deposited at the entrance to the place of meeting.

Here stands a shed to *fend* the show'rs,　　　*ward off*
An' screen our countra gentry[1];
There "Racer Jess[2]," an' twa-three whores,
Are blinkin at the entry.
Here sits a raw o' *tittlin' jads*,　　　*tittering jades*
Wi' heavin' breasts an' bare neck;
An' there a batch o' *wabster* lads,　　　*weaver*
Blackguardin frae Kilmarnock,
　　　For fun this day.

Here some are thinkin' on their sins,
An' some upo' their *claes;*　　　*clothes*
Ane curses feet that *fyl'd* his shins,　　　*bedaubed*
Anither sighs an' prays:
On this hand sits a chosen *swatch*,　　　*sample*
Wi' screw'd up, grace-proud faces;
On that a set o' chaps, at watch,
Thrang winkin' on the lasses　　　*busy*
　　　To chairs that day.

O happy is that man, an' blest!
Nae wonder that it pride him!
Whase ain dear lass, that he likes best,　　　*whose own*
Comes *clinkin'* down beside him!　　　*claps herself*
Wi' arm repos'd on the chair back,
He sweetly does compose him;
Which, by degrees, slips round her neck,
An's loof upon her bosom,　　　*and his palm*
　　　Unkend that day[3].　　　*accidentally*

Now a' the congregation o'er
Is silent expectation;
For Moodie *speels* the holy door[4],　　　*climbs*
Wi' tidings o' damnation:
Should *Hornie*, as in ancient days,　　　*Satan*
'*Mang* sons o' God present him,　　　*among*
The vera sight o' Moodie's face,
To 's *ain het hame* had sent him　　　*own hot home*
　　　Wi' fright that day.　　　*with*

[1]The communion used to be celebrated out of doors in the churchyard or a field near the church, and a temporary shed was put up to give shelter from the weather to the aristocracy who attended. The whole thing was not unlike an American camp-meeting, excepting that in Scotland the communion was celebrated, and the out-of-doors services lasted only one day.

[2]February, 1813, died at Mauchline, Janet Gibson, the Racer Jess of Burns' "Holy Fair," remarkable for her pedestrian feats. She was a daughter of Poosie Nansie, who figures in "The Jolly Beggars."

[3]"This verse sets boldly out with a line of a psalm. It is the best description ever was drawn. 'Unkend that day' surpasses all."

[4]The "holy door" is the door giving entrance to the tent whence the ministers preached.

Hear how he clears the points o' Faith
Wi' rattlin' and thumpin'!
Now meekly calm, now wild in wrath,
He's stampin', an' he's jumpin'!
His lengthen'd chin, his turned-up snout,
His *eldritch* squeel an' gestures,   *unearthly*
O how they fire the heart devout,
Like *cantharidian plaisters*   *mustard plasters*
       On sic a day!

But hark! the tent has chang'd its voice;
There's peace an' rest nae langer;
For a' the real judges rise,
They *canna* sit for anger.   *cannot*
Smith opens out his cauld harangues,
On practice and on morals;
An' aff the godly pour in *thrangs*,   *and off; throngs*
To *gie* the jars an' barrels   *give*
       A lift that day.

What signifies his barren shine,
Of moral pow'rs an' reason?
His English style, an' gesture fine
Are a' clean out o' season.
Like Socrates or Antonine,
Or some auld pagan heathen,
The moral man he does define,
But ne'er a word o' faith in
       That's right that day.

In *guid* time comes an antidote   *good*
Against *sic* poison'd nostrum;   *such*
For Peebles, frae the water-fit,
Ascends the holy rostrum:
See, up he's got the word o' God,
An' meek an' *mim* has view'd it,   *mild*
While "Common-sense[1]" has *taen* the road,   *taken*
An' aff an' up the Cowgate[2]
       Fast, fast that day.

---

[1]We learn from Chambers, who states it on local authority, that Mr. Mackenzie, surgeon of Mauchline, and friend of Burns, had recently written on some topic under the pseudonym of "Commonsense." He was engaged this day to dine at Dumfries House with the Earl of Dumfries, so, after listening to some of the harangues, he left the meeting and set off along the Cowgate to keep his appointment.

[2]A street so called which faces the tent in Mauchline.

Wee Miller[1] *niest*, the Guard relieves,   *next*
An' Orthodoxy *raibles*,   *gabbles*
Tho' in his heart he *weel* believes,   *well*
An' thinks it auld wives' fables:
But faith! the *birkie* wants a manse,   *smart fellow*
So, cannilie he *hums* them;   *humbugs*
Altho' his carnal wit an' sense
Like *hafflins-wise* o'ercomes him   *half*
　　　At times that day.

Now *butt an' ben* the change-house fills,   *kitchen and parlour*
Wi' *yill-caup* commentators;   *ale-mug*
Here's crying out for *bakes* an' *gills*,   *biscuits; whiskey*
An' there the *pint-stowp* clatters;   *pint-measure*
While thick an' *thrang*, an' loud an' lang,   *busily*
Wi' logic an' wi' scripture,
They raise a din, that in the end
Is like to breed a rupture
　　　O' wrath that day.

Leeze me on drink! it *gies* us mair   *commend me to; gives*
Than either school or college;
It *ken'les* wit, it *waukens lear*,   *kindles; awakens learning*
It *pangs* us *fou* o' knowledge: *crams; full*
Be't whisky-gill or *penny-wheep*,   *very small ale*
Or ony stronger potion,
It never fails, on drinkin deep,
To *kittle* up our notion   *tickle*
　　By night or day.

The lads an' lasses, blythely bent
To mind *baith saul* an' body,   *both soul*
Sit round the table, weel content,
An' *steer* about the *toddy*;   *stir; hot Scotch*
On this *ane's* dress, an' that ane's *leuk*,   *one's; look*
They're makin observations;
While some are cozie i' the *neuk*,   *corner*
An' forming assignations
　　　To meet some day.

But now the L——'s ain trumpet *touts*,   *sounds*
Till a' the hills are *rairin'*,   *roaring with echoes*
And echoes back-return the shouts;
Black Russell is *na* spairin':   *not*

[1] A short, paunchy minister, suspected of a New Light tendency.

His piercin' words, like highlan' swords,
Divide the joints an' marrow;
His talk o' Hell, whare devils dwell,
Our vera "*sauls* does harrow"   *souls*
          Wi' fright that day!

A vast, unbottom'd, boundless pit,
Fill'd *fou o' lowin'* brunstane,   *full of blazing*
Whase ragin' flame, an' scorchin' heat,
Wad melt the hardest *whun-stane!*   *whinstone*
The half-asleep start up wi' fear,
An' think they hear it roaran;
When presently it does appear,
'Twas but some neibour snoran
          Asleep that day.

'Twad be *owre* lang a tale to tell,   *too*
How mony stories past;
An' how they crouded to the *yill*,   *ale*
When they were a' dismist;
How drink *gaed* round, in *cogs an' caups*,   *went; wooden cups*
Amang the *furms* an' benches;   *forms*
An' cheese an' bread, frae women's laps,
Was dealt about in lunches,
An' *dawds* that day.   *large slices*

In comes a *gawsie, gash* guidwife,   *portly; sagacious*
An' sits down by the fire,
Syne draws her *kebbuck* an' her knife;   *then; cheese*
The lasses they are shyer:
The auld *guidmen*, about the grace,   *heads of families*
Frae side to side they bother[1];
Till some ane *by* his *bonnet* lays,   *aside; Scotch cap*
An' *gies* them't, like a tether   *gives*
          Fu' lang that day.   *full long*

Waesucks! for him that gets nae lass,   *alas*
Or lasses that hae naething!
Sma' need has he to say a grace,
Or *melvie* his braw claithing!   *soil with crumbs*

[1]It is the custom in Scotland to ask a blessing before eating in any way, and to return thanks after. It is a mark of respect to ask a person to say grace; generally, he modestly declines and suggests another, who in turn names a third and so on. Thus they "bother about frae side to side," till one gives them it, in length "like a tether."

O wives, be minfu' ance yoursel
How bonie lads ye wanted;
An' dinna for a *kebbuck-heel*   *end of a cheese*
Let lasses be affronted
         On *sic* a day!   *such*

Now "*Clinkumbell,*" wi' rattlin *tow,*   *bell-ringer; rope*
Begins to *jow* an' *croon;*   *toll; sound*
Some swagger hame the best they *dow,*   *are able*
Some wait the afternoon.
At slaps the billies halt a blink[1],
Till lasses strip their *shoon;*   *shoes*
Wi' faith an' hope, an' love an' drink,
They're a' in famous tune
         For *crack* that day.   *talk*

How mony hearts this day converts
O' sinners and o' lasses!
Their hearts o' stane, *gin night,* are gane   *by night-time*
As saft as ony flesh is:
 There's some are *fou* o' love divine;   *full*
There's some are fou o' brandy;
An' mony jobs that day begin,
May end in "*houghmagandie*"   *breaking commandments*
         Some ither day.

TO A MOUNTAIN DAISY [1786]

On turning one down with the plough in April, 1786

This poem was composed at the plough. The field where he crushed, the "Wee, modest, crimson-tipped flower," lies next to that in which he turned up the nest of the mouse, and both are on the farm of Mossgiel, and still shown to anxious inquirers by the neighbouring peasantry. (*Chambers.*)

I have seldom met with an image more truly pastoral than that of the lark in the second stanza. Such strokes as these mark the pencil of the Poet, which delineates nature with the precision of intimacy, yet with the delicate colouring of beauty and of taste. (*Henry Mackenzie,* **1745-1831,** author of *The Man of Feeling.*)

---

[1]At gaps in the fences which offer convenience for sitting down, the young fellows halt a moment till the lasses strip off their shoes. Scotch girls in Burns' day walked more easily barefooted than with shoes; besides, there was the question of economy.

Wee, modest, crimson-tippèd flow'r,
Thou's met me in an evil hour;
For I maun crush amang the *stoure*   dust
      Thy slender stem:
To spare thee now is past my pow'r,
      Thou bonie gem.

Alas! it's no thy neibour sweet,
The bonie lark, companion meet,
Bending thee 'mang the dewy *weet,*   wet
      Wi' *spreckl'd* breast!   speckled
When upward-springing, blythe, to greet
      The purpling east.

Cauld blew the bitter-biting north
Upon thy early, humble birth;
Yet cheerfully thou *glinted* forth   glanced
      Amid the storm,
Scarce rear'd above the parent-earth
      Thy tender form.

The flaunting flow'rs our gardens yield,
High shelt-ring woods and *wa's maun* shield;   walls must
But thou, beneath the random *bield*   shelter
      O' clod or stane,
Adorns the *histie stibble* field,   parched; stubble
      Unseen, alane.

There, in thy scanty mantle clad,
Thy *snawie* bosom sun-ward spread,   snowy
Thou lifts thy unassuming head
  In humble guise;
But now the share uptears thy bed,
  And low thou lies!

  Such is the fate of artless maid,
  Sweet flow'ret of the rural shade!
  By love's simplicity betray'd,
      And guileless trust;
  Till she, like thee, all soil'd, is laid
      Low i' the dust.

Such is the fate of simple bard,
On life's rough ocean luckless starr'd!
Unskilful he to note the card
                Of prudent lore,
Till billows rage, and gales blow hard,
                And whelm him o'er!

Such fate to suffering worth is giv'n,
Who long with wants and woes has striv'n,
By human pride or cunning driv'n
                To mis'ry's brink;
Till wrench'd of ev'ry stay but Heav'n,
                He, ruin'd, sink!

Ev'n thou who mourn'st the Daisy's fate,
That fate is thine—no distant date;
Stern Ruin's plough-share drives elate,
                Full on thy bloom,
Till crush'd beneath the furrow's weight,
                Shall be thy doom!

An intelligent observer of his own courses of action and the causes leading up to them will often trace these to the pervading tone or colour of his mind at the time.   Burns, when plowing the grass-rigs of Mossgiel on this April morning, was carrying in his bosom the reflection that Jean Armour had renounced him, and that her father was taking steps to unchain on him the sleuthhounds of the law. His whole mental horizon was tinged with gloom, and his exquisitely sympathetic nature led him to see a type of his own fate in the destruction of "the meanest flower that blows."   He had plowed down a thousand daisies before this, but not one of them all ever roused reflection like this, or tuned his lyre to sing so sweet and sad a song.

DESPONDENCY [1786]

An Ode

The darkening views of his lot, expressed in this deeply-affecting poem, point with sufficient distinctness to the period of its composition.   The concluding couplet of the fourth stanza harmonizes too well with a passage regarding Jean Armour, in a letter to David Bryce, dated June 12, 1786, to be for a moment doubted.   "May Almighty God forgive her ingratitude and perjury to me, as I from my very soul forgive her; and may His grace be with her and bless her all her future life."   The destruction of the marriage-lines, and her refusal to see him, were then rankling in his mind.

Oppress'd with grief, oppress'd with care,
A burden more than I can bear,
I set me down and sigh;
O life! thou art a galling load,
Along a rough, a weary road,
To wretches such as I!
Dim-backward as I cast my view,
What sick'ning scenes appear!
What sorrows yet may pierce me through,
Too justly I may fear!
 Still caring, despairing,
 Must be my bitter doom;
 My woes here shall close ne'er
 But with the closing tomb!

Happy! ye sons of busy life,
Who, equal to the bustling strife,
No other view regard!
Ev'n when the wishèd end's denied,
Yet while the busy means are plied,
They bring their own reward:
Whilst I, a hope-abandon'd wight,
Unfitted with an aim,
Meet ev'ry sad returning night,
And joyless morn the same!
 You, bustling and justling,
 Forget each grief and pain;
 I, listless, yet restless,
 Find ev'ry prospect vain.

How blest the solitary's lot,
Who, all-forgetting, all-forgot,
Within his humble cell,
The cavern wild with tangling roots—
Sits o'er his newly-gather'd fruits,
Beside his crystal well!
Or haply to his ev'ning thought,
By unfrequented stream,
The ways of men are distant brought,
A faint, collected dream;
 While praising, and raising
 His thoughts to heav'n on high,
 As wand'ring, meand'ring,
 He views the solemn sky.

Than I, no lonely hermit plac'd
Where never human footstep trac'd,
Less fit to play the part;
The lucky moment to improve,
And just to stop, and just to move,
With self-respecting art:
But ah! those pleasures, loves, and joys,
Which I too keenly taste,
The solitary can despise—
Can want, and yet be blest!
    He needs not, he heeds not,
    Or human love or hate;
    Whilst I here must cry here
    At perfidy ingrate!

O enviable early days,
When dancing thoughtless pleasure's maze,
To care, to guilt unknown!
How ill exchang'd for riper times,
To feel the follies, or the crimes,
Of others, or my own!
Ye tiny elves that guiltless sport,
Like linnets in the bush,
Ye little know the ills ye court,
When manhood is your wish!
    The losses, the crosses,
    That active man engage;
    The fears all, the tears all,
    Of dim declining Age!

A BARD'S EPITAPH [1786]

Of this beautiful epitaph, which Burns wrote for himself, Wordsworth (1770-1850) says: "Here is a sincere and solemn avowal—a public declaration from his own will—a confession at once devout, poetical and human—a history in the shape of a prophecy."

Is there a whim-inspirèd fool,
Owre fast for thought, owre hot for rule,   *too*
Owre *blate* to seek, owre proud to *snool*,   *bashful; cringe*
    Let him draw near;
And *owre* this grassy heap sing *dool*,   *over; lamentations*
    And drap a tear.

Is there a bard of rustic song,
Who, noteless, steals the crowds among,
That weekly this area throng,
    O, pass not by!
But, with a frater-feeling strong,
    Here, heave a sigh.

Is there a man, whose judgment clear
Can others teach the course to steer,
Yet runs, himself, life's mad career,
    Wild as the wave,
Here pause—and, thro' the starting tear,
    Survey this grave.

The poor inhabitant below
Was quick to learn and wise to know,
And keenly felt the friendly glow,
    And softer flame;
But thoughtless follies laid him low,
    And stain'd his name!

Reader, attend! whether thy soul
Soars fancy's flights beyond the pole,
Or darkling grubs this earthly hole,
    In low pursuit;
Know, prudent, cautious self-control
    Is wisdom's root.

EPISTLE TO A YOUNG FRIEND [1786]

This epistle, in which so much knowledge of the world and the human heart is displayed, was addressed to Andrew Aiken, son of Mr. Robert Aiken, writer in Ayr, to whom "The Cotter's Saturday Night" is inscribed. Mr. Andrew Aiken was a successful merchant in Liverpool (said Chambers). Allan Cunningham relates that he rose to distinction and affluence in the service of his country.   He died in St. Petersburg.

I lang *hae* thought, my youthfu' friend,   *have*
A something to have sent you,
Tho' it should serve *nae ither* end   *no other*
Than just a kind memento:
But how the subject-theme may *gang*,   *go*
Let time and chance determine;
Perhaps it may turn out a sang,
Perhaps turn out a sermon.

Ye'll try the world *fu'* soon, my lad,   *full*
And, Andrew dear, believe me,
Ye'll find mankind an *unco* squad,   *strange*
And *muckle* they may grieve ye: *much*
For care and trouble set your thought,
Ev'n when your end's attained;
And a' your views may come to nought,
Where ev'ry nerve is strained.

I'll no say men are villains a';
The real, harden'd wicked,
Wha *hae nae* check but human law,   *have no*
Are to a few *restricket;*   *restricted*
But, och! mankind are *unco* weak,   *uncommonly*
An' little to be trusted;
If SELF the wavering balance shake,
It's rarely right adjusted!

Yet they wha *fa'* in fortune's strife,   *fall*
Their fate we should *na* censure;   *not*
For still th' important end of life
They equally may answer:
A man may hae an honest heart,
Tho' *poortith* hourly stare him;   *poverty*
A man may tak a neibour's part,
Yet hae nae cash to spare him.

Ay free, *aff han'*, your story tell,   *off hand*
When wi' a bosom crony;
But still keep something to yoursel
Ye scarcely tell to *ony:*   *any*
Conceal yoursel as weel's ye can
Frae critical dissection;
But *keek* thro' ev'ry other man,   *look keenly*
Wi sharpen'd, sly inspection.

The sacred *lowe o'* weel-plac'd love,   *flame of*
Luxuriantly indulge it;
But never tempt th' illicit rove,
Tho' naething should divulge it:
I waive the quantum o' the sin,
The hazard of concealing;
But, och! it hardens a' within,
And petrifies the feeling!

To catch dame Fortune's golden smile,
Assiduous wait upon her;
And gather *gear* by ev'ry wile   *wealth*
That's justify'd by honour;
Not for to hide it in a hedge,
Nor for a train-attendant;
But for the glorious privilege
Of being independent.

The fear o' hell's a hangman's whip,
To *haud* the wretch in order;   *hold*
But where ye feel your honour grip,
Let that ay be your border:
Its slightest touches, instant pause—
Debar a' side-pretences;
And resolutely keep its laws,
Uncaring consequences.

The great Creator to revere,
Must sure become the creature;
But still the preaching cant forbear,
And ev'n the rigid feature:
Yet ne'er with wits profane to range,
Be complaisance extended;
An atheist-laugh's a poor exchange
For Deity offended!

When ranting round in pleasure's ring,
Religion may be blinded;
Or if she *gi'e* a random sting,   *give*
It may be little minded;
But when on life we're tempest driv'n—
A conscience *but* a canker—   *without*
A correspondence fix'd wi' Heav'n,
Is sure a noble anchor!

Adieu, dear, amiable youth!
Your heart can ne'er be wanting!
May prudence, fortitude, and truth,
Erect your brow undaunting!
In ploughman phrase, "God send you speed,"
Still daily to grow wiser;
And may ye better *reck the rede*   *attend to the counsel*
Than ever did th' adviser!

THE BONNIE LASS O' BALLOCHMYLE [1786]

Ballochmyle on the Ayr is about two and a half miles from Mauchline. It was the seat at one time of Sir John Whitefoord, and was afterward occupied by Claude Alexander, a brother of Miss Wilhelmina Alexander in whose honour the song was composed.

The song was sent to Miss Alexander, November 18, 1786, accompanied by a letter in which Burns said:

I had roved out as chance directed, in the favourite haunts of my muse, the banks of Ayr, to view Nature in all the gayety of the vernal year. The evening sun was flaming o'er the distant western hills: not a breath stirred the crimson opening blossom, or the verdant spreading leaf. 'Twas a golden moment for a poetic heart. Such was the scene, and such was the hour—when, in a corner of my prospect, I spied one of the fairest pieces of Nature's workmanship that ever crowned a poetic landscape or blest a poet's eye. . . . The inclosed song was the work of my return home: and perhaps it but poorly answers what might have been expected from such a scene.

'Twas even—the dewy fields were green,
On every blade the pearls hang;
The zephyr wanton'd round the bean,
And bore its fragrant sweets alang:
In ev'ry glen the *mavis* sang,   *thrush*
All Nature list'ning seem'd the while,
Except where greenwood echoes rang,
Amang the braes o' Ballochmyle.

With careless step I onward stray'd,
My heart rejoic'd in nature's joy,
When, musing in a lonely glade,
A maiden fair I chanc'd to spy:
Her look was like the morning's eye,
Her air like Nature's vernal smile;
Perfection whisper'd, passing by,
"Behold the lass o' Ballochmyle!"

Fair is the morn in flowery May,
And sweet is night in autumn mild;
When roving thro' the garden gay,
Or wand'ring in the lonely wild:
But woman, Nature's darling child!
There all her charms she does compile,
Even there her other works are foil'd
By the bonnie lass o' Ballochmyle.

O had she been a country maid,
And I the happy country swain,
Tho' shelter'd in the lowest shed
That ever rose on Scotland's plain!
Thro' weary Winter's wind and rain,
With joy, with rapture, I would toil;
And nightly to my bosom strain
The bonnie lass o' Ballochmyle.

Then pride might climb the slipp'ry steep,
Where fame and honours lofty shine;
And thirst of gold might tempt the deep,
Or downward seek the Indian mine:
Give me the cot below the pine,
To tend the flocks or till the soil;
And ev'ry day have joys divine
With the bonnie lass o' Ballochmyle.

NATURE'S LAW [1786]

Humbly inscribed to Gavin Hamilton, Esq., this characteristic effusion celebrates a ruling quality in the soul of Burns, and reminds us of the epigram he afterwards wrote in Dumfries:

I'm better pleased to make one more,
Than be the death of twenty.

Let other heroes boast their scars,	
The marks of *sturt* and strife;	*turmoil*
And other poets sing of wars,	
The plagues of human life;	
Shame *fa'* the fun; wi' sword and gun	*befall*
To *slap* mankind like lumber!	*cut down*
I sing his name, and nobler fame,	
Wha multiplies our number.	

Great Nature spoke, with air benign,—
"Go on, ye human race;
This lower world I you resign;
Be fruitful and increase.
The liquid fire of strong desire
I've pour'd it in each bosom;
Here, on this hand, does Mankind stand,
And there, is Beauty's blossom."

The Hero of these artless strains,
A lowly bard was he,
Who sung his rhymes in Coila's plains,
With *meikle* mirth an' glee;   *much*
Kind Nature's care had given his share
Large, of the flaming current;
And, all devout, he never sought
To stem the sacred torrent.

He felt the powerful, high behest
Thrill, vital, thro' and thro';
And sought a correspondent breast,
To give obedience due:
Propitious Powers screen'd the young flow'rs,
From mildews of abortion;
And lo! the bard—a great reward—
Has got a double portion[1]!

Auld *cantie* Coil may count the day,   *frisky*
As annual it returns,
The third of Libra's equal sway,
That gave another B(urn)s[2],
With future rhymes, an' other times,
To emulate his sire;
To sing auld Coil in nobler style,
With more poetic fire.

Ye Powers of peace, and peaceful song,
Look down with gracious eyes;
And bless auld Coila, large and long,
With multiplying joys;
Lang may she stand to prop the land,
The flow'r of ancient nations;
And B(urns)es spring, her fame to sing,
To endless generations!

THE BRIGS OF AYR [1786]

The "Auld Brig of Ayr" consists of four arches, and is said to have
been erected in 1252 by two maiden ladies named Love, after the sweet-
heart of one of them had been drowned in crossing the ford during a flood.
It was in 1785 that the venerable pile began to show signs of giving way,
and in May, 1786, the first stone of a new structure was laid a little lower

[1]Jean Armour begot the Bard twins September 3, 1786.
[2]Robert Burns, Junior, one of the twins.

down the river. This was the origin of the poem, "The Brig of Ayr."
In the dialogue between the "conceited gowk" or New Brig, and the Auld
Vandal, as the Auld Brig is called, the latter prophesies that it will be a brig
when the other is "a cairn of stones," and this has proved true. In 1877
the "new" bridge of 1786 was found to be in a dangerous condition; it was
accordingly taken down, and another has since been built on the old site.
The view from the Old Brig on a quiet summer evening is a very pleasant
one.

The gentleman to whom the poem is inscribed was Mr. John Ballantine
of Ayr, by profession a banker, and Dean of Guild at that period, and
afterwards Provost of Ayr. The erection of a new bridge was proceeding
under his chief magistracy in the latter portion of 1786, and Burns, apparently taking a hint from Fergusson's "Dialogue between the Plainstanes
and Causeway," composed his poem, "The Brigs of Ayr," about the
end of September.

This brilliant satirical fiction is remarkable for three things: (1) The beauty of
its impersonations, the vividness of its descriptions, the humour of its morals;
(2) The considerable inter-mixture of the English idiom with the richest and most
expressive Scotch; and (3) The singular fact that it finishes without an appropriate
close, and dies away like a dream, in—nothing. [*Waddell.*]

Mr. John Ballantine lived a bachelor, and died at his villa of Castlehill,
on July 15, 1812.

> The simple Bard, rough at the rustic plough,
> Learning his tuneful trade from ev'ry bough;
> The chanting linnet, or the mellow thrush,
> Hailing the setting sun, sweet, in the green thorn bush;
> The soaring lark, the perching red-breast shrill,
> Or deep-ton'd plovers grey, wild-whistling o'er the hill;
> Shall he—nurst in the peasant's lowly shed,
> To hardy independence bravely bred,
> By early poverty to hardship steel'd,
> And train'd to arms in stern Misfortune's field—
> Shall he be guilty of their hireling crimes,
> The servile, mercenary Swiss of rhymes?
> Or labour hard the panegyric close,
> With all the venal soul of dedicating prose?
> No! though his artless strains he rudely sings,
> And throws his hand uncouthly o'er the strings,
> He glows with all the spirit of the Bard,
> Fame, honest fame, his great, his dear reward!
> Still, if some patron's gen'rous care he trace,
> Skill'd in the secret to bestow with grace;

When Ballantine befriends his humble name,
And hands the rustic stranger up to fame,
With heartfelt throes his grateful bosom swells,
The godlike bliss, to give, alone excels.

'Twas when the stacks get on their winter *hap*,   *covering*
And *thack and rape* secure the toil-won *crap;*   *thatch and rope; crop*
Potato *bings* are snuggèd up frae *skaith*   *heaps; danger*
O' coming Winter's biting, frosty breath;
The bees, rejoicing o'er their summer toils,
Unnumber'd buds an' flow'rs' delicious spoils,
Seal'd up with frugal care in massive waxen piles,
Are doom'd by Man, that tyrant o'er the weak,
The death o' devils, *smoor'd* wi' brimstone *reek:*   *smothered; smoke*
The thundering guns are heard on ev'ry side,
The wounded coveys, reeling, scatter wide;
The feather'd field-mates, bound by Nature's tie,
Sires, mothers, children, in one carnage lie:
(What warm, poetic heart but inly bleeds,
And execrates man's savage, ruthless deeds!)
Nae mair the flow'r in field or meadow springs;
Nae mair the grove with airy concert rings,
Except, perhaps, the Robin's whistling glee,
Proud o' the height o' some bit *half-lang* tree: *half-grown*
The hoary morns precede the sunny days,
Mild, calm, serene, wide spreads the noontide blaze,
While thick the gossamer waves wanton in the rays.

'Twas in that season, when a simple Bard,
Unknown and poor—simplicity's reward!—
Ae night, within the ancient *brugh* of Ayr,   *burgh*
By whim inspir'd, or haply prest wi' care,
He left his bed, and took his wayward route,
And down by Simpson's[1] wheel'd the left about:
(Whether impell'd by all-directing Fate,
To witness what I after shall narrate;
Or whether, rapt in meditation high,
He wander'd out, he knew not where nor why:)
The drowsy Dungeon-clock[2] had number'd two,
And Wallace Tower[3] had sworn the fact was true:
The tide-swoln Firth, with sullen-sounding roar,
Through the still night dash'd hoarse along the shore.

[1] A noted tavern at the Auld Brig end.
[2] A tower on the Old Jail, now removed.
[3] An antique erection in the High Street, now replaced by an elegant tower so named.

All else was hush'd as Nature's closèd e'e;
The silent moon shone high o'er tower and tree;
The chilly frost, beneath the silver beam,
Crept, gently-crusting, o'er the glittering stream—

When, lo! on either hand the list'ning Bard,
The *clanging sugh* of whistling wings is heard;   *rushing sound*
Two dusky forms dart thro' the midnight air,
Swift as the *gos* drives on the wheeling hare: *falcon*
Ane on th' Auld Brig his airy shape uprears,
The ither flutters o'er the rising piers:
Our warlock Rhymer instantly descried
The Sprites that owre the Brigs of Ayr preside.
(That Bards are second-sighted is nae joke,
And ken the lingo of the sp'ritual folk;
Fays, Spunkies, Kelpies, a'[1], they can explain them,
And ev'n the *vera deils* they *brawly ken* them.)   *very devils; well know*

AULD BRIG appear'd of ancient Pictish race,
The vera wrinkles Gothic in his face;
He seem'd as he wi' Time had *warstl'd* lang,   *wrestled*
Yet, teughly doure, he bade an unco bang[2].
NEW BRIG was *buskit* in a *braw* new coat,   *dressed; fine*
That he, at Lon'on, *frae ane* Adams[3] got;   *from one*
In's hand five taper staves as smooth's a bead,
Wi' virls an' whirlygigums at the head[4].
The Goth was stalking round with anxious search,
Spying the time-worn flaws in ev'ry arch;
It chanc'd his new-come neibour took his e'e,
And e'en a vex'd and angry heart had he!
Wi' *thieveless* sneer to see his modish mien,   *unconcealed*
He, down the water, gies him this *guid-een:*—   *good-evening*

AULD BRIG

I doubt na, frien', ye'll think ye're nae sheepshank,[5]
Ance ye were *streekit owre* frae bank to bank!   *stretched across*
But *gin ye be* a Brig as auld as me—   *when you are*
Tho' faith, that date, I doubt, ye'll never see—
There'll be, if that day come, I'll *wad a boddle*,   *bet a penny*
Some fewer *whigmaleeries* in your noddle.   *conceits*

---

[1] Varieties of sprites.   The fays are fairies; spunkies, or Will o' the Wisps; Kelpies, Water-spirits.

[2] Toughly stubborn, he withstood Time's heavy stroke.

[3] Robert Adams, Esq., an eminent Scottish architect, resident in London, from whose designs this New Brig was erected 1786-1788.

[4] Five lamp-posts with rings and ornaments at the top.

[5] You no doubt think you are somebody.

NEW BRIG

Auld Vandal! ye but show your little *mense*,	*civility*
Just much *about it* wi' your scanty sense:	*on par*
Will your poor, narrow, foot-path of a street,	
Whare twa wheel-barrows tremble when they meet,	
Your ruin'd, formless bulk o' stane and lime,	
Compare wi' bonnie Brigs o' modern time?	
There's men o' taste would tak the Ducat stream[1],	
Tho' they should cast the vera *sark* and swim,	*shirt*
E'er they would grate their feelings wi' the view	
O' *sic* an ugly, Gothic hulk as you.	*such*

AULD BRIG

Conceited *gowk!* puff'd up wi' windy pride!	*fool*
This mony a year I've stood the flood and tide;	
And tho' wi' crazy *eild* I'm sair *forfairn*,	*old age; worn*
I'll be a Brig when ye're a shapeless cairn!	
As yet ye little ken about the matter,	
But twa-three winters will inform ye better.	
When heavy, dark, continued, a'-day rains,	
Wi' deepening deluges o'erflow the plains;	
When from the hills where springs the brawling Coil,	
Or stately Lugar's mossy fountains boil;	
Or where the Greenock winds his moorland course,	
Or haunted Garpal[2] draws his feeble source,	
Arous'd by blustering winds an' spotting *thowes*,	*thaws*
In mony a torrent down the *snaw-broo rowes;*	*snow-water rolls*
While crashing ice, borne on the roaring spate,	
Sweeps dams, an' mills, an' brigs, *a' to the gate;*	*all away*
And from Glenbuck[3] down to the Ratton-key[4]	
Auld Ayr is just one lengthen'd, tumbling sea—	
Then down ye'll hurl, deil nor ye never rise!	
And dash the *gumlie jaups* up to the pouring skies!	*muddy splashes*
A lesson sadly teaching, to your cost,	
That Architecture's noble art is lost![5]	

NEW BRIG

Fine Architecture! trowth, I needs must say't o't,	
The L——d be thankit that we've *tint* the *gate o't!*	*lost; way of it*
Gaunt, ghastly, ghaist-alluring edifices,	
Hanging with threat'ning jut like precipices;	

[1]A noted ford, just above the Auld Brig.

[2]The banks of Garpal Water is one of the few places in the West of Scotland where those scaring visions, known by the name of Ghaists, still continue pertinaciously to inhabit.

[3]The source of the River Ayr.   [4]A small landing place above the large quay.

[5]This whole passage—penned ninety years ago—has turned out to be strikingly prophetic. The "New Brig," which was not yet "streekit owre frae bank to bank" when the poem was

O'er-arching, mouldy, gloom-inspiring coves,
Supporting roofs fantastic, stony groves;
Windows and doors in nameless sculptures drest,
With order, symmetry, or taste unblest;
Forms like some bedlam Statuary's dream,
The craz'd creations of misguided whim:
Forms might be worship'd on the bended knee,
And still the second dread command be free;
Their likeness is not found on earth, in air, or sea!
Mansions that would disgrace the building taste
Of any mason reptile, bird or beast:
Fit only for a *doited* monkish race,   *stupid*
Or frosty maids forsworn the dear embrace,
Or *cuifs* of later times, wha held the notion   *blockheads*
That sullen gloom was sterling true devotion:
Fancies that our *guid Brugh* denies protection,[1]   *good burgh*
And soon may they expire, unblest wi' resurrection!

AULD BRIG

O ye, my dear-remember'd, ancient *yealings*,   *fellows*
Were ye but here to share my wounded feelings!
Ye worthy *Proveses*, an' mony a Bailie,   *provosts*
Wha in the paths o' righteousness did toil ay;
Ye dainty Deacons, an' ye *douce* Conveeners[2],   *solemn*
To whom our moderns are but *causey-cleaners;*   *scavengers*
Ye godly Councils, wha hae blest this town;
Ye godly Brethren o' the sacred gown,
Wha meekly *gie* your *hurdies* to the smiters;   *give; buttocks*
And (what would now be strange)[3], ye godly *Writers;*   *lawyers*
A' ye douce folk I've borne *aboon* the *broo,*   *above; water*
Were ye but here, what would ye say or do?
How would your spirits groan in deep vexation,
To see each melancholy alteration;
And, agonizing, curse the time and place
When ye begat the base degenerate race!
Nae langer rev'rend men, their country's glory,
In plain braid Scots hold forth a plain, braid story;

composed, has, on at least one occasion, been closed from all traffic, a threatening rent having been discovered in its masonry. On the other hand, the "Auld Brig" with its "poor narrow foot-path of a street," which for eighty years has been used for foot passengers only, has again been opened for wheel carriages, and may yet be "a brig," when its proud neighbour is "a shapeless cairn."

[1] A compliment to the "advanced liberalism" of the Ayr clergy.
[2] Deacons and Conveners are trade or guild dignitaries.
[3] A sly hit at the Ayr lawyers (writers) of Burns' day.

Nae langer thrifty citizens, an' douce,
Meet owre a pint, or in the Council-house;
But *staumrel*, corky-headed, graceless Gentry,   *stupid*
The *herryment* and ruin of the country;   *robbers*
Men three-parts made by tailors and by barbers,
Wha waste your *weel-hain'd gear* on damn'd new brigs *savings*
        and harbours!

NEW BRIG

Now *haud* you there! for faith ye've said enough,   *hold*
And *muckle* mair than ye can *mak to through.*   *much; prove*
As for your Priesthood, I shall say but little,
Corbies and Clergy are a shot right *kittle:*   *crows; ticklish*
But, under favour o' your langer beard,
Abuse o' Magistrates might weel be spar'd;
To liken them to your auld-warld squad,
I must needs say, comparisons are odd.
In Ayr, wag-wits nae mair can hae a handle
To mouth "a Citizen," a term o' scandal;
Nae mair the Council waddles down the street,
In all the pomp of ignorant conceit;
Men wha grew wise *priggin'* owre hops an' raisins,   *haggling*
Or gather'd lib'ral views in Bonds and Seisins:
If haply Knowledge, on a random tramp,
Had *shor'd* them with a glimmer of his lamp,   *guided*
And would to Common-sense for once betray'd them,
Plain, dull Stupidity stept kindly in to aid them.

What further clish-ma-claver might been said,
What bloody wars, if Sprites had blood to shed,
No man can tell; but, all before their sight,
A fairy train appear'd in order bright;
Adown the glittering stream they featly danc'd;
Bright to the moon their various dresses glanc'd:
They footed o'er the wat'ry glass so neat,
The infant ice scarce bent beneath their feet:
While arts of Minstrelsy among them rung,
And soul-ennobling Bards heroic ditties sung.

O had M'Lauchlan[1], *thairm*-inspiring sage,   *fiddle*
Been there to hear this heavenly band engage,
When thro' his dear strathspeys[2] they bore with Highland rage;
Or when they struck old Scotia's melting airs,
The lover's raptured joys or bleeding cares;

[1] A well-known performer of Scottish music on the violin.
[2] A general term for cheerful Scottish dance-tunes, from Strathspey (or the Vale of the

How would his Highland *lug* been nobler fir'd,   *ear*
And ev'n his matchless hand with finer touch inspir'd!
No guess could tell what instrument appear'd,
But all the soul of Music's self was heard;
Harmonious concert rung in every part,
While simple melody pour'd moving on the heart.

The Genius of the Stream in front appears,
A venerable Chief advanc'd in years;
His hoary head with water-lilies crown'd,
His manly leg with garter-tangle bound.
Next came the loveliest pair in all the ring,
Sweet Female Beauty hand in hand with Spring;
Then, crown'd with flow'ry hay, came Rural Joy,
And Summer, with his fervid-beaming eye;
All-cheering Plenty, with her flowing horn,
Led yellow Autumn wreath'd with nodding corn;
Then Winter's time-bleach'd locks did hoary show,
By Hospitality with cloudless brow:
Next follow'd Courage with his martial stride,
From where the Feal wild woody coverts hide[3];
Benevolence, with mild, benignant air,
A female form, came from the tow'rs of Stair[4];
Learning and Worth in equal measures trode,
From simple Catrine, their long-lov'd abode[5],
Last, white-rob'd Peace, crown'd with a hazel wreath,
To rustic Agriculture did bequeath
The broken, iron instruments of death:
At sight of whom our Sprites forgat their kindling wrath.

A WINTER NIGHT [1786]

Not man only, but all that environs man in the material and moral universe, is lovely in his sight: the "hoary hawthorn," the "troop of gray plover," the "solitary curlew," are all dear to him, all live in this earth along with him, and to all he is knit in mysterious brotherhood. How touching is it, for instance, that amidst the gloom of personal misery, brooding over the wintry desolation without him and within him, he thinks

river Spey) in Inverness-shire. Originally the word meant dance-music for the bagpipe, but it is now applied to all Scottish tunes of this character.
[3]A compliment to the warlike Montgomeries of Coilsfield. The Feal, or Faile Water, flows through the grounds behind the mansion, and joins the Ayr at Fealford.
[4]A compliment to Mrs. Stewart of Stair.
[5]Catrine is a manufacturing village near Mauchline on the Ayr. Professor Dugald Stewart dwelt in Catrine House, the adjoining villa or mansion.

of the "ourie cattle" and "silly sheep" and their sufferings in the pitiless storm.   .   .   .   The tenant of the mean hut, with its rugged roof, and chinky wall, has a heart to pity even there!   This is worth several homilies on mercy: for it is the voice of mercy itself.   (*Thomas Carlyle.*)

When biting Boreas, *fell* and *dour,*   *keen; stern*
  Sharp shivers thro' the leafless bower;
When Phœbus gies a short-liv'd *glower,*   *stare*
     Far south the *lift,*   *sky*
  Dim-dark'ning thro' the flaky shower,
     Or whirling drift:

Ae night the storm the steeples rocked,
  Poor Labour sweet in sleep was locked,
  While *burns,* wi' snawy-wreaths up-choked,   *streamlets*
     Wild-eddying swirl;
  Or thro' the mining outlet *bocked,*   *gurgled*
     Down headlong hurl:

List'ning, the doors an' *winnocks* rattle,   *windows*
  I thought me on the *ourie* cattle,   *huddling*
  Or *silly* sheep, wha bide this *brattle*   *helpless; rage*
     O' winter war,
  And thro' the drift, deep-*lairing, sprattle*   *sinking; scramble*
     Beneath a *scaur.*   *cliff*

Ilk happing bird—wee, helpless thing!   *each hopping*
  That, in the merry months *o'* spring,   *of*
  Delighted me to hear thee sing,
     What comes o' thee?
  Whare wilt thou cow'r thy *chittering* wing,   *shivering*
     An' close thy e'e?

Ev'n you, on murdering errands toiled,
  Lone from your savage homes exil'd,
  The blood-stain'd roost, and sheep-cote spoiled,
     My heart forgets,
  While pitiless the tempest wild
     Sore on you beats!

Now Phœbe, in her midnight reign,
  Dark-muffled, viewed the dreary plain;
Still crowding thoughts, a pensive train,
     Rose in my soul,
  When on my ear this plaintive strain,
     Slow, solemn, stole:

"Blow, blow, ye winds, with heavier gust!
And freeze, thou bitter-biting frost!
Descend, ye chilly, smothering snows!
Not all your rage, as now united, shows
More hard unkindness unrelenting,
Vengeful malice, unrepenting,
Than heaven-illumin'd Man on brother Man bestows!

"See stern Oppression's iron grip,
Or mad Ambition's gory hand,
Sending, like bloodhounds from the slip,
Woe, Want and Murder o'er a land!
Ev'n in the peaceful rural vale,
Truth, weeping, tells the mournful tale,
How pamper'd Luxury, Flatt'ry by her side,
The parasite empoisoning her ear,
With all the servile wretches in the rear,
Looks o'er proud Property, extended wide:
And eyes the simple rustic hind,
Whose toil upholds the glitt'ring show—
A creature of another kind,
Some coarser substance, unrefin'd—
Plac'd for her lordly use, thus far, thus vile, below!

"Where, where is Love's fond, tender throe,
With lordly Honour's lofty brow,
The powers you proudly own?
Is there, beneath Love's noble name,
Can harbour dark the selfish aim,
To bless himself alone!
Mark maiden innocence a prey
To love-pretending snares:
This boasted Honour turns away,
Shunning soft Pity's rising sway,
Regardless of the tears and unavailing pray'rs!
Perhaps this hour, in Misery's squalid nest,
She strains your infant to her joyless breast,
And with a mother's fears shrinks at the rocking blast!

"O ye! who, sunk in beds of down,
Feel not a want but what yourselves create,
Think, for a moment, on his wretched fate,
Whom friends and fortune quite disown!
Ill-satisfy'd keen Nature's clamorous call,
Stretch'd on his straw, he lays himself to sleep
While thro' the ragged roof and chinky wall,
Chill, o'er his slumbers, piles the drifty heap!

Think on the dungeon's grim confine,
Where Guilt and poor Misfortune pine!
Guilt, erring man, relenting view,
But shall thy legal rage pursue
The wretch, already crushèd low
By cruel Fortune's undeservèd blow?
Affliction's sons are brothers in distress;
A brother to relieve, how exquisite the bliss!"

I heard nae mair, for Chanticleer
Shook off the *pouthery* snaw,   *powdery*
And hail'd the morning with a cheer,
A cottage-rousing *craw*.   *crow*

But deep this truth impress'd my mind—
Thro' all His works abroad,
The heart benevolent and kind
The most resembles God.

ADDRESS TO EDINBURGH [1786]

This beautiful address was composed on the Poet's first visit to Edinburgh, in November, 1786.   Allusion is here made to Elizabeth Burnett, daughter of Lord Monboddo, a young lady of surpassing beauty, who at the time formed the charm and ornament of Edinburgh society.   Burns was a frequent guest at the table of the venerable judge, Lord Monboddo.

Edina! Scotia's darling seat!
All hail thy palaces and towers,
Where once, beneath a Monarch's feet,
Sat Legislation's sovereign powers:
From marking wildly-scatt'red flowers,
As on the banks of Ayr I strayed,
And singing, lone, the lingering hours,
I sheltered in thy honoured shade.

Here Wealth still swells the golden tide,
As busy Trade his labour plies;
There Architecture's noble pride
Bids elegance and splendour rise:
Here Justice, from her native skies,
High wields her balance and her rod;
There Learning, with his eagle eyes,
Seeks Science in her coy abode.

THE BONNIE LASS O' BALLOCHMYLE

NITHSDALE

AYR, THE TWA BRIGS

EDINBURGH CASTLE FROM THE GRAY FRIAR'S CHURCHYARD

Thy sons, Edina! social, kind,
With open arms the stranger hail;
Their views enlarged, their liberal mind,
Above the narrow, rural vale:
Attentive still to Sorrow's wail,
Or modest Merit's silent claim;
And never may their sources fail!
And never Envy blot their name!

Thy daughters bright thy walks adorn,
Gay as the gilded summer sky,
Sweet as the dewy, milk-white thorn,
Dear as the raptured thrill of joy!
Fair Burnet strikes th' adoring eye,
Heaven's beauties on my fancy shine;
I see the Sire of Love on high,
And own His work indeed divine!

There, watching high the least alarms,
Thy rough, rude fortress gleams afar;
Like some bold veteran, grey in arms,
And mark'd with many a seamy scar:
The pond'rous wall and massy bar,
Grim rising o'er the rugged rock,
Have oft withstood assailing war,
And oft repell'd th' invader's shock.

With awe-struck thought, and pitying tears,
I view that noble, stately Dome,[1]
Where Scotia's kings of other years,
Famed heroes! had their royal home:
Alas, how chang'd the times to come!
Their royal name low in the dust!
Their hapless race wild-wand'ring roam!
Tho' rigid Law cries out, "'twas just!"

Wild beats my heart to trace your steps,
Whose ancestors, in days of yore,
Thro' hostile ranks and ruin'd gaps
Old Scotia's bloody lion bore:
Ev'n I who sing in rustic lore,
Haply my sires have left their shed,
And fac'd grim Danger's loudest roar,
Bold-following where your fathers led!

[1] Holyrood.

R.B.—17

Edina! Scotia's darling seat!
All hail thy palaces and tow'rs;
Where once, beneath a Monarch's feet,
Sat Legislation's sovereign pow'rs:
From marking wildly scattered flowers,
As on the banks of Ayr I strayed,
And singing, lone, the lingering hours,
I shelter in thy honoured shade.

ADDRESS TO A HAGGIS [1786]

A Haggis is a pudding, supposed to be peculiar to Scotland, composed of minced offal of mutton, mixed with oatmeal and suet, seasoned with salt and pepper, and boiled in a sheep's stomach. Its appearance is very apt to startle an Englishman, however bold he may be as a trencher-man; but by a Scotsman, who knows its intrinsic worth, and knows the country to which it belongs, it is always welcomed at table with hearty applause.

In Burns' time, and before it, when the style of living in Scotland was simpler and humbler than it now is, the Haggis was one of the principal luxuries of the farmer and labouring man, and the Poet's description of the enthusiasm with which it is devoured is not overcharged. At the present day, however, it forms a much less prominent figure in rustic diet, and is rarely to be met with in town life except on particular convivial occasions.

The Edinburgh *Literary Journal* (1829) made the following statement:

About sixteen years ago, there resided in Mauchline, Mr. Robert Morrison, a cabinet-maker. He was a great crony of Burns, and it was at Mr. Morrison's house that the Poet usually spent the 'mids o' the day on Sunday. It was in this house that he wrote his celebrated "Address to a Haggis" after partaking liberally of that dish as prepared by Mrs. Morrison.

Fair fa' your honest, *sonsie* face,	*blessings on; plump*
Great chieftain o' the pudding-race!	
Aboon them a' ye tak your place,	*above*
Painch, tripe, or thairm:	*paunch*
Weel are ye *wordy* o' a grace	*worthy*
As lang's my arm.	

The groaning trencher there ye fill,	
Your *hurdies* like a distant hill,	*rear*
Your pin[1] wad help to mend a mill	
In time o' need,	
While thro' your pores the dews distil	
Like amber bead.	

[1] Wooden pin used to close the opening in the haggis-bag.

His knife see rustic Labour *dight*,   *wipe*
An' cut you up wi' ready sleight,
Trenching your gushing entrails bright
    Like ony ditch;
And then, O what a glorious sight,
    Warm-*reekin'*, rich!   *smoking*

Then, horn for horn[2], they stretch an' strive:
Deil *tak* the hindmost! on they drive,   *take*
Till a' their *weel-swall'd kytes belyve*   *full stomachs; soon*
    Are bent like drums;
Then auld Guidman, maist like to *rive*,   *burst*
    "*Bethanket!*" hums.   *grace after meat*

Is there that owre his French ragout,
Or olio that *wad staw* a sow,   *would sicken*
Or fricassee wad mak her spew
    Wi perfect *scunner*,   *disgust*
Looks down wi' sneering, scornfu' view
    On *sic* a dinner?   *such*

Poor devil! see him owre his trash,
As *feckless* as a withered *rash*,   *feeble; rush*
His spindle *shank* a *guid* whip-lash,   *leg; good*
    His *nieve* a *nit;*   *fist; nut*
Thro' *bluidy* flood or field to dash,   *bloody*
    O how unfit!

But mark the Rustic, haggis-fed,
The trembling earth resounds his tread,
Clap in his *walie nieve* a blade,   *powerful fist*
    He'll mak it whissle:
An' legs, an' arms, an' heads will *sned*,   *shear off*
    Like *taps o' thrissle*.   *thistle-tops*

Ye Pow'rs wha mak mankind your care,
And dish them out their bill o' fare,
Auld Scotland wants nae *skinking* ware   *watery*
    That *jaups* in *luggies;*   *splashes; bowls*
But, if ye wish her gratefu' prayer
    Gie her a Haggis!   *give*

[2]In the time of Burns, haggis, and other spoon-food, was supped with horn spoons.

vein. What a masterful stroke of satiric humour lies in the doubt, that scarcely a greater calamity could be conceived to befall the terror-stricken inhabitants of Kilmarnock, than that of a certain popular clergyman "thrawing his heel," or of a certain unpopular one getting weel, "to preach and read!"

When the worthy old sportsman went out last muir-fowl season, he supposed it was to be, in Ossian's phrase, "the last of his fields," and expressed an ardent wish to die and be buried in the muirs. On this hint the author composed his elegy and epitaph.

Burns, it is said, recited the elegy to the worthy old sportsman whose name it bears. He exclaimed vigorously against being thus prematurely conveyed to the tomb. The Poet, willing to gratify the "game old cock," retired to the window and added the *per contra*.

> Has auld Kilmarnock seen the deil?
> Or great Mackinlay[1] *thrawn* his heel?   *sprained*
> Or Robertson[2] again grown *weel*   *well*
>   To preach an' read?
> "Na, *waur* than a'!" cries *ilka chiel*,   *worse; every fellow*
>   "Tam Samson's dead!"

[1] A certain preacher, a great favourite with the crowd. The phrase, "Thrawn his heel," alludes to a scandal regarding Dr. Mackinlay.

[2] Another preacher, an equal favourite with the few, who was at that time ailing. He was especially unpopular because he read his sermons.

Kilmarnock lang may grunt an' *graen*,	*groan*
An' sigh, an' sab, an' *greet her lane*,	*weep alone*
An' *cleed* her bairns, man, wife an' *wean*,	*clothe; babe*
In mourning weed;	
To Death she's dearly pay'd the *kane*[1]	*tribute*
Tam Samson's dead!	

The Brethren, o' the *mystic level*	*Freemasons*
May hing their head in woefu' bevel,	
While by their nose the tears will revel,	
Like *ony bead;*	*any brook*
Death's gi'en the Lodge an unco *devel*—	*blow*
Tam Samson's dead!	

When Winter muffles up his cloak,	
And binds the mire like a rock;	
When to the *lochs* the curlers flock,	*lakes*
Wi' gleesome speed,	
Wha will they station at the cock[2]?	
Tam Samson's dead!	

He was the king o' a' the *core*,	*group*
To guard, or draw, or wick a bore,	
Or up the rink like Jehu roar	
In time o' need;	
But now he lags on Death's hog-score	
Tam Samson's dead!	

Now safe the stately *sawmont* sail,	*salmon*
And trouts be-*dropp'd* wi' crimson hail,	*speckled*
And eels, *weel-ken'd* for souple tail,	*well-known*
And *geds* for greed,	*pikes*
Since dark in Death's fish-creel we wail	
Tam Samson dead!	

Rejoice, ye *birring paitricks* a';	*whirring partridges*
Ye *cootie* muircocks, *crousely* craw;	*feather-footed; proudly*
Ye *maukins*, cock your *fud* fu' braw,	*hares; tails*
Withouten dread;	
Your mortal *fae* is now awa'—	*foe*
Tam Samson's dead!	

[1]Kane is rent paid in produce.

[2]These are all technical terms in Curling. The "cock," called also the "tee," is the point aimed at, and the skip or captain stands there to direct. To "wick a bore" is to cause your stone to come in contact with one that has been played, and so pass through an opening towards the tee. The "rink" is the course. The "hog-score" is a line drawn across the course some yards before the tee. The stones that do not pass it are thrown out as disgraced.

That woefu' morn be ever mourn'd,
Saw him in shootin *graith* adorn'd,   *garb*
While pointers round impatient burn'd,
    Frae couples free'd;
But och! he *gaed* and ne'er return'd!   *went*
    Tam Samson's dead!

In vain auld age his body batters,
In vain the gout his ancles fetters,
In vain the *burns* cam' down like *waters*   *brooks; rivers*
    An acre *braid!*   *broad*
Now ev'ry auld wife, *greetin'*, clatters   *weeping; repeats*
    "Tam Samson's dead!"

Owre mony a weary *hag* he limpit,   *morass*
An' ay the *tither* shot he thumpit,   *other*
Till coward Death behint him jumpit,
    Wi' deadly *feide;*   *hate*
Now he proclaims, wi' *tout* o' trumpet,   *sound*
    "Tam Samson's dead!"

When at his heart he felt the dagger,
He reel'd his wonted bottle-swagger,
But yet he drew the mortal trigger,
    Wi' weel-aim'd heed;
"L—d, five!" he cry'd, an' owre did stagger—
    "Tam Samson's dead!"

Ilk hoary hunter mourn'd a brither;   *each*
Ilk sportsman-youth bemoan'd a father;
Yon auld gray stane, amang the heather,
    Marks out his head,
Whare Burns has wrote, in rhyming *blether*,   *nonsense*
    "Tam Samson's dead!"

There, low he lies in lasting rest;
Perhaps upon his mould'ring breast
Some spitefu' muirfowl *bigs* her nest   *builds*
    To hatch an' breed:
Alas! nae mair he'll them molest!
    Tam Samson's dead!

When August winds the heather wave,
And sportsmen wander by yon grave,
Three volleys let his memory crave,
    O' *pouther* an' lead,   *powder*
Till Echo answer frae her cave,
    "Tam Samson's dead!"

Heav'n rest his *saul* whare'er he be!   *soul*
Is th' wish o' *mony mae* than me: *many more*
He had twa *fauts*, or maybe three,   *faults*
    Yet what *remead?*   *remedy*
    Ae social, honest man want we:
    Tam Samson's dead!

THE EPITAPH

Tam Samson's weel-worn clay here lies,
Ye canting zealots, spare him!
If honest worth in Heaven rise,
Ye'll mend or ye *win* near him.   *get*

PER CONTRA

Go, Fame, an' canter like a filly
Thro' a' the streets an' *neuks* o' Killie[1];   *nooks*
Tell ev'ry social, honest *billie*   *comrade*
    To cease his grievin';
For, yet unskaith'd by Death's *gleg gullie*,   *sharp knife*
    Tam Samson's *leevin'!*   *living*

EPISTLE TO THE GUIDWIFE OF WAUCHOPE HOUSE [1787]

This delightful poem was called forth by way of "Answer," in March, 1787, to a lengthy rhymed complimentary letter which the Poet received, about three months after his arrival in Edinburgh, from a Mrs. Scott, the wife of a wealthy Roxburghshire farmer, who was an amateur in literature and the fine arts. Her maiden name was Elizabeth Rutherford, and she was niece to Mrs. Cockburn, author of the popular lyric, "I've seen the smiling of Fortune beguiling."

The reference in the third stanza is to the charming incident related in the "Poet's Autobiography" about Handsome Nell (Nelly Kilpatrick), who initiated him in the mysteries of love.   Burns visited Mrs. Scott while

---

[1] Killie is a phrase the country folks sometimes use for Kilmarnock.

on his Border tour in May following the date of his poem, but seems not
to have been peculiarly taken with her.

The Guidwife of Wauchope House died February 29, 1789, about two
years after inditing her letter to Burns. The collected poems of Mrs.
Scott were published, in 1801, by her relatives.

I mind it weel in early date,
When I was beardless, young and *blate*,   *bashful*
An' first could thresh the barn;
Or haud a yokin at the pleugh[1],
An' tho' *forfoughten* sair eneugh,   *tired out*
Yet *unco* proud to learn: *very*
When first amang the yellow corn
A man I reckon'd was,
An' wi' the *lave ilk* merry morn   *rest; each*
Could rank my rig and lass[2],
    Still *shearing*, and clearing   *reaping*
    The *tither* stookèd *raw*,   *other; row*
    Wi' *claivers*, an' *haivers*,   *gossip; nonsense*
    Wearing the day awa.

E'en then, a wish, (I mind its pow'r),
A wish that to my latest hour
Shall strongly heave my breast,
That I, for poor Auld Scotland's sake,
Some usefu' plan or book could make,
Or sing a sang at least.
The rough burr-thistle, spreading wide
Amang the bearded *bear*,   *barley*
I turn'd the weeder-clips aside,
An' spar'd the symbol dear[3]:
    No nation, no station,
    My envy e'er could raise;
    A Scot still, *but* blot still,   *without*
    I knew nae higher praise.

[1]Do a day's work at the plough.   There are properly two "yokins" in the day—one from
morning till midday, one from dinner till night.

[2]A "haflins man" (a lad) or, more frequently, a woman was put on each ridge along with
an able-bodied man in reaping-time, the youngster or female getting the easier half, or "clean
side" of the ridge.   Burns could take the heavier part and, with his lass, keep up his ridge
with those of the others.

[3]The thistle is the emblem of Scotland, as the rose is of England and the shamrock of
Ireland.   The motto is as appropriate allegorically, as it is true historically.   *Nemo me impune
lacessit.*

But still the elements o' sang,
In formless jumble, right an' wrang,
Wild floated in my brain;
Till on that *har'st* I said before,   *harvest*
My partner in the merry *core*,   *group*
She rous'd the forming strain;
I see her yet, the *sonsie* quean,   *pretty and gay*
That lighted up my *jingle*,   *rhymes*
Her witching smile, her *pauky een*   *roguish eyes*
That gart my heart-strings tingle:
    I firèd, inspirèd,
    At every kindling *keek*,   *sly glance*
    But *bashing* and *dashing*,   *abashed; ashamed*
    I fearèd ay to speak.

Health to the sex! *ilk* guid *chiel* says,   *each; fellow*
Wi' merry dance in winter days,
An' we to share in common:
The gust o' joy, the balm of woe,
The *saul* o' life, the heaven below,   *soul*
Is rapture-giving woman.
Ye surly *sumphs*, who hate the name,   *dolts*
Be mindfu' o' your mither;
She, honest woman, may think shame
That ye're connected with her:
    Ye're *wae* men, ye're *nae* men   *poor; not*
    That slight the lovely dears;
    To shame ye, disclaim ye,
    Ilk honest *birkie* swears.   *fellow*

For you, no bred to barn and *byre*,   *cow-stable*
Wha sweetly tune the Scottish lyre,
Thanks to you for your line:
The *marled* plaid ye kindly spare,   *chequered*
By me should gratefully be *ware;*   *worn*
'Twad please me *to the nine.*   *to perfection*
I'd be mair *vauntie* o' my *hap*,   *boastful; covering*
Douce hingin owre my curple[1],
Than ony ermine ever *lap*,   *leaped*
Or proud imperial purple.
    Farewell then, lang *hale* then,   *health*
    An' plenty be your *fa';*   *lot*
    May losses and crosses
    Ne'er at your *hallan* ca'!   *threshold*

[1]Hanging decently over my back and loins.

INSCRIPTION ON THE TOMBSTONE [1787]

ERECTED BY BURNS TO THE MEMORY OF

ROBERT FERGUSSON, POET.

BORN, 5TH SEPTEMBER, 1751—DIED 16TH OCTOBER, 1774.

By special grant of the Managers to Robert Burns, who erected this stone, this burial place is to remain for ever sacred to the memory of Robert Fergusson.—R. B.

No sculptured marble here, nor pompous lay,
"No storied urn nor animated bust";
This simple stone directs pale Scotia's way
To pour her sorrows o'er her Poet's dust.

She mourns, sweet tuneful youth, thy hapless fate:
Tho' all the powers of song thy fancy fired,
Yet Luxury and Wealth lay by in State,
And thankless starved what they so much admired.

This humble tribute with a tear now gives,
A brother Bard, who can no more bestow:
But dear to fame thy Song immortal lives,
A nobler monument than Art can show.

THE FIRST KISS AT PARTING [1788]

Humid seal of soft affections,
Tenderest pledge of future bliss,
Dearest tie of young connections,
Love's first snowdrop, virgin kiss!

Speaking silence, dumb confession,
Passion's birth, and infants' play,
Dove-like fondness, chaste concession,
Glowing dawn of brighter day!

Sorrowing joy, adieu's last action,
When lingering lips no more must join;
What words can ever speak affection
So thrilling and sincere as thine?

PEGGY'S CHARMS [1787]

The heroine of this poem is Miss Margaret Chalmers

> Where, braving angry winter's storms,
> The lofty Ochils rise,
> Far in their shade my Peggy's charms
> First blest my wondering eyes;
> As one who, by some savage stream,
> A lovely gem surveys,
> Astonish'd doubly, marks it beam
> With art's most polish'd blaze.
>
> Blest be the wild, sequester'd shade,
> And blest the day and hour,
> Where Peggy's charms I first survey'd,
> When first I felt their power!
> The tyrant death with grim control
> May seize my fleeting breath;
> But tearing Peggy from my soul
> Must be a stronger death.

UP IN THE MORNING EARLY [1788]

These lines by Burns are in his best manner.   It is interesting to observe that the Poet, in his complaint of winter, cannot forget the birds.

> Cauld blaws the wind frae east to west,
> The drift is driving *sairly;*   *sorely*
> Sae loud and *shill's* I hear the blast,   *shrill*
> I'm sure it's winter fairly.

Chorus.

> Up in the morning's no for me,
> Up in the morning early;
> When a' the hills are cover'd wi' snaw,
> I'm sure it's winter fairly.
>
> The birds sit chittering in the thorn,
> A' day they fare but sparely;
> And lang's the night frae e'en to morn—
> I'm sure it's winter fairly.
>
> Up in the morning's, etc.

I LOVE MY JEAN [1788]

This song, beginning—Of a' the airts the wind can blaw, I composed out of compliment to Mrs. Burns. It was during the honeymoon.—ROBERT BURNS.

Of a' the *airts* the wind can blaw,   *points*
I dearly like the west,
For there the bonnie lassie lives,
The lassie I lo'e best:
There's wild-woods grow, and rivers *row*,   *roll*
And mony a hill between:
But day and night my fancy's flight
Is ever wi' my Jean.

I see her in the dewy flowers,
I see her sweet and fair:
I hear her in the tunefu' birds,
I hear her charm the air:
There's not a bonnie flower that springs
By fountain, *shaw*, or green;   *woodland*
There's not a bonnie bird that sings,
But minds me o' my Jean.

AULD LANG SYNE [1788]

Burns' words go straight to the heart. He grasped the truth, that every human being has an Auld Lang Syne, and that it is human nature to look back lovingly to the days that are gone. That Burns struck a universal chord in the song is proved by the fact, that his "Auld Lang Syne" has been translated into many languages and will be sung by generations yet unborn.

Auld Lang Syne! Magic words, that carry us across leagues of space and back over years of time; that make the grey-haired grandfather in a far-off land more of a bonneted boy in a Scottish braeside, spending a careless summer day with school friends, all unthinking of the weary path of life in the years to come.

Should auld acquaintance be forgot,
And never brought to mind?
Should auld acquaintance be forgot,
And *auld lang syne*?   *olden time, days of other years*

Chorus.

> For auld lang syne, my dear,
> For auld lang syne,
> We'll tak a cup o' kindness yet,
> For auld lang syne!

And surely ye'll be your pint *stowp*,   *flagon*
And surely I'll be mine;
And we'll tak a cup o' kindness yet,
For auld lang syne.

We *twa hae* run about the braes,   *two, have*
And *pu'd* the *gowans* fine;   *pulled; daisies*
But we've wander'd mony a weary foot
Sin' auld lang syne.   *since*

We twa hae *paidl'd* i' the burn,   *waded*
Frae morning sun till *dine;*   *noon*
But seas between us *braid* hae roar'd   *broad*
Sin' auld lang syne.

And there's a hand, my trusty *fiere!*   *comrade*
And *gie's* a hand o' thine!   *give me*
And we'll tak a right *gude*-willie *waught*,   *good; draught*
For auld lang syne.

JOHN ANDERSON, MY JO [1788]

The best song ever written on the happiness of married life, which glorifies the life-long devotion of a husband and wife to each other.

John Anderson, the hero of this song, lies buried in the churchyard of Fort Augustus, a quiet spot embosomed in hills, and sloping down towards the wide expanse of Loch Ness. He was a native of Ayrshire, a carpenter by trade, and is commonly said to have made Burns' coffin, at the latter's own request, many years before his death.

Anderson, to whom Burns was warmly attached, went to Inverness-shire, after his wife's death, to reside with his daughter Kate, who had married the innkeeper of Invergarry, some eight miles from this village. There he spent his declining years; and thither the Poet, on one of his visits to the Highlands, came to visit his humble friend. He rested for a night at his house; and local tradition still tells how his pony wandered astray during the night, and points out the spot, in the wildest part of the romantic glen of Garry, where it was found and restored to its master. From Invergarry

Burns rode over the hills to Foyers, where he penned, or rather pencilled (as he tells us himself) the well-known lines with which the sight of the majestic falls inspired his muse.

The following inscription marks the grave of John Anderson in Fort Augustus churchyard:

SACRED TO THE MEMORY OF JOHN ANDERSON,

WHO DIED AT INVERGARRY, THE 4 MAY, 1832,

AGED 84 YEARS:

ALSO HIS DAUGHTER CATHERINE, WHO DIED AT INVERGARRY, THE 20 DECEMBER, 1832,

AGED 52 YEARS.

RELICT OF THE JAMES GREARSON,

WHO WAS LOST IN THE "COMET" OF GREENOCK POINT

THE 21 OCTOBER, 1825.

This stone is erected by their affectionate children.

John Anderson, my *jo*, John,	*dear*
When we were first *acquent*,	*acquainted*
Your locks were like the raven,	
Your bonnie brow was *brent*;	*smooth*
But now your brow is *beld*, John,	*bald*
Your locks are like the snaw;	
But blessings on your frosty *pow*,	*head*
John Anderson, my jo.	
John Anderson, my jo, John,	
We *clamb* the hill *thegither*;	*climbed; together*
And mony a *cantie* day, John,	*happy*
We've had wi' *ane anither*:	*one another*
Now we *maun* totter down, John,	*must*
And hand in hand we'll go,	
And sleep thegither at the foot,	
John Anderson, my jo.	

TO MARY IN HEAVEN [1789]

This celebrated poem was composed in September, 1789, on the anniversary of the day in which Burns heard of the death of his early love, Mary Campbell.

According to Mrs. Burns, he spent the day, though labouring under a cold, in the usual work of his harvest, and apparently in excellent spirits. But as the twilight deepened, he appeared to grow "very sad about something," and at length wandered out to the barn-yard, to which his wife, in her anxiety for his health, followed him, entreating him, in vain, to observe that the frost had set in, and to return to the fireside.   On being again and again requested to do so, he always promised compliance—but still remained where he was, striding up and down slowly, and contemplating the sky, which was singularly clear and starry.   At last Mrs. Burns found him stretched on a mass of straw, with his eyes fixed on a beautiful planet "that shone like another moon," and prevailed on him to come in.   He immediately, on entering the house, called for his desk, and wrote as they now stand, with all the ease of one copying from memory, these sublime and pathetic verses.

Highland Mary, as Burns called her, resided with her parents in Campbelltown, in Argyllshire.   At the time (1786) Burns became acquainted with her, she was servant in Coilsfield House (not far from Mossgiel), the seat of Colonel Montgomery, afterwards Earl of Eglinton.

My Highland Lassie was a warm hearted charming young creature, as ever blessed a man with generous love.   After a pretty long trial of the most ardent reciprocal attachment, we met by appointment on the second Sunday of May, in a sequestered spot on the banks of Ayr, where we spent the day in taking a farewell before she would embark for the West Highlands, to arrange matters among her friends for our projected change of life.   At the close of the Autumn following, she crossed the sea to meet me at Greenock, when she had scarce landed when she was seized with a malignant fever, which hurried my dear girl to her grave in a few days, before I could even hear of her illness.—*Robert Burns.*

Thou ling'ring star, with less'ning ray,
That lov'st to greet the early morn,
Again thou usher'st in the day
My Mary from my soul was torn.
O Mary! dear departed shade!
Where is thy place of blissful rest?
See'st thou thy lover lowly laid?
Hear'st thou the groans that rend his breast?

That sacred hour can I forget,
Can I forget the hallowed grove,
Where by the winding Ayr we met,
To live one day of parting love!
Eternity can not efface
Those records dear of transports past,
Thy image at our last embrace,
Ah! little thought we 'twas our last!

Ayr, gurgling, kiss'd his pebbled shore,
O'erhung with wild woods, thick'ning green;
The fragrant birch and hawthorn hoar,
'Twin'd amorous round the raptur'd scene:
The flowers sprang wanton to be prest,
The birds sang love on every spray,
Till too, too soon, the glowing west
Proclaim'd the speed of wingèd day.

Still o'er these scenes my mem'ry wakes,
And fondly broods with miser care!
Time but th' impression stronger makes,
As streams their channels deeper wear.
My Mary, dear departed shade!
Where is thy place of blissful rest?
See'st thou thy lover lowly laid?
Hear'st thou the groans that rend his breast?

THE WOUNDED HARE [1789]

In a letter to Alexander Cunningham, May 4, 1789, Burns says:

I have just put the last hand to a little poem, which I think will be something
to your taste. One morning lately, as I was out pretty early in the fields, sowing
some grass seeds I heard a burst of a shot from a neighbouring plantation, and
presently a little wounded hare came crippling by me. You will guess my indigna-
nation at the inhuman fellow who would shoot a hare at this season, when all of
them have young ones. Indeed, there is something in this business of destroying,
for our sport, individuals in the animal creation that do not injure us materially,
which I could never reconcile to my ideas of virtue.

It is only when his emotions are greatly moved that Burns appears
in all his power, and then he stirs the emotions of all mankind. Tenderness to animals is the feeling most conspicuous in his verses after
the passion of love.

Inhuman man! curse on thy barb'rous art,
And blasted be thy murder-aiming eye;
May never pity soothe thee with a sigh,
Nor never pleasure glad thy cruel heart!

Go live, poor wand'rer of the wood and field!
The bitter little that of life remains:
No more the thickening brakes and verdant plains
To thee a home, or food, or pastime yield.

AULD LANG SYNE

And we'll tak' a cup o' kindness yet
For Auld Lang Syne.

AULD LANG SYNE

We twa ha'e paidl'd i' the burn
Frae morning sun till dine.

WILLIE'S MILL, TARBOLTON

TO MARY IN HEAVEN
See'st thou thy lover lowly laid?

Seek, mangled wretch, some place of wonted rest,
No more of rest, but now thy dying bed!
The sheltering rushes whistling o'er thy head,
The cold earth with thy bloody bosom prest.

Perhaps a mother's anguish adds its woe;
The playful pair crowd fondly by thy side;
Ah! helpless nurslings, who will now provide
That life a mother only can bestow!

Oft as by winding Nith I, musing, wait
The sober eve, or hail the cheerful dawn,
I'll miss thee sporting o'er the dewy lawn,
And curse the ruffian's aim, and mourn thy hapless fate.

LINES [1790]

Written in a wrapper, enclosing a letter to Captain Grose

Burns, not knowing Grose's address at the time, enclosed a letter to him under cover to Mr. Cardonnel, a well-known antiquary, in order that he might forward it to his "fat friend." What was written in the wrapper was done extemporaneously, and proves, as strongly as any of his longer poems, the fertile and daring humour of the author. Mr. Cardonnel read the "Lines" everywhere, much to the annoyance of Captain Grose and to the amusement of his friends. Mr. Cardonnel published a quarto volume on ancient Scottish coins, which accounts for the allusion in the last verse.

Ken ye *ought* o' Captain Grose?   *anything*
Igo, and ago,
If he's amang his friends or foes?
Iram, coram, dago.

Is he South, or is he North?
Igo, and ago,
Or drownèd in the river Forth?
Iram, coram, dago.

Is he slain by Highland bodies?
Igo, and ago,
And eaten like a wether-haggis?
Iram, coram, dago.

Is he to Abram's bosom *gane?*   *gone*
Igo, and ago,
Or *haudin* Sarah by the *wame?*   *holding; waist*
Iram, coram, dago.

Where'er he be, the Lord be near him!
Igo, and ago,
As for the de'il, he *daur* na *steer* him.   *dare; molest*
Iram, coram, dago.

But please transmit th' enclosèd letter,
Igo, and ago,
Which will oblige your humble debtor.
Iram, coram, dago.

So may ye hae auld *stanes* in store,   *stones*
Igo, and ago,
The very stanes that Adam bore.
Iram, coram, dago.

So may ye get in glad possession,
Igo, and ago,
The coins o' Satan's coronation!
Iram, coram, dago.

REPLY TO A GENTLEMAN

Who Asked Burns if He Would Not Like to be a Soldier [1790]

I murder hate by field or flood,
Tho' glory's name may screen us;
In wars at hame I'll spend my blood,
Life-giving wars of Venus.

The deities that I adore
Are social Peace and Plenty;
I'm better pleased to make one more,
Than be the death of twenty.

THANKSGIVING FOR VICTORY

Ye hypocrites! are these your pranks?
To murder men, and give God thanks?
Desist for shame! proceed no further!
God won't accept your thanks for murther.

TAM O' SHANTER [1790]

A Tale

Of Brownyis and of Bogilis full is this Buke.—GAWIN DOUGLAS.

Written late in the Autumn of 1790, when the Poet was near the close of his thirty-second year.

Captain Grose, in the introduction to his *Antiquities of Scotland*, says:

> To my ingenious friend, Mr. Robert Burns, I have been seriously obligated; he was not only at the pains of making out what was most worthy of notice in Ayrshire, the county honoured by his birth, but he also wrote, expressly for this work, the pretty tale annexed to Alloway Church.

In a letter to Captain Grose, Burns gives the legend which formed the groundwork of the poem:

> On a market day in the town of Ayr, a farmer from Carrick, and consequently whose way lay by the very gate of Alloway kirkyard, in order to cross the River Doon at the old bridge, which is about two or three hundred yards on than the said gate, had been detained by his business, till by the time he reached Alloway it was the wizard hour, between night and morning.—Though he was terrified with a blaze streaming from the kirk, yet it is a well-known fact that to turn back on these occasions is running by far the greatest risk of mischief,—he prudently advanced on the road. When he had reached the gate of the kirkyard, he was surprised and entertained, through the ribs and arches of an old Gothic window, which still faces the highway, to see a dance of white witches merrily footing it round their old sooty blackguard master, who was keeping them all alive with the power of his bagpipe. The farmer stopping his horse to observe them a little, could plainly descry the faces of many old women of his acquaintance and neighbourhood. How the gentleman was dressed tradition does not say, but that the ladies were all in smocks; and one of them happening unluckily to have a smock which was considerably too short to answer all the purposes of that piece of dress, our farmer was so tickled that he involuntarily burst out, with a loud laugh, "Weel luppen, Maggie wi' the short sark!" and, recollecting himself, instantly spurred his horse to the top of his speed. I need not mention the universally-known fact that no diabolical power can pursue you beyond the middle of a running stream. Lucky it was for the poor farmer that the river Doon was so near, for notwithstanding the speed of his horse, which was a good one, against he reached the middle of the arch of the bridge, and consequently the middle of the stream, the pursuing, vengeful hags, were so close at his heels that one of them actually sprang to seize him; but it was too late, nothing was on her side of the stream but the horse's tail, which immediately gave way at her infernal grip, as if blasted by a stroke of lightning; but the farmer was beyond her reach. However the unsightless tailless condition of the vigorous steed was, to the last hour of the noble creature's life, an awful warning to the Carrick farmers not to stay too late in Ayr markets.

According to Mrs. Burns, the poem was composed in one day.   She informed Cromek that:

The Poet had lingered longer by the river side than his wont, and that taking the children with her, she went out to join him, but perceiving that her presence was an interruption to him, she lingered behind him; her attention was attracted by his wild gesticulations and ungovernable mirth, while he was reciting the passages of the poem as they arose in his mind.

Burns speaks of "Tam o' Shanter" as his first attempt at a tale in verse—unfortunately it was his last.   He himself regarded it as the masterpiece of all his poems, and posterity has not, says Principal Shairp, reversed the judgment.   Lockhart wrote:

In the inimitable tale of Tam o' Shanter, Burns has left us sufficient evidence of his abilities to combine the ludicrous with the awful and even the horrible.

Douglas Graham of Shanter Farm was the hero of the poem, and John Davidson, a shoemaker of Kirkoswald, is said to have been his companion during the evening, before he took the memorable ride.

When *chapman billies* leave the street,	*merchant; fellows*
And *drouthy* neibours, neibours meet;	*thirsty*
As market days are wearing late,	
An' folk begin to *tak the gate;*	*set out homeward*
While we sit bowsing at the *nappy*,	*ale*
An' gettin' fou and unco happy,	
We think na on the lang Scots miles,	
The mosses, waters, *slaps*, and styles,	*gaps*
That lie between us and our hame,	
Where sits our sulky, sullen dame,	
Gathering her brows like gathering storm,	
Nursing her wrath to keep it warm.	
This truth *fand* honest TAM o' SHANTER,	*found*
As he *frae* Ayr *ae* night did canter:	*from; one*
(Auld Ayr, wham ne'er a town surpasses,	
For honest men and bonnie lasses.)	
O Tam! had'st thou but been sae wise,	
As ta'en thy *ain* wife Kate's advice!	*own*
She tauld thee weel thou was a *skellum*,	*worthless fellow*
A bletherin', blusterin', drunken *blellum;*	*windbag*
That frae November till October,	
Ae market-day thou was na sober;	

That *ilka melder*, wi' the miller,	*every grist*
Thou sat as lang as thou had *siller;*	*money*
That ev'ry naig was ca'd a shoe on	
The smith and thee gat roarin fou on;	
That at the Lord's house, ev'n on Sunday,	
Thou drank wi' Kirkton[1] Jean till Monday.	
She prophesied, that late or soon,	
Thou wad be found, deep drown'd in Doon;	
Or catch'd wi' warlocks in the *mirk*,	*dark*
By Alloway's auld haunted kirk.	

Ah, gentle dames! it *gars* me *greet*,	*makes; weep*
To think how mony counsels sweet,	
How mony lengthen'd, sage advices,	
The husband frae the wife despises!	

But to our tale:—Ae market night,	
Tam had got planted, unco right,	
Fast by an *ingle*, bleezing finely,	*fire-side*
Wi' *reaming swats*, that drank divinely;	*frothing; ale*
And at his elbow, *Souter* Johnie,	*shoemaker*
His ancient, trusty, drouthy crony;	
Tam *lo'ed* him like a very brither;	*loved*
They had been *fou* for weeks *thegither*.	*full; together*
The night drave on *wi'* sangs an' clatter:	*with*
And ay the ale was growing better:	
The Landlady and Tam grew gracious,	
Wi' favours secret, sweet and precious:	
The Souter tauld his queerest stories;	
The Landlord's laugh was ready chorus:	
The storm without might *rair* and rustle,	*roar*
Tam did *na* mind the storm a whistle.	*not*

Care, mad to see a man sae happy,	
E'en drown'd himsel amang the *nappy!*	*ale*
As bees flee hame wi' lades o' treasure,	
The minutes wing'd their way wi' pleasure:	
Kings may be blest but Tam was glorious,	
O'er a' the ills o' life victorious!	

But pleasures are like poppies spread,	
You seize the flow'r, its bloom is shed;	
Or like the snowfalls in the river,	
A moment white—then melts for ever;	

[1]Any little village where a parish church is erected is called "the Kirkton."

Or like the Borealis race,
That flit ere you can point their place;
Or like the Rainbow's lovely form
Evanishing amid the storm.
Nae man can tether Time nor Tide;
The hour approaches Tam *maun* ride—   *must*
That hour, o' night's black arch the key-stane,
That dreary hour Tam mounts his beast in;
And *sic* a night he taks the road in   *such*
As ne'er poor sinner was abroad in.

The wind blew as *'twad* blawn its last;   *it would*
The rattling show'rs rose on the blast:
The speedy gleams the darkness swallow'd;
Loud, deep, and lang the thunder bellow'd:
That night, a child might understand,
The Deil had business on his hand.

Weel mounted on his gray meare Meg,   *well*
A better never lifted leg,
Tam *skelpit* on thro' *dub* and mire,   *rushed; pools*
Despising wind, and rain, and fire;
Whiles holding fast his gude blue bonnet,   *sometimes*
Whiles crooning o'er an auld Scots sonnet,
Whiles *glow'ring* round wi' prudent cares,   *gazing*
Lest *bogles* catch him unawares;   *spirits*
Kirk-Alloway was drawing nigh,
Where ghaists and *houlets* nightly cry.   *owls*

By this time he was cross the ford,
Where in the snaw the chapman *smoor'd ;*   *smothered*
And past the *birks* and *meikle* stane,   *birches; big*
Where drunken Charlie brak's neck-bane;
And thro' the *whins,* and by the cairn,   *gorse*
Where hunters fand the murder'd bairn;
And near the thorn, *aboon* the well,   *above*
Where Mungo's mither hang'd hersel'.
Before him Doon pours all his floods,
The doubling storm roars thro' the woods,
The lightnings flash *frae* pole to pole,   *from*
Near and more near the thunders roll,
When, glimmering thro' the groaning trees,
Kirk-Alloway seem'd in a breeze,
Thro' *ilka bore* the beams were glancing,   *every crevice*
And loud resounded mirth and dancing.

Inspiring bold John Barleycorn!
What dangers thou canst make us scorn!
Wi' *tippenny*, we fear nae evil;   *twopenny ale*
Wi' *usquabae*, we'll face the devil!   *whiskey*
The swats sae ream'd in Tammie's noddle[1],
Fair play, he car'd na deils a *boddle*.   *cent*
But Maggie stood, right *sair* astonish'd,   *sore*
Till, by the heel and hand admonish'd,
She ventur'd forward on the light;
And, wow! Tam saw an *unco* sight!   *strange*

Warlocks and witches in a dance;   *wizards*
Nae cotillon *brent* new frae France,   *brought*
But hornpipes, jigs, strathspeys and reels,
Put life and mettle in their heels.
A *winnock-bunker* in the east,   *window-recess*
There sat auld Nick, in shape o' beast;
A *towzie tyke*, black, grim and large,   *shaggy dog*
To gie them music was his charge:
He screw'd the pipes and *gart* them skirl,   *made*
Till roof and rafters a' did *dirl*.   *vibrate*
Coffins stood round like open presses,
That shaw'd the dead in their last dresses;
And (by some devilish *cantraip* sleight)   *magic*
Each in its cauld hand held a light,
By which heroic Tam was able
To note upon the haly table,
A murderer's banes in gibbet-*airns;*   *irons*
Twa spang-*lang*, wee, unchristen'd bairns;   *two; long*
A thief, new-cutted frae a rape,
Wi' his last gasp his *gab* did gape;   *mouth*
Five tomahawks, wi' blude red-rusted;
Five scymitars, wi' murder crusted;
A garter, which a babe had strangled:
A knife, a father's throat had mangled,
Whom his *ain* son of life bereft,   *own*
The grey-hairs yet *stack* to the *heft;*   *stuck; haft*
Wi' mair o' horrible and awfu',
Which even to name wad be unlawfu'.

As Tammie glowr'd, amaz'd, and curious,
The mirth and fun grew fast and furious;
The Piper loud and louder blew,
The dancers quick and quicker flew;

[1]The frothing new ale so worked in Tammie's head that he was fit for anything.

They reel'd, they set, they cross'd, they *cleekit*,   *linked*
Till *ilka* carlin swat and reekit,   *every*
And *coost* her *duddies* on the wark,   *cast; clothing*
And linket at it in her *sark!*   *shirt*

Now Tam, O Tam! had *thae* been queans,   *they*
A' plump and strapping in their teens!   *all*
Their *sarks*, instead o' *creeshie* flannen,   *shirts; greasy*
Been snaw-white seventeen-hunder linen[1]!
Thir breeks o' mine, my only pair,   *these*
That ance were plush, *o' guid* blue hair,   *of good*
I wad hae gi'en them off my *hurdies*,   *hips*
For ae *blink* o' the bonnie burdies!   *glimpse*
But wither'd beldams, auld and droll,
Rigwoodie[2] hags wad *spean* a foal   *wean*
Louping an' flinging on a *crummoch*,   *leaping; staff*
I wonder did na turn thy stomach.

But Tam kent what was what *fu brawlie:*   *full well*
There was ae winsome wench and *waulie*,   *loveable*
That night enlisted in the *core*,   *company*
Lang after kenn'd on Carrick shore!
(For *mony* a beast to dead she shot,   *many*
And perish'd mony a bonnie boat,
And shook baith meikle corn and *bear*,   *barley*
And held the country-side in fear;)
Her *cutty* sark, o' Paisley *harn*,   *short; flax*
That while a lassie she had worn,
In longitude tho' sorely scanty,
It was her best, and she was *vauntie*.   *proud*
Ah! little *kent* thy reverend grannie,   *knew*
That sark she *coft* for her wee Nannie,   *bought*
Wi' twa pund Scots ('twas a' her riches),
Wad ever grac'd a dance of witches!

But here my Muse her wing maun cow'r,
Sic flights are far beyond her power;
To sing how Nannie lap and flang,
(A souple jade she was and strang),
And how Tam stood, like ane bewitch'd,
And thought his very een enrich'd;

---

[1] The manufacturer's term for very fine linen woven in a reed of 1,700 divisions.
[2] The rigwoodie was the band (originally of plaited withes) that passed over a horse's back, hooking it to a cart. The witches were as dry and tough as this.

Even Satan glowr'd, and fidg'd fu' fain,
And *hotch'd* and blew wi' might and main: *hitched*
Till first *ae* caper, *syne* anither,   *one; then*
Tam *tint* his reason *a' thegither*,   *lost; all together*
And roars out, "Weel done, *Cutty-sark!*"   *short-shirt*
And in an instant all was dark:
And scarcely had he Maggie rallied,
When out the hellish legion sallied.

As bees bizz out wi' angry *fyke*,   *fuss*
When plundering herds assail their *byke*;   *nest*
As open *pussie's* mortal foes,   *hares*
When, pop! she starts before their nose;
As eager runs the market-crowd,
When "Catch the thief!" resounds aloud;
So Maggie runs, the witches follow,
Wi' mony an *eldritch* skriech and hollow.   *unearthly*

Ah, Tam! Ah, Tam! thou'll get thy *fairin'!*   *reward*
In hell they'll roast thee like a herrin'!
In vain thy Kate awaits thy coming!
Kate soon will be a woefu' woman!
Now, do thy speedy utmost, Meg,
And win the key-stane o' the brig;
There, at them thou thy tail may toss,
A running stream they dare na cross.
But ere the key-stane she could make,
The *fient* a tail she had to shake!   *deuce*
For Nannie, far before the rest,
Hard upon noble Maggie prest,
And flew at Tam wi' furious *ettle*;   *attempt*
But little *wist* she Maggie's mettle!   *guessed*
Ae spring brought off her master *hale*,   *one; whole*
But left behind her *ain* grey tail: *own*
The *carlin* claught her by the rump,   *huzzy*
And left poor Maggie scarce a stump.

Now, wha this tale o' truth shall read,
Ilk man, and mother's son, tak heed:
Whene'er to Drink you are inclin'd,
Or *cutty-sarks* rin in your mind,   *short-shirts*
Think! ye may buy the joys *o'er* dear,   *over*
Remember Tam o' Shanter's *meare*.   *mare*

LAMENT FOR JAMES, EARL OF GLENCAIRN [1791]

Here we have the Poet, released from the trammels of pure English verse, paying a tribute of sorrow, gratitude and love, on the occasion of the death of his patron, who died January 30, 1791, aged forty-one, after a vain effort to restore health by a voyage to Lisbon.

Sir John Whitefoord's letter to the Poet, acknowledging receipt of the finished poem, is dated October 16, 1791, so we must conclude that Burns produced it only after long musing.

His letter, March 19, 1791, to Mr. Dalzell, the late Earl's factor, has the following passage:

I had a packet of poetic bagatelles ready to send to Lady Betty (his lordship's sister) when I saw the fatal tidings in the newspapers. I see, by the same channel, that the honoured Remains of my noble patron are designed to be brought to the family burial-place. Dare I trouble you to let me know privately before the day of interment, that I may cross the country, and steal among the crowd, to pay a tear to the last sight of my ever remembered benefactor? It will oblige me beyond expression.

The wind blew hollow frae the hills,	
By fits the sun's departing beam	
Look'd on the fading yellow woods,	
That wav'd o'er Lugar's winding stream:	
Beneath a *craigy* steep, a Bard,	*rocky*
Laden with years and *meikle* pain,	*much*
In loud lament bewail'd his lord,	
Whom Death had all untimely *ta'en*.	*taken*
He lean'd him to an ancient *aik*,	*oak*
Whose trunk was mould'ring down with years;	
His locks were bleachèd white with time,	
His hoary cheek was wet *wi'* tears!	*with*
And as he touched his trembling harp,	
And as he tuned his doleful sang,	
The winds, lamenting thro' their caves,	
To echo bore the notes alang:	
"Ye scatter'd birds that faintly sing,	
The reliques o' the vernal *queire!*	*choir*
Ye woods that shed on a' the winds	
The honours o' the aged year!	
A few short months, and glad and gay,	
Again ye'll charm the ear and *e'e*	*eye*
But *nocht* in all revolving time	*nothing*
Can gladness bring again to me.	

"I am a bending aged tree,
  That long has stood the wind and rain;
  But now has come a cruel blast,
  And my last hold of earth is gane;
  Nae leaf o' mine shall greet the spring,
  Nae simmer sun exalt my bloom;
  But I *maun* lie before the storm,   *must*
  And others plant them in my room.

"I've seen *sae* mony changefu' years,   *so*
  On earth I am a stranger grown:
  I wander in the ways of men,
  Alike unknowing, and unknown:
  Unheard, unpitied, unreliev'd,
  I bear *alane* my *lade* o' care,   *alone; load*
  For silent, low, on beds of dust,
  Lie a' that would my sorrows share.

"And last (the sum of a' my griefs!)
  My noble master lies in clay;
  The flow'r amang our barons bold,
  His country's pride, his country's stay:
  In weary being now I pine,
  For a' the life of life is dead,
  And hope has left my aged ken,
  On forward wing forever fled.

"Awake thy last sad voice, my harp!
  The voice of woe and wild despair!
  Awake, resound thy latest lay,
  Then sleep in silence evermair!
  And thou, my last, best, only friend,
  That fillest an untimely tomb,
  Accept this tribute from the Bard
  Thou brought from Fortune's *mirkest* gloom.   *darkest*

"In poverty's low barren vale,
  Thick mists, obscure, involv'd me round;
  Though oft I turn'd the wistful eye,
  Nae ray of fame was to be found:
  Thou found'st me, like the morning sun
  That melts the fogs in limpid air,
  The friendless Bard and rustic song
  Became alike thy fostering care.

"O! why has worth so short a date,
    While villains ripen grey with time?
Must thou, the noble, gen'rous, great,
    Fall in bold manhood's hardy prime!
Why did I live to see that day—
    A day to me so full of woe?
O! had I met the mortal shaft
    That laid my benefactor low!

"The bridegroom may forget the bride
    Was made his wedded wife *yestreen;*   *yesternight*
The monarch may forget the crown
    That on his head an hour has been;
The mother may forget the child
    That smiles sae sweetly on her knee;
But I'll remember thee, Glencairn,
    And a' that thou hast done for me!"

SWEET AFTON [1786]

The Kilmarnock edition of the *Poems* appeared in July, 1786, and one of the first persons of superior condition (Gilbert, indeed, says the first) who courted the Poet's acquaintance in consequence of having read them, was the beautiful and accomplished lady, Mrs. Stewart of Stair, afterwards of Afton, and heiress of the estate. Burns presented her on this occasion with some manuscript songs, and among them with one in which her own charms were celebrated in that warm strain of compliment which the Poet seems always to have considered the most proper whenever fair lady was to be addressed in rhyme.

Burns calls it simply "Sweet Afton" and adds no explanation. None was needed; the song explains itself. The lady was aware of the ways of the muse, and smiled at the images of beauty with which she was associated as she slumbered on the banks of her native stream. Unlike some other ladies of whom the Poet sang, she looked upon his strains as a mark of respect, and felt them as a work of genius.

Afton is a small stream in Ayrshire, one of the tributaries of the Nith; Afton-lodge stands upon its bank. The scenes of the Afton are beautiful, and merit the painter's pencil as much as the Poet's song.

Flow gently, sweet Afton, among thy green braes,
Flow gently, I'll sing thee a song in thy praise:
My Mary's asleep by thy murmuring stream,
Flow gently, sweet Afton, disturb not her dream.

Thou stock-dove, whose echo resounds thro' the glen;
Ye wild whistling blackbirds in yon thorny den;
Thou green crested lapwing, thy screaming forbear,
I charge you disturb not my slumbering Fair.

How lofty, sweet Afton, thy neighbouring hills,
Far mark'd with the courses of clear, winding rills;
There daily I wander as noon rises high,
My flocks and my Mary's sweet cot in my eye.

How pleasant thy banks and green valleys below,
Where, wild in the woodlands, the primroses blow;
There oft, as mild ev'ning weeps over the *lea*,   *pastures*
The sweet-scented *birk* shades my Mary and me.   *birch*

Thy crystal stream, Afton, how lovely it glides,
And winds by the cot where my Mary resides;
How wanton thy waters her snowy feet lave,
As, gathering sweet flowerets, she stems thy clear wave.

Flow gently, sweet Afton, among thy green braes,
Flow gently, sweet river, the theme of my lays;
My Mary's asleep by thy murmuring stream,
Flow gently, sweet Afton, disturb not her dream.

THE SOLDIER'S RETURN [1793]

A correspondent of Thomson's says, regarding the origin of this song:

Burns, I have been informed, was one summer evening at the Inn at Brownhill
with a couple of friends, when a poor wayworn soldier passed the window; of a
sudden it struck the Poet to call him in, and get the story of his adventures, after
listening to which, he all at once fell into one of those fits of abstraction not unusual
with him. He was lifted to the region where he had his garland and singing robes
about him, and the result was the admirable song. Chambers says, that the spot
where the Poet imagined the meeting of the lovers to have taken place was Mill
Mannock, a sweet pastoral scene on the Coyl, near Coylton Kirk.

Brownhill was a posting station some fifteen miles from Dumfries.
Dining there on one occasion, the Poet met a Mr. Ladyman, a commercial
traveller who solicited a sample of his "rhyming ware."

At dinner beans and bacon were served, and the landlord, whose name was Bacon, had as was his wont pressed himself somewhat offensively into the company of his guests:

> At Brownhill we always get dainty good cheer,
> And plenty of bacon each day in the year;
> We've all things that's neat, and mostly in season
> But why always Bacon? come, give me a reason.

> When wild war's deadly blast was *blawn*,   *blown*
> And gentle peace returning,
> *Wi' mony* a sweet babe fatherless,   *with many*
> And mony a widow mourning;
> I left the lines and tented field,
> Where lang I'd been a lodger,
> My humble knapsack a' my wealth,
> A poor and honest *sodger*.   *soldier*

> A *leal*, light heart was in my breast   *true; loyal*
> My hand unstain'd wi' plunder;
> And for fair Scotia, hame again,
> I cheery on did wander:
> I thought upon the banks o' Coyl,
> I thought upon my Nancy,
> I thought upon the witching smile
> That caught my youthful fancy.

> At length I reach'd the bonnie glen,
> Where early life I sported;
> I pass'd the mill and trysting thorn,
> Where Nancy aft I courted:
> Wha spied I but my ain dear maid,
> Down by her mother's dwelling!
> And turn'd me round to hide the flood
> That in my *e'en* was swelling.   *eyes*

> Wi' alter'd voice, quoth I, "Sweet lass,
> Sweet as yon hawthorn's blossom,
> O! happy, happy may he be,
> That's dearest to thy bosom:
> My purse is light, I've far to *gang*,   *go*
> And fain wad be thy lodger;
> I've serv'd my king and country lang—
> Take pity on a sodger!"

Sae wistfully she gaz'd on me,
And lovelier was than ever;
Quo' she, "A sodger ance I lo'ed,
Forget him shall I never:
Our humble cot, and hamely fare,
Ye freely shall partake it;
That gallant badge—the dear cockade,
Ye're welcome for the sake o't."

She gaz'd—she redden'd like a rose—
Syne pale like *ony* lily;   *then; any*
She sank within my arms, and cried,
"Art thou my ain dear Willie?"
"By Him who made yon sun and sky!
By whom true love's regarded,
I am the man; and thus may still
True lovers be rewarded!

"The wars are o'er, and I'm come hame,
And find thee still true-hearted!
Tho' poor in gear, we're rich in love,
And *mair*, we'se ne'er be parted."   *more*
Quo' she, "My grandsire left me *gowd*,   *gold*
A *mailen plenish'd* fairly;   *farm stocked*
And come, my faithfu' sodger lad,
Thou'rt welcome to it dearly!"

For gold the merchant ploughs the main,
The farmer ploughs the manor;
But glory is the sodger's prize,
The sodger's wealth is honour:
The brave poor sodger ne'er despise,
Nor count him as a stranger;
Remember he's his country's stay,
In day and hour of danger.

LINES

Written extempore in a lady's pocketbook

Grant me, indulgent-Heaven, that I may live
To see the miscreants feel the pains they give;
Deal Freedom's sacred treasures free as air,
Till slave and despot be but things which were.

WANDERING WILLIE [1793]

Chambers tells us that the Poet, in composing the following song, "gave expression to the supposed feelings of Clarinda, by throwing himself sympathetically into the circumstances of that unhappy lady, in seeking a reunion with her aberrant husband."

Here awa', there awa', wandering Willie,
Here awa', there awa', *haud awa*' hame;   *hold away*
Come to my bosom, my *ain* only dearie,   *own*
Tell me thou bring'st me my Willie the same.

Winter winds blew loud and cauld at our parting;
Fears for my Willie brought tears in my *e'e:*   *eye*
Welcome now *simmer,* and welcome my Willie;   *summer*
The simmer to nature, my Willie to me.

Rest, ye wild storms, in the cave of your slumbers,
How your dread howling a lover alarms!
Wauken ye breezes, *row* gently ye billows,   *awake; roll*
And waft my dear laddie *ance* mair to my arms.   *once*

But oh, if he's faithless, and minds *na* his Nannie,   *not*
Flow still between us thou wide-roaring main;
May I never see it, may I never *trow* it,   *believe*
But, dying, believe that my Willie's my ain.

SCOTS WHA HAE [1793]

Robert Bruce's address to his army before the battle of Bannockburn

"I have borrowed the last stanza from the common stall edition of Wallace (Hamilton of Gilbertfields—a mere travesty of Minstrel Harry's):

A false usurper sinks in every foe,
And liberty returns with every blow;
   —a couplet worthy of Homer."

—ROBERT BURNS.

Scots, *wha hae wi*' Wallace bled!   *who have with*
Scots, *wham* Bruce has *aften* led!   *whom; often*
Welcome to your gory bed,
Or to Victory!

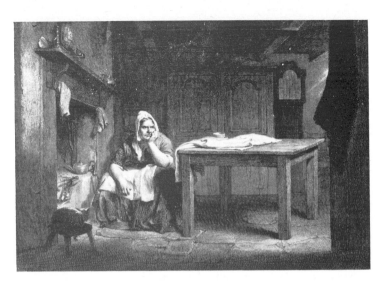

TAM O' SHANTER

Nursing her wrath to keep it warm

TAM O' SHANTER

The Souter tauld his queerest stories

TAM O' SHANTER

Nae man can tether Time nor Tide

TAM O' SHANTER

And, wow! Tam saw an unco sight!

In French

Eccossais, qui avec saigne sous Wallace,
Eccossais, qui Bruce a souvent conduits,
Soyes les bienvenus a votre lit sanglant,
Ou a la victoire glorieuse.

(M. De Wailly, 1843.)

In German

Schotten, die Wallace Blut geweiht,
Bruce so oft gefuhrt zum Streit;
Grab sind Sieg, sie sind bereit,
Auf deme, schliezt die Reih!

(Dr. Legerlotz, 1893.)

In Czech

Skoti, ketere Wallace ved;
Skoti, s ninaiz Bruce sel v pred,
Vitejte mi naposled
V hrob, nel vitezstvi.

(M. Sladek, 1893.)

Now's the day, and now's the hour;
See the front o' battle lour!
See approach proud Edward's power—
Chains and slaverie!

Wha will be a traitor knave?
Wha can fill a coward's grave?
Wha sae base as be a slave?
Let him turn and flee!

Wha for Scotland's king and law
Freedom's sword will strongly draw,
Freeman stand, or freeman *fa'?*   *fall*
Let him follow me!

By oppression's woes and pains!
By your sons in servile chains!
We will drain our dearest veins,
But they shall be free!

Lay the proud usurpers low!
Tyrants fall in every foe!
Liberty's in every blow!
Let us do or die!

SONNET [1793]

Written on January 25, 1793, the birthday of the Poet, on hearing a thrush sing in a morning walk.

> Sing on, sweet Thrush, upon the leafless bough;
> Sing on, sweet bird, I listen to thy strain:
> See agèd winter, 'mid his surly reign,
> As thy blithe carol clears his furrow'd brow.
>
> So in lonely poverty's dominion drear,
> Sits meek content with light unanxious heart,
> Welcome the rapid moments, bids them part,
> Nor asks if they bring aught to hope or fear.
>
> I thank thee, Author of this opening day!
> Thou whose bright sun now gilds the orient skies!
> Riches denied, thy boon was purer joys,
> What wealth could never give nor take away!
>
> Yet come, thy child of poverty and care;
> The mite high Heaven bestowed, that mite with thee I'll share.

DOES HAUGHTY GAUL INVASION THREAT? [1795]

In the early part of 1795, two companies of volunteers were raised by Dumfries, as its quota for defending the fatherland, while the bulk of the regular army was engaged abroad. By War Office intimation, dated 24th March, A. S. De Peyster, Esq., was appointed "Major Commandant" of the Dumfries Volunteers, and various gentlemen of the district were nominated as Captains and Lieutenants. Many of the liberal residents who had incurred the suspicion of the government were fain to enrol themselves in these corps, in order to show they were well affected towards their country. Syme, Maxwell, and other of the Poet's friends, became volunteers. Burns followed suit, and the noble effusion, following, was soon thereafter composed.

The ballad appeared in the *Dumfries Journal* of May 5th, as well as in the May number of the *Scots Magazine;* and printed copies of it, in form of a sheet-song, set to music by Mr. Stephen Clarke, were soon distributed to members of the corps to which the Poet belonged. In thanking Johnson for a packet of the music sent to him, Burns thus wrote:

Our friend Clarke has indeed done his part well: 'tis chaste and beautiful. I have not met with anything that has pleased me so much. You know I am no connoisseur; but that I am an amateur, will be allowed me.

In the last stanza, the difficult problem of combining democratic opinions with stirring patriotism has here found an artistic solution, in which Burns has conceded nothing, yet which was calculated to make people forget many an indiscretion committed in the heat of party warfare.

Does haughty Gaul invasion threat?	
Then let the *loons* beware, Sir,	*rascals*
There's wooden walls upon our seas,	
And volunteers on shore, Sir.	
The Nith shall run to Corsincon[1],	
And Criffel sink in Solway[2],	
Ere we permit a foreign foe	
On British ground to rally!	

O let us not like snarling tykes	
In wrangling be divided,	
Till, slap! come in an *unco loon*	*strange rascal*
And wi' a *rung* decide it.	*bludgeon*
Be Britain still to Britain true,	
Amang oursels united;	
For never but by British hands	
Maun British wrangs be righted!	*must*

The kettle o' the kirk and state,	
Perhaps a *clout* may fail in't;	*patch*
But deil a foreign tinkler loon	
Shall ever ca' a nail in't.	
Our father's blude the kettle bought,	
An' wha wad dare to spoil it?	
By heavens! the sacrilegious dog	
Shall fuel be to boil it!	

The wretch that would a tyrant own,
And the wretch, his true-born brother,
Who'd set the mob aboon the throne,—
May they be damned together!
Who will not sing "God save the King!"
Shall hang as high's the steeple;
But while we sing "God save the King!"
We'll not forget the people!

[1]Corsincon, a high hill at the source of the river Nith.
[2]Criffel, a mountain at the mouth of the same river, where it flows into the Solway.

YE BANKS AND BRAES O' BONNIE DOON [1791]

This beautiful song is familiar in every land, and was in the Poet's day known as "The Caledonian Hunt's Delight." It appeared in Johnson's *Museum* in 1792. No song that Burns ever composed enjoys greater popularity than this. A portion of its success must, in fairness, be attributed to the air, which was produced by an amateur musician in Edinburgh —Mr. James Miller, with a few helping touches from Stephen Clarke, the organist. Shortly after Burns' arrival in Edinburgh, he sent the song to Mr. Ballantyne.

Ye banks and braes o' bonnie Doon,
How can ye bloom sae fresh and fair?
How can ye chant, ye little birds,
And I sae weary *fu'* o' care!   *full*
Thou'll break my heart, thou warbling bird,
That wantons thro' the flowering thorn:
Thou minds me o' departed joys,
Departed—never to return!

Aft hae I rov'd by bonnie Doon,   *oft have*
To see the rose and woodbine twine;
And *ilka* bird sang o' its luve,   *every*
And fondly sae did I o' mine.
Wi' lightsome heart I pu'd a rose,
Fu' sweet upon its thorny tree;
And my *fause* Lover staw my rose,   *false*
But ah! he left the thorn wi' me.

A MAN'S A MAN FOR A' THAT [1795]

Written January 1, 1795, this is one of the greatest songs ever composed in any language. Pierre Jean Béranger (1770-1857), the French poet, declared: "This song is not a song for an age, but for all eternity." It has frequently been called the World's Anthem, and had Burns written nothing else, this one song would have immortalized his name. It is known, and has been sung and recited, in every part of the civilized world.

In a letter dated January 15, 1795, Burns wrote to Thomson thus:

The foregoing has lain by me this fortnight, for want of a spare moment. . . . I do not give you the song for your book, but merely by way of *vive la bagatelle;* for the piece is not really poetry.

The performance, nevertheless, is so characteristic of Burns, that of all the poems and songs he ever wrote, it could be least spared from a collection of his works.   People abroad of every nation quote its generous and powerful couplets whenever they speak of Burns.   The French Revolution was now emerging from its bloody baptism.   On July 28th preceding, Robespierre, with his chief partisans, perished on the guillotine which they had so freely and wantonly kept in perpetual motion.

In October the Jacobin Club had been suppressed, and the trials of Horne Tooke, of Hardy, Thelwall and others for treason in England closely followed.   The sentiments therefore which are embodied in Burns' song found an echo in many a British heart.

> Is there for honest Poverty
> That hings his head, an' a' that?
> The coward slave—we pass him by,
> We dare be poor for a' that!
> For a' that, and a' that,
> Our toils obscure, an' a' that,
> The rank is but the guinea's stamp,
> The man's the *gowd* for a' that.   *gold*

> What though on hamely fare we dine,
> Wear hoddin grey, an' a' that;
> Gie fools their silks, and knaves their wine,
> A man's a man for a' that!
> For a' that, an' a' that,
> Their tinsel show, an' a' that;
> The honest man, tho' e'er sae poor,
> Is king o' men for a' that!

> Ye see yon *birkie* ca'd a lord,   *proud fellow*
> Wha struts, an' stares, an' a' that;
> Tho hundreds worship at his word,
> He's but a *coof* for a' that: *blockhead*
> For a' that an' a' that,
> His ribband, star, an' a' that;
> The man of independent mind,
> He looks and laughs at a' that.

> A prince can mak' a belted knight,
> A marquis, duke, an' a' that;
> But an honest man's *aboon* his might,   *above*
> Gude faith, he *mauna fa'* that!   *must not attempt*

For a' that, an' a' that,
Their dignities an' a' that;
The pith o' sense, an' pride o' worth,
Are higher rank than a' that.

Then let us pray that come it may
As come it will for a' that
That sense and worth, o'er a' the earth,
Shall *bear the gree*, an' a' that!   be the victors
For a' that, an' a' that,
It's comin' yet for a' that,
That Man to Man, the world o'er,
Shall brothers be for a' that!

The late Rev. Dr. Norman Macleod (1812-1872), in reference to his occasional visits to Balmoral Castle, by invitation of Queen Victoria (1819-1901), noted in his diary how some of those autumnal evenings were spent. Not the least interesting glimpse of Balmoral life is that which shows Her Majesty sitting at her spinning wheel, *tête à tête* with the genial Scotch parson, and listening intently, while he read to her from Burns' poems, such pieces as "Tam o' Shanter," and "A Man's a Man for a' That." Dr. Macleod records that this latter was declared by the Queen to be her "favourite" among Burns' productions. (*Memoirs of Dr. Macleod*, 1876).

THE RED, RED ROSE [1796]

This love song has been a universal favourite since it was first given to the world. It is one of those lyrics, in imitation of the old minstrels, which calls forth the commendations of Hazlitt in his critical remarks on Burns' poetry. The lines and sentiments are so exceeding simple that one, on seeing them for the first time, naturally imagines that he has seen or heard them before. Burns wrote the song in 1796.

My Luve is like a red, red rose,
That's newly sprung in June:
My Luve is like the melodie,
That's sweetly play'd in tune.

As fair art thou, my bonie lass,
So deep in luve am I;
And I will luve thee still, my Dear,
Till a' the seas gang dry.

Till a' the seas gang dry, my Dear,
And the rocks melt wi' the sun;
And I will luve thee still, my Dear,
While the sands o' life shall run.

And fare-thee-well, my only Luve!
And fare-thee-well, a while!
And I will come again, my Luve,
Tho' 'twere ten thousand mile!

FAIREST MAID ON DEVON BANKS [1796]

On July 12, 1796, Burns, nine days before his death, penned this, his last song, and laid aside his harp for ever. He left Dumfries for Brow on the 4th of July, and returned home on the 18th. Early in the day on the 21st, all was over.

Chorus

Fairest maid on Devon banks,
Crystal Devon, winding Devon,
Wilt thou lay that frown aside,
And smile as thou wert wont to do?

Full well thou know'st I love thee dear,
Couldst thou to malice lend an ear?
O did not Love exclaim: "Forbear,
Nor use a faithful lover so"?
    Fairest maid, etc.

Then come, thou fairest of the fair,
Those wonted smiles, O let me share;
And by thy bounteous self I swear,
No love but thine my heart shall know.
    Fairest maid, etc.

YOUTH

An unpublished Poem by Burns

"There is every reason to believe" (says the *Dramatic Review*) "that the following charming little poem by Robert Burns has never until now been printed. In no edition of his works is it to be found. A correspondent copied it verbatim many years ago from a page of one of the Poet's M.S. Excise Books, which were then, and are doubtless still, preserved in the Burns Memorial in Edinburgh. Though this positive evidence were wanting, the authenticity of the verses would be sufficiently attested by their style. The pathetic grace of sentiment, the passionate love of nature, the surprising wealth of rural imagery, the elegant simplicity of diction, and even the occasional negligence of rhyme, so characteristic of his free, untutored Muse, all proclaim the author. The poem is an admirable example of Burns in his pensive vein. His death in 'the noon of life' gives a melancholy personal significance to the last two lines."

Youth is the vision of a morn
That flies the coming day;
It is the blossom on the thorn,
Which wild winds sweep away:
It is the image of the sky,
In glassy waters seen,
When not a cloud appears to fly
Across the blue serene.
But when the waves begin to roar
And lift their foaming head,
The morning star appears no more,
And all the heaven is fled.
'Tis fleeting on the passing rays
Of bright electric fire
That flash about with sudden blaze
And in that blaze expire

It is the morning's gentle gale
That as it swiftly blows
Scarce seems to sigh across the vale
Or bend the blushing rose.
But soon the gathering tempests soar,
And all the sky deform;
The gale becomes the whirlwind's roar,
The sigh an angry storm.
For Care and Sorrow's morbid gloom,
And heart-corroding Strife,
And Weakness, pointing to the tomb,
Await the "Noon of Life."

POEM BY ROBERT BURNS

Hitherto Unpublished

"It is seldom in these days," says *The Dundee Courier*, "that a hitherto unpublished poem of the great Poet comes to light. But Mrs. John Moffatt, St. Andrews, is the happy possessor of such. The poem below was copied by Mrs. Moffatt's grandfather, the late Mr. Edward Sanderson, well nigh 100 years ago."

The verses are prefaced with the following words:

Composed by Robert Burns, and presented to the nobleman addressed, upon being called up from the servant's hall (where he had been sent to dine along with them), to add to the entertainment of his company, along with which company he had been asked to go on an excursion to the Bass Rock.   On presenting which he put on his hat, turned on his heel, and retired.

> My Lord, I would not fill your chair,
> Tho' ye be proudest noble's heir!
> I came this night to join your feast
> As equal of the best at least!
> 'Tis true that cash with me is scant
> And titles trifles that I want:
> The King has never made me kneel
> To stamp my manhood with his seal:
> But what of that?   The King on high
> Who took less pains with you than I,
> Has filled my bosom and my mind
> With something better of its kind
> Than your broad acres, something which
> I cannot well translate to speech.
> But by its impulse I can know
> 'Tis deeds, not birth, that make men low.
> Your rank, my Lord, is but a loan:
> But mine, thank heaven, is all my own!
> A peasant this my pride to be—
> Look round and round your halls and see
> Who boasts a higher pedigree.
> I was not fit, it seems, to dine
> With these fox-hunting heroes fine,
> But only came to bandy jests
> Among your Lordship's hopeful guests.
> There must be here some sad mistake—
> I would not play for such a stake.
> Be a buffoon for drink and meat
> And a poor earl's tax paid seat?
> No, die my heart, 'ere such a shame
> Descend on Robert Burns' name.

XVI

The Burns Festival

AYR, 1844

IT SEEMED as if all classes had spontaneously assembled to join hands above the grave of Robert Burns, then and there to renew the vow of enduring reconciliation and love.

Among the vast multitude present were:

ROBERT BURNS (1786-1857)
WILLIAM NICOL BURNS (1791-1872) }—Sons of Burns
JAMES GLENCAIRN BURNS (1794-1865)
(ISABELLA BURNS) MRS. JOHN BEGG (1771-1858)—Sister of Burns
ROBERT BURNS BEGG (1798-1876)—Nephew of Burns
AGNES BROWN BEGG (1800-1877) }—Nieces of Burns
ISABELLA BURNS BEGG (1806-1877)
JAMES BURNES (1780-1852)—Cousin of Burns and father of DR. JAMES BURNES (1801-1862), SIR ALEXANDER BURNES (1805-1841) and CHARLES BURNES (1812-1841)
JESSIE LEWARS (1778-1855)—MRS. THOMSON of Dumfries, who attended the Poet at his dying bed
EARL OF EGLINTON (1812-1861)—13th Earl—ARCHIBALD WILLIAM MONTGOMERIE
THE COUNTESS OF EGLINTON
    and
PROFESSOR JOHN WILSON (1785-1854)—CHRISTOPHER NORTH

BLACKWOOD'S DESCRIPTION OF THE GREAT FESTIVAL

We have once more been joyous spectators of a truly national gathering. Once more we have seen Scotsmen, of every grade and degree, assemble together without a tinge of party purpose, to do honour to the memory of a poet who sprang from the ranks of the people, and who was heart and soul a Scotsman in his feelings, his inspiration and, it may be, in his errors and his prejudices also. It was a stirring and exciting spectacle, such as no other country could have exhibited—to behold peer and senator, poet and historian and peasant—the great and the small, the lettered and the simple of the land—unite, after fifty years of silence, in deep and sincere homage to the genius of one humble man. Nor did they assemble there because his genius was greater than God in his bounty had bestowed upon others, but because he had used it for the glory and exaltation of his country; because he loved her with an ardour the most vivid and extreme; because he had shed the light entrusted to his charge both on the lofty dwelling and on the lowly hearth, but most brightly and cheeringly upon the latter, for that was his peculiar charge. We feel assured that the events of that day, and the sentiments which were then inspired and uttered, will produce a marked effect upon the disposition of the country at large. It seemed as if all classes had spontaneously assembled to join hands above the grave of Robert Burns, and then and there to renew the vow of enduring reconciliation and love.

We shall now proceed to give a short account of the proceedings of the day. In our climate, the state of the weather on public occasions is always regarded with anxiety; for enthusiasm, however warm, is apt to expire beneath a deluge of northern rain. On the previous evening the sky promised well. A brilliant sunset and a warm wind seemed security for a placid morrow; and although the glare of the great furnaces in the neighbourhood of Glasgow glowed somewhat ominously large as the night wore on, we retired to rest rather in hope than resignation. But dismal, indeed, was the prospect when we awoke. A vaporous grey mist had entirely usurped the heavens, and the flash of weary rain resounded through the pluvious metropolis of the west. Fortunately, we were not ignorant of the fact that Glasgow is under the peculiar tutelage of the Pleiades; and accordingly we proceeded to the railway, trusting that matters might mend so soon as we lost sight of the stupendous chimney-stalk of St. Rollox. Notwithstanding the inclemency of the weather, and the early hour, every town, as we passed along, seemed in a state of the greatest excitement. There were bands of music, deputations of mason lodges, and the rival brotherhood of Odd Fellows, with hundreds of men and women, all clad in holiday attire, awaiting the arrival of the train at every station. It is a marvel to us, how half of these expectants could have found their way to Ayr. Carriage after carriage was linked to the already exorbitant train, until the engine groaned audibly, and almost refused to proceed. Still the rain continued to fall, and it was not until after we had left Irvine, and were rounding the margin of the bay towards Ayr, that the sky brightened up and disclosed the great panorama of the sea, with Ailsa and Arran looming in the distance, and steamers from every direction ploughing their way into the port.   The streets of Ayr were swarming with people, and sounding with the crash of music.   There were arches on the bridge, flags streaming from windows, and bells tolling from the steeples—symptoms of a jubilee as great as if Royalty had descended unawares, and the whole district had arisen to pay honour to its Queen.   The inns were thronged to excess, and the waiters in absolute despair.   What a multitude of salmon must have died to furnish that morning meal.   Yet every face looked bright and happy, as became those who had engaged in such a pilgrimage.   Then the burst of music became louder and more frequent, as band after band, preceding the trades and other public bodies, filed past towards the rendezvous of the great Procession.   This was on what is called the Low Green; and the admirable arrangements made by the committee of management— of which Mr. Ballantine of Castlehill was convener, and Messrs. Bone and Gray secretaries—were manifest.   Mr. Thwaites undertook the marshalling of the whole.   Here, first, the grandeur of the National Festival was displayed, while the immense multitudes that had come trooping in from all quarters stood congregated in orderly muster, a mighty host, bound in unity by one soul, stretching far and wide from the towers of Ayr to the sea.   Suddenly, at signal given, the Procession began to deploy, in admirable order, with streaming banners and crashes of music and shouts from the accompanying thousands that rent the sky; and we were warned that it was time to proceed, if we wished to obtain a place upon the Platform erected on the banks of the Doon.

A unit in the stream of population, we skirted the noble race-course, and reached the Platform just before the head of the Procession arrived.   It was erected in a magnificent situation.   Behind was the monument of Burns, and the sweet habitation of Mr. Auld, with old Alloway Kirk a little farther off.   Behind it was the immense pavilion erected for the banquet, all gay with flags and streamers.   To the right, were the woods that fringe the romantic Doon, at that point concealed from sight; but not so the Old Bridge, which spans it, with its arch of triumphal evergreen.   Every slope beyond was studded with groups of people, content to view the spectacle from afar.   The Carrick hills reached far away beyond; and, on the other side, were the town and broad bay of Ayr, and Arran with all its mountains.   But we had little leisure to look around us.   On the Platform were collected many of the Ladies and Gentlemen of the country—Sir David Hunter Blair; James Campbell, Esq. of Craigie; W. A. Cunninghame, Esq. of Fairlie; A. Boyle, Esq. of Shewalton, etc.; Archibald Hastie, Esq., M.P.; A. Buchanan, Esq., Charles Neaves, Esq., Mr. Sheriff Campbell, Mr. Sheriff Bell, Mr. Carruthers, etc., etc.; some of the most distinguished of those who had come from afar, and conspicuous in front, the surviving Kindred of Burns. There stood with his beautiful Countess, the noble and manly Eglinton, preux chevalier of his day, and fitting representative of that ancient house of Montgomery, so famous in the annals and peerage of Scotland, and of France. There was the venerable and venerated Lord Justice-General Boyle, the President of the Scottish Courts, and chief magistrate of the land, with the snows of more than seventy winters lying lightly and gracefully upon his head. There stood Wilson, never more fitting in his place than here; for of the many who have interposed to shield the memory of Burns from detraction, he had spoken with the most generous spirit and collected purpose, and came now to rejoice in the common triumph. There, too, were Alison, the sound and strong historian, Chambers, whose delicate generosity to the relatives of Burns, independently of the services he has rendered to our national literature, made him one of the fittest spectators of the scene; and a host of other distinguished men, well and aptly representing the aristocracy and the learning of our country. Many strangers, too, had come to grace the festival; amongst whom, it may be allowed us to specify the names of Mrs. S. C. Hall, the charming authoress, and her accomplished husband. We looked in vain for some whose presence there would have given an additional interest to the scene. We would fain have seen the poets of the sister countries represented by Wordsworth and Moore. That might not be; but their sympathies were not withheld.

Among that brilliant group, there stood an elderly female, dressed in deep black, and three men, all past the meridian of life, with quiet thoughtful looks, and unpretending aspect. These were the sister and the sons of Burns. His sister!—and half a century has well-nigh gone past since the hot heart of the brother was stricken cold, and the manly music of his voice made dumb for ever! Was it too much to believe that, through these many long years of her earthly pilgrimage—sometimes, we fear, darkened by want and neglect—that sister had always clung to the memory of the departed dead, in the hope that the day would always arrive when his genius should receive the homage of a new generation, to atone for the apathy and coldness of that which had passed away? What emotions must have thrilled the bosom of that venerable woman, as she gazed on the stirring spectacle before her, and saw her lingering hopes far more than thoroughly realized! What a glorious welcome, too, for the sons to their native land! They had left it—not quite as the poor man does—but with heavy difficulties before them. They had wrestled their way onwards through half the journey of life, and now, on their return, they were greeted with a welcome which it were almost worth the struggles of a life to obtain. All this they owed to their father; and honoured among the honourable that day were the lineage and kindred of Burns.

Beneath and around the Platform there were thousands already congregated. If any one had wished to paint the character of the Scottish peasantry in its loftiest and most endearing light, the subjects were there before him. Old patriarchal men, on whose venerable temples time had bleached the white locks of age to the softness of those of infancy, stood leaning upon their grandchildren, proud and yet wondering at the honours which were that day paid to him, whom, long, long ago, reaching away through the vista of memory, they remembered to have seen in their youth. So familiarized were they with his image, and the glorious language he had uttered, that they had almost forgotten the greatness and universality of his fame; and now, when brought forth from their cottages in the far glens and mainlands of the south, they could scarcely believe that the great, and gifted, and beautiful of the land, had come together for no other purpose than to celebrate the genius of their old companion. But they were proud, as they well might be; for it was a privilege even to have beheld him, and in that homage they recognized and felt the tribute that was paid to their order. The instinctive decency of Scottish feeling had accorded to these men, a fitting and conspicuous place. Around them were the women of their families of all ages—from the matron in her coif to the bashful maiden with the snood—and even children; for few were left at home on that day of general jubilee. These, and a vast concourse of strangers, already occupied the ground.

Meanwhile the Procession had wound its enormous length from Ayr along a road almost choked up with spectators. Every wall and gate had its burden, and numerous Flibbertigibbets sat perched upon the branches of the trees. The solitary constable of the burgh was not present to preserve order, or, if he was, his apparition was totally unrequired. The old bell of Alloway Kirk was set in motion as the head of the column appeared, and continued ringing until all were past. The whole land was alive. Each road and lane poured forth its separate concourse to swell the ranks of the great Procession. The weather, after one heavy final shower, cleared up; or, if not clear, resolved itself into that indescribable mixture of sunshine and cloud which sets off the beauties of the undulating landscape so well, light alternating with shadow, and, on the ridges of the distant hills, contending radiance and gloom.

On they went, with banners flying and a perfect storm of music, across the new Bridge of Doon, deploying along the road on the opposite side of the river, and finally recrossing by the old bridge, from which they filed past in front of the Platform. The order of the Procession was as follows:

Band the 87th Fusiliers
Provost, Magistrates, Town Council and Trades of Ayr
Five Bagpipers in Highland Costume

Farmers and Shepherds
Dalrymple Burns' Club, with banners and music
Motto, "Firm"
Kilwinning Band
Kilwinning Mother Lodge of Freemasons
Cumnock Band
Loudoun Newmilns Lodge
Irvine Band
Troon Navigation Lodge
Girvan Masons
St. James' Tarbolton
St. John's, Ayr
Thistle and Rose, Stevenston
St. John's Largs
Glasgow Star
St. Andrew's Band
Royal Arch, Maybole
St. Paul's, Ayr
St. Andrew's, Ayr
St. John's, Girvan
St. James', Kilmarnock
St. Peter's, Galston
St. John's, New Cumnock
Junior or Knights Templars, Maybole
Saltcoats Band
St. John's Dairy
Kilbarchan Band
St. John's, Greenock
Shoemakers as follows:
    Champion
    British Prince and Attendants
    Indian Prince and Train

Catrine Band
King Crispin and Train
Souter Johnie, in character
Highland Chieftains
Greenock Band
Lodge of Odd Fellows
Band
Robert Burns Lodge, Beith
Ayr Band
Banks of Ayr Lodge of Odd Fellows
St. I. Makdougall Brisbane Lodge, Largs
Ancient Order of Foresters, Glasgow
Captain mounted, with Bow and Arrows
Kilmarnock Band

Kilmarnock Burns Lodge of Foresters
Weavers from Maybole
Maybole Band
Tailors of Maybole
Mauchline Band
Boxmakers of Mauchline

(with large Scotch Thistle, carried shoulder-high
by Four Men and Banner inscribed:

I turn'd my weeder-clips aside,
And spared the Symbol dear.

The party were from the Establishment of
Messrs. W. and A. Smith. The Thistle grew near
to Mossgiel.)

Caledonia Union Odd Fellows, Dunlop

(Deputations of the Magistrecy joined in the
Procession from Dumbarton, Dunlop, Maybole and
Irvine.)

The effect of the Procession as seen from the Platform almost baffles
the power of description. The wailing of the bagpipes and the crash of
the bands were heard from the bosom of deep wood-thicket behind, long
before the ranks became visible. At length, among the trees that skirted
the opposite banks, there was a glittering of lances, and a lifting of banners,
and a dark-growing line of men, in closest order, marching as if to battle.
Gradually it flowed on, in continuous stream, file succeeding to file without
gap or intermission, until the head of the column appeared recrossing by
the Old Br:dge, and winding up the road towards the Platform; and still
new banners rose up behind, and fresh strains of music burst forth amidst
the leafy screen. And now they reached the Platform; lance and flap were
lowered in honour of those who stood bareheaded above, and deafening
were the cheers that ushered in the arrival of the national pageant. The
spectacle was most imposing, and must have conveyed to the minds of
the strangers present a vivid impression of the energy and enthusiasm so
deeply implanted in the Scottish character, and always so irresistibly
manifested at the touching of a national chord. The most interesting
part of the Procession by far was the array of Farmers and Shepherds, the
flower of the west-country yeomanry, attired in the graceful plaid. Of
that same breed of men, of tall and compact mould and hardy sinew,
was Robert Burns; nor is it possible to imagine anything more animated
than the appearance of those stalwart sons of the soil, as they lingered for a
moment before the Platform, and looked with wistful eyes at the sons of
the Poet, if haply they might trace in their lineaments some resemblance
to the features of him whom, from their infancy, they had learned to love.
Then came the Freemasons, and King Crispin with his train, and the

TAM O' SHANTER

But scarcely had he Maggie rallied

TAM O' SHANTER

Ae spring brought off her master hale

THE HORRORS OF WAR

Wi' mony a sweet babe fatherless
And mony a widow mourning.

THE SOLDIER'S RETURN

Archers, and much more of old Scottish device, until there seemed no end to the flowing tide of population, all keen and joyful, and exultant. But the full burst of enthusiasm was reserved for the close. In the rear of all appeared an enormous Thistle borne shoulder high; and no sooner was the national emblem in sight, than a universal and long-continued cheer burst forth from the many thousands who were now congregated in the plain beyond. Alas, for that thistle! Though Burns, as the inscription bore,

> Had turn'd his weeder-clips aside,
> And spared the symbol dear,

such was not the fate of the offspring plant. Scarcely had it reached the Platform, when Christopher North violently possessed himself of one branch, the Lord Justice-General seized upon another, and in the twinkling of an eye it was torn into fragments, and its rough leaves and rougher flowers displayed upon manly bosoms, from which it would have been difficult to wrest them again. So closed the Procession—but not the gathering. Deafening were the cheers which followed for Burns—for his Sons—for Professor Wilson—for Lord Eglinton; until the last remnant of reserve gave way, and a torrent of people swept forward to obtain, if possible, a pressure of their hands that were gladly and gratefully held forth. Descending from the Platform, we entered the meadow-ground beyond, where the multitude were now assembled. One of the bands struck up the beautiful air—"Ye banks and braes o' bonny Doon"; and immediately the People, as if actuated by one common impulse, took up the strain, and a loftier swell of music never rose beneath the cope of heaven. We thought of the fine lines of Elliott—

> To other words, while forest echoes ring,
> Ye banks and braes o' bonny Doon, they sing;
> And far below, the drover, with a start
> Awaking, listens to the well-known strain,
> Which brings Schehallion's shadow to his heart
> And Scotia's loveliest vales: then sleeps again,
> And dreams on Loxley's banks of Dunsinane.

Few could abstain from tears as the last glorious note died solemnly away into the skies. We looked down from the top of the pavilion-stairs upon the vast multitude beneath. There could not have been less than eighty-thousand souls collected upon the ground. Of all that mighty mass, not one man had thrown discredit upon the harmony and order of the day. Every face glowed with happiness and congratulation, as if conscious that a good work had been done, and that the nation had at length discharged the duty which she owed to one of her most gifted sons.

THE BANQUET

The company began to enter the pavilion almost immediately after the close of the Procession and the chair was taken about two o'clock. The Pavilion was erected in a field of twenty-two acres, adjoining to the Monument and was a magnificent building. It measured not less than 120 feet by 110, forming nearly a perfect square. The roof, supported by two rows of pillars, was covered with waterproof felt, and the building inside was lined with white cloth festooned with crimson. In the centre of the roof was a radiation of the same colours. The tables and seats were arranged in parallel lines from the head to the foot of the apartment, rising with a gentle inclination from the middle on both sides. At each end there was an elevated table for the Chairman, Croupier, and their respective supporters; and on the two remaining sides of the square there were *vis-a-vis* galleries for the instrumental band and glee-singers, a pianoforte for the accompaniment to Mr. Templeton being placed in front of the latter, at which Mr. Blewitt took his station. Mr. Templeton, between the speeches, sang, with great power and sweetness, appropriate songs from Burns; and Mr. Blewitt's performance was admirable. Mr. John Wilson (Scottish Vocalist) came from Paris to the Festival; but unfortunately was prevented by severe illness from delighting the assembly with his exquisite strains. The hall was lighted by twenty-two glass windows, shaded with white cloth. The chairman and croupier's seats were of oak, made of the rafters of Alloway Kirk; and several splendid silver vases decorated their tables. The hall was seated to accommodate 2,000 persons, and was entirely filled, although not inconveniently crowded.

The distinguishing feature of the pavilion was the number of ladies who were present. A great room exclusively filled with men, is at best a dull and sombre spectacle; and so far from social, that it always conveys to us a gross idea of selfishness. The mere scenic effect on this occasion was immensely heightened by the adoption of the polite rule; nor can it be doubted that the tone of the meeting underwent a similar improvement.

The Chairman, the Right Hon. the Earl of Eglinton, was supported on the right by Robert Burns, Esq., (58) late of the Stamps and Taxes, Somerset House, London, eldest son of the poet; Major James Glencairn Burns (50), youngest son of the poet; Miss Agnes Brown Begg (44), niece of the poet; Henry Glassford Bell, Esq., Sheriff-Substitute of Lanarkshire; Rev. Mr. Cuthill, Ayr; Mr. Robert Burns Begg (46), teacher, Kinross, nephew of the poet; Miss Isabella Burns Begg (38), the younger niece of the poet; Mr. & Mrs. Thomson of Dumfries, (the latter the Jessie Lewars (66) of the bard, who tended his deathbed);—on the left, Colonel William Nicol Burns (53), third son of the poet; Isabella Burns (73), Mrs. John Begg, sister of the poet; Sir John McNeill, Bart., late Plenipotentiary to the Court of Persia; the Right Hon. Lord Justice-General Boyle; the Countess of Eglinton; Sir David Hunter-Blair, Bart., of Blairquhan. The Croupier, Professor John Wilson, was supported on the right by Archibald Alison, Esq., Sheriff of Lanarkshire, and author of the *History of Europe*, afterwards Sir Archibald Alison; Colonel Mure of Caldwell, author of *Travels in Greece;* William E. Aytoun, Esq., Advocate; A. Hastie, Esq., M.P. for Paisley; James Oswald, Esq., M.P. for Glasgow;—on the left by Sir James Campbell, Glasgow; Provost Miller, Ayr; James Ballantine, Esq., of Castlehill; Charles Mackay, Esq., London; James Campbell, Esq., of Craigie.

The Rev. Mr. Cuthill of Ayr asked the blessing.

The Earl of Eglinton, after the usual loyal toasts, rose and spoke as follows:

Ladies and gentlemen: The subject of the toast which I have now the honour to bring before your notice, is one of such paramount importance on this occasion, and is so deeply interesting, not only to those whom I am addressing, but to all to whom genius is dear, that I could have wished that it had been committed to more worthy hands; more especially when I see the great assemblage collected here—the distinguished persons who grace our board today. It is only because I conceive that my official position renders me the most formal and fitting, though most inefficient, mouthpiece of the inhabitants of this country, that I have ventured to present myself before you on this occasion, and to undertake the onerous, though most gratifying, duty of proposing, in such an assemblage, the thrilling toast— "The Memory of Burns."

This is not a meeting for the purpose of recreation and amusement—it is not a banquet at which a certain number of toasts are placed on paper, which must be received with due marks of approbation—it is the enthusiastic desire of a whole people to pay honour to their greatest countryman. It is the spontaneous out-pouring of a nation's feeling towards the illustrious dead, and the wish to extend the hand of welcome and of friendship to those whom he has left behind. Here on the very spot where the Poet first drew breath, on the very ground which his genius has hallowed, beside the Old Kirk which his verse has immortalized, beneath the monument which an admiring and repentant people have raised to his memory, we meet after the lapse of years, to pay our homage at the shrine of genius. The master-mind who has sung the "Isle of Palms"—who has revelled in the immortal "Noctes"—and who has already done that justice to the memory of Burns which a brother poet alone can do—Christopher himself is here, anxious to pay his tribute of admiration to a kindred spirit. The historian who has depicted, with a Gibbon's hand, the eventful period of the French empire, and the glorious victories of Wellington is here—a Clio, as it were, offering a garland to Erato. The distinguished head of the Scottish bench is here. In short, every town and every district, every class and every age, has come forward to pay homage to their poet. The honest lads whom he so praised, and whose greatest boast it is that they belong to the land of Burns, are here. The fair lasses whom he so loved and sung, have flocked hither to justify, by their loveliness, their poet's words. While the descendant of those who dwelt in the "Castle o' Montgomerie," feels himself only too highly honoured by being permitted to propose the memory of him who wandered then unknown along the banks of Fail.

How little could the pious old man who dwelt in yon humble cottage, when he read the "big ha' bible"—"his lyart haffets wearing thin and bare"—have guessed that the infant prattling on his knee was to be the pride and admiration of his country; that that infant was to be enrolled a chief among the poetic band; that he was to take his place as one of the brightest planets that glitter round the mighty sun of the Bard of Avon! In originality second to none, in the fervent expression of deep feeling, and in the keen perception of the beauties of nature, equal to any who ever revelled in the bright fairyland of poesy, well may we rejoice that Burns is our own—well may we rejoice that no other land can claim to be the birthplace of our Homer except the hallowed spot on which we stand!

Oh! that he could have forseen the futurity of fame he has created to himself—Oh! that he could have forseen this day, when the poet and the historian, the manly and the fair, the peer and the peasant, vie with each other in paying their tribute of admiration to the untaught but mighty genius whom we hail as the first of Scottish poets! It might have alleviated the dreary days of his sojourn at Mossgiel—it might have lightened the last hours of his pilgrimage upon earth. And well does he deserve such homage. He has portrayed the "Cotter's Saturday Night" in strains that are unrivalled in simplicity, and yet fervour—in solemnity, and in truth—He has breathed forth the patriotic words which tell of the glories of Wallace, and immortalize alike the poet and the hero—He who called inspiration from the modest daisy, and yet thundered forth the heroic strains of "The Song of Death"—He who murmured words which appear the very incarnation of poetry and of love, and yet hurled forth the bitterest shafts of satire—a Poet by the bard of nature, despising, as it were, the rules of art, and yet triumphing over those very rules which he set at nought—at whose name every Scottish heart beats high—whose name has become a household word in the cottage as in the palace—to whom shall we pay our homage, of whom shall we be proud, if it is not our own immortal Burns? But I feel that I am detaining you too long, I feel that, in the presence of a Wilson and an Alison, I am not a fit person to dilate upon the genius of Burns. I am but an admirer of the poet like yourselves. There are some present who are brother poets and kindred geniuses—men who, like Burns, have gained for themselves a glorious immortality. To them will I commit the grateful task of more fully displaying before you, decked out in their eloquence, the excellencies of the poet, the genius of the man, and to welcome his sons to the land of their father: and I will only ask you, in their presence—on the ground which his genius has rendered sacred—on the "banks and braes o' bonny Doon"—to join with me in drinking an overflowing bumper, and giving it every expression of enthusiasm which you can, to "The memory of Burns."

Mr. Robert Burns rose, along with his brothers, William Nicol Burns and James Glencairn Burns, and was received with enthusiastic cheering. He said:

My lord, ladies and gentlemen: Of course it cannot be expected, at a meeting such as the present, that the sons of Burns should expatiate on the merits and genius of their deceased father.   Around them are an immense number of admirers, who, by their presence here this day, bear a sufficient testimony to the opinion in which they hold his memory, and the high esteem in which they hold his genius.   In the language of the late Sir Christopher Wren, though very differently applied, the sons of Burns can say, that to obtain a living testimony to their father's genius they have only to look around them.   I beg, in name of my Aunt (Mrs. John Begg), brothers and myself, to return our heartfelt and grateful thanks for the honour that has this day been paid to my father's memory.

Professor John Wilson (1785-1854) then rose and said:

Were this Festival but to commemorate the genius of Burns, and it were asked, what need now for such commemoration, since his fame is coextensive with the literature of the land, and enshrined in every household? I might answer, that although admiration of the poet be wide as the world, yet we, his compatriots, to whom he is especially dear, rejoice to see the universal sentiment concentered in one great assemblage of his own people: that we meet in thousands and tens of thousands to honour him, who delights each single one of us at his own hearth.   But this commemoration expresses, too, if not a profounder, a more tender sentiment; for it is to welcome his sons to the land he has illustrated, so that we may at once, indulge our national pride in a great name, and gratify in filial hearts the most pious of affections.   There was, in former times, a custom of crowning great poets.   No such ovation honoured our bard, though he too tasted of human applause, felt its delights, and knew the trials that attend it.   Which would Burns himself have preferred, a celebration like this in his lifetime, or fifty years after his death?   I venture to say, he would have preferred the posthumous as the finer incense.   The honour and its object are then seen in juster proportion, for death confers an elevation which the candid soul of the poet would have considered, and such honour he would rather have reserved for his manes than have encountered it with his living infirmities. And could he have forseen the day, when they for whom at times he was sorely troubled, should, after many years of separation, return to the hut where himself was born, and near it, within the shadow of his monument, be welcomed for his sake by the lords and ladies of the land; and—dearer thought still to his manly breast—by the children and the children's children of people of his own degree, whose hearts he sought to thrill by his first voice of inspiration; surely had the Vision been sweeter to his soul than even that immortal one, in which the Genius of the Land bound the holly round his head, the lyric crown that it will wear for ever.

Of his three Sons sitting here, one can remember their father's face—those large lustrous eyes of his, so full of many meanings, as they darkened in thought, melted in melancholy, or kindled in mirth, but never turned on his children, or on their excellent mother, but with one of intense affection.   That son may even on this day have remembrance of his father's head, with its dark clusters not unmixed with gray, and those eyes closed, lying upon the bed of death.   Nor, should it for a moment placidly appear, is such image unsuitable to this festival.   For in bidding welcome to his sons to their father's land, I feel that, while you have conferred on me a high honour, you have likewise imposed on me a solemn duty and, however inadequately I may discharge it, I trust that in nought shall I do any violence to the spirit either of humanity or of truth.

I shall speak reverently of Burns' character in hearing of his sons; but not even in their hearing must I forget what is due always to established judgment of the everlasting right. Like all other mortal beings, he had his faults—great even in the eyes of men—grievous in the eyes of Heaven. Never are they to be thought of without sorrow, were it but for the misery with which he himself repented them. But as there is a moral in every man's life, even in its outward condition imperfectly understood, how much more affecting when we read it in confessions wrung out by remorse from the greatly gifted, the gloriously endowed! But it is not his faults that are remembered here—assuredly not these we meet to honour. To deny error to be error, or to extenuate its blame, that makes the outrage upon sacred truth, but to forget that it exists, or if not wholly so, to think of it along with that under-current of melancholy emotion at all times accompanying our meditations on the mixed characters of men—that is not only allowable, but it is ordered—it is a privilege dear to humanity—and well indeed might he tremble for himself who should in this be deaf to the voice of nature crying from the tomb.

And mark how graciously in this does time aid the inclinations of charity! Its shadows soften what they may not hide. In the distance, discordances that once jarred painfully on our ears are now undistinguishable—lost in the music sweet and solemn, that comes from afar with the sound of a great man's name. It is consolatory to see, that the faults of them whom their people honour grow fainter and fainter in the national memory, while their virtues wax brighter and more bright; and if injustice have been done to them in life, (and who now shall dare to deny that cruelest injustice was done to Burns?) each succeeding generation becomes more and more dutiful to the dead—desirous to repair the wrong by profounder homage. And it is by his virtues that man may best hope to live in the memory of man. Is there not something unnatural, sometimes monstrous, in seeking to eternize here below, that of which the proper doom is obscurity and oblivion? How beneficent thus becomes the power of example! The good that men do then indeed "lives after them"—all that was ethereal in their being alone survives—and thus ought our cherished memories of our best men—and Burns was among our best—to be invested with all consistent excellencies; for far better may their virtues instruct us by the love which they inspire, than ever could their vices by aversion.

To dwell on the goodnesses of the great shows that we are at least lovers of virtue—that we may ourselves be aspiring to reach her serene abodes. But to dwell on their faults, and still more to ransack that we may record them, that is the low industry of envy, which, grows into a habit, becomes malice, at once hardening and embittering the heart. Such beyond all doubt, in the case of our great poet, was the source of many "a malignant truth and lie," fondly penned, and carefully corrected for the press, by a class of calumniators that may never be extinct; for, by very antipathy of nature, the mean hate the magnanimous, the groveling them who soar. And thus, for many a year, we heard "souls ignoble born to be forgot" vehemently expostulating with some puny phantom of their own heated fancy, as if it were the majestic shade of Burns evoked from his Mausoleum for contumely and insult.

Often, too, have we been told by persons somewhat presumptuously assuming the office of our instructors, to beware how we suffer our admiration of genius to seduce us from our reverence of virtue. Never cease to remember—has been still their cry—how far superior is moral to intellectual worth. Nay, they have told us that they are not akin in nature. But akin they are; and grief and pity 'tis that ever they should be disunited. But mark in what a hateful, because hypocritical spirit, such advices as these have not seldom been proffered, till salutary truths were perverted by misapplication into pernicious falsehoods. For these malignant counsellors sought not to elevate virtue, but to degrade genius; and never in any other instance have they stood forth more glaringly self-convicted of the most wretched ignorance of the nature both of the one and the other, than in their wilful blindness to so many of the noblest attributes of humanity in the character of Burns. Both gifts are alike from heaven, and both alike tend heavenward. Therefore we lament to see genius soiled by earthly stain; therefore we lament to see virtue, where no genius is, fall before the tempter. But we, in our own clear natural perceptions, refuse the counsels of those who with the very breath of their warning would blight the wreath bound round the heads of the Muses' sons by a people's gratitude—who, in affected zeal for religion and morality, have so deeply violated the spirit of both, by vile misrepresentations, gross exaggeration, and merciless denunciations of the frailties of our common nature in illustrious men—men who, in spite of their aberrations, more or less deplorable, from the right path, were not only in their prevailing moods devout worshippers of virtue, but in the main tenor of their lives exemplary to their brethren. And such a man was Burns. In boyhood—youth—manhood—where such peasant as he? And if in trouble and in trial, from which his country may well turn in self-reproach, he stood not always fast, yet shame and sin it were, and indelible infamy, were she not now to judge his life as Christianity commands. Preyed upon, alas! by those anxieties for the sakes—even on account of the very means of subsistence—of his own household and his own hearth—yet was he in his declining, shall we call them disastrous years, on the whole faithful to the divine spirit with which it had pleased Heaven to endow him—on the whole obedient to its best inspirations; while he rejoiced to illumine the paths of poverty with light which indeed was light from heaven, and from an inexhaustible fancy, teeming to the genial warmth of the heart in midst of chill and gloom, continued to the very last to strew along the weary ways of this world flowers so beautiful in their freshness, that to eyes too familiar with tears they looked as if dropped from heaven.

These are sentiments with which I rejoice to hear the sympathy of this great assemblage thus unequivocally expressed—for my words but awaken thoughts lodged deep in all considerate hearts. For which of us is there in whom, known or unknown, alas! there is not much that needs to be forgiven? Which of us that is not more akin to Burns in his fleshly frailties than in his diviner spirit? That conviction regards not merely solemn and public celebrations of reverential memory—such as this; it pervades the tenor of our daily life, runs in our heart's blood, sits at our hearths, wings our loftiest dreams of human exaltation. How, on this earth, could we love, or revere, or emulate, if, in our contemplation of the human being, we could not sunder the noble, the fair, the gracious, the august, from the dregs of mortality, from the dust that hangs perishably about him the imperishable? We judge in love, and in love we may be judged. At our hearthsides, we gain more than we dared desire, by mutual mercy; at our hearthsides, we bestow and receive a better love, by this power of soft and magnanimous oblivion. We are ourselves the gainers, when thus we honour the great dead. They hear not—they feel not, excepting by an illusion of our own moved imaginations, which fill up chasms of awful, impassable separation; but we hear—we feel; and the echo of the acclaim which hills and skies have this day repeated, we can carry home in our hearts, where it shall settle down into the composure of love and pity, and admiration and gratitude, felt to be due for ever to our great poet's shade.

In no other spirit could genius have ever dared, in elegies and hymns, to seek to perpetuate at once a whole people's triumph, and a whole people's grief, by celebration of king, sage, priest, or poet, gone to his reward. From the natural infirmities of his meanest subject, what King was ever free? Against the golden rim that rounds his mortal temples come the same throbbings from blood in disease or passion hurrying from heart to brain, as disturb the aching head of the poor kind on his pallet of straw. But the king had been a guardian, a restorer, a deliverer; therefore his sins are buried or burned with his body; and all over the land he saved, generation after generation continues to cry aloud—"O king, live for ever!" The Sage, who, by loud meditation on man's nature and man's life, has seen how liberty rests on law, rights on obligations, and that his passions must be fettered, that his will be free—how often has he been overcome, when wrestling in agony with the powers of evil, in that seclusion from all trouble in which reverent admiration, nevertheless believes that wisdom for ever serenely dwells! The Servant of God, has he always kept his heart pure from the world, nor ever held up in prayer other than spotless hands? A humble confession of his own utter unworthiness would be his reply alike to scoffer and to him who believes. But unterrified by plague and pestilence, he had carried comfort unto houses deserted but by sin and despair; or he had sailed away, as he truly believed for ever, to savage lands, away from the quiet homes of Christian men—among whom he might have hoped to lead a life of peace, it may be of affluence and honour—for his Divine Master's sake, and for sake of them sitting in darkness and in the shadow of death. Therefore his name dies not, and all Christendom calls it blest. From such benefactors as these there may seem to be, but there is not, a deep descent to them who have done their service by what one of the greatest of them all has called "the vision and the faculty divine"—them to whom largely have been given the powers of fancy and imagination and creative thought, that they might move men's hearts, and raise men's souls, by the reflection of their own passions and affections in poetry, which is still an inspired speech. Nor have men, in their judgment of the true Poets, dealt otherwise with them than with patriot kings, benign legislators and holy priests. Them, too, when of the highest, all nations and ages have reverenced in their gratitude. Whatever is good and great in man's being seems shadowed in the name of Milton; and though he was a very man in the storms of civil life that shook down the throne at the shedding of the blood of kings, nevertheless, we devoutly believe with Wordsworth, that "His soul was like a star, and dwelt apart." But not of such as he only, who "in darkness, and with danger compassed round 'soared' beyond this visible diurnal sphere," and whose song was of mercy and judgment, have men wisely resolved to dwell only on what is pure and high and cognate with their thoughts of heaven. Still, as we keep descending from height to height in the regions of song, we desire to regard with love the genius that beautifies wherever it settles down; and if pity will steal in for human misfortunes, or for human frailties reproach, our love suffers no abatement, and religious men feel that there is piety in pilgrimage to such honoured graves. So feel we now at this commemoration. For our Poet we now claim the privilege, at once bright and austere, of death. We feel that our Burns is brought within the justification of all celebrations of human names; and that, in thus honouring his memory, we virtuously exercise the imaginative rights of enthusiasm owned by every people that has produced its great men.

And with a more especial propriety do we claim this justice in our triumphal celebration of poets, who like Burns, were led by the character of their minds to derive the matter and impulse of their song, in a stricter sense from themselves. For they have laid bare to all eyes many of their own weaknesses at the side of their higher and purer aspirations. Unreserved children of sincerity, by the very open-heartedness which is one great cause of their commanding power, and contagiously diffuses every zealous affection originating in their nobility of nature—by this grown to excess, made negligent of instinctive self defence, and heedless of mis-construction, or overcome by importunate and clinging temptations—to what charges have they not been exposed from that proneness to disparaging judgments so common in little minds! For such judgments are easy indeed to the very lowest understandings, and regard things that are visible to eyes that may seldom have commerced with things that are above. But they who know Burns as we know him know that by this sometimes unregulated and unguarded sympathy with all appertaining to his kind, and especially to his own order, he was enabled to receive into himself all modes of their simple, but not undiversified life, so that his poetry murmurs their loves and joys from a thousand fountains. And suppose—which was the case—that this unguarded sympathy, this quick sensibility, and this vivid capacity of happiness which the moment brings, and the frankness of impulse, and the strength of desire, and the warmth of blood, which have made him what he greatly is, which have been fire and music in his song, and manhood, and courage, and endurance, and independence in his life, have at times betrayed or over-mastered him—to turn against him all this self-painting and self-revealing, is it not ungrateful, barbarous, inhuman? Can he be indeed a true lover of his kind, who would record in Judgment against such a man words that have escaped him in the fervour of his pleading designed to uphold great causes dear to humanity?—who would ignobly strike the self-disarmed?—scornfully insult him who, kneeling at the Muses' confes-sional, whispers secrets that take wings and fly abroad to the uttermost parts of the earth? Can they be lovers of the people who do so? Who find it in their hearts true to think, and speak, and write of Robert Burns?—He who has reconciled poverty to its lot, toil to its taskwork, care to its burden—nay, I would say even—grief to its grave? And by one Immortal Song has sanctified for ever the poor man's Cot—by such a picture as only genius, in the inspiring power of piety, could have painted; has given enduring life to the image—how tender and how true!—of the Happy Night passing by sweet transition from this worky world into the Hallowed Day, by God's appointment breathing a heavenly calm over all Christian regions in their rest—nowhere else so profoundly—and may it never be broken!—as over the hills and valleys of our beloved, and yet religious land!

It cannot be said that the best biographers of Burns, and his best critics, have not done, or desired to do, justice to his character as well as to his genius; and, according as the truth has been more entirely and fearlessly spoken, has he appeared the nobler and nobler man. All our best poets too, have exultingly sung the worth, while they mourned the fate of him, the brightest of the brotherhood. But above, and below, and round about all that they have been uttering, has all along been heard a voice, which they who know how to listen for it can hear, and which has pronounced a decision in his favour not to be reversed; for on earth it cannot be carried to a higher tribunal. A voice heard of old on great national emergencies, when it struck terror into the hearts of tyrants, who quaked and quailed, and quitted for aye our land before "the unconquered Caledonian spear"—nor, since our union with noblest England, ever slack to join with her's and fervid Erin's sons, the thrice-repeated cry by which battle-fields are cleared; but happier, far happier to hear, in its low deep tone of peace. For them, it is like the sound of distant waterfalls, the murmur of summer woods, or the sea rolling in its rest. I mean the Voice of the People of Scotland—the Voice of her Peasantry and her Trades—of all who earn their bread by the sweat of their brow—her Working Men.

I presume not to draw their character. But this much I will say, that in the long run they know whom it is fitting they should honour and love. They will not be dictated to in their choice of the names that with them shall be household words. Never, at any period of their history, have they been lightly moved; but, when moved, their meaning was not to be mistaken; tenacious their living grasp as the clutch of death; though force may wrench the weapon from their hands, no force can wrench the worship from their hearts. They may not be conversant with our written annals; but in our oral traditions they are familiar with historic truths—grand truths conceived according to the People's idea of their own national mind, as their hearts have kindled in imagination of heroic or holy men. Imaginary, but real—for we all believe that men as good, as wise, as brave, have been amongst us as ever fancy fabled for a people's reverence. What manner of men have been their darlings? It would be hard to say; for their love is not exclusive—it is comprehensive. In the national memory live for ever characters how widely different!—with all the shades, fainter or darker, of human infirmity! For theirs is not the sickly taste that craves for perfection where no frailties are. They do not demand in one and the same personage inconsistent virtues. But they do demand sincerity, and integrity, and resolution, and independence, and an open front, and an eye that fears not to look in the face of day! And have not the grave and thoughtful Scottish people always regarded with more especial affection those who have struggled with adversity—who have been tried by temptations from without or from within—now triumphant, now overcome—but, alike in victory or defeat, testifying by their conduct that they were animated by no other desire so steadily as by love of their country and its people's good? Not those who have been favourites of fortune, even though worthy of the smiles in which they basked; but those who rose superior to fortune, who could not frown them down. Nor have they withheld their homage from the unfortunate in this world of chance and change, if, in abasement of condition, by doing its duties they upheld the dignity of their own nature, and looked round them on their honest brethren in poverty with pride.

And how will such a people receive a great National Poet? How did they receive Burns? With instant exaltation. At once, they knew of themselves, before critics and philosophers had time to tell them, that a great Genius of their own had risen, and they felt a sudden charm diffused over their daily life. By an inexplicable law, humour and pathos are dependent on the same constitution of mind; and in his Poems they found the very soul of mirth, the very soul of sadness, as they thought it good with him to be merry, or to remember with him, "that man was made to mourn." But besides what I have said of them, the people of Scotland hold in the world's repute—signally so—the name of a religious people. Many of them the descendants of the old covenanters, heirs of the stern zeal which took up arms for the purity of the national faith—still tinged, it may be, by the breath of the flame that then passed over the land—retain a certain serverity of religious judgment in questions of moral transgression, which is known to make a part of hereditary Scottish manners—especially in rural districts, where manners best retain their stamp. But the sound natural understanding of the Scottish peasant, I use the liberty to say, admits, to take their place at the side of one another, objects of his liberal and comprehensive regard, which might appear, to superficial observation and shallow judgment, to stand upon such different grounds, so that the approbation of the one should exclude the admiration of the other. But not so. Nature in him is various as it is vigorous. He does not, with an over-zealous scrutiny, vainly try to reduce into seeming consistency affections spontaneously springing from many sources. Truth lies at the bottom; and, conscious of truth, he does not mistrust or question his own promptings. An awful reverence, the acknowledgment of a Law without appeal or error—Supreme, Sacred, Irresistible—rules in his judgment of other men's actions, and of his own. Nevertheless, under shelter and sanction of that rule, he feels, loves, admires, like a man. Religion has raised and guards in him—it does not extinguish—the natural human heart. If the martyrs of his worship to him are holy—holy, too, are his country's heroes. And holy her poets—if such she have—who have sung—as during his too short life above them all sang Burns—for Scotland's sake. Dear is the band that ties the humbly educated man to the true national poet. To many in the upper classes he is, perhaps, but one among a thousand artificers of amusement who entertain and scatter the tedium of their idler hours. To the peasant the book lies upon his shelf a household treasure. There he finds depicted himself— his own works and his own ways. There he finds a cordial for his drooping spirits, nutriment for his wearied strength. Burns is his brother—his helper in time of need, when fretfulness and impatience are replaced with placidity by his strains, or of a sudden with a mounting joy. And far oftener than they who know not our peasantry would believe, before their souls awakened from torpor he is a

luminous and benign presence in the dark hut; for, in its purity and power, his best
poetry is felt to be inspired, and subordinate to the voice of heaven.

And will such a people endure to hear their own Poet wronged? No, no! Think
not to instruct them in the right spirit of judgment. They have read the Scriptures, perhaps, to better purpose than their revilers, and know better how to use
the lessons learned there, applicable alike to us all—the lessons, searching, and
merciful, which prescribe mutual judgment amongst beings, all, in the eye of absolute
Holiness and Truth, stained, erring, worthless: And none so well as aged religious
men in such dwellings know, from their own experience, from what they have
witnessed among their neighbours, and from what they have read of the lives of
good and faithful servants, out of the heart of what moral storms and shipwrecks,
that threatened to swallow the strong swimmer in the middle passage of life, has
often been landed safe at last, the rescued worshipper upon the firm land of quiet
duties, and of years exempt from the hurricane of the passions! Thus thoughtfully
guided in their opinion of him, who died young—cut off long before the period when
others, under the gracious permission of overruling mercy, have begun to redeem
their errors, and fortified perhaps by a sacred office, to enter upon a new life—they
will for ever solemnly cherish the memory of the Poet of the Poor. And in such
sentiments there can be no doubt but that all his countrymen share; who will,
therefore, rightfully hold out between Burns and all enemies a shield which clatter-
ing shafts may not pierce. They are proud of him, as a lowly father is proud of an
illustrious. The rank and splendour attained reflects glory down, but resolves not,
nor weakens one single tie.

Ay, for many a deep reason the Scottish people love their own Robert Burns.
Never was the personal character of poet so strongly and endearingly exhibited in
his song. They love him, because he loved his own order, nor ever desired for a
single hour to quit it. They love him because he loved the very humblest condition
of humanity, where everything good was only the more commended to his manly
mind by disadvantages of social position. They love him, because he saw with
just anger, how much the judgments of "silly coward man" are determined by such
accidents, to the neglect or contempt of native worth. They love him for his
independence. What wonder! To be brought into contact with rank and wealth—
a world inviting to ambition, and tempting to a thousand desires—and to choose
rather to remain lowly and poor, than seek an easier or a brighter lot, by courting
favour from the rich and great—was a legitimate ground of pride, if any ground of
pride be legitimate. He gave a tongue to this pride, and the boast is inscribed in
words of fire in the Manual of the Poor. It was an exuberant feeling, as all his
feelings were exuberant, and he let them all overflow. But sometimes, forsooth!
he did not express them in sufficiently polite or courteous phrase! And that too
was well. He stood up not for himself only, but for the great class to which he
belonged, and which in his days—and too often in ours—had been insulted by the
pride of superior station, when unsupported by personal merit, to every bold
peasant a thing of scorn. They love him, because he vindicated the ways of God to
man, by showing that there was more genius and virtue in huts, than was dreamt
of in the world's philosophy. They loved him for his truthful pictures of the poor.
Not there are seen slaves sullenly labouring, or madly leaping in their chains; but

in nature's bondage, content with their toil, sedate in their sufferings, in their recreations full of mirth—are seen Free Men. The portraiture, upon the whole is felt by us—and they know it—to demand at times pity as a due; but challenges always respect, and more than respect, for the condition which it glorifies. The Land of Burns! What mean we by the words? Something more, surely, than that Fortune, in mere blindness had produced a great poet here? We look for the inspiring landscape, and here it is; but what could all its beauties have availed, had not a people inhabited it possessing all the sentiments, thoughts, aspirations, to which nature willed to give a voice in him of her choicest melody? Nothing prodigious after all, in the birth of such a poet among such a people. Was anything greater in the son than the austere resignation of the father? In his humble compeers there was much of the same tender affection, sturdy independence, strong sense, self-reliance, as in him; and so has Scotland been prolific, throughout her lower orders, of men who have made a figure in her literature and her history; but to Burns nature gave a finer organization, a more powerful heart, and an ampler brain, imbued with that mystery called genius, and he stands forth conspicuous above all her sons.

From the character I have sketched of the Scottish people of old and at this day, it might perhaps be expected that much of her poetry would be of a stern, fierce, or even ferocious kind—the poetry of bloodshed and destruction. Yet not so. Ballads enow, indeed, there are, embued with the true warlike spirit—narrative of exploits of heroes. But many a fragmentary verse, preserved by its own beauty, survives to prove that gentlest poetry has ever been the produce both of heathery mountain and broomy brae; but the names of the sweet singers are heard no more, and the plough has gone over their graves. And they had their music too, plaintive or dirge-like, as it sighed for the absent, or wailed for the dead. The fragments were caught up, as they floated about in decay; and by him, the sweetest lyrist of them all, were often revivified by a happy word that let in a soul, or, by a few touches of his genius; the fragment became a whole, so exquisitely moulded, that none may tell what lines belong to Burns, and what to the poet of ancient days. They all belong to him now, for but for him they would have perished utterly; while his own matchless lyrics, altogether original, find the breath of life on the lips of a people who have gotten them all by heart. What a triumph of the divine faculty thus to translate the inarticulate language of nature into every answering modulation of human speech! And with such felicity, that the verse is now as national as the music! Throughout all these exquisite songs, we see the power of an element which we, raised by rank and education into ignorance, might not have surmised in the mind of the people. The love-songs of Burns are prominent in the poetry of the world by their purity. Love, truly felt and understood, in the bosom of a Scottish peasant, has produced a crowd of strains which are owned for the genuine and chaste language of the passion, by highly as well as by lowly born—by cultured and by ruder minds—that may charm in haughty saloons, not less than under smoke-blackened roofs. Impassioned beyond all the songs of passion, yet, in the fearless fervour of remembered transports, pure as hymeneals; and dear, therefore, for ever to Scottish maidens in hours when hearts are wooed and won; dear, therefore, for ever to Scottish matrons, who, at household work, are happy to hear them from their daughters' lips. And he, too, is the Poet of their friendships. At stanzas instinct with blythe and cordial amities, more brotherly the grasp of peasant's in peasant's toil-hardened hands! The kindliness of their nature, not chilled, though oppressed with care, how ready at his bidding—at the repeated air of a few exquisite but unsought-for words of his—to start up all alive! He is the Poet of all their humanities. His Daisy has made all the flowers of Scotland dear. His moorland has its wild inhabitants, whose cry is sweet. For sake of the old dumb fellow-servant which his farmer gratefully addresses on entering on another year of labour, how many of its kind have been fed or spared? In the winter storm 'tis useless to think of the sailor on his slippery shrouds; but the "outland eerie cattle" he teaches his feres to care for in the drifting snow. In what jocund strains he celebrates their amusements, their recreations, their festivals, passionately pursued with all their pith by a people in the business of life grave and determined as if it left no hours for play! Gait, dress, domicile, furniture, throughout all his poetry, are Scottish as their dialect; and sometimes, in the pride of his heart, he rejoices by such nationality to provoke some alien's smile. The sickle, the scythe, and the flail, the spade, the mattock, and the hoe, have been taken up more cheerfully by many a toil-worn cottar, because of the poetry with which Burns has invested the very implements of labour. Now and then, too, here and there peals forth the clangour of the war-trumpet. But Burns is not, in the vulgar sense, a military poet; nor are the Scottish, in a vulgar sense, a military people. He and they best love tranquil scenes and the secure peace of home. They are prompt for war, if war be needed,—no more. Therefore two or three glorious strains he has that call to the martial virtue quiescent in their bosoms—echoes from the warfare of their ancient self-deliverance—menacings—a prophetical *Nemo me impune lacessit*, should a future foe dare to insult the beloved soil. So nourishes his poetry all that is tender and all that is stern in the national character. So does it inspire his people with pride and contentment in their own peculiar lot; and as that is at once both poetical and practical patriotism, the poet who thus lightens and brightens it is the best of patriots.

I have been speaking of Burns as the poet of the country—his is the rural, the rustic muse. But we know well that the charm of his poetry has equal power for the inhabitants of towns and cities. Occupations, familiar objects, habitual thoughts, are indeed very different for the two great divisions of the people; and there is a brotherhood both of consanguinity and of lot. Labour—the hand pledged to constant toil—the daily support of life, won by its daily wrestle with a seemingly adverse but friendly necessity—in these they are all commoners with one another. He who cheers, who solaces, who inspirits, who honours, who exalts the lot of the labourer, is the poet alike of all the sons of industry. The mechanic who inhabits a smoky atmosphere, and in whose ear an unwholesome din from workshop and thoroughfare rings hourly, hangs from his rafter the caged linnet; and the strain that should gush free from blossomed or green bough, that should mix in the murmur of the brook, mixes in and consoles the perpetual noise of the loom or the forge. Thus Burns sings more especially to those whose manner of life he entirely shares; but he sings a precious memento to those who walk in other and less pleasant ways. Give then the people knowledge, without stint, for it nurtures the soul. But let us never forget, that the mind of man has other cravings—that it draws nourishment from thoughts, beautiful and tender, such as lay reviving dews on the drooping fancy, and are needed the more by him to whom they are not wafted fresh from the face of nature. This virtue of these pastoral and rural strains to penetrate and permeate conditions of existence different from those in which they had their origin, appears wheresoever we follow them. In the mine, in the dungeon, upon the great waters, in remote lands under fiery skies, Burns' poetry goes with his country-men. Faithfully portrayed, the image of Scotland lives there; and thus she holds, more palpably felt, her hand upon the hearts of her children, whom the constraint fortune or ambitious enterprise carries afar from the natal shores. Unrepining and unrepentant exiles, to whom the haunting recollection of hearth and field breathes in that dearest poetry, not with homesick sinkings of heart, but with home-invigorated hopes that the day will come when their eyes shall have their desire, and their feet again feel the greensward and the heatherbent of Scotland. Thus is there but one soul in this our great National Festival; while to swell the multitudes that from morning light continued flocking towards old Ayr, till at midday they gathered into one mighty mass in front of Burns' Monument, came enthusiastic crowds from countless villages and towns, from our metropolis, and from the great City of the West, along with the sons of the soil dwelling all round the breezy uplands of Kyle, and in regions that stretch away to the stormy mountains of Morven.

Sons of Burns! Inheritors of the name which we proudly revere, you claim in the glad solemnity which now unites us, a privileged and more fondly affectionate part. To the honour with which we would deck the memory of your father, your presence, and that of your respected relatives, nor less that of her (Jessie Lewars, now Mrs. Thomson of Dumfries), sitting in honour by their side, who, though not of his blood, did the duties of a daughter at his dying bed, give an impressive living reality; and while we pay this tribute to the poet, whose glory, beyond that of any other, we blend with the renown of Scotland, it is a satisfaction to us, that we pour not out our praises in the dull cold ear of death. Your lives have been past for many years asunder; and now that you are freed from the duties that kept you so long from one another, your intercourse, wherever and whenever permitted by your respective lots to be renewed, will derive additional enjoyment from the recollection of this day—a sacred day indeed to brothers, dwelling—even if apart—in unity and peace. And there is one whose warmest feelings, I have the best reason to know, are now with you and us, as well on your own account as for the sake of your great parent, whose character he respects as much as he admires his genius, though it has pleased Heaven to visit him with such affliction as might well deaden even in such a heart as his all satisfaction even with this festival. But two years ago, and James Burnes (cousin of the Poet) was the proud and happy father of three sons, all worthy of their race. One only (Dr. James Burnes) now survives, and may in due time return from India to be a comfort, if but for a short, a sacred season, to his old age! But Sir Alexander Burnes—a name that will not die—and his gallant brother (Charles) have perished, as all the world knows, in the flower of their life—foully murdered in (Cabool, India) a barbarous land. For them many eyes have wept; and their country, whom they served so faithfully, deplores them among her devoted heroes. Our sympathy may not soothe such grief as his; yet it will not be refused, coming to him along with our sorrow for the honoured dead. Such a father of such sons has far other consolations.

In no other way more acceptable to yourselves could I hope to welcome you, than by thus striving to give an imperfect utterance to some of the many thoughts and feelings that have been crowding into my mind and heart concerning your father. And I have felt all along that there was not only no impropriety in my doing so, after the address of our Noble Chairman, but that it was even the more required of me that I should speak in a kindred spirit, by that very address, altogether so worthy of his high character, and so admirably appropriate to the purpose of this memorable day. Not now for the first time, but many times, has he shown how well he understands the ties by which, in a country like this, men of high are connected with men of humble birth, and how amply he is endowed with the qualities that best secure attachment between the Castle and the Cottage. We rise to welcome you to your Father's Land.

Mr. Robert Burns replied in the following terms:

My lord, and ladies and gentlemen: You may be assured that the sons of Burns feel all that they ought to feel on an occasion so peculiarly gratifying to them, and on account of so nobly generous a welcome to the Banks of Doon. In whatever land they have wandered—wherever they have gone—they have invariably found a kind reception prepared for them by the genius and fame of their father; and under the providence of Almighty God, they owe to the admirers of his genius all that they have, and what competencies they now enjoy. We have no claim to attention individually—we are all aware that genius, and more particularly poetic genius, is not hereditary, and in this case the mantle of Elijah has not descended upon Elisha. The sons of Burns have grateful hearts, and will remember, so long as they live, the honour which has this day been conferred upon them by the noble and the illustrious of our own land, and many generous and kind spirits from other lands—some from the far West, a country composed of the great and the free, and altogether a kindred people. We beg to return our most heartfelt thanks to this numerous and highly respectable company for the honour which has been done us this day.

OTHER SPEAKERS WERE

Sir John McNeill, Bart. (1795-1883), British Diplomat.
Henry Glassford Bell (1803-1874), Poet and Judge.
Sir Archibald Alison (1792-1867), Author of *History of Europe*.
William Edmonstoune Aytoun (1813-1865), Poet and Humorist.
Sir David Hunter-Blair, Bart., of Blairquhan (-1857).
Colonel William Mure of Caldwell (1799-1860), Author.
Sir James Campbell, of Glasgow (1773-1845), British General.
Provost Miller of Ayr.
Lord David Boyle (1772-1853), President of the Scottish Court of Sessions.

XVII

Humour

BURNS, like true steel, was ever ready to give fire at the touch of the flint, and being present in a company where an ill-educated *parvenu* was boring every one by boasting of the many great people he had lately been visiting, the Poet gave vent to his feelings in the following impromptu stanza, which we may be sure effectively silenced the babbling snob before him:

> No more of your titled acquaintances boast,
> And in what lordly circles you've been;
> An insect is only an insect at most,
> Though it crawl on the curls of a queen.

His humour was irrepressible to the last. A little before his death an officer of volunteers, in whose company he had been an enthusiast, called on Burns. The Poet's last message was:

> When arranging about my funeral, dinna let the awkward squad fire owre me!

Having been storm-staid one Sunday at Lamington, in Clydesdale, the Poet went to church, but the day was so cold, the place so uncomfortable, and the sermon so poor, that he left this protest on the pew which he had occupied:

> As cauld a wind as ever blew,
> A caulder kirk, and in't but few;
> As cauld a preacher's ever spak'—
> Ye'll a' be het ere I come back.

303

Burns while in Edinburgh visited at the studio of a well-known painter, who was at the time engaged on a picture of Jacob's dream. Burns embodied his criticism of the work in the following lines, which he wrote on the back of a sketch still preserved in the painter's family:

> Dear—I'll gie ye some advice,
> You'll tak' it no uncivil;
> You shouldna paint at Angel's mair,
> But try and paint the devil.
> To paint an Angel's *kittle* wark,   *difficult*
> Wi' auld Nick there's less danger;
> You'll easy draw a *weel-kent* face,   *well-known*
> But no sae weel a stranger.

EPIGRAM ON BAD ROADS (1786)

> I'm now arrived, thanks to the Gods!
> Thro' pathways rough and muddy;—
> A certain sign that making roads
> Is not the people's study:
> And tho' I'm not with Scripture crammed,
> I'm sure the Bible says
> That heedless sinners shall be damned
> Unless they mend their ways.

THE HENPECKED HUSBAND (1784)

> Curs'd be the man, the poorest wretch in life,
> The crouching vassal to the tyrant wife,
> Who has no will but by her high permission;
> Who has not sixpence but in her possession;
> Who must to her his dear friend's secret tell;
> Who dreads a curtain-lecture worse than hell.
> Were such a wife had fallen to my part,
> I'd break her spirit, or I'd break her heart;
> I'd charm her with the magic of a switch,
> I'd kiss her maids, and kick the perverse bitch.

ON CAPTAIN FRANCIS GROSE (1790)

In a moment of festivity, Grose is said to have asked Burns to produce an epigram or epitaph on him. Burns eyed the Antiquarian for a moment, and then hurled the following at him amid roars of laughter.

The Devil got notice that Grose was a-dying,
So whip! at the summons, old Satan came flying;
But when he approached where poor Francis lay moaning,
And saw each bed-post with its burden a-groaning,
Astonish'd! confounded! cry'd Satan, "By ——!
"I'll want 'im, ere I take such a damnable load!"

EXTEMPORE IN THE COURT OF SESSION
Composed in 1787

Lord Advocate

He clench'd his pamphlets in his fist.	
He quoted and he hinted,	
Till in a declamation-mist,	
His argument he *tint* it;	*lost*
He gapèd for't, he grapèd for 't,	
He *fand* it was awa, man;	*found*
But what his common sense came short,	
He eke'd out wi' law, man.	

Mr. Erskine

Collected Harry stood *awee*	*a little time*
Then open'd out his arm, man;	
His lordship sat *wi' ruefu' e'e*,	*with rueful eye*
And eyed the gathering storm man:	
Like wind-driv'n hail it did assail,	
Or torrents *owre a linn*, man;	*over a waterfall*
The Bench *sae* wise, lift up their eyes,	*so*
Half-wauken'd wi the din, man.	

ON COMMISSARY GOLDIE'S BRAINS

Lord, to account who dares thee call,
Or e'er dispute thy pleasure?
Else why within so thick a wall
Enclose so poor a treasure?

ON BURNS' HORSE BEING IMPOUNDED

Was e'er poor poet sae befitted,
The maister drunk,—the horse committed;
Puir harmless beast! tak' thee nae care,
Thou'lt be a horse when he's nae mair (mayor).

KATHERINE JAFFRAY

He's tell'd her father and mother baith,
As I hear sindry say, O;
But he has na tell'd the lass hersel'
Till on her wedding day, O.

GREEN GROW THE RASHES

Auld Nature swears, the lovely dears,
Her noblest work she classes O;
Her prentice han' she tried on man,
An' then she made the lasses O.

EPITAPH ON JAMES GRIEVE LAIRD OF BOGHEAD, TARBOLTON
(Original Common-Place Book, 1784)

Here lies Boghead[1] amang the dead,
In hopes to get salvation;
But if such as he, in Heav'n may be,
Then welcome—hail! damnation.

This is the earliest sample of an extensive crop of like facetiæ which the author, to the close of his life, was fond of producing. It is not very complimentary to the poor laird who provoked it; yet, by adopting a very slight variation, the poet, in his Kilmarnock volume, converted this quatrain into a rich compliment to his friend, Gavin Hamilton, thus:

The poor man weeps—here Gavin sleeps,
Whom canting wretches blamed;
But with such as he, where'er he be,
May I be saved or damned!

EPITAPH ON WILLIAM HOOD, SENR., IN TARBOLTON
(Kilmarnoch Edition, 1786)

Here *Souter* Hood in death does sleep;	*shoemaker*
To hell if he's *gane* thither,	*gone*
Satan, gie him thy *gear* to keep;	*cash*
He'll *haud* it weel *thegether*.	*hold; together*

The poet printed this with the title, "On a Celebrated Ruling Elder." One of the Tarbolton elders provoked the poet's hostility—not by his hypocrisy, but by his extreme penuriousness. The epitaph is recorded in the Commonplace-Book, under date April, 1784.

[1]Boghead lies upwards of a mile due west from Lochlea, and near Adamhill.

LINES ON THE AUTHOR'S DEATH

Written with the supposed view of being handed to John Rankine after the Poet's interment.

(Stewart, 1801)

> He who of Rankine sang, lies stiff and dead,
> And a green grassy hillock hides his head;
> Alas! Alas! A devilish change indeed.

These lines must be regarded as a counterpart to the poet's elegy on himself, composed shortly afterwards, beginning:

> Now Robin lies in his last lair,
> He'll gabble rhyme and sing nae mair.

WRITTEN TO A GENTLEMAN

Who had Sent the Poet a Newspaper and Offered to Continue It Free of Expense

Chambers considers that this jocular rhyming epistle was addressed in Feb., 1790, to Peter Stuart, editor of the *Star* newspaper, London, to whom the poet had previously "sent various contributions in prose and verse." The closing couplet does not mean that he returns the paper to the sender; but that he gratefully sends back a rhyming abstract of the news. The text shows, moreover, that he had read the paper to some purpose; for his summary of the history of Europe at that period is most comprehensive and correct.

Kind Sir, I've read your paper through,	
And faith, to me 'twas really new!	
How guess'd ye, sir, what *maist* I wanted?	*most*
This *mony* a day I've *graned and gaunted*	*many; groaned and grunted*
To *ken* what French mischief was brewin;	*know*
Or what the *drumlie* Dutch were doin';	*confused*
That vile *doup-skelper*, Emperor Joseph	*one that strikes the breech*
If Venus yet had got his nose off;	
Or how the *collieshangie* works	*quarrelling*
Atween the Russians and the Turks;	*between*
Or if the Swede, before he halt	
Would play *anither* Charles the *Twalt*	*another; Twelfth*
If Denmark, anybody *spak'o't;*	*did speak of it*
Or Poland, *wha* had now the *tack o't;*	*who; slight hold of it*
How cut-throat Prussian blades were *hingin*	*hanging*
How *libbet* Italy was singin';	*castrated*

If Spaniard, Portuguese, or Swiss,
Were sayin' or takin' aught amiss:
Or how our merry lads at *hame*   *home*
In Britain's court, kept up the game;
How Royal George—the Lord *leuk o'er him!*   *look over him*
Was managing St. Stephen's quoram
If *sleekit* Chatham Will was livin',   *cunning*
Or *glaikit* Charlie got his *nieve* in;   *foolish; fist*
How Daddie Burke the plea was cookin',
If Warren Hastings' neck was *yeukin';*   *itching*
How *cesses, stents,* and fees were *raxed,*   *taxes; rates; stretched*
Or if bare—yet were taxed;
The news o' princes, dukes, and earls,
Pimps, sharpers, bawds and opera-girls;
If that daft buckie, Geordie Wales,
Was *threshin'* still at *hizzies'* tails;   *thrashing; young women's*
Or if he was grown *oughtlins douser*   *of necessity more prudent*
And no' a perfect *kintra cooser;*   *country stallion*
A' this and *mair* I never heard of,   *more*
And but for you I might despaired of:
So gratefu', back your news I send you,
And pray, *a' gude* things may attend you!   *all good*

[Ellisland, Monday morning, 1790]

XVIII

Memories of Burns: Dorothy Wordsworth and Her Brother, William

When DOROTHY WORDSWORTH
toured Scotland with her poet brother, William Wordsworth (1770-
1850), her keen observant eyes noted every detail of the journey
which she carefully wrote down in her diary. A visit to the home
and grave of Burns, shortly after his death, gives a vivid description
of the great Scottish Bard's surroundings.

This is what Miss Wordsworth has written about "poor Burns":

Went to the churchyard where Burns is buried. A book-seller accompanied us. He showed us the outside of Burns' house, where he had lived
the last three years of his life and where he died. It has a mean appearance,
and is in a bye situation, whitewashed; dirty about the doors; flowering
plants in the windows. . . . Mrs. Burns was gone to spend some
time by the seashore, with the children. We spoke to the servant-maid at
the door, who invited us forward, and we sat down in the parlour. The
walls were coloured with a blue wash; on one side of the fire was a mahogany
desk, opposite to the window a clock, and over the desk, a print from the
"Cotter's Saturday Night," which Burns mentions in one of his letters
having received as a present.

The house was cleanly and neat in the inside, the stairs of stone, scoured
white, the kitchen on the right side of the passage, the parlour on the left.
In the room above the parlour the poet died and his son after him in the
same room. We were glad to leave Dumfries which is no agreeable place
to them who do not love the bustle of a town that seems to be rising up to
wealth. We could think of little else but poor Burns and his moving
about on that unpoetic ground.

Upon visiting the grave, Dorothy Wordsworth states that "there was no stone to mark the spot; but a hundred guineas have been collected to be expended on some sort of monument."

Standing there by this humble grave, Dorothy and William Wordsworth repeated to one another Burns' own verses:

> Is there a man whose judgment clear
> Can others teach the course to steer,
> Yet runs himself life's mad career
>   Wild as the wave?
> Here pause, and thro' the starting tear,
>   Survey this grave.
>
> The poor inhabitant below
> Was quick to learn and wise to know,
> And keenly felt the friendly glow
>   And softer flame;
> But thoughtless follies laid him low,
>   And stain'd his name.

The years have passed, that name is numbered among the great immortals and gilded with the light of beloved memory which will never fade in the hearts of Scotland's worthy sons and daughters.

XIX

Memories of Burns: Sir Walter Scott

$\mathcal{S}$HORTLY AFTER Burns' arrival in Edinburgh Sir Walter Scott met him at Dr. Adam Ferguson's home, and gives his recollections in a letter to Mr. Lockhart:

I was a lad of fifteen, in 1786-1787, when he first came to Edinburgh, but had sense and feeling enough to be much interested in his poetry, and would have given the world to know him; but I had very little acquaintance with any literary people, and still less with the gentry of the west country, the two sets whom he most frequented. Mr. Thomas Grierson was at that time a clerk of my father's. He knew Burns, and promised to ask him to his lodgings to dinner, but had no opportunity to keep his word; otherwise I might have seen more of the distinguished man. As it was, I saw him one day at the late venerable Professor Ferguson's, where there were several gentlemen of literary reputation, among whom I remember the celebrated Mr. Dugald Stewart. Of course we youngsters sat silent, looked, and listened. The only thing I remember, which was remarkable in Burns' manner, was the effect produced upon him by a print of Bunbury's representing a soldier lying dead on the snow, his dog sitting in misery on one side—on the other, his widow, with a child in her arms. These lines were written beneath:

> Cold on Canadian hills, or Minden's plain,
> Perhaps that parent wept her soldier slain;
> Bent o'er her babe, her eye dissolved in dew,
> The big drops mingling with the milk he drew,
> Gave the sad presage of his future years,
> The child of misery baptized in tears.

Burns seemed much affected by the print, or rather the idea which it suggested to his mind. He actually shed tears. He asked whose the lines were, and it chanced (but nobody but myself remembered), that they occur in a half-forgotten poem of Langhorne's, called by the unpromising title of "The Justice of Peace." I whispered my information to a friend present, who mentioned it to Burns, who rewarded me with a look and a word, which, though of mere civility, I then received, and still recollect, with very great pleasure.

His person was strong and robust; his manners rustic, not clownish; a sort of dignified plainness and simplicity, which received part of its effect, perhaps, from one's knowledge of his extraordinary talents. His features are represented in Mr. Nasmyth's picture; but to me it conveys the idea that they are diminished, as if seen in perspective. I think his countenance was more massive than it looks in any of the portraits. I would have taken the poet had I not known what he was, for a very sagacious country farmer of the old Scotch school; i.e. none of your modern agriculturists, who keep labourers for their drudgery, but the douce gudeman who held his own plough. There was a strong expression of sense and shrewdness in all his lineaments; the eye alone, I think, indicated the poetical character and temperament. It was large, and of dark cast, which glowed (I say literally glowed) when he spoke with feeling or interest. I never saw such another eye in a human head, though I have seen the most distinguished men of my time.

His conversation expressed perfect self-confidence, without the slightest presumption. Among the men who were the most learned of their time and country, he expressed himself with perfect firmness, but without the least intrusive forwardness; and when he differed in opinion, he did not hesitate to express it firmly, yet at the same time with modesty. I do not remember any part of his conversation distinctly enough to be quoted; nor did I ever see him again, except in the street, where he did not recognize me, as I could not expect he should. He was much caressed in Edinburgh, but (considering what literary emoluments have been since his day) the efforts made for his relief were extremely trifling.

I remember, on this occasion, I thought Burns' acquaintance with English poetry was rather limited, and also, that having twenty times the abilities of Allan Ramsay and of Ferguson, he talked of them with too much humility as his models; there was, doubtless national predilection in his estimate.

This is all I can tell you about Burns. I have only to add, that his dress corresponded with his manner. He was like a farmer dressed in his best to dine with the laird. I do not speak in a *malam partem*, when I say, I never saw a man in company with his superiors in station and information, more perfectly free from either the reality or the affectation of embarrassment. I was told, but did not observe it, that his address to females was extremely deferential, and always with a turn either to the pathetic or humorous, which engaged their attention particularly.   I have heard the late Duchess of Gordon remark this.   I do not know anything I can add to these recollections of forty years since.

XX

Tributes

BURNS HAS BEEN HAILED as one
of the immortals. Far beyond the confines of his native Scotia has
the fame of the National Bard extended. Burns has been widely
acclaimed as one of the world's great souls, and the most effective
poetic voice that the cause of world brotherhood and international
peace has ever found, and one whom men delight to honour. Men
and women of various nationalities have vied with one another in
heaping praise upon the Peasant Poet of Scotland, and have not
hesitated to link his name with the most famous of mankind.

When William Burns confided to the Poet's mother his paternal
expectations of the future greatness of their eldest born, or when
the Poet himself made to his Jean the prediction that a day would
come when his place as a poet would receive a juster recognition, there
did not seem too much ground for such anticipations; but the series
of tributes which follow show that these hopes of future fame were
not, after all, so ill-founded or extravagant.

		PAGE
MME. JULIETTE LAMBER ADAM	1836-1936 (French)	367
SIR ARCHIBALD ALISON	1757-1839	365
DR. HARRY B. ANDERSON (Toronto)	1868-	377
AUGUSTE JEAN ANGELLIER	1848-1911 (French)	367
SIR ALFRED AUSTIN	1835-1913	350
LORD (ARTHUR JAMES) BALFOUR	1848-1930	353, 365
HUBERT STEWART BANNER	1891-	359, 365
AMELIA EDITH HUDDLESTON BARR	1831-1919	336
HENRY WARD BEECHER	1813-1887 (U.S.A.)	349-350

		PAGE
HENRY GLASSFORD BELL	1803-1874	354
ENOCH ARNOLD BENNETT	1867-1931	337
PIERRE JEAN BÉRANGER	1780-1857 (French)	274
PROFESSOR JOHN STEWART BLACKIE	1809-1895	353
JAMES GILLESPIE BLAINE	1830-1893 (U.S.A.)	363
LEON PAUL BLOUET (MAX O'RELL)	1848-1903 (French)	356
SIR DAVID BRAND	1837-1908	361
GEORG MORRIS-COHEN BRANDES	1842-1927 (Danish)	362
LORD (HENRY PETER) BROUGHAM	1778-1868	366
JOHN BROWN, M.D.	1810-1882	368
SIR JAMES CRICHTON-BROWNE	1840-1938	340
ROBERT BROWNING	1812-1889	324
WILLIAM JENNINGS BRYAN	1860-1925 (U.S.A.)	349
WILLIAM CULLEN BRYANT	1794-1878 (U.S.A.)	350
COLONEL JAMES GLENCAIRN BURNS	1794-1865	327
COLONEL WILLIAM NICOL BURNS	1791-1872	327
BURNS CENTENARY (1859)		326
Burnsiana, 1892 (J. D. ROSS)		357
LORD BYRON	1788-1824	352
ROBERT BURNS	1786-1857	302
GIOSUE CARDUCCI	1802-1871 (Italian)	337
THOMAS CARLYLE	1795-1881	369, 185
ALEXANDER CARMICHAEL, LL.D.	1833-1912	1
ANDREW CARNEGIE	1835-1919	342
JOSEPH CHAMBERLIN	1836-1914	339
ROBERT CHAMBERS	1802-1871	4
WILLIAM CHAMBERS	1800-1883	4
CHANG-YON-TONG (June 13, 1904)	(Chinese)	334
GILBERT KEITH CHESTERTON	1874-1936	347
LUIGI CHIARINI	1789-1834 (Italian)	353
JULES ARESENE ARNAND CLARETIE	1840-1913 (French)	368
RICHARD COBDEN	1804-1865	352
PRESIDENT HENRY JOHN CODY (University of Toronto)	1868-	320
SAMUEL TAYLOR COLERIDGE	1772-1834	368
REV. DR. FRANK WILLARD COURT	1875- (U.S.A.)	354
HON. SAMUEL SULLIVAN COX	1824-1889 (U.S.A.)	362
PROFESSOR GEORGE LILLIE CRAIK	1798-1868	357
ROBERT HARTLEY CROMEK	1770-1812	337
DR. JAMES CURRIE	1756-1805	137, 139
GEORGE WILLIAM CURTIS	1824-1892 (U.S.A.)	335
ALPHONSE DAUDET	1840-1897 (French)	356
RT. REV. JAMES B. DOLLARD (Toronto)	1872-	324
SIR ARTHUR CONAN DOYLE	1859-1930	357
PROFESSOR HENRY DRUMMOND	1851-1897	360
WILLIAM JAMES DUNLOP (Toronto)	1881-	322
GEORGES EEKOUD	1854-1927 (Flemish)	353
ELIZABETH, QUEEN OF ROUMANIA	1843-1916	351
EARL OF EGLINTON (13TH EARL)	1812-1861	289
EBENEZER ELLIOTT	1781-1849	351
RALPH WALDO EMERSON	1803-1882 (U.S.A.) 348, 364	
EDWARD FITZGERALD	1809-1883	335
ANTONIO FOGAZZARO	1842-1910 (Italian)	354
GEORGE WILLIAM FOOTE	1850-1915	325
ARCHDEACON J. B. FOTHERINGHAM (Toronto)	1879-	318

PAGE

CHARLES JAMES FOX 1749-1806   339
DUNCAN CAMERON FRASER (Nova Scotia) 1845-1910   368
SARAH MARGARET FULLER (Countess Ossoli) . . . . . 1810-1850 (U.S.A.)   363
SENATOR WILLIAM PIERCE FYRE . . . . 1831-1911 (U.S.A.)   364
W. B. GARDNER (MAX PHILPOT)   352
JAMES ABRAM GARFIELD . . . . 1831-1881 (U.S.A.)   349
GUISEPPE GARIBALDI . . . . 1807-1882 (Italian) 353
THOMAS A. GILLEN (Toronto) 1869-   30
W. KING GILLIES, M.A., LL.D. (Edinburgh, 1938)   90
WILLIAM EWART GLADSTONE 1809-1898   365
VON JOHAN WOLFGANG GOETHE . . . . 1749-1832 (German)   363
ARTURO GRAF . . . . 1848-1913 (Italian) 337
JAMES GRAY 1770-1830   366
HORACE GREELY . . . . 1811-1872 (U.S.A.)   350
WILLIAM GUNNYON   355
SIR JOHN ALEXANDER HAMMERSTON 1871-   359
NATHANIEL HAWTHORNE . . . . 1804-1864 (U.S.A.)   359
WILLIAM HAZLITT 1778-1830   180
HANS HECHT 1876-   (German)   347
EMMANUEL HEIL . . . . 1834-1899 (Flemish) 356
HON. GEORGE F. HOAR . . . . 1826-1904 (U.S.A.)   359
OLIVER WENDELL HOLMES . . . . 1809-1894 (U.S.A.) 347, 354
ROBERT GREEN INGERSOLL . . . . 1833-1899 (U.S.A.) 358, 360
REV. DR. JOHN GIBSON INKSTER (Toronto) 1867-   323
A. BAINE IRVINE   90
LORD (FRANCIS) JEFFREY 1773-1850   364
MAURUS JOKAI . . . . 1825-1904 (Hungarian) 362
JOHN KEATS 1795-1821   337
LORD KELVIN 1824-1907   363
REV. DR. H. BEVERLEY KETCHEN (Hamilton, Ont.) 1872-   326
CHARLES KINGSLEY 1819-1875   357
JAMES PROCTOR KNOTT . . . . 1830-1911 (U.S.A.)   361
LAJOS KOSSUTH . . . . 1802-1894 (Hungarian) 356
CHARLES LAMB 1775-1834   364
THOMAS C. LATTO   358
HON. FRANCIS ROBERT LATCHFORD (Toronto) 1853-1938   325
SIR HARRY LAUDER 1870-   339
SIR WILFRID LAURIER 1841-1919   180
RICHARD LE GALLIENE 1866-   352
ABRAHAM LINCOLN . . . . 1809-1865 (U.S.A.)   363
JOHN GIBSON LOCKHART 1794-1854   337-8, 368
HENRY WADSWORTH LONGFELLOW . . . . 1807-1882 (U.S.A.)   348
JAMES RUSSELL LOWELL . . . . 1819-1891 (U.S.A.)   362
LORD LYTTON (BULWER-LYTTON) 1803-1873   348
HUGH MACDONALD 1817-1860   347
JAMES RAMSAY MACDONALD 1866-1937   362
CHARLES MACKAY 1814-1889   324
ALEXANDER M'LACHLAN (Toronto) 1818-1896   333
REV. DR. NORMAN MACLEOD 1812-1872   358
KUNO MEYER . . . . 1858-1919 (German) 354
HUGH MILLER 1802-1856   335
MARY RUSSELL MITFORD 1786-1855   358
LORD (JOHN) MORLEY 1838-1923   351
HENRY VOLLAM MORTON 1892-   348

PAGE

WILLIAM HENRY HARRISON MURRAY . . . . 1840-1904 (U.S.A.) 363
LORD (CHARLES NEATE) NEAVES 1800-1876 335
JOHN NESS (Toronto) 1883- 321
THOMAS POWER O'CONNOR ("TAY-PAY") 1848-1929 353
MRS. MARGARET OLIPHANT 1828-1897 335
MARIO PILO . . . . 1859-1920 (Italian) 355
WILLIAM PITT 1759-1806 350
WILLIAM POWER 1873- 345
SIR HENRY RAEBURN, R.A. 1756-1823 127
PETER ROSS 1847-1902 74
WILLIAM ROBERTSON 1721-1793 350
LORD ROSEBERY 1847-1929 369
WILLIAM MICHAEL ROSSETTI 1829-1919 366
JOHN DAWSON ROSS 1853- 357
JOHN RUSKIN 1819-1900 348
EDMOND HENRY ADOLPHE SCHERER . . . . 1815-1889 (French) 356
SIR WALTER SCOTT 1771-1832 311, 339
The Scotsman (1892) 367
J. STEWART SEGGIE (Sunderland, 1938) 351
PROFESSOR WILLIAM YOUNG SELLER 1825-1890 354
REV. RICHARD SKIPSEY (Sunderland, 1859) 329
ALEXANDER SMITH 1830-1867 360
GRANT F. O. SMITH (Toronto) 1877- 325
REV. DR. WALTER CHALMERS SMITH 1824-1908 355
S.M.T. Magazine (January, 1936) 349
PROFESSOR FRANKLYN BLISS SNYDER . . . . 1884- (U.S.A.) 336
WILLIAM THOMAS STEAD 1849-1912 351
ROBERT LOUIS STEVENSON 1850-1890 338
ALGERNON CHARLES SWINBURNE 1837-1909 352
HIPPOLYTE ADOLPHE TAINE . . . . 1828-1893 (French) 323
REV. DR. THOMAS DE WITT TALMADGE . . . . 1832-1902 (U.S.A.) 336
ROBERT TANNAHILL 1774-1810 336
JAMES BAYARD TAYLOR . . . . 1825-1878 (U.S.A.) 350
ALFRED, LORD TENNYSON 1809-1892 363
JOSEPH THOMAS . . . . 1811-1891 (U.S.A.) 361
A. A. THOMSON 1894- 364
FRANCIS THOMPSON 1859-1907 366
QUEEN VICTORIA 1819-1901 276
REV. DR. PETER HATELY WADDELL . . . . 1817-1891 (U.S.A.) 365
WILHELM RICHARD WAGNER . . . . 1813-1883 (German) 352
DR. WILLIAM WALLACE 1860- 366
W. STEWART WATSON 1800-1880 76
THE RIGHT REV. LAUGHLAN MACLEAN WATT 1867- 151
ALEXANDER WEBSTER 1707-1784 336
WALTER (WALT) WHITMAN . . . . 1819-1892 (U.S.A.) 350
JOHN GREENLEAF WHITTIER . . . . 1807-1892 (U.S.A.) 361
JAMES WILKIE, B.L. 366
WILLIAM WILL (London, 1918) 53
SIR DANIEL WILSON 1816-1892 330
GENERAL JAMES GRANT WILSON . . . . 1832-1914 (U.S.A.) 338
PROFESSOR JOHN WILSON 1785-1854 291, 335
WILLIAM WORDSWORTH 1770-1850 356, 368
DUDLEY WRIGHT 1868- 355

1

"Is the Burns' cult ending?" was the headline in a literary journal that caught my eye as I was starting out for a summer holiday at Murray Bay on the St. Lawrence River. I did not read what followed but there flashed into my mind the Auld Brig's taunt of the New Brig in the "Brigs of Ayr": "I'll be a brig when ye're a shapeless cairn," and that is exactly how I feel when I read "new" poetry—much of it "the crazed creations of misguided whim." I had proof within myself and within my packed trunk that the Cult of Burns could not end. I am not yet sixty but for fifty years of that sixty the shrine of Robert Burns has found me kneeling there year in and year out and of the two or three books chosen to be the companions of my vacation the one inevitable companion was "The Poems of Robert Burns." Sentiment? I am not ashamed of sentiment: it is sentiment and not reason that makes the wheels of life go round and while I am prepared to break a lance with any critic regarding the art and technique of Burns as a lyric poet I plead guilty to a worship that may be as blind as that of a religious devotee but as satisfying as springs of water in a dry and thirsty land.

The years confirm my critical judgment: life itself—its tears and tragedies, confirms my emotional appreciation. A. E. Housman, in his *Art of Poetry*, speaks of the making of poetry as a "physical" sensation; I add that the reading of Burns' poetry—especially when read aloud—has always given me physical reactions. At times it is as when a great ship plunges deeper and ever deeper into the trough of the sea and there comes a deeper sinking within—the breath held tense, the pain in the pit of the stomach—the sense of unescapable doom. Can you explain the tremulous awe that presses the brain and thrills the body as the soul when Bach's Mass is sung? It is as easy or difficult to explain the "pins and needles," the uncanny throb of heart and tingling of spine when reading Burns. Can you explain the reaction—the physical reaction—that comes when you read:

> Had we never loved sae kindly,
> Had we never loved sae blindly,
> Never met—or never parted
> We had ne'er been broken-hearted

or the sheer sense of rollicking dancing delight "when neist outspak a raucle carlin'"

> A Highland lad my love was born
> The Lawland laws he held in scorn;

the feet dance, the hands are flung high in the air: it is a world of motion.

But why emphasize the bodily sensation when the appeal to other senses is so poignant? Burns has an instinct for the nuances of beauty that is unerring. There is the beauty that comes of contrast:

> How can ye chant, ye little birds,
> And I sae weary, fu' o' care.

There is the delicacy of the eye of the artist that notes "the *crimson-tipped* flower"; of the ear that discriminates the breeze: "Of a' the airts the wind can blow I dearly loe the West"; of the soul that raptures in colour: "My luve is like a red red rose that's newly sprung in June." There are native poets *and* native poets but give me Burns as guide and interpreter: "While waters wimple to the sea," "the dewy flowers," "the tuneful birds," "the woodbine twine," "There wild woods grow, and rivers row and monie a hill between" create a landscape of beauty, shot through with emotions of love, of pity, of tragedy. "The simmer first unfauld her robes" for the worshipper of Nature; "The gay, green birk," "the hawthorn's blossom," "the waters never drumlie" reward the kneeling spirit.

But as a true lyric poet he gives not only the scene but sets in the foreground or background human emotion of which he plumbs the depths. In 1938 we live in a strange world listening to the clash of nations, beholding the arrogance of wealth and of power and hearing ever the sorrowful sighing of the poor. In the last half of the eighteenth century the sensitive heart of Burns was stirred by the strange winds of his own day and his poetry catches its music. Born in poverty, reared in adversity, wrestling from the unwilling soil a scanty living he kept his own soul and dared to sing the simple annals of the poor. Seduced on occasion by wealth and society, he knew the true worth of man ("See yon birkie ca'd a lord") though himself was born in a clay biggin' and clad in hoddin grey. I do not know that had Burns lived to-day he would have sung the "Red International" but he is the uncrowned King of the common folk and will remain the seer and prophet of the day when "man to man the war'd o'er shall brithers be for a' that." A lover of his own land he gave the Scot his battle-hymn, "Scots wha hae," but the deep diapason of one of its stanzas could be transmuted into a battle-hymn of humanity: "By oppression's woes and pains, by your sons in servile chains, we will drain our dearest veins, but they shall be free."

But what of the man himself, his character, the things by which he lived? The life of a poet need not be a cudgel to belay the poet, yet how often has this been done and in the case of Burns none more so. "Rantin', rovin' Robin." Yes! But what of his service to truth and to religion? "All hail Religion! Maid divine! To stigmatize false friends of thine, can ne'er defame thee." R. L. Stevenson has said he "was not devoted to

religion, he was haunted by it" but what a servant of the Lord he was in
exposing Holy Willies, or ridding the theology of his day of its God,—

> Wha in the heavens dost dwell
> Wha', as it pleases best Thysel,
> Sends ane to heaven, and ten to hell
> A' for Thy glory
> And no for ony guid or ill
> They've done afore Thee.

and of the positive side of giving to the world in "The Cotter's Saturday
Night" the beauty and stability of "a correspondence fix'd wi' heaven."
A mixture of dirt and deity he was undoubtedly but are not we all? If
he was at times the scandal of the world, was he not at times the glory of
the world? In the fire-burnt areas about Murray Bay the first flower
that raises its head is the "Fire-weed"—a brilliant red bloom challenging
the avid blackness around it and from the ground of Burns' life there springs
the beauty of a soul unconquerable in life and tragically triumphant even
in death.

But why go further? He has written his own epitaph: "leave the fire
ashes, what survives is gold." A "helpless smoke of words" comes
between Burns and the men and women of succeeding generations but
through the smoke there is an altar sacred to the heart of every Scot,
where Burns is high and lifted up. I could write as a critic and argue
that he is the greatest of all lyric poets, I prefer to write as a devotee. I
would rather lose a library of lyrics than part with "To Mary in Heaven."
His songs will live

> Till a' the seas gang dry, my dear
> And the rocks melt wi' the sun.

—VEN. ARCHDEACON J. B. FOTHERINGHAM, Toronto.
(Written for this book, July, 1938.)

2

That Burns commemorations occur year by year is itself a marvel. So
is fulfilled Burns' own prophecy that people would think more of him a
hundred years later than they did in his lifetime.

1. He was a true patriot, loving his own country, yet not despising other
countries. He made a contribution to the restoration and upbuilding
of a worthy national sentiment in Scotland.

2. He was a broad humanitarian. In him, as in all great poets, there
is a universal element, an appeal to what is deepest in every man. He
sought to awaken the sense of human brotherhood, of the unity and dignity
of human nature. Even the animals fell under his kindly care and observa-

tion. He was a teacher of democracy in its noblest form, based on the intrinsic worth of man, which in turn is based on man's kinship to God. Respecting man as man, he worthily interpreted the life of the common people. Among his themes were the thoughts, feelings and manners of the Scottish peasantry, their virtues and their vices.

3. His love of nature was simple and intense. With clear eye and responsive heart, he painted it without subtlety as the background of his pictures of human life and character.

He represents the age-long warfare between the flesh and the spirit. The contradiction between noble gifts and actual life represents a painful, yet not uncommon human tragedy. On the one side is a man with a noble nature, with singular endowments of head and heart, with strong intellectual force, broad sympathy and tender sensibility. On the other side is a fierce and passionate lower nature, hard to restrain and fatal to indulge. Between these contrasted natures is a will too weak, too irresolute to obey the voice of conscience. He "sees the better and approves it, but he follows the worse" (as the Roman poet Ovid phrases this human situation). Burns is not one of Scotland's saints; to try to canonize him is to provoke a counter-verdict. We know his defects; but it is not ours to judge him. "What's done we partly may compute, we know not what's resisted." Let us, human beings, judge him by his best, not by his worst, even while we do not forget the warning of his weakness. "Thoughtle s folly laid him low and stained his name."

5. He was not one of Scotland's religious teachers, yet he expressed the fundamental truths of national religion—belief in God and in the immortality of the soul. He emphasized the difference between right and wrong; and with righteous indignation lashed hypocrisy and inhumanity. With humour he portrayed the incongruities of life and with satire scorched its shams.

6. If "the greatest thing possessed by any nation is its own rendering of the universal heart of man," then Scotland found its fullest utterance in the songs and poetry of Robert Burns.

—Canon H. J. Cody, Rector of St. Paul's Church, Toronto.
(Now, 1940, President of the University of Toronto, spoken at the meeting of the Burns Literary Society, Toronto, January 25, 1918.)

3

With the lave o' Scotsmen I have made the pilgrimage to Burns' Cottage; I've gaped at the scenes he immortalized, I've sat in his "neuk" and stood by his grave as a matter of course; I sang a boyish alto to his love-songs at school and recited his verses with great gusto and little comprehension in later years.

But I had to travel 3,000 miles to appreciate him.

Perhaps it's not to be wondered at. Few there were who realized the beauty of the mountain daisy till Burns painted it for them: to most folks field-mice were vermin till he endowed one of them with an ego; the menial tasks of the farm and the home became votive offerings of thankful hearts to the great God of all creation when he wove his magic spell about them; commonplace sights and scenes glowed in the sunlight of his sympathetic touch and the mean, the false and the vile shrivelled and died under his caustic pen.

So he ministers to the expatriated Scot. We span the ocean and wander again by some crystal stream which he calls "Afton" but which we know by many another name; we take the road over the hill, careless of the weather, to just such a trysting place as he describes; we plight our troth or say our tender farewells under the green birk or hawthorn blossom where he met and parted with "Highland Mary"; we put our finger on some "Holy Willie" of our own acquaintance, or kneel in some humble cot for family worship as the Priest of our now-scattered household commends us to the Eternal care.

Time may dim such memories; new interests may intrude; the busy world may claim our attention to the exclusion of sentiment and romance, but, when we sit down to re-read or recall Burns, the flood-gates are opened and there pours over us a healing and cleansing spate of remembrance which carries us back to the rock from whence we are hewn.

Robert Burns is loved at home, but he is revered abroad.

—JOHN NESS.
(Toronto, August 5, 1938.)

4

When occupying the chair and directing the affairs of his lodge, Robert Burns was a model of dignity and decorum, a fact easily gleaned from the stories that have persisted through the years. He greatly valued Masonry and realized that it was a great honour to be elected by his brethren to a position of responsibility in his lodge.

In those days, as has been the case in all ages, there were dues to be paid (small in amount then as now), and inevitably there were a few brethren who were slow in attending to this rather important duty. When such delinquents were under discussion, Burns always pleaded for leniency. With him sympathy and Masonic charity were instinctive.

And how greatly he enjoyed meeting and greeting his brethren and spending an evening in cheerful good fellowship. He was one of the friendliest of Masons.

Dignity and reverence in the lodge room; jollity and buoyancy after the lodge was closed; generous sympathy and assistance at all times to those in need—such were the characteristics of Robert Burns, the Mason.

—W. J. Dunlop.

Toronto,   (Grand Master, 1937-1939, of the Grand Lodge
August 30, 1938.   A.F. & A.M. of Canada in the Province of Ontario.)

5

By universal consent Robert Burns has been given an abiding place among the Immortals of all ages. He is one of the world's great humans. His message came from his heart. It has reached the heart of mankind. And, as he himself said, "The heart aye's the part aye, that maks us right or wrang."

The letters of Burns are good. His poems are better. But his songs are the best. He started Scotland singing her own songs, and she has sung herself into that high place which she now occupies among the great nations of the earth. Songs such as "Scots wha hae wi' Wallace bled," "Ye banks and braes of Bonnie Doon," and many more, will thrill and stir any real people to the things that are highest and best.

"Tam o' Shanter" is perhaps Burns' masterpiece as a work of imaginative art. "The Cotter's Saturday Night" is selected as his greatest didactic poem. But the piece which has influenced young men who have fared forth to foreign fields, and inspired them to become truly great citizens, not only of the Empire, but of the world, is "An Epistle to a Young Friend." This short poem is replete with words of wisdom and grace. It closes on this high and holy strain:

> When ranting round in pleasure's ring,
> Religion may be blinded,
> Or if she gie a random sting,
> It may be little minded.
> But when on life we're tempest driven,
> A conscience but a canker;
> A correspondence fix'd with heaven,
> Is sure a noble anchor.

—Rev. Dr. John Gibson Inkster.
(Knox Church, Toronto, July 18, 1938.)

6

At last, after so many years, we escape from the measured declamation— we hear a man's voice! Much better, we forget the voice in the emotion which it expresses, we find this motion reflected in ourselves, we enter into relations with a soul. Then form seems to fade away and disappear; I will say that this is the great feature of modern poetry; Burns has reached it seven or eight times.

—Hippolyte Adolphe Taine.

7

Burns is the greatest peasant—next perhaps to King David of the Jews—whom any age has produced.

—Charles MacKay.

8

Scotland has many reasons to be proud of her national bard. It was surely to his credit that as a humble ploughman, unaided by the teachings of schools and universities, he was able to lift his voice in seraphic song that echoed around the admiring world! His songs have a simplicity and a charm that move the hearts and the affections of men of every country and of every race. His adoring love for his native land is well displayed in every line of his simple and gracious lyrics. He stirs every heart as he praises "the banks and braes of bonnie Doon," and the lovely scenery of Maxwelton, and of Afton Water. His love of the wild things of nature, such as the lark, the laverock, the field-mouse, or the mountain daisy, is so feelingly expressed as to bring tears to the reader's eyes. His "Cotter's Saturday Night" is an enduring monument to the Poet's reverence for God and for the teachings of Religion, and with this he couples a manly and ineradicable love of his native and beloved Scotia. Hear him in his full tide of patriotic song!

> O Thou Who poured the patriotic tide
> That streamed thro' Wallace's undaunted heart;
> Who dared to nobly stem tyrannic pride,
> Or nobly die, the second glorious part;
> (The patriot's God peculiarly Thou art,
> His friend, inspirer, guardian and reward!)
> O never, never Scotia's realm desert;
> But still the patriot and the patriot's bard
> In bright succession raise, her ornament and guard!

—Monsignor James B. Dollard.
(Lady of Lourdes Church, Toronto, written for this book, July, 1938.)

9

Shakespeare was of us, Milton was for us, Burns, Shelley, were with us—they watch from Their graves!

—Robert Browning.

10

Once admit that an honest man is as fit for any other world as he is for this one, and creeds become not only superfluous, but impertinent. Burns, therefore, does not belong to any Faith; he belongs to Humanity.

—GEORGE WILLIAM FOOTE.
(Editor of the *Freethinker*.)

11

It was the aim of Burns to "touch the heart," to ingratiate himself into the thought, and if possible to stimulate the reader to aspire unto a noble sphere. He repeats this again and again,

> The heart aye's the part . . .
> Then man my soul with firm resolves . . .
> The heart benevolent and kind the most resembles God . . .

It is "as counsel for poor mortals" that Burns has conquered the English-speaking world. He is the defender of that vast company of sinners called mankind, and he defends them all the more effectively because he shares not only their sins but their aspirations after virtue. He had a mind endowed with such a gift of sympathy, that it enabled him to say what good and bad men think better than they could say it themselves.

You will find all through his works every argument in favour of good morals, and many allowances made for bad.

Burns penned his own biograph, which is illuminating and probably as good as any of the critiques that have been penned about him. And also he jotted down a poem regarding a certain mendicant "wise woman," who is supposed to have prophesied at his birth,

> He'll hae misfortunes great and sma',
> But aye a heart aboon them a';
> He'll be a credit to us a',
>   We'll a' be proud o' Robin.

Four brief lines, which likely bespeak better the intent of the career of Burns than does his actual impress upon the imagination of humanity, or than any of the fat tomes that have been written upon these topics.

—G.F.O.S.

12

I admire Burns because he loved and defended the common people as one of themselves; he loved flowers, and he loved animals, and any man who could not admire a man like that, is not worthy of the name.

—HON. FRANCIS ROBERT LATCHFORD.
(Chief Justice in Appeal of Supreme Court of Ontario.)

13

. . . Has there ever appeared a poet with a greater emotional appeal than Robert Burns? How do you account for the indisputable fact that his birthday is celebrated more widely than that of any other human being? Why is it that the 25th of December is the only date that overshadows the popularity of the 25th of January?

He wasn't a greater genius than Byron or Shakespeare. He never wrote anything finer than Gray's "Elegy" or Goldsmith's "Deserted Village." As a matter of fact Burns wrote a lot of stuff that even we could scarcely recommend for the curriculum of Bishop Strachan's School. He drank more than the W.C.T.U. would approve. Some of his love affairs were unconventional to say the least. And yet his memory is honoured above that of any king or statesman. More toasts are drunk to the "Immortal Memory" of that plowman Poet than to any other writer ancient or modern.

Burns with all his faults wrote songs that will go echoing through the world till "a' the seas gang dry"—and it would be impossible to estimate his humanitarian influence. The sentiment of "a man's a man for a' that" is working away like leaven, and

> It's coming yet for a' that
> When man to man the world o'er
> Shall brothers be for a' that.

That dream of a poor obscure Scottish plowman has become the trumpet call of civilization.

—Rev. Dr. H. Beverley Ketchen.
(McNab Presbyterian Church, Hamilton, Ontario, at the luncheon of St. Andrew's Society of Toronto, 1937.)

14

The Burns Centenary (1859)

The celebration of the hundredth birthday of Robert Burns, on the 25th January, 1859, presented a spectacle unprecedented in the history of the world.

The utmost enthusiasm pervaded all ranks and classes. Villages and hamlets, unnoticed in statistical reports, unrecorded in Gazetteers, had their dinners, suppers and balls. City vied with hamlet, peer with peasant, philanthropist with patriot, philosopher with statesman, orator with poet, in honouring the memory of the Ploughman Bard.

The meetings were no less remarkable for their numbers than for their unanimity of sentiment; the number of speakers at each meeting being greatly over the average on other public occasions.

There were 872 meetings held, according to James Ballantine in his excellent *Chronicle of the Hundredth Birthday of Robert Burns.*

Scotland	676
England	76
Ireland	10
Colonies	48
United States	61
Copenhagen	1

At a great meeting held at the City Hall, Glasgow, presided over by Sir Archibald Alison, Bart., Colonel James Glencairn Burns said:

I humbly thank my God that he has spared me to live and see this glorious day, a day on which so many thousands in almost every part of the globe are paying homage to the genius of the Bard of Scotia. My mother told the late Mr. M'Diarmid of Dumfries that my father once said to her—"Jean, one hundred years hence they'll think mair o' me than they do now." How truly his prophecy has been fulfilled the proceedings here and elsewhere amply testify. I feel most grateful to you for the opportunity you have afforded me of being present at this, one of the most influential of these gatherings, presided over, as it is, by the celebrated and talented author of the *History of Europe*—supported by such well-known and distinguished men as Judge Haliburton, Principal Barclay, Sir David Brewster, Mr. Monckton Milnes, and Mr. Glassford Bell. In no place will the day be hailed and celebrated with more enthusiasm than in the Far East, where I spent so many and such happy years. In proof of this I may quote a few lines written by my old friend, Colonel George Anderson Vetch, the author of many a Burns birthday ode. In a poem of his, entitled "The Exile in India," he says:

> The music of Scotia is sweet—'midst the scene,
> But ah! could you hear it when seas roll between!
> Tis then, and then only, the soul can divine
> The rapture that dwells in the songs o' lang syne.

As a leal and true Scot, and a warm admirer of the genius of the Bard, I have joined in doing honour to his memory. As his son, permit me to return you my most sincere thanks for the same.

At the conclusion of Colonel James Glencairn Burns' speech, the band struck up "The Campbells are Coming."

Colonel William Nicol Burns, at a great meeting at Dumfries Assembly Rooms, said:

I beg to thank you very sincerely for the honour you have done us in drinking so cordially my brother's health and mine. We were brought up in humble life, but we have attained in our profession the rank of field officers. I would ask what is the cause of this? I do not hesitate to reply, the genius of Robert Burns. Two distinguished Scotsmen, Sir James Shaw, London, and Sir John Reid, one of the directors of the East India Company, and at one time governor of the Bank of England, gave my brother and myself our cadetships in the Indian Army. We went out to India, and the fame of our father pursued us in good fortune. While I was only an ensign the adjutancy of my regiment became vacant, and the Highland Society of Madras asked of the commander-in-chief the appointment for me. His Excellency could not then accede to the request, and the appointment was given to an officer much my senior. On the appointment, however, of the army of the Deccan at the time of the Pindaree war, Sir Thomas Hyslop conferred on me the temporary appointment of Field-assistant-quartermaster-general. The fame of Burns did still more for us. I was afterwards placed on the general staff in the commissariat, to which my brother had been appointed some time previously by the Marquis of Hastings. After a long residence in India we have been spared in the providence of God to come to spend the evening of our days in our native land. And can I say this, that wherever the sons of Burns have appeared—even at this late period—whether in England, in Scotland, or in Ireland, they have always been received with the most affectionate enthusiasm as the sons of Burns; and even Americans, wherever we have met them, have exhibited almost as much enthusiasm in responding to the names of the sons of Burns as our own countrymen.

When Colonel William Nicol Burns rose to speak, the band played "Wandering Willie," and at the conclusion of his address "Willie brew'd a peck o' maut," was sung by Mr. Lee.

At this stage of the proceedings, the Chairman, Dr. W. A. F. Browne, intimated that a deputation had been appointed to proceed to the great meeting in the Nithsdale Mills to show that meeting that, though separated by place, they were one in sentiment, and to express the best wishes for their enjoyment. The deputation, consisting of Colonel William Nicol Burns, and Messrs. William Gordon, Robert Scott, and W. R. M'Diarmid, thereupon left.

At Nithsdale Mills, Colonel William Nicol Burns was received with most rapturous demonstrations, and his health, as well as that of his brother, was the occasion of these demonstrations being renewed.

Colonel Burns, in rising to respond, was full of emotion. He only uttered a few words of thanks, his heart being too full to say anything more. His appearance was venerable and his countenance very like the countenance of a Burns.

The Chairman of the Nithsdale Mills gathering, sat in the arm-chair in which Burns himself had so often reclined when full of care and oppressed with grief.

At Sunderland in County Durham, England, the interest excited upon the centenary of the birth of the poet Burns manifested itself in various forms. The votaries of the theatre celebrated the event upon the stage. Other parties commemorated the event at their inns. At the Crown and Sceptre, Mr. Bewick provided a grand Burns supper. But the largest and most generally attractive entertainment took place in the great hall of the Athenæum. There about 500 of the *élite* of the borough assembled to do honour to the memory of genius, poetry, wit and humour. The chief promoter of this soirée was Mr. George Hardcastle, who, along with Mr. St. John Crookes, devoted every possible attention to it, to make a memorable celebration. The assembly consisted of ladies and gentlemen, representing the wealth, literature, taste and fashion of the borough.

The Chairman was the Rev. Richard Skipsey, incumbent of St. Thomas's Church, whose wife was a Miss Robinson and sister-in-law to Colonel James Glencairn Burns. He opened the proceedings with an elaborate and interesting historical speech. He said that Robert Burns was the greatest poet of the people of his nation, not excepting George Crabbe, who has always been so designated. He gave a graphic sketch of the Poet's life, and said there was one thread that was most conspicuous,—that of great industry and undoubted honesty. He had been told that the Poet's excise reports had been examined by one who was formerly in Sunderland, and that not one mark of disapprobation was attached to them, and that this fact was borne out by the evidence of Mr. Findlater, who knew him from the time of his appointment to his death. He always fulfilled the duties of his office till disabled by disease, which rendered him unable to discharge them. To the kindness of his disposition ample testimony had been borne. He took the most anxious care of the education of his family, devoting himself personally to it, as one of his most pleasing engagements. He instructed his eldest son Robert in the English poets—from Shakespeare to Gray. He was seldom intoxicated, and it was impossible that a man could be a drunkard who so devoted himself to home duties and to the education of his children.

Sunderland, England, was the first place that held a public celebration of the anniversary of the birth of the Poet, Robert Burns, February 3, 1821. So early as 1803 a Burns Club was held in the borough of Sunderland. A son of the Bard, James Glencairn Burns, married in April, 1818, Sarah, a daughter of James Robinson, the Postmaster of Sunderland. James Glencairn Burns and his wife, on more than one occasion, paid dutiful calls on their relatives in Sunderland.

Toronto, Canada: The centennial dinner took place in the Rossin House, now the Prince George Hotel. The dinner was supplied in Mr. Joslin's best style and gave general satisfaction. Daniel Wilson (1816-1892), afterwards Sir Daniel Wilson and President of University College, Toronto, from 1880 to 1892, and President of the University of Toronto from

1889 to 1892, took the chair. The Vice-Chairmen were the Hon. J. H. Cameron, Q.C., Hon. Oliver Mowat (1820-1903), afterwards Sir Oliver Mowat, and Prime Minister of Ontario from 1872 to 1896, and Hon. G. W. Allan. On the right of the chair sat Sir John Beverley Robinson, Bart., Chief Justice of the Court of Queen's Bench, Vice-Chancellor Spragge, Hon. J. C. Cameron, Hon. Mr. Cayley, the President of St. George's Society, and the President of St. Patrick's Society. On the Chairman's left were Hon. Mr. Chief Justice Draper, C.B., Hon. George Skeffington Connor, Q.C., M.P.P. (1810-1863), Chancellor of the University of Toronto in 1863, Mr. Justice Richards, and Hon. F. M. Vankoughnet. At the other tables were Hon. George Brown, M.P.P., J. B. Robinson, M.P.P., Colonel Thompson, Angus Morrison, M.P.P., M. Talbot, M.P.P., Alderman Ewart, Vice-Chancellor Langton, W. McMaster, William Henderson, Dr. Thorburn, Daniel Morrison, M. C. Cameron, William Hay, T. G. Ridout, W. Dickson (Galt, Ontario), A. H. Armour, Rice Lewis, Mr. Sheriff Jarvis, Mr. Ex-Sheriff Jarvis, W. B. Lindsay, T. G. O'Neill, George Michie, R. Milroy, John Watson, John Bell, John Fisken, Alexander Grant, Seeker Brough, J. McMichael, etc., etc.

After the usual loyal and patriotic toasts the Chairman said:

Gentlemen: I have now to invite your attention to the special object to which we owe our assembling here on this high festival of genius. This day we mark by a peculiarly significant symbol—the lapse of another century of time. Throughout the world-wide empire won to itself by the Anglo-Saxon race, it is being commemorated this day that, one hundred years ago, the mean clay bigging of a Scottish peasant became, by the birth of Robert Burns, one of the sacred shrines—the Meccas of the world. The hard lot of toiling poverty was his heritage from the cradle to the grave. In the world's broad field of battle, life was to him one stern warfare sweeping onward through all its brief scenes as a grand but fearful tragedy— gloomy, yet lighted up with the glory and beauty of a loving and gifted soul. For Burns, art and culture, the sophistical philosophy and the refined artificialities of the eighteenth century, did nothing. All the sterling worth of Scotland's peasant Bard was born of her rugged soil, and of the genial nurture of that sainted father of her "Cotter's Saturday Night." Life to him was real and earnest. With a tenderness tearfully tremulous as the loving pity of a mother, there was sunshine still behind the clouds; there was wealth of treasure for his large heart in the sympathies of nature; and he seems to us as if sent into the eighteenth century to reveal once more to men where the true beauty of life lay; and to tell us how the daisy in the furrow, and the man of honest independent worth, are alike fulfilling great Nature's plan. In the genius of Scotland's peasant Bard we discern the pulsations of a musical instrument of the widest compass. From his rustic lyre come notes joyous and earnest—laughter—moving and tremulous with tears. Alas! its heavenly notes were jarred in the dread struggle with temptations, with passions, with the social environments of that poor century to which he was so vainly given as a teacher and a guide. It is not for us to pity him, who, tried before the impartial tribunal of posterity, has been adjudged one of those whose memory and whose works posterity will not willingly let die. It is not for us to pity—to blame the mighty dead; neither is it for us now to attempt his panegyric. Nay, rather, may we say of his poems, they are imperfect, and of very small extent; for his life itself was a mere broken fragment. His sun went down ere it was noon, darkening on one of the saddest tragedies of the eighteenth century; and the world only learned when too late the priceless value of the treasure it had cast beneath its feet and trodden in the mire. Robert Burns had only attained his thirty-seventh year, when, casting one lingering look of anguish on the orphanage of his love, he lay down amid the stern realities of life's battlefield to die.

Let us think of this if we would estimate rightly what he did accomplish. Was there not, in the genial drollery, and pregnant life of that "Tam o' Shanter" of his, the promise of a whole series of Scottish *Canterbury Tales*, had he but lived to the maturity to which Chaucer attained ere he gave form and utterance to his immortal song? Dying at thirty-seven, Milton would have left to us no *Paradise Lost* or *Regained*. Dryden at that age would only have been known, if known at all, as the courtly sycophant who penned his "*Annus Mirabilis*"; and even Pope, who lisped in numbers, would have left unaccomplished the poems on which chiefly rest the enduring foundations of his fame. Yet the author of the "Cotter's Saturday Night" stands in need of no such apology. Burns has bequeathed to us his songs, and that is fame enough to win for him the poet's immortality. His songs were a noble patriotic offering—and how generously bestowed on that country for which her poet mourned that he could do so little, while laying on her altar the priceless tribute. What lyric in any language surpasses in pathetic tenderness his "Mary in Heaven?" What glorious battle-song ever rang with more thrilling patriotic fervour than his "Scots Wha Hae wi' Wallace Bled?" or what noble manly lay can equal in pith and power his "Man's a Man for a' That"?

The songs of Burns are already a part of the living language of our common race; and may not our hearts thrill within us this night, when gathered here around this festive board, on a spot hewn in our own day out of the old savage-haunted pines of Ontario's wooded shores—as we think that the same songs are being this night sung wherever the free banner of England floats on the breeze; and wherever the language is spoken inherited by her sons. Under the straw-clad roofs of Scotland, in the cottage homes of England and of Ireland, the songs of Burns have been chanted in triumph today. By the echoes of their music, repeated from land to land, may fancy follow the flag of British freedom round the world.

Where it proudly floats above the rocky heights of Gibraltar, and on Malta's ancient knightly towers, there their music has given voice to the breeze. At Aden, on the old Red Sea; in Africa, on her Atlantic coasts and her far-southern Cape of storms; in India, where the rush of the Ganges replies to the answering shouts of Britain's triumphant and dauntless sons; on that island-continent of Australasian seas—a newer world than our own—on solitary rocks like the low historic St. Helena; on clustering groups like the Antilles; and where the flag of a great republic flaunts proudly over the hardy descendants of our common stock—to each and all of these, as to ourselves, the peasant's voice, sweeping along the electric wires of genius, is heard thrilling this night with the pregnant utterances of that inspired song,

> Then let us pray that come it may,
> As come it will for a' that,
> That man to man, the world o'er,
> Shall brothers be for a' that.

The lot of Burns was proud, yet also a most sad one. One of Nature's great high-priests, he was taken in early youth from the sickle and the plough, and plunged into temptation; and suffering, and ineffectual self-guidance. His spirit was jarred in all its melodies, and the coarse hand of a mean prosaic age swept rudely over the broken strings. It is not for us to judge the strong man, if he yielded before the wiles of the world's Philistines ere he passed away forever beyond reach of the wrongs heaped on him by an unappreciating age. But let us never forget this, that amid the mean necessities of the humblest peasant lot; in poverty, in weary toil, in sorrow, and even in shame, Burns had still an eye for the beauty and the poetry of life; and built up for himself a glorious and immortal monument out of those very materials of his suffering and his toil.

Therefore is it that this day, with joyous pride, we look back on him whose footsteps we trace in the sands of the completed century; whose influence lives and shall live in the world's coming centuries; and above all in that dear native land, for which his warmest wish to heaven was sent, and amid whose bleak and rugged wilds he won for himself an everlasting name.

Nor let us judge hardly even of those who took their Poet from the sickle and the plough "to gauge ale firkins," and who only learned to discern his true worth when the toil-worn reaper had lain down to his last sleep, and the greatest of a nation's poets had gone to join the great departed. The case of Burns is no solitary one. The world has had her Dante, and Cameons, and Milton, and Dryden, and Chatterton, as well as its Burns. He, too, is now ranked among the benefactors of his race. For him the gorgeous temple has been reared, where, living, he almost wanted bread. The scene of his brief and chequered career is now the land of song, the land of Burns—known by his name and visited for his sake, by pilgrims from many a distant scene; and for him, and seeking to honour ourselves by rendering a just tribute to his fame, we, in this distant nook of Britain's world-wide empire, hold high festival to-night.

The glory dies not, and the grief is past. Not in sorrow as over the kingly dead struck down amid the vanquished in the highest places of the field; but with joyous acclamations as welcoming the victor in triumph, returning laden with the spoil, let us now pledge the immortal memory of Scotland's peasant Bard.

The Chairman resumed his seat amid great cheering, which was again renewed.

The toast was given with three times three. Hon. J. H. Cameron here read sentiments which had just been brought on the telegraph wires from different parts of the United States. He also remarked that the lines of telegraph from one end of America to the other were open, free to-night for the transmission of messages connected with the Burns Centenary.

Those who celebrated the centennial anniversary of the great Poet in the St. Lawrence Hall, Toronto, were by no means behind their brethren of the Rossin House in the magnificence of the preparation. Without exaggeration, the whole affair was a triumph from end to end. The platform was occupied by several members of the Toronto Highland Society in their national costume. Besides these gentlemen were Lieut. Colonel Irvine, A.D.C., Colonel Macdougall, Sir James Leith Hay, Bart., President of the Burns Club; Thomas D'Arcy McGee, M.P.P., Rev. Professor John McCaul, President of King's College 1848 to 1849, President of the University of Toronto, 1850 to 1853, and President of University College, Toronto, 1853 to 1880, George Duggan, Recorder, George Gurnett, County Magistrate, Captain Goodwin, Thomas Sellars, and Alexander M'Lachlan, author of *Canadian Lyrics*.

Mr. Alexander M'Lachlan (1818-1896), concluded an eloquent and feeling address on the life and character of Burns by reading a very beautiful poem composed by himself for the occasion. The first three stanzas are as follows:

> All hail! prince and peasant,
> The hour that gave birth
> To the heart whose wild beatings
> Resound through the earth;
> Whose sympathies nations
> Nor creeds could not bind,
> But gushed out in torrents
> Of love to mankind.
>
> All hail! mighty Minstrel,
> Thy magical art
> Was the breathings of love through
> The strings of the heart;
> And all thine own burdens
> Of sorrow and grief
> Were charmed into music
> For mortals' relief.
>
> Let the poor and the lowly
> Look up and rejoice;
> The dumb and down-trodden
> Find in thee a voice;
> And the high and the lordly,
> In palace and hall—
> For thou wert the playmate
> And brother of all.

Several speeches were made and songs were sung, and precisely at ten o'clock, Mayor Adam Wilson of Toronto gave "The Memory of Burns," a toast which it had been agreed upon to drink at that moment throughout America.

15

O kindred soul of humble birth,
Divine, though of the lowly earth,
Forgotten thou art not today
Nor yet neglected:—here's the bay!

Thy cottage home hid from the proud,
Nor thought of by the vulgar crowd
In thine own time, now claims a place
For universal eyes to gaze.

Nor changed its homely rugged lines
Where closely crept thy tender vines;
But men have changed; no more deplore:—
Where once they spurn'd we now adore.

Thy life and work and destiny
Contain a meaning deep for me:
Though fame be darken'd by a fate,
The laurel wreath comes soon or late.

Thy splendid fame shall ever rise
With undimm'd glory o'er the skies:—
To struggling souls a hope shall yield
On sailing seas and ploughing field.

I'm a foreign unknown bard,
Whose devious course is rough and hard,
But cheer'd at times by thy sweet song
I sing away nor mind the throng.

Like thee I'll toil with manly hand;
Like thee by manhood ever stand;
And guided by thy spirit brave,
Shall wait for verdict in the grave.

—CHANG-YON-TONG.
(Chinese Commissioner at opening of Burns' Cottage,
St. Louis Exposition, June 13, 1904.)

16

With all my admiration for about a score of the Frenchman's almost perfect songs, I would give all of them up for a score of Burns' couplets, stanzas, or single lines scattered among those quite imperfect lyrics of his.

—EDWARD FITZGERALD.

17

Johnson and Burns . . . strongly resembled each other. Both were men of strong passions and kindly affections—both were lovers of truth and lovers of independence.

—LORD (CHARLES NEATE) NEAVES.

18

Just so in "Tam o' Shanter." We know not what some German genius like Goethe might have made of him; but we much mistake the matter if "Tam o' Shanter" at Alloway Kirk be not as exemplary a piece of humanity as Faustus on "May-day Night upon the Hartz Mountains."

—PROFESSOR JOHN WILSON.

19

Although Burns was of all poets the most unschooled, he belongs in poetry with Raphael in painting, and Mozart in music, and there is no fourth.

—GEORGE WILLIAM CURTIS.

20

The two most remarkable men who rose from among the people during the last century were Robert Burns and Benjamin Franklin.

—HUGH MILLER.

21

Burns came, like Homer, from the very fountain-head of life.

—MRS. (MARGARET) OLIPHANT.

22

Yes, Burns, thou dear departed shade!"
When rolling centuries have fled,
Thy name shall still survive the wreck of Time,
Shall rouse the genius of thy native clime;
Bards yet unborn, and patriots shall come,
And catch fresh ardour at thy hallow'd tomb—
There's not a cairn-built cottage on our hills,
Nor rural hamlet on our fertile plains,
But echoes to the magic of his strains,
While every heart with highest transport thrills.
Our country's melodies shall perish never,
For, Burns, thy songs shall live for ever.
Then, once again, ye vocal few,
Give the song to merit due.

—ROBERT TANNAHILL.
(Written for Robert Burns Birthday Celebration,
Paisley, January 29, 1807.)

23

His art—at its best—was that supreme sort which conceals itself in its own perfection.

—PROFESSOR FRANKLYN BLISS SNYDER.

24

Life is a struggle, and any one who can, like Robert Burns, ease it, is a benefactor.

—REV. DR. THOMAS DE WITT TALMADGE.

25

The genius and influence of Robert Burns is beyond analysis and beyond criticism.

—AMELIA EDITH HUDDLESTON BARR.

26

The lark of Scotia's morning sky!

—OLIVER WENDELL HOLMES.

27

His writings represent the mother-wit of the Scottish intellect.

—ALEXANDER WEBSTER.

28

Robert Burns seems to me to be worthy to be admired among the most admired, for he became and remained a great poet in a condition of life in which others would have become less than man.

—ARTURO GRAF.

29

I confess that Burns bowled me over.   For weeks I kept saying, "This man stands alone."

—ARNOLD BENNETT.

30

Search Scotland over, from the Pentland to the Solway, and there is not a cottage but so poor and wretched as to be without its Bible; and hardly one that, on the same shelf, and next to it, does not treasure a Burns.

—JOHN GIBSON LOCKHART.

31

O smile among the shades, for this is fame!

—JOHN KEATS.
(At Burns' Cottage, Alloway.)

32

Burns was a very singular man in the strength and variety of his faculties. I saw him, and once only, in the year 1792.   We conversed together for about an hour in the street of Dumfries, and engaged in some very animated conversation.   We differed in our sentiments sufficiently to be rather vehemently engaged—and this interview gave me a more lively as well as forcible impression of his talents than any part of his writings.   He was a great orator, an original and very versatile genius.

—ROBERT HARTLEY CROMEK.

33

Robert Burns appears to me to have laid open in the poetry of his country both doors and windows to the breath of revolution.   In rough outline, in idyllic emotion, in sarcasm and in tenderness, in blasphemy and in prayer, in negation and in aspiration, he seems to conjure up the ethics and æsthetics of a new philosophy.

—GIOSUE CARDUCCI.

34

What may we not suppose that Burns would have produced had he lived till the age of three score and ten, or even the age at which Shakespeare and Milton gave to the world their greatest works?

—General James Grant Wilson (U.S.A.).

35

It needs no effort of imagination, to conceive what the sensation of an isolated set of scholars (almost all either clergymen or professors) must have been in the presence of this big-boned, black-browed, brawny stranger, with his great flashing eyes, who, having forced his way among them from the plough-tail at a single stride, manifested, in the whole strain of his bearing and conversation, a most thorough conviction, that, in the society of the most eminent men of his nation, he was exactly where he was entitled to be; hardly designed to flatter them by exhibiting even an occasional symptom of being flattered by their notice; by terms calmly measured himself against the most cultivated understandings of his time in discussion; overpowered the "bon-mots" of the most celebrated convivialists by broad floods of merriment, impregnated with all the burning fire of genius; astounded bosoms habitually enveloped in the thrice-plied folds of social reserve by compelling them to tremble—nay to tremble visibly—beneath the fearless touch of mutual pathos; and all this without indicating the smallest willingness to be ranked among those professional ministers of excitement, who are content to be paid in money and smiles for doing what the spectators and auditors would be ashamed of doing in their own persons, even if they had the power of doing it.

—John Gibson Lockhart.

36

The dialect of Burns was fitted to deal with any subject; and whether it was a stormy night, a shepherd's collie, a sheep struggling in the snow, the conduct of cowardly soldiers in the field, the gait and cogitations of a drunken man, or only a village cockcrow in the morning, he could find language to give it freshness, body and relief. He was always ready to borrow the hint of a design, as though he had a difficulty in commencing—a difficulty—let us say, in choosing a subject out of a world which seemed all equally living and significant to him; but once he had the subject chosen, he could cope with nature single-handed, and make every stroke a triumph. Again his absolute mastery in his art enabled him to express each and all of his different humours, and to pass smoothly and congruously from one to another.   Many men invent a dialect for only one side of their nature— perhaps their pathos or their humour, or the delicacy of their senses—and, for lack of a medium, leave all the others unexpressed.   You meet such an one, and find him in conversation full of thought, feeling and experience, which he has lacked the art to employ in his writings.   But Burns was not thus hampered in the practice of his literary art; he could throw the whole weight of his nature into his work, and impregnate it from end to end.

—ROBERT LOUIS STEVENSON.

37

Burns was about as clever a man as ever lived.

—CHARLES JAMES FOX.

38

No poet of our tongue ever displayed higher skill in marrying melody to immortal verse than Robert Burns.

—SIR WALTER SCOTT.

39

Burns, you claim, and claim rightly, as your National Poet; but that does not exclude us as Englishmen from claiming him as one of the glories of the United Kingdom.

—JOSEPH CHAMBERLAIN.

40

Burns' works are eternal.   His words will live forever.   I make bold to say his memory is celebrated by more men, in Burns societies and kindred bodies, than that of any other man that ever lived, excepting Jesus Christ. No other man, King or commoner, has more monuments, the world over, to his name than Robert Burns.   Justly, for he lifted his nation on to a pedestal, made it great in song and story.   "Tam o' Shanter" is matchless. The "Cotter's Saturday Night" is a domestic star that will shine forever. His beautiful songs will be sung as long as the burn wimples to the sea and the bonnie, bloomin' heather blossoms on the hills of Caledonia. An honest man was Burns, and "an honest man's the noblest work of God." I can picture Burns in the field, at the plough, or the harrow, or walking at his horse's head along a country road.   He might be riding on top of his cart-load and he would never belabour his horse.   I can see him in innocent conversation with his horse or his dog; trudgin' hame at nicht wi' the craws; gettin' his bowl o' brose, his cup o' tea, and his bannock of butter; loshin' himself up for the evenin'; sethin' out for a quiet walk;

feastin' on the pleasures of the day's observations, and pennin' his ever-lastin' lines:

> Had we never lov'd sae kindly,
> Had we never lov'd sae blindly,
> Never met or never parted,
> We had ne'er been broken-hearted.

He was always sincere. His sincerity was his success. His sincerity made him anxious at all times to speak the truth. His truthfulness created a sensitiveness over which he had no control. It made him discontented. His discontent made him miserable. He was intensely human, therefore he suffered enormously in the world. He never courted pity. His nature was independent. His independence made him grave. He was a fearless, outspoken critic. His honesty was never questioned, he believed what he said, and never said what he did not believe. "A man's a man for a' that." I am convinced that Robert Burns often thought about death, and that it pained him mortally, while he surveyed the beauties of the landscape, listened to the laverock, admired the hills and valleys of his beloved Scotia, to realise that one day his eyes would be dimmed in death, and that he would no more feast on these sequestered scenes. And he would pray inwardly, faithfully:

> Where with intention I have err'd,
> No other plea I have,
> But Thou are good; and Goodness still
> Delighteth to forgive. *Amen.*

—Sir Harry Lauder.

41

Burns from a New Point of View

. . . Burns had heart disease of rheumatic origin, which cut him off at middle age, and no doubt dated from childhood. In all likelihood it was in the "auld clay biggin'," in the damp Ayrshire climate, and not very weathertight, some "Janwar blast" blew in the germ of lifelong perturbation. The offspring of Scottish peasants in these days were left to harden as best they could, and no particular notice would be taken of an inconspicuous illness. But if on the occurrence of that first inconspicuous illness Burns had been put to bed in blankets for three months, the whole tenor of his days might have been different from what it was.

At Mount Oliphant, from his thirteenth to his fifteenth year, the heart trouble was well declared. "He was almost constantly," says Gilbert, "afflicted in the evenings with a dull headache, which at a future period of his life was exchanged for a palpitation of the heart, and a threatening of fainting and suffocation in his bed in the night-time." Then, too, he became subject to those attacks of despondency which recurred from time to time during the rest of his life. These were no doubt connected with the condition of the heart, but were in some degree, as Gilbert thought, due to the hardships and privations he had to undergo. At thirteen he had to assist in threshing the corn, and at fifteen was the principal labourer on the farm, for there were no other hired servants, male or female, while all this time, like the rest of the family, he had to live very sparingly. "The anguish of mind we felt," says Gilbert, "at our tender years under these straits and difficulties was very great."

From the Mount Oliphant period onwards, through the Lochlee and Mossgiel time, although the records are scant, we have indications that his malady was still with him. At Irvine, when engaged in flax-dressing, in 1781, and twenty-two years of age, he had a three months' attack of "vapours," which he said he shuddered to recall, and about which he wrote to his father, December, 1781: "My health is nearly the same as when you were here, only my sleep is a little sounder, and on the whole I am rather better than otherwise, though I mend by very slow degrees. The weakness of my nerves has so debilitated my mind that I dare neither review my past wants nor look forward into futurity, for the least anxiety in my breast produces most unhappy effects on my whole frame. P.S.—My meal is nearly out but I am going to borrow till I get more." At Mossgiel, in 1784, there was an exacerbation of his disease. The movement of the heart was seriously affected; he became liable to fainting fits, particularly in the night-time, and as a remedy he resorted to cold baths. A barrel of cold water stood near his bedside, and into this he was obliged to plunge when threatened with an access of his ailment. His sensations, which only those who have thus suffered can fully realize, were terrible, kept him in fear of sudden death and led to acute compunction for errors real or imaginary, and to religious reflections.

Timor mortis conturbat me.

Like Dunbar, in great sickness he was moved to poesy, and composed, as he tells us, a prayer, "when fainting fits and other alarming symptons of pleurisy or some other dangerous disorder," which still threatened him, first put nature on the alarm.

> O Thou unknown, Almighty Cause
> Of all my hope and fear!
> In whose dread presence, ere an hour,
> Perhaps I must appear!
> If I have wander'd in those paths
> Of life I ought to shun;
> As something, loudly in my breast,
> Remonstrates I have done; . . .

. . . It will not, I think, be disputed that Burns died of rheumatic endocarditis; with the origin of which alcohol had nothing to do; nor will it be denied, that if he had had the advantage of the guidance which modern medical science and practice afford in cardiac disease, his life might have been freed from many disquietudes and considerably prolonged. He and his fair fame were to a large extent the victims of a faulty diagnosis, and it is the consequent incomprehension of his real state and sufferings that has permitted the harsh and unjust judgment so generally passed on him. . . . He was truly a painful example of the neglect of rheumatism in early life. . . . Reviewing his history, the wonder is that he struggled on and survived as long as he did. It was his splendid constitution that upheld him. . . . No poet ever lived a life as arduous and thorny as did Burns. He had to earn his living and that of his family. From *res augusta domi* he was never free. It was only on loiterings by the wayside that he could toy with the Muse, and yet he gathered a goodly garland. He had what was practically six months' holiday at Mossgiel, leaving the management of the farm to Gilbert, and that was his most prolific and potential time. He took one whole day off at Ellisland, and we have "Tam o' Shanter." Had he been able to live the life poetical, as Byron and Shelley and Wordsworth and Keats and Tennyson and Browning and Swinburne did, what might he not have achieved? Burdened and harassed as he was, he did nobly. He was not unspotted from the world. What poet ever was? But he has been, as I have tried to show in some respects, sadly misunderstood and vilified for faults which were fatalities.
                                                —SIR JAMES CRICHTON-BROWNE, M.D.

NOTE: Sir James Crichton-Browne and Dr. H. B. Anderson independently arrived at similar conclusions.

42

It was not his genius, his insight, his vision, his wit or spirit of manly independence, nor all of these combined, which captured the hearts of men. It was his spontaneous, tender, all-pervading sympathy with every form of misfortune, pain, or grief; not only in man, but in every created form of being. He loved all living things, both great and small. Repeated are the proofs of this overflowing tenderness. The nest of the mouse destroyed by the plough which had "cost many a weary nibble," appeals to his heart, and the lesson is enforced:

> But Mousie, thou art no thy-lane,
> In proving foresight may be vain:
> The best laid schemes o' mice an' men
>   Gang aft agley,
> An' lea'e us nought but grief an' pain
>   For promis'd joy!

Burns seems to have divined what science to-day proclaims, that all life is kin; listen to this outburst of emotion:

> I'm truly sorry Man's dominion
> Has broken Nature's social union,
> An' justifies that ill opinion,
>> Which makes thee startle
> At me, thy poor, earth-born companion,
>> And fellow-mortal!

We murmur to ourselves, "beyond this it is impossible for mortal to go, this must be the utmost limit." But wait a moment. We are told that talent does what it can but genius what it must, and Burns, sweeping upward and onward under this law, startled the world by his next leap, clear out of all bounds, at which it still keeps wondering, for no mortal before or since has ever dared to entertain the idea of reformation and pardon for the Evil One:

> But fare-you-weel, auld "Nickie-ben!"
> O wad ye tak' a thought an' men!
> Ye aiblins nicht—I dinna ken—
>> Still hae a stake;
> I'm wae to think upo' yon den,
>> Ev'n for your sake.

The Poet was ever the reformer, and, true to his mission, he ventures to intimate that his "Infernal Majesty" might vary one of his recreations with advantage:

> I'm sure sma' pleasure it can gie,
>> E'en to a deil,
> To skelp and scaud poor dogs like me,
>> An' hear us squeal!

A RELIGIOUS TEACHER

In such familiar terms Burns addresses the Arch Fiend, enemy of God and Man—whom Milton thus describes:

> Incensed with indignation, Satan stood
> Unterrified, and, like a comet, burned
> In the arctic sky, and from his horrid hair
> Shakes pestilence and war.

Fortunately the stern doctrines literally interpreted in the Poet's day remain with us in our day only as helpful allegories in man's progress to higher conceptions.   Not till another poet reaches this towering height upon which to-day one sits alone in solitude can the ascendency of Burns ever be questioned as the genius of the overflowing, sympathetic heart, ever alive to the sorrows of man, beast, mouse, or devil.   There are two stanzas which give Burns high place as a truly religious teacher of men:

> The feat o' Hell's a hangman's whip,
> To hand the wretch in order,
> But where you find your honour grip,
> Let that aye be your border;
> Its slightest touches, instant pause,
> Debar a' side pretences;
> And resolutely keep its laws,
> Uncaring consequences.

In the "Cotter's Saturday Night" we have the finest picture of humble life ever painted, inculcating the most truly religious lesson:

> Compar'd with this, how poor Religion's pride,
> In all the pomp of method, and of art;
> When men display to congregations wide
> Devotion's ev'ry grace, except the heart:
> The Power, incens'd, the pageant will desert,
> The pompous strain, the sacredotal stole;
> But haply, in some cottage far apart,
> May hear, well pleas'd, the language of the soul;
> And in His Book of Life the inmates poor enrol.

I venture to submit that one line of Burns has not received due attention as constituting a rule of life—a pure gem:

> Thine own reproach alone do fear.

Having from our own conscience—the Judge within—received a verdict of approval, we have little to fear from any other tribunal.   The "Judge within" sits in the Supreme Court.   The prophets in days past were stoned as Burns was, but the assailants of Burns in his day were wrong. He saw the great light before they did, as the prophets and leaders of mankind invariably do and must do, else they were not prophets.   The day has now arrived when he, the proclaimer of the royalty of man, stands revealed to us as the true Poet-Prophet of his age.   What he proclaimed has proved to be the needed gospel for the advancement of man, especially for us as the English-speaking race.   I have ventured to hail him as the Poet-Prophet of his age.   That he was a Poet will pass unquestioned, but was he not also a Prophet?   Did he not see, in advance of his fellows, the certain growth of the rights of man through the spread of democracy, and was he not awake to the crude and repulsive theology of his day, and at the same time saw the coming of the better day in which we now live, when the God of wrath who condemned man to everlasting torment has become displaced by the Heavenly Father, who can be trusted to deal mercifully even with the sinner? In these changes we recognise the work of Burns; it was he who laid the axe to the root of the tree of ignorance and superstitition, and in doing so made mankind his debtor. Burns's political gospel rules our English-speaking race, which is marching steadily, though more slowly than we could wish, to the full fruition of the ideal of our Poet-Prophet. You honour yourselves in honouring the man who has proved himself the Poet-Prophet of his age.

—Andrew Carnegie.
(As he unveiled the Montrose Burns Statue on
August 7, 1912.)

43

By one section of his fellow-countrymen Burns was regarded as a miracle of genius, a pattern of manhood, and an apostle of freedom, by another as a lewd fellow of the baser sort, with a knack of rhyming and an itch for notoriety.

The Burnsites have gained in strength recently. They now include members of all classes and political parties. The high priest of the Burns cult for many years was the Earl of Rosebery. Professor W. P. Ker, whose sympathies were strongly Conservative, wrote a pamphlet to prove that Burns, had he lived to-day, would have been an ardent Imperialist—and Unionist, resolutely opposed to Scottish Home Rule, and rejoicing in the concentration of all political and social and literary interests in London.

The average Burns Club is solidly middle class in composition and sentiment, and a proposer of "The Immortal Memory" would be reasonably safe in combining his laudation of Burns with a denunciation of Socialist doctrines. It is to a staunch Conservative, Sir James Crichton-Browne, that we owe the removal of the stigma of intemperance which, since the time of Currie, his first biographer, has dimmed the fame of Burns.

Burns' works are no longer the Bible of any one faction; they are industriously exploited by propagandists of all colours and shades. Under the industrious band of biographers and commentators his real personality is slowly vanishing, and is being replaced by a figure which has the property of taking on the lines and shapes of its surroundings. Burns, in fact, is on the way to becoming an eponymous hero, a rustic Fingal or Arthur.

But we are as far as ever from being able to assign him his rightful place in European, British, or even Scottish literature.

His life, from birth to death, has been exposed to the prying eyes of all and sundry. He, not the essential Burns, but the transient Burns that represented an imperfect compromise between personality and outward circumstance—has been put to the question by a heterogeneous and wrangling bench of poets and critics, ministers, doctors, judges, peers, M.P.'s, bailies, journalists, scribes and Pharisees, publicans, and sinners, and deadheads and "buddies" and axe-grinders of all sorts. For nearly a century a continuous post-mortem examination has been held over him, and at every Burns supper the poor corpse is torn to pieces afresh.

> They wasted, o'er a scorching flame,
> The marrow of his bones;
> But a miller us'd him worst of all,
> For he crush'd him 'tween two stones.

The miller is the Burns expert, whose mill grinds slowly and exceeding small; but nothing but dust comes out of it.

But the big world to which Burns now belongs has no interest in the nobodies whose great grandfather sold a sheep to Burns or had a drink with him in a country pub.

Burns opens a window on infinity, or he would not be a poet; but he does it by revealing, in imperishable form, the interest, intensity, and dignity of ordinary human life.

He was the first great poet to write of the common people as one of themselves, and of the animal creation as a lover of all life. He definitely extended the range of human sympathy. His countrymen's worship of him has been indiscriminate and uninformed, but it has not been misplaced. In him a powerful and intrepid intelligence and a virile artistry were combined with the biggest and warmest heart that beat in a human breast.

Burns is a terminus not a junction, in the system of Scottish Poetry; the form in which he excelled he filled so full with his own genius and personality as to leave no room in them for his successors. His human sympathies were widened, his passionate yearnings tempered, his philosophy of life kept sane and sweet by direct contact with Mother Earth and worthy, hard working folk. He did not refine upon his feelings or subtilise his egotism. He took the goods the gods provided him, passed cheerfully and thankfully from flower to flower, and acknowledged his own place in the social scheme of things.

—WILLIAM POWER.

44

The glow of immortality rests upon Burns' modest farm. The mouse which he startled with the plough-share in November, 1785, the daisy which he had to crush "among the stoure" while working in the fields in April, 1786, will live transfigured through the ages. Wherein does the compelling force of this art consist? To answer this question we must take various factors into account. The first is that the Poet's personality is never lost to view behind the scenes depicted in the Kilmarnock Volume. This personality is so great, so discerning, so courageous, so sincere, and inwardly so gripped by the subjects which it sets out to describe, that a wave of warmest life passes from it to them. Burns sets down not only what he has observed, but also what he has experienced, and so what he writes acquires a vital strength corresponding with the keenness with which these experiences were felt.

—HANS HECHT.'

45

Till through the cloud of fortune's wrong
He soared to fields of glory;
But left his land her sweetest song
And earth her saddest story.

—OLIVER WENDELL HOLMES.

46

The High Priest of loving, erring, yet repentant hearts . . . the bard the warmest, deepest passion-thrilling with the wand of fellow-feeling the heights and the depths of our glorious though imperfect nature. His failings were the fruits of an overly warm, rich heart; they are the failings of a noble nature; excess in love, excess in friendly sociality. Mean vice was a stranger to him.

—HUGH MACDONALD.

47

Songs of his nation became the song of all nations. Burns was perhaps the one writer—certainly the one poet—who gave the impression of writing slapdash and always hitting the right word.

His love songs were the only love-songs simple enough to be true. He was the one most striking example of the fact that the more narrowly national a poet was the more universal he became.

—GILBERT KEITH CHESTERTON.

48

He went through life in a kind of childish nudity. No one is competent to judge him until he has read his letters and his unexpurgated poems. Even when he is posing he is revealing himself in his pretences. He was a peasant who had to bear the pain of voicing the inarticulateness of centuries of peasants. In his voice, clear and unhesitant, one heard all the joys and sorrows which lay unspoken for generations in the heart of men who work with their hands. This great silence he broke magnificently. He sang in thirty-six years all the things that men like him in every other particular but that of expression had failed to sing for centuries. No wonder he died young. It was a great strain on the throat. Critics say that he was born out of his station, that had he been in Byron's position his life would have been happier. Surely Burns was first and last a peasant. Surely Byron's possibilities would have meant no greater happiness for him and as short a life.

—HENRY VOLLAM MORTON.

49

The books that have most influenced me are Coleridge and Keats in my youth, Burns as I grew older and wiser.

—JOHN RUSKIN.

50

But still the music of his song
Rises o'er all elate and strong,
Its master chords
Are Manhood, Freedom, Brotherhood,
Its discords, but an interlude
Between the words.

—HENRY WADSWORTH LONGFELLOW.

51

Not Latimer nor Luther, struck more telling blows against false theology than did this grave singer. The "Declaration of Independence" and the "Marseillaise" are not more weighty documents in the history of Freedom than the songs of Burns.

—RALPH WALDO EMERSON.

52

Burns is one of the most correct poets that the world has known.

—LORD LYTTON.

53

Only those who speak from the heart and to the heart employ a universal language. Burns was a past master in the use of this language; he gave poetic expression to a sympathy that embraced the entire world; his words live because they glow with the love that makes all mankind kin.

—WILLIAM JENNINGS BRYAN.

54

The nation which read Burns in the nursery could never have tyrants in the Parliament House.

—REV. HENRY WARD BEECHER.

55

The more we know of Burns' life, the deeper grows the essential mystery of his genius and the minute and inexhaustible researches of Burns' scholars seem like desperate attempts to solve the insoluble. For Burns' poems, songs and letters, immortal though they be, are no more than the literary expressions of an extraordinary personality which was genius incarnate.

All we can say in the last resort about Burns is that he was Man raised to an incalculably high power. There are passages in his poems which show that Burns himself was somehow aware of this.

That this at least expresses or suggests the mystery of Burns, is shown by the positive nature of his whole life and achievement. There was nothing negative, inhibitory, grudging or coldly analytic about him—of jealousy and envy he had not the slightest trace.

He is one of the world's greatest humorists, and his humour is invariably corrective of the world's injustices.

—*S.M.T. Magazine*, Edinburgh, January, 1936.

56

Rising above the trammels of birth and poverty, Burns spoke to the great nameless class of labouring men throughout the world, while kings and countries listened in amazement. He lived close to the beating heart of Nature; and all the rich and deep sympathies of life grew and blossomed in his own.

—JAMES ABRAM GARFIELD.
(U.S.A. President.)

57

Burns was great because God breathed into him in greater measure than any other man the spirit of that love which constitutes his own essence, and made him more than any other man a living soul.   Burns was great by the greatness of his sympathies.

—William Cullen Bryant.

58

Burns has taught me the thoughts of God in nature more than a great many pulpits have.

—Henry Ward Beecher.

59

The stranger in a foreign land comes to love Scotland and her people because Burns loved them.

—James Bayard Taylor.

60

He was the most flesh and blood chiel ever cast upon the sands of time.

—Walt Whitman.

61

Of all the men who ever lived Burns nestles closest to the bosom of humanity.

—Horace Greely.

62

Others may be the favourites of a class or clique, Burns is the favourite of the whole world.

—Sir Alfred Austin.

63

Of Burns' poetry I can think of none since Shakespeare's that had so much the appearance of sweetly coming from nature.

—William Pitt.

64

I scarcely ever met any man whose conversation displayed greater vigour.

—William Robertson.

65

O Burns, thou joy of my young heart!
Thou lark, thou soul of Nature's song!
A spark of thee, and of thine art,
Hath wandered with me so far and long!

—ELIZABETH, QUEEN OF ROUMANIA (CARMEN SYLVA).

66

How much more respectable human nature appears in our eyes after reading Burns than after reading Byron.

—EBENEZER ELLIOTT.

67

A few lines from Burns has done more to form and maintain the present improved political and social conditions of the people than all the millions of editorials ever written.

—LORD (JOHN) MORLEY.

68

The right of Burns to a place amongst the Immortals is as uncontestable as the right of Scotland to a place amongst the nations.

—WILLIAM THOMAS STEAD.

69

They had only to peruse the works of Burns to find something that would appeal to everyone of whatever class or kind.

Without imagination they could not appreciate poetry fully. Burns was a hard worker and died at an early age, not from his own failings, but from a rheumatic condition of the heart which had nothing to do with imbibing alcohol. It was the result of hard work in the fields of Ayrshire for 16 hours a day.

Though not a descriptive poet, Burns gave them descriptions of nature of a unique kind. He transformed the commonplace into the sublime, and helped them to appreciate the simple beauties of the countryside.

In his satirical poems—such as "Holy Fair" and "Holy Willie's Prayer"—Burns did for Scotland what Dickens did for England. His object was to bring the sword of satire down on the country's hypocrites.

Burns as a great "organist" touched many chords of human feeling and emotion. It was a tragedy that he died at so early an age. During the last six months of his life he wrote some of his best works—therefore the view which some had taken that he left the world at the right time because of his own failings was undoubtedly wrong.

—J. STEWART SEGGIE.

(Of Edinburgh, at the Sunderland Burns dinner, January 25, 1938.)

70

The rank of Burns is the very first of his art.

—LORD BYRON.

71

The total impression of his poems is, and remains always, that of a candid, healthy, tender, fresh and mirthful soul—of a fine, free reflecting character and clear mind.

—WILHELM RICHARD WAGNER.

72

Wallace and Bruce emancipated the nation; Burns emancipated the man.

—W. B. GARDNER (MAX PHILPOT).

73

There can be no question that Burns is the most popular great poet in the world.

—RICHARD LE GALLIENE.

74

Burns was one who equally delighted and astonished the world.

—RICHARD COBDEN.

75

Above the storms of praise and blame,
That blur with mist his wondrous name,
His thunderous laughter went and came
And lives and flies;
The roar that follows on the flame
When lightning dies.

—ALGERNON CHARLES SWINBURNE.

76

When Scotland forgets Burns, then history will forget Scotland.

—Professor John Stewart Blackie.

77

Let us for a thousand years from now do honour to the genius and character of Robert Burns. It has not the power of curtailing by one second all his journey to his Calvary; we ever remain his debtors who will never be able to pay to him the debt we owe him.

—T. P. O'Connor (Tay Pay).

78

Burns, . . . Carlyle, . . . Stevenson, . . . Scott, . . . I do not suppose that four more different geniuses could be found in the literature of any other country. Of all these four men, without doubt the one which is nearest to the hearts of his fellow-countrymen is Robert Burns.

—Lord (Arthur James) Balfour.

79

Such his life, and such his verse, in which beat all the affections, all human sentiments—love, enthusiasm, compassion, indignation: And all speak the language of truth.

—Luigi Chiarini.

80

I consider your Burns one of the most beautiful poets of whom humanity has cause to be proud. I admire and love him as a friend, as a brother in the spirit. He is at one and the same time strong and sweet, and has nothing in common with those scribblers in metre, these rhetoricians, those imposters who are the plague of literature, and who, unfortunately, too often usurp the place and influence of the poets of Nature, artists and born geniuses.

—Georges Eekoud

81

. . . This very great Scottish poet.

—Guiseppe Garibaldi.

82

Little wonder is it that Burns is worshipped.   .   .   .   He has extraordinary richness in language, wealth of imagery, gracefulness, vivacity, tenderness of feeling, and a sincerity, which sometimes, as in the "Tragic Fragment," becomes affecting.

—Antonio Fogazzaro.

83

I find in Burns that Celtic fire and power of imagination, that humour—now delicate, now light, now grotesque—but above all that wonderful eye for Nature, which was peculiar to the Celtic mind.

—Kuno Meyer.

84

Carlyle was not quite finished in his prenatal existence.   The bricklayer's mortar of his father's calling stuck to his fingers through life, but only, as the soil he turned up with his ploughshare, clung to the fingers of Burns.   We do not wish either to have been other than what he was.   Their breeding brings them to the average level, carries them more nearly to the heart, makes them a simple expression of our common humanity.

—Oliver Wendell Holmes.

85

Tennyson and Longfellow deign to borrow jewelry from Burns to make their own verses shine.

—Rev. Dr. Frank Willard Court.

86

Show me the song writer, from the days of Anacreon to the days of Béranger, who comes within a thousand miles of Burns?

—Henry Glassford Bell.

87

Among modern poets Catullus has been compared to   .   .   .   Burns. In general intellectual power, in the breadth of his human sympathies, the modern poet is much the greater.   He is, in all ways, the larger man.

—Professor William Young Sellar.

88

Homer, Virgil, Dante, and Shakespeare have, perhaps more than any other poets, left the impress of their minds on their compatriots, but none of them has learned the thought and speech of the great mass of his countrymen so thoroughly as Burns.

—WILLIAM GUNNYON.

89

I do not say Burns was a Homer, a Dante, a Shakespeare, or a Goethe, or that he could ever have done what they did. Yet it is among them that we picture him now, for he has flashes, at least, of a light which we only find in them, notes of tender melody which only such as they awaken, and he rouses the echoes with a large mirth which only one of them can rival. That is his place by almost universal consent.

—REV. DR. WALTER CHALMERS SMITH.

90

To me the fundamental basis of the æsthetic worth of a work of art lies in its form and meaning, and this in the songs of Burns is perfect. His verses sound easy and sweet, like a piece of music, the rhythms and refrains, the majors and minors move and follow and alternate with a graceful and alluring playfulness that combines the smoothness of a reed with the stately march of lofty poetry.

—MARIO PILO.

91

No anniversary is more zealously and joyously observed by Scots throughout the world than the 25th January, Burns' birthday, which is regarded as one of the most notable days in the Scottish calendar. Nor is the observance confined to Scotsmen. Burns in his writings, appeals to all, because he is the Poet of Humanity. He wrote of man's virtues and failings, of loving kindness and of vice. He possessed the supreme gift of understanding and of sympathy. He was a Humanitarian and a Reformer. . . . He embodied all that was best in the study of man as man and of nature in all its aspects. His variety is the greatest in the poetry of his time and he gave a fresh impulse to Scottish patriotism, while, at the same time he set standards which appeal to the whole of the human family. He was the foe of bigotry, but he was, at the same time, intensely religious.

—DUDLEY WRIGHT.

92

Deep in the general heart of man,
His power survives.

—WILLIAM WORDSWORTH.

93

It may safely be said that more touching, sublime poetry than that of Burns was never written.

—LEON PAUL BLOUET (MAX O'RELL).

94

.   .   .   But the Scotch bagpipe has more power and resonance than the pipe of Pierre Dupont of Lyons; and, in addition, your Robert Burns lived a hundred years too soon.

—ALPHONSE DAUDET.

95

Burns has nothing to learn and nothing to unlearn; he shot up as spontaneously as the daisy of his own mountains.

—EDMUND HENRY ADOLPHE SCHERER.

96

.   .   .   Your great National Poet, Robert Burns, who is so well known in Flemish Belgium.   I have translated several of his most beautiful songs, and my very good friend, Frans de Cort, the Flemish poet, has translated at least fifty.   On the occasion of his centenary, my daughter and I have composed several verses in honour of the illustrious Poet and inimitable songster of the whole world.

—EMMANUEL HEIL.

97

From Lajos Kossuth in exile, to Robert Burns in immortality.

The man o' independent mind
Is king o' men for a' that.

—KOSSUTH.

(Inscription by the Hungarian Patriot in Album at
Alloway Cottage.)

98

Nothing in Horace, in the way of curious felicity of phrase, excels what we find in the compositions of this Ayrshire ploughman.

—Professor George Lillie Craik.

99

Referring to Mr. J. B. Reid's *Burns' Concordance*, an Edinburgh newspaper says: "It occurred to us in running over the closely-printed pages to measure by the amount of space occupied what was Burns' favourite word. Every author has his favourite words; it has been remarked, for example, as characteristic that Goldsmith had a peculiar liking for the words 'bliss' and 'blest.' It is surely no less characteristic of Burns that his favourite word should be 'heart'; the quotations under this word fill no less than nearly six of the minutely-printed columns. It will give some idea of the hugeness of this proportion to mention that even such a common auxiliary as 'hae' has little more than a column and a half. 'Lass,' 'friend,' and 'Heaven,' come next to 'heart,' as far as my observation goes, each having about two columns. 'Lassie' has one column; and it is curious that 'frien,' with its seven entries, occupies only about an eighth of a column. Such are the revelations of accurate statistics; one would have said offhand that the Scots form 'frien' occurred oftener than friend. It seems a curious illustration of Burns' tendency to use English for an expression of his more serious sentiment."

—John D. Ross.
(Burnsiana, 1892.)

100

Burns is supreme in the qualities of the heart.

—Sir Arthur Conan Doyle.

101

Burns' face, to judge of it by the early portrait of him by Nasmyth, must have been a face like that of Joseph of old, of whom the Rabbis related that he was mobbed by the Egyptian ladies whenever he walked the streets. The magic of that countenance, making Burns at once tempter and tempted, may explain many a sad story.

—Charles Kingsley.

102

Had but a penny each been set aside
By all who thrill'd with joy at Robin's lay,
That paltry tribute had been ample pay,
Enabling him hard fortune to deride.
How bravely, then, would he have stemm'd the tide
Of penury that rolled in day to day;
The modest competence for which men pray
He had enjoyed by Nith's clear silvery side;
That grinding poverty of which they tell us
Had been no legend to the wide world's end;
His head been raised erect among his fellows;
No borrowing one pound notes from pitying friend;
"Laird" Burns had ta'en his independent stand
With Jean Armour, Queen of Ellisland.

—Thomas C. Latto.

103

There are two things which to me make Burns sufficiently memorable. One is his noble protest for the independence and dignity of humanity; another is his intense nationality—a noble sentiment, springing like a plant deeply rooted for ages in the soil and bearing fruit which nourishes the manliest virtues of a people.

—Rev. Dr. Norman Macleod.

104

Not Ariosto's, no, nor Shakespeare's strain
Could sooner raise or sooner quell a tear:
Only one tear thy magic cannot chain;—
Burns, Burns! for thee it falls! thee on thy bier!

—Mary Russell Mitford.

105

The name of Robert Burns can never die. He is enrolled among the immortals and will live forever. This man left a legacy of riches untold, not only to Scotland, but the whole world. He enriched our language, and among succeeding generations he has scattered the gems of thought. His heart blossomed in a thousand songs, songs of all time, all seasons, suited to every experience of the heart and to every phase of thought, songs for the dawn of life, songs of the cradle, songs for growing boys and girlhood, songs for the hours of courtship, and for the sweet and sacred relationship of man and wife; songs for the cheerless and songs for the vanished days, and songs that were filled with light and hope for days to come, songs for the sunshine and for the storm; songs that set the pulse throbbing and stir the heart of man.   —ROBERT GREEN INGERSOLL.

106

There never was a poet at once so local and so universal in his appeal. He brought the quality of pity into poetry and stirred it in the hearts of men when the blighting shadow of Calvinism *cum* Knoxism still lay upon Scotland and made its religion bleak and forbidding. For every lowly thing, for all down-trodden unhappy folk, Burns was full of pity. And that pity has immortal expressions in many of his poems, while there is also a wistfulness about much that he wrote which goes straight to our hearts.

—SIR JOHN ALEXANDER HAMMERSTON.

107

Burns brought to the world the best message ever brought since Bethlehem, and humanity the world over walks more erect for what he said and sung. Genius sings through the soul of Burns like the wind through an Æolian harp.   —GEORGE F. HOAR.
(U.S.A. Senator.)

108

Long before his school days were finished he was seen as often trudging behind the plough as occupied with his studies, and already at that early period the glories of Nature were stirring his soul within him in preparation for his special mission to make articulate the heart of his native land. Burns was "mystic from the first, breathing poetry before he knew it himself." A marked feature of Burns' early life was the consuming interest he took in the simple heart affairs of his fellow rustics. A courtship in the neighbourhood was to him something touched with the ray of the divine. A passionate fellow himself, the sight of others' passion exalted his spirit to the lyrical plane. He was for ever falling in love himself; love was as necessary to his temperamental nature as the sunshine to some exotic flower.   —HUBERT STEWART BANNER.

109

In this humble nook, of all places in the world, Providence was pleased to deposit the germ of the richest human life which mankind had then within its circumference.   —NATHANIEL HAWTHORNE.
(At Burns' birthplace.)

110

Though Scotland boasts a thousand names
Of patriot, king, and peer,
The noblest, grandest of them all
Was loved and cradled here;
Here lived the gentle, peasant prince,
The loving cotter-king,
Compared with whom the greatest lord
Is but a titled thing.

'Tis but a cot roofed in with straw,
A hovel made of clay;
One door shuts out the snow and storm,
One window greets the day.
And yet I stand within this room
And hold all thrones in scorn;
For here, beneath this lowly thatch,
Love's sweetest Bard was born.

—Robert Green Ingersoll.
(Wrote the above lines in Burns' Cottage.)

111

There was no truer gentleman in Europe than the ploughman poet.
. . . He loved everything—the mouse and the daisy, and all things
great and small God had made. So with this simple passport he could
mingle with any society, and enter courts and palaces from his little
cottage on the banks of the Ayr.

—Professor Henry Drummond.

112

Of all poets Burns was, perhaps, the most directly inspired. His poems
did not grow—like stalactites—by the slow process of accretion; like
Adam, they had no childhood—they awoke complete. Burns produced
all his great efforts by single strokes. In his best things there is an impetus,
a hurry, which gives one the idea of boundless resource. To him a song
was the occupation of a morning; his best epistles drive along in a fiery
sleet of words and images; his "Tam o' Shanter" was written in a day—since
Bruce fought Bannockburn, the best single day's work done in Scotland.
Burns was never taken by surprise; he was ready for all calls and emergencies. He had not only—like Addison—a thousand-pound note at
home, but he had—to carry out the image—plenty of loose intellectual
coin in his pocket. A richer man—with plenty of money in his purse, and
able to get the money out of his purse when swift occasion required—
Nature has seldom sent into the world.

Born and bred as he was in the country, we find in Burns the finest of pictures in rural life. We smell continually the newly turned earth, the hawthorn blossom, the breath of kine. His shepherds and shepherdesses are not those who pipe and make love in Arcady and on Sèvres china—they actually work, receive wages, attend markets, hear sermons, go sweet-hearting, and, at times, before the congregation endure rebuke. The world he depicts is a real world, and the men and women are also real.

—ALEXANDER SMITH.

113

Through all his tuneful art, how strong,
The human feeling gushes!
The very moonlight of his song
Is warm with smiles and blushes!

Robert Burns lives on with a vitality which gathers strength from time. His fame broadens and deepens every year. The world has never known a truer singer.

—JOHN GREENLEAF WHITTIER.

114

Burns possessed as no other man ever did the universal alchemy of genius which enabled him to bring to light the fine virgin gold in everything he touched.

—JAMES PROCTOR KNOTT.

115

The most striking characteristics of Burns' poetry are simplicity and intensity,—an intensity not limited to feeling or passion merely, but belonging equally to his imagination and his thoughts,—in which qualities he is scarcely, if at all, inferior to any of the greatest poets that ever lived. Some of his expressions are like brilliant flashes of light: in an instant the thought or sentiment is impressed upon the mind, never to be forgotten. His power of concentration is perfectly marvellous. In two short lines—

The rank is but the guinea stamp,
The man's the gowd for a' that,

he says more than many able men could do in an elaborate essay.

—JOSEPH THOMAS.

116

Knighthood was the theme of Scott,
Manhood the theme of Burns.

—SIR DAVID BRAND.

117

If Watt in invention, Adam Smith in economy, Brougham in eloquence, Knox in theology, Hume in history,   . . .   Jeffrey in criticism, and Scott in fiction, were all combined in one effulgent star, it would not equal the splendors of Burns!

—Hon. Samuel Sullivan Cox (U.S.A.).

118

. . .   This great Genius, who has rendered himself immortal throughout all free nations.

—Maurus Jokai.
(Hungarian novelist.)

119

. . .   Scotland's greatest poetic Genius.

—Georg Morris-Cohen Brandes.

120

The most ordinary of men could have mused as Burns mused, when he made a plea for understanding and charity, and yet his case is not Burns' case.   Only a Burns could have imparted the tragic sorrow of being the circumstance.   The protest of Burns' bowed heart was a protest of the gods themselves.   The God-given gifts which were the genius of Burns made his way distressing and his life tormented with remorse.

The gold in the crown of Burns was his struggle with poverty, and the gold bore a dross of its own.   His hardship scarred him and broke his naturally robust frame.   If he had had the advantage of the guidance which modern medical science and practice afford in cardiac disease, his life might have been freed from many disquietudes and considerably prolonged.

—James Ramsay MacDonald.

121

His magic was not far to seek:—
He was so human, whether strong or weak,
Far from his kind he neither sank nor soared,
But sat an equal guest at every board;
No beggar ever felt him condescend
Nor prince presume; for still himself he bare
At manhood's simple level, and whene'er
He met a stranger, there he left a friend.

—James Russell Lowell.

122

His like we ne'er again will find,—
Such kings have no successors;
But of the treasures of his mind
All nations are possessors:

And while the vault of heaven glows,
And earth endures below it,
So long resplendent, lives and grows
The fame of Scotland's poet.

—WILLIAM HENRY HARRISON MURRAY.

123

Burns never touched a sentiment without carrying it to its ultimate expression, and leaving nothing further to be said.

—ABRAHAM LINCOLN.

124

It were impossible to increase the fame of Robert Burns.

—LORD KELVIN.

125

We esteem the highly praised Burns amongst the first poetical spirits which the past century has produced.

—VON JOHAN WOLFGANG GOETHE.

126

Read the exquisite songs of Burns. In shape each of them has the perfection of the berry; in light the radiance of the dew-drop.

—ALFRED, LORD TENNYSON.

127

Since Adam there has been none that approached nearer fitness to stand up before God and angels in the naked majesty of manhood than Robert Burns.

—SARAH MARGARET FULLER (COUNTESS OSSOLI).

128

Genius is not confined to lands and latitude. Burns belongs to the world.

—HON. JAMES GILLESPIE BLAINE.

129

The name of Robert Burns has been, and is, dearer to more hearts than any other except alone that of Him who was born in a manger and died that we might live.

—WILLIAM PIERCE FYRE.
(U.S.A. Senator.)

130

Reputations rise and fall. Literary fashions blow hot and cold. Great men of one age become the little men of the next. But a man's a man for a' that. The stature of Burns will never shrink. Men of high birth honoured him. Great ladies spoke of his power, not in poetical achievements, but in a kind of magic of personality. Men of all ranks were proud to call him brother. Children adored him.

There was glamour in the man, but it was no false and flashy glamour. Behind the warm-hearted geniality was the strength, the steadfastness of a man's man. So great was the force of his personality that everything he touched remains memorable, not only because he was a poet, but because he was a man.

Times change and institutions topple, but the living force of a tremendous personality endures, and will endure, till a' the seas gang dry.

—A. A. THOMSON.

131

In my early days I had a passionate fondness for the poetry of Burns. Burns was the god of my idolatry.

—CHARLES LAMB.

132

Do you think Burns has had no influence on the life of men and women in Scotland, has opened no eyes and ears to the face of nature and the dignity of man and the charm and excellence of women?

—RALPH WALDO EMERSON.

133

We think Burns entitled to the rank of a great and original genius. He has great humour, great powers of description, great pathos, and great discrimination of character.

—LORD (FRANCIS) JEFFREY.

134

The Scottish people love him for his independence.

—Professor John Wilson.

135

The child of Nature, Burns told us like Homer, or the Hebrew poet in the book of Job, what he saw and what he felt, uninfluenced by the greatness, unbought by the wealth, undeterred by the criticism of the world.

—Sir Archibald Alison.

136

Shakespeare and Homer together could not supply the place of Burns.

—Rev. Dr. Peter Hately Waddell.

137

He is the daily companion of hundreds of thousands of men.   He holds the first place in the hearts of his fellow country-men.

—Lord (Arthur James) Balfour.

138

He came when poets had forgot
How rich and strange the human lot,
How warm the tints of life, how hot
Are love and hate.
And what makes Truth divine, and what
Makes Manhood great.

—Sir William Watson.

139

His works bear impressed upon them, beyond the possibility of mistake, the stamp of true genius.

—William Ewart Gladstone.

140

He was given the rare quality of Wisdom that could interpret the plan of the Great Architect Divine in the tiniest and humblest of his creatures, and the Beauty of a tongue that could give voice to a nation's soul.

—Hubert Stewart Banner.

141

Education has a necessary tendency to mature and disclose rare capacity of the highest order—all that is called genius: A Watt to alter the whole face of the world, . . .   adding to the happiness of mankind; a Burns whose immortal verse makes the solace and the delight of his countrymen in every age and every country where their lot may be cast.

—Lord (Henry Peter) Brougham.

142

Conquerors like Napoleon live only in the pages of history, but this rude, unlettered poet, who sang because he must, lives on in the hearts and affections of men, and is honoured more and more as the years roll by.

—James Wilkie.

143

Burns, like Homer, is not merely a poet, but a literature. He has succeeded in fulfilling the old savage ideal—he has swallowed up all his predecessors, and become possessed of their united powers.

—Francis Thompson.

144

There are probably ten Scotsmen to whom Burns and his work are breathing and potential realities, for one Englishman to whom Shakespeare is more than a name.

—William Michael Rossetti.

145

It came under my own view professionally, that he superintended the education of his children with a degree of care that I have never seen surpassed by any parent in any rank of life whatever.

—James Gray.
(Rector of the Dumfries Academy.)

146

The most magnetic personality the world has ever seen.

—Dr. William Wallace.

147

His poems show Burns at his extremest. They exhibit him in his happiest, tenderest, most indignant, most dignified moods. They represent the summits of his life. His ordinary work-a-day range and level are revealed to us in his prose. There we have in a long scarcely broken series of views *the man Robert Burns*, divested of his singing robes, his laurel crown, and his lyre-handling, the rude implements of his earthly toil, and wearing hodden grey and a' that. We surprise him at his work, and look in upon him at his leisure. We find him in taverns and at trysting-trees. We meet him in the world's ways, in crowded streets and on country roads. We observe his bearing in the various relations of life—which in his case are necessarily numerous. We watch the rise and growth of his sympathies and raptures; we see his actions; we listen to his free, offhand remarks, his ever-returning earnest questionings, his half-formed opinions, his firm decisions. Above all, we share his frank confidences on the four great topics of life, love, politics and religion.

—*The Scotsman.*

148

Weigh his defects, his faults, as heavily as you like, the scale where the pure gold is, easily turns the balance. Admiration increases as we examine his qualities. When one thinks of his sincerity, his uprightness, his kindness towards peoples and animals, his contempt for anything base, his hatred of any trickery—which in itself would be an honour—his disinterestedness, the many beautiful impulses that form his heart, the high inspirations of his mind, the intensity, the idealism which was necessary to him to keep his soul above his fate; when one thinks that he felt all these generous feelings so intensely that they formed part of his intellectual life, that they came from him as jewels, so keenly did he feel them, so like was his soul to a furnace where precious metals were molten, that it might be said he was one of Nature's Noblemen, and of great goodness.

When it is remembered how much he suffered, how much he overcame, and how much he accomplished, with what misery his genius had to fight to be born and to live, the perseverance of his class of apprenticeship, his intellectual exploits, and, after all, his glory, one says to one self that what he did not succeed in or what he did not undertake, was as nothing compared to what he achieved, and that he was a man that accomplished much. And what remains to be said except that the clay of which he was made was full of diamonds, and that his life was one of the most valiant and the proudest that any poet ever lived.

—Auguste Jean Angellier.

149

In the whole of English literature there is no more beautiful tribute than his rendered to the virtues of the peasant, nor any finer description of labour's rewards.

—Mme. Juliette Lamber Adam.

150

. . . This noble, sincere, powerful spirit—powerful, because he has drawn from his native soil the inspiration of his songs and the patriotic sentiment of his writings.

—JULES ARESENE ARNAND CLARETIE.

151

The freedom-ringing songs of Burns have without doubt helped to build the great British Empire.

—DUNCAN CAMERON FRASER.
(Lieut.-Governor of Nova Scotia.)

152

His written word persists through the changeful years, and is dear to the heart of humanity.

—SAMUEL TAYLOR COLERIDGE.

153

Fresh as the flower whose modest worth
He sang, his genius glinted forth,
Rose like a star that, touching earth,
For so it seems,
Doth glorify its humble birth
With matchless beams.

—WILLIAM WORDSWORTH.

154

Burns makes you feel the reality, the depths and truth of his passion. We have no love songs in English of the same class as those of Burns.

—JOHN BROWN, M.D.
(Author of *Rab and His Friends*.)

155

Mr. David M'Culloch, of Ardwell, has often told me that he was seldom more grieved, than when riding into Dumfries one fine summer evening to attend a county ball, he saw Burns walking alone, on the shady side of the principal street, while the opposite side was gay with successive groups of gentlemen and ladies, all drawn together for the festivities of the night, not one of whom appeared willing to recognise him.

—JOHN GIBSON LOCKHART.

156

We see in him a freer, purer development of whatever is noblest in our-selves; his life is a rich lesson to us, and we mourn his death as that of a benefactor who lived and taught us.

He was often advised to write a tragedy; time and means were not left for this; but through life he enacted a tragedy, and one of the deepest.

No poet of any age or nation is more graphic than Burns . . . three lines from his hand and we have a likeness. . . . It seems a draughts-man working with a burnt stick, and yet the burin of Retzsch is not more expressive or exact.

Burns is a theme that cannot easily become either trite or exhausted.

The largest soul of all the British lands.

Our peasant Burns showed himself among us, a soul like an Æolian harp, in whose strings the vulgar wind, as it passed through them, changed itself into articulate melody.

There is reason to believe that in his latter years, the Dumfries Aris-tocracy had partly withdrawn themselves from Burns, as from a tainted person, no longer worthy of their acquaintance. That painful class, stationed in all provincial cities, behind the utmost breast-work of gentility, there to stand siege and do battle against the intrusions of grocerdom and grazierdom, had actually seen dishonour in the society of Burns, and branded him with their veto,—had as we vulgarly say, cut him! Alas! when we think that Burns now sleeps "where bitter indignities can no longer lacerate his heart," and that those fair dames and frizzled gentlemen already lie at his side,—where the breast-work of gentility is quite thrown down,—who would not sigh over the thin delusions and foolish toys that divide heart, and make man unmerciful to his brother!

—Thomas Carlyle.

157

Lord Rosebery's Tribute

I have sometimes asked myself, if a roll-call of fame were read over at the beginning of every century, how many men of eminence would answer a second time to their names. But of our poet there is no doubt or question. The *adsum* of Burns rings out clear and unchallenged. There are few before him on the list, and we cannot now conceive a list without him. He towers high, and yet he lived in an age when the average was sublime.

It sometimes seems to me as if the whole eighteenth century was a constant preparation for, a constant working up to, the great drama of the revolution which closed it. The scenery is all complete when the time arrives—the dark volcanic country; the hungry desperate people; the firefly nobles; the concentrated splendour of the Court—in the midst, in her place as heroine, the dazzling Queen. And during long previous years brooding nature had been producing not merely the immediate actors, but figures worthy of the scene. What a glittering procession it is! We can only mark some of the principal figures. Burke leads the way; then come Fox and Goethe; Nelson and Mozart; Schiller, Pitt, and Burns; Wellington and Napoleon. And among these Titans, Burns is a conspicuous figure, the figure which appeals most of all to the imagination and affection of mankind. Napoleon looms larger to the imagination, but on the affection he has no hold. It is in the combination of the two powers, that Burns is supreme.

What is his secret? We are always discussing him and endeavouring to find it out. Perhaps, like the latent virtue of some medicinal baths, it may never be satisfactorily explained. But, at any rate, let us discuss him again. What pleasanter or more familiar occupation can there be for Scotsmen?

The clue to Burns' extraordinary hold on mankind is possibly a complicated one; it has, perhaps, many developments. But I believe the causes are, like most great causes, simple; though it might take long to point out all the ways in which they operate. The secret, as it seems to me, lies in two words—inspiration and sympathy. I must proceed then in a more summary way.

Now there seems to me to be two great natural forces in British literature. I use the safe adjective of British. I use it partly because hardly any of Burns' poetry is strictly English; partly because he hated, and was perhaps the first to protest against, the use of the word English as including Scottish. There are in that literature two great forces of which the power seems sheer inspiration and nothing else—Shakespeare and Burns. This is not the place or the time to speak of that miracle called Shakespeare, but one must say a word of the miracle called Burns.

Try and reconstruct Burns as he was, a peasant, born in a cottage that no sanitary inspector in these days would tolerate for a moment; struggling with desperate effort against pauperism, almost in vain; snatching at scraps of learning in the intervals of toil, as it were with his teeth; a heavy silent lad, proud of his ploughing. All of a sudden, without preface or warning, he breaks out into exquisite song, like a nightingale from the brushwood, and continues singing as sweetly—with nightingale pauses—till he dies. A nightingale sings because he knows no other. So it was with Burns. What is this but inspiration? One can no more measure or reason about it than measure or reason about Niagara.

Under the limitations which I have imposed on myself, we must take for granted the incomparable excellence of his poetry. But the poetry is only a fragment of Burns. Amazing as it may seem, all contemporary testimony is unanimous that the man was far more wonderful than his works. "It will be the misfortune of Burns' reputation," writes an accomplished lady, who might well have judged him harshly, "in the records of literature, not only to future generations and to foreign countries, but even with his native Scotland and a number of his contemporaries, that he has been regarded as a poet, and nothing but a poet. Poetry," she continues, "was actually not his forte. . . . None, certainly, ever outshone Burns in the charms—the sorcery, I would almost call it—of fascinating conversation, the spontaneous eloquence of social argument, or the unstudied poignancy of brilliant repartee." And she goes on to describe the almost superhuman fascination of his voice and of his eyes, those balls of black fire which electrified all on whom they rested.

It seems strange to be told that it would be an injustice to judge Burns by his poetry alone; but as to the magnetism of his presence and conversation there is only one verdict. "No man's conversation ever carried me so completely off my feet," said the Duchess of Gordon—the friend of Pitt and of the London wits, the Queen of Scottish society. Dugald Stewart says that "all the faculties of Burns' mind were, so far as I could judge, equally vigorous, and his predilection for poetry was rather the result of his own enthusiastic and impassioned temper than of a genius exclusively adapted to that species of composition. From his conversation I should have pronounced him to be fitted to excel in whatever walk of ambition he had chosen to exert his abilities." And of his prose compositions the same severe judge speaks thus—"Their great and varied excellences render some of them scarcely less objects of wonder than his poetical performances. The late Dr. Robertson used to say that, "considering his education, the former seemed to him the more remarkable of the two." "I think Burns," said Principal Robertson to a friend, "was one of the most extraordinary men I ever met with. His poetry surprised me very much, his prose surprised me still more, and his conversation surprised me more than both his poetry and prose." We are told, too, that "he felt a strong call towards oratory, and all who heard him speak—and some of them were excellent judges—admitted his wonderful quickness of apprehension and readiness of eloquence." All this seems to be marvellous. It surely ratifies the claim of inspiration without the necessity of quoting a line of his poetry.

If his talents were universal, his sympathy was not less so. His tenderness was not a mere selfish tenderness for his own family, for he loved all mankind except the cruel and the base. Nay, we may go further and say that he placed all creation, especially the suffering and despised part of it, under his protection. The oppressor in every shape, even in the comparatively innocent embodiment of the factor and the sportsman, he regarded with direct and personal hostility. But above all he saw the charm of the house; he recognised it as the basis of all society, he honoured it in its humblest form, for he knew, as few know, how unpretentiously, but how sincerely, the family in the cottage is welded by mutual love and esteem. "I recollect once," said Dugald Stewart, speaking of Burns, "he told me, when I was admiring a distant prospect in one of our morning walks, that the sight of so many smoking cottages gave a pleasure to his mind which none could understand who had not witnessed, like himself, the happiness and worth which they contained." He dwells repeatedly on the primary sacredness of the home and the family, the responsibility of fatherhood and marriage. "Have I not," he once wrote to Lord Mar, "a more precious stake in my country's welfare than the richest dukedom in it? I have a large family of children, and the prospects of many more." The lines in which he tells his faith are not less memorable than the stately stanzas in which Gray sings the "short and simple annals of the poor." I must quote them again, often quoted as they are—

> To mak' a happy fireside clime
> To weans and wife,
> That's the true pathos and sublime
> Of human life.

His verses, then, go straight to the heart of every home; they appeal to every father and mother. But that is only the beginning, perhaps the foundation, of his sympathy. There is something for everybody in Burns. He has a heart even for vermin; he has pity for even the arch-enemy of mankind. And his universality makes his poems a treasure-house in which all may find what they want. Every wayfarer in the journey of life may pluck strength and courage from it as he passes. The sore, the weary, the wounded will all find something to heal and soothe. For this great master is the universal Samaritan. Where the priest and the Levite may have passed by in vain, this eternal heart will still afford a resource. But he is not only for the sick in spirit. The friend, the lover, the patriot will all find their choicest refreshment in Burns. His touch is everywhere, and it is everywhere the touch of genius. Nothing comes amiss to him. What was said of the debating power of his eminent contemporary, Dundas, may be said of his poetry—"He went out in all weathers." And it may be added that all weathers suited him; that he always brought back something precious, something we cherish, something that cannot die.

He is, then, the universal friend in an unique sense. But he was, poetic-ally speaking, the special friend of Scotland, in a sense, which recalls a profound remark of another eminent Scotsman, I mean Fletcher of Saltoun. In an account of a conversation between Lord Cromarty, Sir Edward Seymour, Sir Christopher Musgrave, and himself, Fletcher writes—"I said I knew a very wise man, so much of Sir Christopher's sentiment that he believed if a man were permitted to make all the ballads, he need not care who should make the laws of a nation." This may be rudely paraphrased, that it is more important to make the songs of a nation than to frame its laws, and this again may be interpreted to mean that in the days of Fletcher, at any rate, as in the days of Burns, it is the familiar songs of the people that mould their thoughts, their manners, and their morals. If this be true, can we exaggerate the debt that we Scotsmen owe to Burns? He had bequeathed to his country the most exquisite casket of songs in the world; primarily to his country, though others cannot be denied their share. We give only one example, but it is a signal one. From distant Roumania the queen of that country wrote that she had no copy of Burns with her, but that she knew his songs by heart.

We must remember, too, that there is more than this to be said. Many of Burns' songs were already in existence in the lips and minds of the people—rough and coarse and obscene. Our benefactor takes them, and with a touch of inspired alchemy transmutes them and leaves them pure gold. He loved the old catches and the old tunes, and into these gracious moulds he poured his exquisite gifts of thought and expression. But for him those ancient airs, often wedded to words which no decent man could recite, would have perished from that corruption, if not from neglect. He rescued them for us by his songs, and in doing so he hallowed the life and sweetened the breath of Scotland.

I have also used the words patriot and lover. These draw me to different lines of thought. The word "patriot" leads me to the political side of Burns. There is no doubt that he was suspected of being a politician; and he is even said to have sometimes wished to enter Parliament. That was perhaps an excusable aberration, and Professor Masson has surmised that had he lived he might have been a great Liberal pressman. My frail thought shall not dally with such surmise, but it conducts us naturally to the subject of Burns' politics. From his sympathy for his own class, from his indignation against nobles like the Duke of Queensberry, and from the toasts that cost him so dear, it might be considered easy to infer his political opinions. But Burns should not be claimed for any party. A poet, be it remembered, is never a politician, and a politician is never a poet—that is to say, a politician is never so fortunate as to be a poet, and a poet is so unfortunate as never to be a politician. I do not say that the line of demarcation is never passed—a politician may have risen for a moment, or a poet may have descended; but where there is any confusion between the two callings, it is generally because the poet thinks he discerns, or the politician thinks he needs something higher than politics. Burns' politics were entirely governed by his imagination. He was at once a Jacobite and a Jacobin. He had the sad sympathy which most of us have felt for the hapless house of Stuart, without the least wish to be governed by it. He had much the same sort of abstract sympathy with the French Revolution, when it was setting all Europe to rights; but he was prepared to lay down his life to prevent it putting this island to rights. And then came his official superiors of the Excise, who, notwithstanding Mr. Pitt's admiration of his poetry, snuffed out his politics without remorse.

The name of Pitt leads me to add that Burns had some sort of relation with three Prime Ministers, Colonel Jenkinson, of the Cinque Ports Fencible Cavalry—afterwards Minister for fifteen years under the title of Liverpool—was on duty at Burns' funeral, though we are told—the good man—that he disapproved of the poet, and declined to make his acquaintance. Pitt, again, passed on Burns one of his rare and competent and literary judgements, so eulogistic, indeed, that one wonders that a powerful Minister could have allowed one whom he admired so much to exist on an exciseman's half pay when dying. And from Addington, another Prime Minister, Burns elicited a sonnet, which, in the Academy of Lagado, would surely have been held a signal triumph of the art of extracting sunshine from cucumbers.

So much for politics in the party sense. "A man's a man for a' that" is not politics—it is the assertion of the rights of humanity in a sense far wider than politics. It erects all mankind; it is the charter of its self-respect. It binds, it heals, it revives, it invigorates; it sets the bruised and broken on their legs, it refreshes the stricken soul, it is the salve and tonic of character; it cannot be narrowed into politics. Burns' politics are indeed nothing but the occasional overflow of his human sympathy into past history and current events.

And now having discussed the two trains of thought suggested by the words "friend" and "patriot," we come to the more dangerous word "lover." There is an eternal controversy which, it appears, no didactic oil will ever assuage, as to Burns' private life and morality. Some maintain that these have nothing to do with his poems; some maintain that his life must be read into his works, and here again some think that his life damns his poems, while others aver that his poems cannot be fully appreciated without his life. Another school thinks that his vices have been exaggerated, while their opponents scarcely think such exaggeration possible. It is impossible to avoid taking a side. We walk on the ashes, knowing the fire beneath, and unable to avoid it, for the topic is inevitable. I must confess myself, then, one of those who think that the life of Burns doubles the interest of his poems, and I doubt whether the failings of his life have been much exaggerated, for contemporary testimony on that point is strong; though a high authority, Mr. William Wallace, has recently taken the other side with much power and point.

But the life of Burns, which I love to read with his poems, does not consist in his vices; they lie outside it. It is a life of work, and truth, and tenderness. And though, like all lives, it has its light and shade, remember that we know it all, the worst as well as the best. His was a soul bathed in crystal, he hurried to avow everything. There was no reticence in him. The only obscure passage in his life is the love passage with Highland Mary, and as to that he was silent not from shame, but because it was a sealed and sacred episode. "What a flattering idea," he once wrote, "is a world to come! There shall I with speechless agony of rapture again recognise my lost, my ever dear Mary! whose bosom was fraught with truth, honour, constancy, and love." He had, as the French say, the defects of his qualities. His imagination was a supreme and celestial gift. But his imagination often led him wrong, and never did Quixote see the heroic in all the common events of life which made Burns (as his brother tells us) see a goddess in every girl he approached. Hence many love affairs, and some guilty ones; but even these must be judged with reference to time and circumstance. This much is certain, that had he been devoid of genius they would not have attracted attention. It is Burns' pedestal that affords a target. And why, one may ask, is not the same measure meted out to Burns as to others? The bastards of great captains and statesmen and princes are treated as historical and ornamental incidents. They strut the scene of Shakespeare, and ruff it with the best. It is for the unlawful children of Burns, though he and his wife cherished them as if born in wedlock, that the vials of wrath are reserved. Take two brilliant figures, both of royal ancestry, who were alive during Burns' life. We occupy ourselves endlessly and severely with the lapses of Burns. We leave an elegant sigh over the kindred frailties of Charles James Fox and Charles Edward Stuart.

Again, it is quite clear that, though exceptionally sober in his earlier days, he drank too much in later life. But this, it must be remembered, was but an occasional condescendence to the vice and habit of the age. The gentry who pressed him to their houses, and who were all convivial, have much to answer for. His admirers, who thronged to see him and who could only conveniently sit with him in a tavern, are also responsible for this habit, so perilously attractive to men of genius. From the decorous Addison and the brilliant Bolingbroke onward, the eighteenth century records hard drinking as the common incident of intellectual eminence.

To a man who had shone supreme in the most glowing society, and who was now an exciseman in a country town, with a home that cannot have been very exhilarating, and with a nervous system highly strung, the temptation of the warm tavern and the admiring circle there, may well have been almost irresistible. Some attempt to say that his intemperance was exaggerated. I neither affirm nor deny. It was not as a sot he drank; that no one insinuated; if he succumbed, it was to good fellowship.

I do not seek to palliate or excuse, and, indeed, none will be turned to dissipation by Burns' example; he paid too dearly for it. But I will say this, that it all seems infinitely little, infinitely remote. Why do we strain, at this distance, to discern this dim spot on the poet's mantle. Shakespeare and Ben Jonson took their cool tankard at the Mermaid; we cannot afford, in the strictest view of literary responsibility, to quarrel with them for that. When we consider Pitt and Goethe we do not concentrate our vision on Pitt's bottles of port or Goethe's bottles of Moselle. Then why, we ask, is there such a chasm between the Mermaid and the Globe, and why are the vintages of Wimbledon and Weimer so much more innocent than the simple punch-bowl of Inveraray marble and its contents?

I should like to go a step further and affirm that we have something to be grateful for even in the weaknesses of men like Burns. Mankind is helped in its progress almost as much by the study of imperfection as by the contemplation of perfection. Had we nothing before us in our futile and halting lives but saints and the ideal, we might well fail altogether. We grope blindly along the catacombs of the world, we climb the dark ladder of life, we feel our way to futurity, but we can scarcely see an inch around or before us. We stumble and falter and fall, our hands and knees are bruised and sore, and we look up for light and guidance. Could we see nothing but distant unapproachable impeccability, we might well sink prostrate in the hopelessness of emulation and the weariness of despair. Is it not then, when all seems blank and lightless and lifeless, when strength and courage flag, and when perfection seems as remote as a star, is it not then that imperfection helps us? When we see that the greatest and choicest images of God have had their weaknesses like ours, their temptations, their hours of darkness, their bloody sweat, are we not encouraged by their lapses and catastrophies to find energy for one more effort, one more struggle? Where they failed we feel it a less dishonour to fail; their errors and sorrows make, as it were, an easier ascent from infinite imperfection to infinite perfection. Man after all is not ripened by virtue alone. Were it so this world were a paradise of Angels. No! Like the growth of the earth, he is the fruit of all the seasons; the accident of a thousand accidents, a living mystery, moving through the seen to the unseen. He is sown in dishonour; he is matured under all the varieties of heat and cold; in mist, and wrath, in sorrow and vapours, in the melancholy of autumn, in the torpor of winter, as well as in the rapture and fragrance of summer, or the balmy affluence of the spring—its breath, its sunshine, its dew. And at the end he is reaped—the product, not of one climate, but of all; not of good alone, but of evil; not of joy alone, but of sorrow—perhaps mellowed and ripened, perhaps stricken and withered and sour. How, then, shall we judge any one? How, at any rate, shall we judge a giant, great in gifts, great in temptation; great in strength and great in weakness? Let us glory in his strength and be comforted in his weakness. And when we thank Heaven for the inestimable gift of Burns, we do not need to remember wherein he was imperfect, we cannot bring ourselves to regret that he was made of the same clay as ourselves.

—EARL OF ROSEBERY

158

ROBERT BURNS, HIS MEDICAL FRIENDS, ATTENDANTS AND BIOGRAPHER
(*Annals of Medical History*, Vol. X. New York, Paul B. Hoeber Co.)

One hundred and twenty-seven years have elapsed since Dr. James Currie, F.R.S., of Liverpool, published the first great biography of Robert Burns.

Dr. Currie had met the poet but once and then only for a few minutes in the streets of Dumfries, so that he was entirely dependent on others for the information on which he based his opinions of the character and habits of Burns. A few days after Burns' death he wrote to John Syme, "Stamp-office Johnnie," an old college friend then living in Dumfries: "By what I have heard, he was not very correct in his conduct, and a report goes about that he died of the effects of habitual drinking." But doubting the truthfulness of the current gossip, he asked Syme pointedly "What did Burns die of?" It is easily seen why he should have gone to Syme for information as Burns had lived for a time over the stamp office and it was known that he and Syme were intimate. Syme, therefore, above all others is responsible for the opinions which Currie afterwards expressed as to Burns' habits; and when the biography was published, it was to Syme that Currie wrote for reassurance that he had done justice to his subject. It is difficult to discern the reason for Syme's attitude, but apparently the cause of the poet's untimely death was a mystery for which some explanation had to be proffered.

Two incidents, however, discredit Syme as a dependable witness: the sword incident, on the occasion of his reproving the poet regarding his habits, of which there are several conflicting accounts, and his apocryphal version of the circumstances under which "Scots Wha Hae" was produced during the Galloway tour. In regard to the latter incident, the letter Burns wrote Thomson in forwarding the poem disposes of Syme's fabrication.

As Burns' biographer, Dr. Currie is known to have been actuated by admiration, friendship, and the benevolent purpose of helping to provide for the widow and family; and it is quite evident that he was willing, if not anxious, to undertake the task. He was especially concerned that Burns' good friend, Mrs. Walter Riddell of Woodley Park, should not be chosen. Therefore, the opinions to which Currie gave currency in the biography, were no doubt received with sorrowful acquiescence by many who would have disputed them, had they emanated from a less friendly source.

Subsequent writers have depended largely upon the material in the way of manuscripts, letters, and information furnished by the poet's family, friends, Masonic brethren and correspondents (along with not a little gossip and tittle-tattle of residents of Dumfries and other casual acquaintances) placed at Currie's disposal, and have thereby been influenced in accepting his conclusions. However, there has been a gradual accumulation of information and criticism, pointing out inaccuracies and statements disputed by reliable witnesses, leading to a growing conviction that Dr. Currie unwittingly, but nevertheless grossly, misrepresented the habits and character of the Scottish poet.

Many who have pondered on the activities and read the poems and letters of Burns find it difficult to believe that these are consistent with a life of drunkenness and debauchery; or that his early death is satisfactorily explained by alcoholism. The question therefore naturally arises: If Burns did not die from alcoholic excess, what was the real cause which lead to the death, at thirty-seven years of age, of a man of his physical strength and vigor? A positive denial must be based on convincing data establishing an intelligent diagnosis. This was the problem which presented itself to me many years ago and led me to consider the sources of information, if such might be traced, which would afford an answer.

On reading Allan Cunningham's *Complete Works of Burns*, one was surprised at the numerous references, in the Poet's correspondence, to his health at various periods of his life. These, collected and pieced together, furnish a clinical record leading to the inevitable conclusion that Dr. Currie's opinions were based on insufficient and unreliable information and that Burns died from rheumatism and heart disease.

Burns was born January twenty-fifth, 1759, the eldest of the seven children of William Burness and Agnes Brown, honest, thoughtful, religious Scottish peasantry. The roof of the "auld clay biggin," built by his father, was blown off a few nights after he was born and the infant was carried through the storm to a neighbour's house, a fitting prelude to the eventful drama of which the closing scene was in the small house in the Mill Vennell, Dumfries, thirty-seven years later.

The medical profession figures much less prominently in Burns' writings than that of either law or divinity.   Neither were his social intimacies as frequent and close with the doctors as with the lawyers and the clergy.   In the convivial gatherings of which he wrote with poetic coloring:

> I've been at drunken writers' feasts,
> Nay, been bitch-fou 'mang godly priests.

the representatives of medicine were conspicuous by their absence.   It was the lawyers and "new licht" ministers who enlisted the inspired ploughboy in the controversy that was then dividing the more liberal from the rigidly orthodox members of the Kirk in the West of Scotland.   While his onslaught on the "auld licht" with the keen satire and unanswerable humour of the "Kirk's Alarm," "Holy Willie's Prayer," "The Holy Fair," and the "Twa Herds," spread the name and heightened the fame of the Poet and set the countryside roaring, the author unfortunately inspired fear and wrath in the minds of a numerous and respected part of the community.

When the fighting spirit was aroused he might boast:

> The mair they talk I'm kenned the better,
> E'en let them clash,

yet in an opposite mood of extreme melancholy and regret, which was so frequent with him, he uttered the prayer:

> If I have wandered in those paths
> Of life I ought to shun,
> As something loudly in my breast
> Remonstrates I have done.   .   .   .
>
> Where with intention I have erred
> No other plea I have;
> But Thou art good and Goodness still
> Delighteth to forgive.

Burns was at Irvine learning flax dressing in 1781, a rustic celebrity of twenty-two years known only to his companions and a few others as a rhymer, and there he made his first medical acquaintance, Dr. Hamilton, who assisted him in the publication of the first edition of his poems at Kilmarnock, five years later.

When his father, harassed by the misfortunes of his farming venture at Lochlea, was dying of consumption, the medical attendant was that excellent man and physician, Dr. John MacKenzie of Mauchline, who afterwards described so sympathetically the Burns' family circle. Attracted by the magnetic personality, and quickly perceiving the genius of the Poet, he became his lifelong friend.

The family removed to the farm of Mossgiel, near Mauchline, in 1784, and Dr. MacKenzie introduced Burns to Dugald Stewart, Professor of Philosophy in the University of Edinburgh, who invited him to dinner in company with Lord Daer, Lord Selkirk's son and heir, an event which he celebrated as that "ne'er to be forgotten day."

A more distinguished medical friend was Dr. John Moore, a Scotsman who had settled in London, the father of Sir John Moore, the hero of Corunna. At the instance of Mrs. Dunlop, the earliest patroness of Burns, Dr. Moore entered into correspondence with him during the Ellisland period. Moore, who was prominent in literary circles at that time, became an admirer, advised him to familiarize himself with the classic mythology and the history of France and Britain, and otherwise assumed the rôle of critic and mentor. He urged him to abandon the provincial dialect and write in English; but happily the independent spirit and good sense of the Poet prevented a transition so inadvisable. It was to Moore that Burns wrote the autobiographical letter later so extensively used by his biographers. The correspondents never met.

On his second visit to Edinburgh, having sprained his knee in August, 1787, Burns was attended by Dr. James Gregory, successor to Cullen as Professor of Medicine, and the most eminent physician of his day in Edinburgh.

Dr. Alexander Wood, "lang Sandy Wood, one of the best hearted of men," was the surgical consultant with Gregory. It was he who urged Burns to write the "Elegy on the Death of Lord President Dundas," and personally delivered the poem and accompanying letter to his Lordship's son. Burns was incensed by the latter's apparent lack of appreciation and attention: "He took no more notice of my poem or me than I had been a strutting peddler." It was Wood who successfully recommended the Poet an appointment in the Excise.

When Burns left Ellisland to live in Dumfries, he made the acquaintance of Dr. William Maxwell, whose father had been out with Prince Charlie in '45. Maxwell was a medical student in Paris at the time of the execution of Louis XVI. Both Burns and Maxwell were under suspicion of sympathy with the French Revolution and Burns feared he would lose his post in the Excise; but when the war broke out between Britain and France in 1793, he joined the Dumfries Volunteers and further showed his patriotism in the stirring poem "Does haughty Gaul invasion threat?"

It was to Maxwell he addressed the well-known quatrain on the recovery of Miss Jessie Staig, the doctor's patient:

> Maxwell, if honour here you crave,
> That merit I deny,
> You save fair Jessie from the grave!
> An angel could not die.

Maxwell attended Burns in his last illness. With Syme and McMurdo he enlisted the services of his colleague, Dr. James Currie, and furnished him with information regarding the Poet's illness and death. He also helped to collect the material for the *Life of Burns* which Currie, after four years' hard work, published in four volumes in 1800, by which £1,500 were raised for the support of the widow and family. Maxwell shares with Syme the responsibility for the misinformation given to Currie.

Dr. James Currie (1756-1805) was himself a literary man of repute, a Scotsman, who had settled in Liverpool and acquired a distinguished place in his profession. As a physician he is best known for having introduced the clinical thermometer into practice and the use of cold baths in the treatment of fever. He was a Liberal, an advocate of the abolition of slavery, and an ardent temperance reformer. He died of tuberculosis and heart disease, the latter due to a severe attack of rheumatism from which he suffered while a student in Edinburgh. His *Life of Burns*, though with all kindliness of intention and the best of motives, has unfortunately been the basis of all subsequent writings which have attributed the Poet's early death to drunkenness and debauchery.

Currie states that "though by nature of an athletic temperament, Burns had in his constitution the peculiarities and the delicacies that belong to the temperament of the genius. He was liable from a very early period of life to that interruption in the process of digestion which arises from deep and anxious thought. Connected with this disorder of the stomach there was a disposition to headache, more especially about the temples and eyeballs and frequently accompanied by violent and irregular movements of the heart." He then traces the gradual decline in the Poet's health: "Perpetually stimulated by alcohol in one or other of its various forms, the inordinate actions of the circulating system became at length habitual . . . and the powers of life began to fail." The circulatory disturbance referred to by Currie is certainly not symptomatic of alcoholism, but is readily explained as a sequel to rheumatism. "Upwards of a year preceding his death his temper became more irritable and gloomy, and he fled from himself into society of the lowest kind," and concludes "He who suffers the pollution of inebriation, how shall he escape other pollution?" These uncharitable and unwarranted insinuations are contradicted by fellow citizens of Burns who were in frequent and intimate contact with him during the period to which Currie has reference. Apparently the statements, in so far as they are not mere assumption, were based on the misinformation of those who failed entirely to recognize the nature of Burns' disease, or on the idle gossip of busybodies.

Currie refers to the tendency on the part of men of genius to indulge in narcotic excesses, which "acting on the system of nerves so as to give a fictitious gaiety to the ideas of imagination, alter the effect of the external impression which we receive. Opium is chiefly employed for this purpose by the disciples of Mahammed and the inhabitants of Asia; but alcohol, the principle of intoxication in vinous and spiritous liquors, is preferred in Europe and is universally used in the Christian world." That he was an extremist is evident: "There are a great number of other substances which may be considered under this point of view. Tobacco, tea and coffee are of the number . . . and an enquiry into the particular effects of each on the health, morals and happiness of those who use them would be curious and useful."

It is not my purpose to picture Burns as a model of sobriety or to state that he was not, as was the custom of the times in which he lived, given to occasional excesses. He frequented convivial gatherings and celebrated these occasions in verse; he extolled the virtues of alcohol in some of his poems, and with poetic license undoubtedly exaggerated his own excesses. These follies represented the exuberance of ardent youth; but we have the testimony of intimate acquaintances, of fellow citizens of Dumfries, and others of unimpeachable character, which should acquit him of the charge of habitual drunkenness that destroyed his health and led to his early death.

Rev. James Grey, minister in Dumfries at the time, says, "The truth is, Burns was seldom intoxicated"; Mr. Alexander Findlater, his superior officer in the Excise, who saw Burns frequently during the Ellisland and Dumfries periods and who was with him the night he died, states emphatically, "I never beheld anything like the gross enormities with which he is now charged"; and Dr. Copland Hutchinson is reported by Allan Cunningham: "I lived in Dumfries during the whole period that Burns lived there. I was much about and saw him daily, but I never saw him even the worse for liquor. He might drink as much as other men but certainly not more." Even Cunningham says, "Burns was no tippler; he loved the excitement of company and to see the bottle circulate to others as well as to himself."

Nanse Tinnock, "Poosie Nansie," the hostess of the Mauchline Howff, famed as the scene of "The Jolly Beggars," adds her testimony regarding Burns' habits when he was under great strain and temptation. (He was deserted for a time by Jean Armour; the marriage lines were burned by her father, who ordered him out of the house when he visited her after the birth of the twins. He was threatened with the law, and his passage was actually taken for Jamaica. Burns had boasted of toasting the Scottish members of parliament at "Auld Nanse Tinnock's nine times a week.") She exclaimed, "The lad hardly ever drank three half-mutchkins under my roof in his life."

It is difficult to believe that a man who rode thirty or forty miles daily as a gauger, of whose work in the Excise no complaint ever was made; who superintended his farm, watched over the education of his children, interested himself in libraries, kept up a large correspondence, collected, rewrote or composed some two hundred and sixty songs with accompanying letters, the last less than a fortnight before his death, was debased and dying from alcoholism. "Tam o' Shanter," "To Mary in Heaven," "Scots Wha Hae," and the "Banks of Devon" show no evidence of having been written by a habitual drunkard and yet they were all composed at that period when bad habits were said to be undermining his health. The pride, spirit, and patriotism of this alleged drunkard were such that he indignantly refused to accept payment from Johnson for the immortal lyrics he was writing or adapting for "The Museum," even though he was in financial distress.

Through his own letters, his brother Gilbert, Professor Dugald Stewart, Rev. Dr. Hugh Blair, John Richmond, Professor Walker, Mrs. Riddell, Burns' wife and servants and others, his life and habits at Mt. Oliphant, Lochlea, Mossgiel and Mauchline, Edinburgh, Ellisland and the final years at Dumfries, can be traced, and the weight of testimony is against the doleful verdict of Currie.

Robert and Gilbert Burns had each an allowance of only seven pounds a year when on the farms of Lochlea and Mossgiel, a modest sum for riotous living!

With what prescience Burns anticipated future events in his letter to Mrs. Dunlop from Edinburgh in 1787:

When proud Fortune's ebbing tide recedes you will bear me witness that, when my bubble of fame was at the highest, I stood unintoxicated with the inebriating cup in my hand, looking forward with rueful resolve to the hastening time when the blow of calumny should dash it to the ground with all the eagerness of vengeful triumph.

The ever present fear was again expressed to Mrs. Riddell, a few days before his death, of the time "when no dread of his resentment would restrain them nor prevent malice or envy from pouring forth their venom to blast his fame."

A critical review of trustworthy information fortunately furnishes a medical history of the long illness that led to his death at thirty-seven years of age, which to my mind shows conclusively that it was rheumatism and endocarditis which, with almost equal certainty, had its inception in his childhood.

In extenuation of the mistaken diagnosis of Currie and Maxwell, it should be remembered that the relationship of rheumatism to heart disease was not widely known at that time, as this was first established by Matthew Baillie in 1786. Further, it is only within the past twenty-five or thirty years that growing pains, tonsillitis, chorea and infected teeth, have been recognized to be very frequently the cause of heart disease, especially in childhood. Clinical thermometers were not commonly in use at that time, so that slight febrile reactions were readily overlooked. As the discovery of the stethoscope by Laënnec was not until 1818, that valuable diagnostic instrument was not then available.

The Poet's brother, Gilbert, supplies suggestive information regarding the beginning of his illness: "My brother at the age of thirteen assisted in the threshing of the crop of corn, and at fifteen was the principal labourer on the farm, for we had no hired servants, male or female. The anguish of mind we felt at our tender years under these straits and difficulties was very great. . . . At this time (Mt. Oliphant, 1774), he was almost constantly afflicted in the evening with a dull headache, which at a future period of his life was to be exchanged for a palpitation of the heart and a threatening of fainting and suffocation in the night time."

Burns evidently had another serious illness when he was engaged in the labour of flax dressing at Irvine in 1781. He wrote to his father:

My health is nearly the same as when you were here only my sleep is a little sounder, and on the whole I am rather better than otherwise though I mend by very slow degrees. The weakness of my nerves has so debilitated my mind that I dare neither review past wants nor look forward into futurity, for the least anxiety or perturbation in my breast produces the most unhappy effect on my whole frame. . . . I am quite transported at the thought that ere long, perhaps very soon, I shall bid an eternal adieu to all the pains and uneasiness and disquietude of this weary life for I assure you I am heartily tired of it; and if I do not very much deceive myself, I could contentedly and gladly resign it.

In his Common Place Book under date of August, 1784, Burns has an entry: "When fainting fits and other alarming symptoms of a pleurisy or some other dangerous disorder, which indeed still threatens me, first put nature on the alarm." He then wrote "The Prayer in Prospect of Death."

John Richmond, with whom Burns lived at Mrs. Carfrae's in Baxter's Close on his first Edinburgh visit in 1786, says that "the Poet was so knocked up by his walk from Mauchline to Edinburgh, that he could not leave his room for the next two days."

Dugald Stewart wrote Dr. Currie of the same period:

> He told me indeed himself that the weakness of his stomach was such as to deprive him of any merit of his temperance. I was, however, somewhat alarmed . . . when he confessed to me the first night he spent in my house . . . that he had been much disturbed in bed by a palpitation of his heart, which he said was a complaint to which he had of late become subject.

On the border tour with Ainslie, May, 1787,[1] there is an entry in his journal: "I am taken extremely ill with strong feverish symptoms . . . embittering remorse scares my fancy at the gloomy forebodings of death."

A letter which Burns wrote to Dr. Moore from Mauchline, August second, 1787, is of special interest: "I am here under the care of a surgeon, with a bruised limb extended on a cushion; a drunken coachman was the cause; I got my fall on Saturday and I am getting slowly better," etc. Three months and a half later he wrote from Edinburgh to Miss Chalmers: "For the first time, yesterday I crossed the room on crutches."

The following extracts from his letters refer to his condition following the accident:

> January twentieth, 1788, he wrote Clarinda of "an old indisposition accompanied by much to make me good for nothing, so that I can scarcely hold up my head.
>
> January twenty-first, 1788, to Mrs. Dunlop: "After six weeks' confinement I am beginning to walk across the room. They have been six horrible weeks, anguish and low spirits make me unfit to read, write or think."

To Rev. John Skinner from Edinburgh, February fourteenth, 1788: "I have been a cripple now near three months, though I am getting vastly better" . . . He refers to the illness following the injury to his knee, for which he was treated by Dr. Gregory and Dr. Wood, and the expression, as we know, is one commonly used by persons suffering from rheumatism. How unfortunate Gregory and Wood left no account of this illness!

To Mr. Cruickshank from Mauchline, March third, 1788: "My unlucky knee is rather worse and I fear for some time will scarcely stand the fatigue of my Excise instructions."

His despondency and anticipation of death are evident again in a letter to Mr. Robert Muir, Kilmarnock, March seventh, 1788: "If we lie down in the grave, the whole man a piece of broken machinery, be it so: at least there is an end of pain, woes and wants."

He wrote Richard Brown from Glasgow, March twenty-sixth, 1788: "Watching, fatigue, and a load of care almost too heavy for my shoulders have in some degree actually fevered me."

[1] It is well known that many of the dates attached to Burns' letters are only approximate, having been added by Dr. Currie.

April twenty-eighth, 1788, to Mrs. Dunlop from Ellisland:

I have slept in an apartment in which the force of the winds and rains were only mitigated by being sifted through the numberless apertures in the windows and walls. In consequence, I was Sunday, Monday and part of Tuesday, unable to stir out of bed with all the miserable effects of a violent cold."

August, 1788, he wrote another letter to Cruickshank from Ellisland: "I fear my knee will never be entirely well, and an unlucky fall this winter has made it still worse." The trouble with his knee therefore lasted more than a year. Evidently the injury to the knee localized the rheumatism in that joint, whence it spread to other parts of the body.

Another phase of his illness is referred to in a letter to William Creech from Ellisland, May thirtieth, 1789: "I had intended troubling you with another long letter, but at present the delightful sensations of an omnipotent toothache so engrosses all my inner man as to put out of my power even to write nonsense. . . . Fifty troops of infernal spirits are driving post from ear to ear along my jaw bones."

About this time the "Address to the Toothache" appeared, from which it is evident that he had personal knowledge of that disease, and it is scarcely necessary at the present time to emphasize the relationship of infection of the teeth to rheumatism:

> My curse upon thy venomed stang
> That shoots my tortured gums alang;
> And through my lugs gaes many a twang
> Wi' gnawing vengeance;
> Tearing my nerves wi' bitter pang
> Like wracking engines.
>
> When fevers burn or ague freezes,
> Rheumatics gnaw or cholic squeezes;
> Our neighbour's sympathy may ease us
> Wi' pitying moan;
> But thee, thou hell of all diseases
> Aye mocks our groan.

To Mrs. Dunlop, September thirteenth, 1789: "I am groaning under the miseries of a diseased nervous system. What is man? Today in the luxuriance of health, exulting in the enjoyment of existence; in a few days, perhaps a few hours, loaded with conscious, painful being, counting the tardy pace of the lingering moments by the re-percussions of anguish."

At this time he had serious financial worries: "With the task of the superlatively damned to make one guinea do the business of three."

February twentieth, 1790, to Clarinda: "I have been ill the whole winter, incessant headache, depression of spirits and deranged nervous system."

In October, 1791, Burns left Ellisland to live in the cramped quarters of the Wee Vennel in Dumfries. He apparently had better health for about three years, at least there is no further reference to ill health until the end of 1793, when he wrote to Lady Glencairn of the "cheerless gloom and sinking despondency of diseased nerves," etc.

February, 1794, to Cunningham: "For these two months I have not been able to lift my pen. My constitution and frame were *ab origine* blasted with a deep taint of hypochondria which poisons my existence. My feelings at times could only be envied by a reprobate spirit listening to the sentence that dooms it to perdition."

June twenty-fifth, 1794, to Mrs. Dunlop: "To tell you that I have been in poor health will not be excuse enough, though it is true. I am afraid that I am about to suffer for the follies of my youth. My medical friends threaten me with a flying gout." Considering the previous and subsequent history of his case, it seems altogether probable that he had a recrudescence of the rheumatism at this time.

Cunningham states that during 1795, "Burns was fallen off indeed, not in brightness of intellect, but in vigor and health. His walks were shorter, his rests more frequent; his smile had something of melancholy in it . . . and among the sons of men he looked like one marked out for an early grave." These symptoms are obviously more suggestive of heart disease than of alcoholism.

January thirty-first, 1796, after the death of his friend Riddell of Friar's Carse, Burns wrote to the widow: "The autumn robbed me of my only daughter, a darling child. . . . I had scarcely begun to recover from the shock when I became myself a victim of a most severe rheumatic fever and long the die spun doubtful, until after many weeks of a sick bed, it seems to have turned up life and I am beginning to crawl across my room." Apparently he was confined to bed, or at least to the house, from about October, 1795, to January 30, 1796.

The disease had now declared itself so definitely that there can be no further doubt regarding the diagnosis, and both he and his friends became alarmed.

Currie states that "From October, 1795, to the January following, Burns was confined to the house by an 'accidental' complaint." We have Burns' own definite statement in contradiction that he suffered from an attack of rheumatic fever.

Currie continues: "A few days after he began to go abroad he dined at a tavern and returned about three o'clock on a very cold morning, benumbed and intoxicated." This was followed by an attack of rheumatism which confined him about a week. "His appearance now began to fail; his hand shook and his voice faltered on any exertion or emotion; his pulse became weaker and more rapid, and pain in the larger joints and in the hands and feet deprived him of the enjoyment of refreshing sleep." Medical men assuredly will recognize in this description the symptoms of rheumatism and heart disease rather than of alcoholism. Currie was evidently in error in his statement of the time when his health began to fail, as Cunningham had noticed it in the previous year. He further entirely overlooked or misrepresented the attack of rheumatic fever in October, 1795. "About the end of June he was advised to go into the country and, impatient of medical advice as well as every control, he determined for himself to try the benefits of bathing in the sea." This statement is not in accord with Burns, who says he went to Brow on Maxwell's advice.

February, 1796, he had a relapse of the rheumatism, apparently following the Globe tavern incident referred to by Currie. That a patient who was just beginning to crawl about after a serious attack of acute rheumatism, which confined him to bed for three months, should have attended a dinner suggests that neither Burns nor his advisers understood the nature of his illness. It is certainly no cause for wonder that he should have fainted, fallen in the snow and suffered a relapse, and it is an arbitrary presumption to attribute such consequences to alcohol.

He was still under the care of Dr. Maxwell. A little later he wrote to Mitchell of the Excise: "Rheumatism, cold and fever have formed to me a terrible combination; I close my eyes in misery and open them without hope."

He was in financial distress and threatened by his creditors. About the end of June, under Maxwell's advice, he went to Brow, a cold, bleak watering place on the Solway, to try the effects of sea-bathing. This unfortunate treatment, as one would expect, aggravated the disease.

Mrs. Riddell, who was residing near Brow at the time, invited him to her house, sending her carriage for him as he was unable to walk. She says:

The stamp of death was impressed on his features. His first words to her were, "Well, Madam, have you any commands for the other world?" His looks were hollow and ghastly; a tremor pervaded his whole frame; his tongue was parched.

July seventh, Burns wrote to Cunningham:

In these eight or nine months I have been ailing, sometimes bedfast, sometimes not. For the past three months I have been tortured with an excruciating rheumatism which has reduced me to nearly the last state. Pale, emaciated, so feeble as to occasionally need help from my chair.

He wrote to James Johnson from Dumfries, July fourth:

The hand of pain and sorrow and care has these many months lain heavy on me.
. . . This protracting, slow, consuming illness which hangs over me will, I
doubt much, my dear friend, ever arrest my sun before he has well reached his
middle career.

A few days later he wrote to his brother, Gilbert:

I am dangerously ill and not likely to get better. . . . An inveterate
rheumatism has reduced me to such a state of debility . . . that I can scarcely
stand on my legs.

He wrote to Mrs. Dunlop from Brow, July twelfth:

An illness which has long hung about me in all probability will speedily send me
beyond that bourne whence no traveller returns. . . . The remembrance (of his
correspondence with her) yet adds one more pulse to my poor palpitating heart.
Farewell!
He grew feverish on the 14th day of July, felt himself sinking, and longed to be
home. . . . He returned from Brow to Dumfries, July 18th, in a small spring
cart. The ascent to the house was steep and the cart stopped at the foot of the
Mill Hole Brae. When he alighted he shook much and stood with difficulty. He
seemed unable to stand upright. He stopped as if in pain and walked tottering
towards the house. (Cunningham.)

To the anxious enquiries of citizens of Dumfries, Dr. Maxwell shook
his head, "He cannot be worse." John Gibson, a fellow member of the
Dumfries volunteers, called on him. Burns appealed to him, "John,
don't let the awkward squad fire over me." "A tremor," says Maxwell,
"pervaded his frame; his tongue, though often refreshed, became parched;
his mind, when not roused by conversation, sank into delirium." On the
second and third days after his return from Brow the fever increased and
his strength diminished. The fourth day, July twenty-first, 1796, he
died at the age of thirty-seven years and seven months.
Even the death scene is obviously misrepresented by Cunningham:
"When his attendant, James Maclure, held a cordial to his lips, he swallowed
it eagerly, rose almost wholly up, spread out his hands, sprang forward
nearly the whole length of the bed, fell on his face and expired." Chamber's
comment is reasonable and evidently true: "The bard was far indeed from
being in a condition to make any violent movement. Though he had been
muttering in delirium for some time before, he died in a state of perfect
calmness, the calmness of exhaustion."
Burns was by nature strong and vigorous, both physically and mentally;
clear of vision; of an intense, nervous temperament; independent, proud,

ambitious, imaginative; he was impatient of restraint and subject to moods varying rapidly from gaiety to the deepest depression.

In a person of this type it is common that mental and nervous stress, worry and other emotional disturbance, produce a characteristic group of symptoms: headache, sleeplessness, digestive disturbance, irritability, apprehensiveness, depression, often ending in a "nervous breakdown." If he is suffering at the same time from organic disease, a vicious circle develops, in which there is a mutual aggravation and intermingling of nervous and organic symptoms. This is clearly evident in Burns' case and it is not difficult to trace a relationship between his various illnesses and coincidental nervous and mental stress. The overwork, worry, privation and exposure of his early years predisposed him to rheumatic infection and endocarditis, reasonably accounting for the significant symptoms which appeared at fifteen years of age.

In his second serious illness at twenty-two years of age the manifestations were mostly nervous, though the phrases "anxiety or perturbation in my breast" and "pains and uneasiness" are at least suggestive of rheumatic and cardiac trouble. Three years later "alarming symptoms of a pleurisy or some other dangerous disorder, fainting fits," etc. point definitely to organic disease, the nature of which is made reasonably manifest two years later when an apparently slight injury to the knee was followed by a "crippling" illness which more or less incapacitated him for a year. During this time there are references to feverish attacks, to toothache, spells of digestive disturbance, nervous depression, irritability and kindred symptoms.

In the middle of 1794 "a flying gout" made its appearance, and a year later an attack of rheumatic fever which confined him to bed for over three months.

Beyond this point the case was an ordinary one of rheumatism with heart complications, shortness of breath, faintness, weakness, rapid, irregular pulse (auricular fibrillation), and toward the end, fever, parched tongue and delirium, presumably due to a bacterial endocarditis which developed as a terminal infection.

One need not look for a complete and accurate clinical description of his case; but it is remarkable that in his correspondence the symptoms Burns describes and the information he furnishes are sufficiently definite to place the diagnosis of his disease beyond reasonable doubt.

—H. B. ANDERSON, M.D.
Toronto.

Direct Descendants of Robert Burns

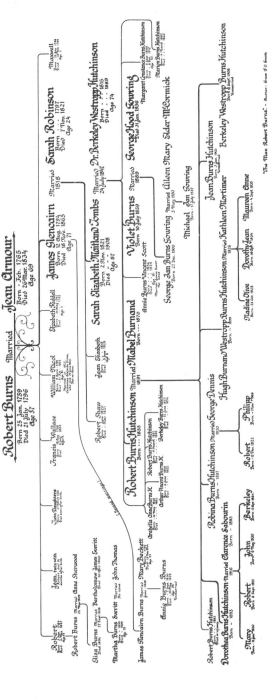

"The Man Robert Burns." - Author: Snow D. C. Smith.

List of Subscribers

Aikenhead, James, Toronto, Ont.
Aitken, William, Toronto, Ont.
Allan, Thomas, Hamilton, Ont.
Allin, R. W., Toronto, Ont.
Anderson, Donald Hume, St. Thomas, Ont.
Anderson, Dr. Duncan MacKenzie, Toronto, Ont.
Anderson, Dr. H. B., Toronto, Ont.
Anderson, John H., Toronto, Ont.
Archibald, Dr. T. D., Toronto, Ont.
Atkinson, J. E., Toronto, Ont.

Baird, J. M., Toronto, Ont.
Bannerman, Donald, Toronto, Ont.
Barber, Eric Edmund, Toronto, Ont.
Barclay, Rt. Rev. William, Hamilton, Ont.
Barnes, Rev. J. H., Toronto, Ont.
Baxter, William, Tranent, Scotland.
Beath, Lance B., Toronto, Ont.
Beatty, Sir Edward, Montreal, Que.
Beattie, Helen, Toronto, Ont.
Bell, David W., Toronto, Ont.
Bertram, Henry, Dundas, Ont.
Black, William Robert, Toronto, Ont.
Blackburn, Peter Allan, Oshawa, Ont.
Bonnell, Franklin H., Vancouver, B.C.
Botterell, Richard F., Montreal, Que.
Bowles, Walter F., Toronto, Ont.
Boyter, J. Bowman, Toronto, Ont.
Bradwin, F. W., Toronto, Ont.
Brewing, Rev. Dr. Richard, Toronto, Ont.
Brewis, Lillie, Hamilton, Ont.
Brown, James C., Hamilton, Ont.
Browne, George R., Toronto, Ont.
Bryce, Very Rev. Dr. Peter, Toronto, Ont.
Bucham, William, Winnipeg, Man.

Buchanan, W. W., Toronto, Ont.
Bulger, John E., Toronto, Ont.
Burness, C. Stuart, Toronto, Ont.
Burness, L. R., Rangoon, Burma.
Burns, Rev. Robert Newton, Toronto, Ont.
Burton, C. L., Toronto, Ont.
Burton, E. G., Toronto, Ont.

Canadian Bank of Commerce Library, Toronto, Ont.
Cameron, A. Kirk, Montreal, Que.
Cameron, Col. H. S., Toronto, Ont.
Cameron, Neil C., Toronto, Ont.
Campbell, Dr. Colin A., Toronto, Ont.
Campbell, J. D., Toronto, Ont.
Campbell, Rev. Dr. Malcolm A., Montreal, Que.
Campbell, William A., Toronto, Ont.
Carlaw, Alec. Lyle, Glasgow, Scotland.
Carlyle, J. A., Toronto, Ont.
Carmichael, Andrew, Toronto, Ont.
Chambers, Mrs. M., Toronto, Ont.
Chambers, William C., Toronto, Ont.
Cheyne, James, Toronto, Ont.
Child, Charles B., Toronto, Ont.
Chisholm, H. H., Oakville, Ont.
Chisholm, Col. James, Hamilton, Ont.
Christie, Rev. Dr. Wallace, Toronto, Ont.
Clark, J. G., Toronto, Ont.
Clendining, Robert H., Toronto, Ont.
Cockburn, J. D., Toronto, Ont.
Cockram, Rev. W. Ewart, Toronto, Ont.
Cody, Rev. Dr. J. H., Toronto, Ont.
Coleman, His Honour D. B., Whitby, Ont.
Colquhoun, Charles W., Toronto, Ont.
Compton, Robert, Toronto, Ont.
Comrie, Robert, Toronto, Ont.

Copeland, J. F., Toronto, Ont.
Copus, Frank A., Stratford, Ont.
Cousins, Edward L., Toronto, Ont.
Cowie, Hedley Vicars, Toronto, Ont.
Cowie, Richard T. F., Toronto, Ont.
Cowie, Robert Wright Ralston, Toronto, Ont.
Craig, John, Toronto, Ont.
Creighton, Thomas Kelso, Oshawa, Ont.
Creighton, T. M., Toronto, Ont.
Crichton, Arthur S., Toronto, Ont.
Crump, John, Toronto, Ont.

Dalton, Mrs. William, Toronto, Ont.
Dandie, Walter, Toronto, Ont.
Davidson, George B., Toronto, Ont.
Davidson, Rev. Dr. Richard, Toronto, Ont.
Davidson, Robert, Toronto, Ont.
Day, Mrs. Elizabeth, Harrogate, England.
Dewar, James A., Oshawa, Ont.
Dewar, James E., Toronto, Ont.
Dickie, Edward, Toronto, Ont.
Dodd, William D., Toronto, Ont.
Dollard, Rt. Rev. Mgr. J. B., Toronto, Ont.
Domm, Rev. Gordon, Toronto, Ont.
Donaldson, A. G., Toronto, Ont.

Doney, Dr. Harvey, Toronto, Ont.
Dow, Dr. James, Toronto, Ont.
Drew, Lieut.-Col. George A., Toronto, Ont.
Duncan, Rev. Phillip, Toronto, Ont.
Duncanson, John, Toronto, Ont.
Dunlap, Mrs. David A., Toronto, Ont.
Dunlop, W. J., Toronto, Ont.
Dunn, Andrew, Toronto, Ont.
Dunn, Robert C., Toronto, Ont.

Eames, Leonard C., Hamilton, Ont.
Eaton, Lady, King, Ont.
Edmonds, Charles E., Toronto, Ont.
Ekblad, Birger E., Toronto, Ont.
Ely, Ernest Frederick, Toronto, Ont.

Ferguson, Hon. G. Howard, Toronto, Ont.
Ferguson, James, Lockerby, Dumfries, Scotland.
Findlay, Mrs. Fred, Toronto, Ont.
Finlay, Rev. James M., Toronto, Ont.
Fleming, Rt. Rev. Dr. A. L., Toronto, Ont.
Fleming, Robert, Toronto, Ont.
Flynn, James, Toronto, Ont.
Forbes, H. M., Toronto, Ont.
Foreman, Rev. Edgar, Toronto, Ont.
Fotheringham, The Venerable Archdeacon J. B., Toronto, Ont.
Fotheringham, John R., Hamilton, Scotland.
Frame, S. J., Toronto, Ont.
Fraser, J. A., Toronto, Ont.
Fraser, Rev. John Young, Toronto, Ont.
Fulton, Robert, Toronto, Ont.
Fyvie, J. M., Toronto, Ont.

Garrow, Frank, Toronto, Ont.
Gauldie, Kenneth, Toronto, Ont.
Gay, John R., Toronto, Ont.
Gibson, John C., Toronto, Ont.
Gibson, R. B., Toronto, Ont.
Gillanders, James F., Toronto, Ont.
Gillen, Alexander S., Toronto, Ont.
Gillespie, Dougald L., Toronto, Ont.
Gillespie, Walter, Toronto, Ont.
Gillies, D. B., Toronto, Ont.
Glover, Allan F., Toronto, Ont.
Gordon, Hon. G. N., Peterborough, Ont.
Gowans, Rev. C. A., Toronto, Ont.
Graham, R. M., Toronto, Ont.
Grainger, Charles E., Toronto, Ont.
Grand Lodge Library, A.F. and A.M., Toronto, Ont.
Grant, Mrs. Arthur, Toronto, Ont.
Grant, David E., Toronto, Ont.
Grant, Peter M., Toronto, Ont.
Gray, Alexander, Toronto, Ont.
Greenfield, Col. T. W., Hamilton, Ont.

Greenslade, Rev. Stanley H., Toronto, Ont.

Grubbe, Talbot P., Toronto, Ont.

Hadden, John, Toronto, Ont.

Haldenby, Brigadier Eric W., Toronto, Ont.

Hall, Irving C., Toronto, Ont.

Hamilton, Miss Emma, Toronto, Ont.

Hamilton, John P., Toronto, Ont.

Hanna, W. E., Toronto, Ont.

Hanna, W. B., Toronto, Ont.

Hardie, Alexander, Toronto, Ont.

Hardy, A. A., Toronto, Ont.

Harrison, James, Toronto, Ont.

Henderson, George, Toronto, Ont.

Henderson, James, Toronto, Ont.

Henderson, W. T. R., Toronto, Ont.

Hepburn, John T., Toronto, Ont.

Hepburn, Hon. Mitchell F., St. Thomas, Ont.

Hewitt, R. L., Toronto, Ont.

Hoban, Mary, Toronto, Ont.

Honeywell, His Honour A. E., Toronto, Ont.

Hope, Hon. Mr. Justice J. A., Toronto, Ont.

Houston, H. C., Toronto, Ont.

Howell, Stephen A., Toronto, Ont.

Howie, Frank, Toronto, Ont.

Howie, George, Toronto, Ont.

Hunnisett, Rev. Wesley A., Toronto, Ont.

Hunt, Miss Doris, Toronto, Ont.

Hunter, Col. A. T., Toronto, Ont.

Hunter, Andrew W., Toronto, Ont.

Hunter, James, Toronto, Ont.

Hunter, Jim, Toronto, Ont.

Hutton, Peter, Toronto, Ont.

Inkster, Rev. Dr. John Gibson, Toronto, Ont.

Innes, Rev. T. Christie, Toronto, Ont.

Inrig, William, Toronto, Ont.

Irish, Mark H., Toronto, Ont.

Izatt, James P., Toronto, Ont.

Jackson, His Honour J. Arthur, Toronto, Ont.

Jackson, Lloyd D., Hamilton, Ont.

James, Dr. F. Cyril, Montreal, Que.

Jamieson, Henry T., Toronto, Ont.

Jardine, W., Toronto, Ont.

Johnston, R. D., Toronto, Ont.

Kemp, Lady, Toronto, Ont.

Ketchen, Rev. Dr. H. Beverley, Hamilton, Ont.

King, Rt. Hon. W. Lyon Mackenzie, Ottawa, Ont.

Kinghorn, Andrew A., Toronto, Ont.

Kirkwood Rev. James T., Toronto, Ont.

Knox, Professor R. S., Toronto, Ont.

Laidlaw, R. A., Toronto, Ont.

Lang, Joseph N., Toronto, Ont.

Langskill, J. Roy, Toronto, Ont.

Lawrence Sam, Hamilton, Ont.

Le Clair, .V. J., Toronto, Ont.

Lee, Thomas, Toronto, Ont.

Leitch, Arthur S., Toronto, Ont.

Leith, Sam, Toronto, Ont.

Lewis, Robert, Toronto, Ont.

Lewis, Ivor R., Toronto, Ont.

Liddle, J., Toronto, Ont.

Logan, Dr. Frederick A., Toronto, Ont.

Logie, Ben., Toronto, Ont.

Logie, James, Toronto, Ont.

Lorimer, Charles S., Toronto, Ont.

Lyon, T. Stewart, Toronto, Ont.

Lyttle, Rev. Robert H., Toronto, Ont.

Mann, Dr. R. W., Toronto, Ont.

Marr, Alfred G., Toronto, Ont.

Marsh, J. F., Toronto, Ont.

Martin, John, Toronto, Ont.

Mary Mellish Archibald Memorial Library, Sackville, N.B.

Masson, Dr. Duncan M., Rochester, Minnesota, U.S.A.

Masson, Thomas M., Toronto, Ont.

Matheson, Dan., Toronto, Ont.

Meighen, Rt. Hon. Arthur, Toronto, Ont.
Melhuish, Arthur E., Toronto, Ont.
Michie, Charles, Toronto, Ont.
Michie, Col. J. F., Toronto, Ont.
Middleton, Hon. Mr. Justice W. E., Toronto, Ont.
Mitchell, B. L., Toronto, Ont.
Mitchell, W. H., Toronto, Ont.
Montgomery, Archibald W., Toronto, Ont.
Moore, G. Cecil, Toronto, Ont.
More, William G., Toronto, Ont.
Morgan, Fred W., Toronto, Ont.
Morgan, Jeremiah, Toronto, Ont.
Morison, W. A., Toronto, Ont.
Morrison, Dr. D. A., Brantford, Ont.
Morrison, Norman A., Toronto, Ont.
Morrow, Graham, Toronto, Ont.
Morrow, G. A., Toronto, Ont.
Moss, Col. Frank, Toronto, Ont.
Mount Dennis Public Library, Mount Dennis, Ont.
Muir, James, Toronto, Ont.
Murdoch, Wallace, Toronto, Ont.
Murray, Arthur, Greenock, Scotland.
Murray, Dr. Charles, The Lythe, Banchory Ternan, Scotland.
Macabe, Thomas J., Toronto, Ont.
MacCulloch, W. L., Toronto, Ont.
MacDermot, T. W. L., Toronto, Ont.
Macdonald, Hugh, Toronto, Ont.
MacDougall, Mrs. Ruth E., Vancouver, B.C.
Macfadyen, Arthur, Toronto, Ont.
Mackay, Hon. Mr. Justice J. Keiller, Toronto, Ont.
Mackellar, E. A., Toronto, Ont.
Mackenzie, G. F., Toronto, Ont.
MacKenzie, Morley E., Toronto, Ont.
MacLachlan, D. C., Toronto, Ont.
MacLellan, William, Toronto, Ont.
MacLennan, Rev. David A., Toronto, Ont.
MacMillan, Christine M., Yorkton, Sask.

Macmillan, John, Toronto, Ont.
Macnab, John, Toronto, Ont.
McArthur, Roderick, Toronto, Ont.
McBride, A. E., Toronto, Ont.
McCrea, Hon. Charles, Toronto, Ont.
McCombie, Mrs. William, Toronto, Ont.
McClelland, D. McK., Toronto, Ont.
McDougall, Neil, Toronto, Ont.
McEwan, Gordon C., Toronto, Ont.
McFadyen, Thomas, Toronto, Ont.
McFarlane, John, Toronto, Ont.
McFarlane, John Jr., Toronto, Ont.
McGhie, Dr. T. B., Toronto, Ont.
McGibbon, Lewis, Toronto, Ont.
McGillivray, Thomas Alexander, Toronto, Ont.
McGolpin, William C., Toronto, Ont.
McIlwraith, Dr. D. G., Hamilton, Ont.
McIntosh, A. A., Toronto, Ont.
McIntosh, Alex. N., Toronto, Ont.
McIntosh, Robert D., Toronto, Ont.
McIntyre, Hugh McD., Hamilton, Ont.
McKay, Harold, Toronto, Ont.
McKean, T., Toronto, Ont.
McKibbon, Lieut. James E., Trenton, Ont.
McLaren, Ian M., Toronto, Ont.
McLaren, Wallace M., Toronto, Ont.
McLean, W. A., Toronto, Ont.
McLeod, John A., Toronto, Ont.
McMynn, Thomas, Alloway, Ayr, Scotland.
McNichol, Dr. Oscar A., Toronto, Ont.
McNish, J. Douglas, Toronto, Ont.
McRobie, George A., Toronto, Ont.

Ness, John, Toronto, Ont.
Newlands, Thomas J., Hamilton, Ont.
Northey, R. K., Toronto, Ont.

Ontario Provincial Legislative Library, Toronto, Ont.
Ontario Dept. of Education Travelling Libraries.

Oshawa Collegiate Institute Library.

Oshawa Public Library.

Owen, His Grace Most Rev. Dr. Derwyn T., Toronto, Ont.

Paget, R. A., Toronto, Ont.

Palmer, H. A., Toronto, Ont.

Parker, Herbert, Toronto, Ont.

Parker, His Honour James, Toronto, Ont.

Parker, J. G., Toronto, Ont.

Parkhill, Clarence O. F., Toronto, Ont.

Parkin, John, Toronto, Ont.

Paton, Hugh, Montreal, Que.

Pauline, J. M., Toronto, Ont.

Pendlebury, H. J., Toronto, Ont.

Pettit, Holland, Toronto, Ont.

Phippen, H. W., Toronto, Ont.

Phipps, Albert E., Toronto, Ont.

Porter, Alexander D., Toronto, Ont.

Rae, Robert, Toronto, Ont.

Reid, C. Gordon L., Toronto, Ont.

Reid, Loftus A., Toronto, Ont.

Richardson, Sinclair G., Hamilton, Ont.

Riddel, John Hutton, Toronto, Ont.

Riddell, W. J., Toronto, Ont.

Riddell, Hon. Mr. Justice W. R., Toronto, Ont.

Roberts, Sir Charles G. D., Toronto, Ont.

Robertson, Alfred J., Toronto, Ont.

Robertson, Charles S., Toronto, Ont.

Robertson, Hon. R. S., Toronto, Ont.

Robertson, William, Toronto, Ont.

Rochester, Rev. William M., Toronto, Ont.

Rogerson, Robert C., Toronto, Ont.

Rose, J. G., Edinburgh, Scotland.

Ross, Bruce D., Toronto, Ont.

Ross, Thomas H., Hamilton, Ont.

Ross, Dr. Victor, Hamilton, Ont.

Rowland, John A., Toronto, Ont.

Roy, W. Ormiston, Montreal, Que.

Russell, John Gordon, Toronto, Ont.

Sachs, Rev. Rabbi Samuel, Toronto, Ont.

Samuel, Dr. Sigmund, Toronto, Ont.

Scott, George McKean, Toronto, Ont.

Scott, Hew M., Toronto, Ont.

Sealy, John D. A., Toronto, Ont.

Sedgwick, Harry, Toronto, Ont.

Sedgwick, Joseph, Toronto, Ont.

Sedgewick, R. M., Toronto, Ont.

Sedgewick, Rev. Dr. W. A., Toronto, Ont.

Selby, Dr. David L., Toronto, Ont.

Shields, Rev. Dr. Thomas T., Toronto, Ont.

Short, Mrs. Robert, Toronto, Ont.

Simpson, James I., Toronto, Ont.

Simpson, Robert B., Toronto, Ont.

Sinclair, Neil, Toronto, Ont.

Singer, George S., Toronto, Ont.

Sloan, T. Reginald, Hamilton, Ont.

Smart, Miss Mary, Toronto, Ont.

Spence, John D., Toronto, Ont.

Spiers, George P., Toronto, Ont.

Springett, Rev. Ernest J., Toronto, Ont.

Summers, W. E. G., Toronto, Ont.

Smith, Albert, Toronto, Ont.

Smith, David, Toronto, Ont.

Smith, Esther Wilson, Hamilton, Ont.

Smith, Mrs. Florence A., Vancouver, B.C.

Smith, Gladstone Joseph, Hamilton, Ont.

Smith, Gladstone Stephen, Hamilton, Ont.

Smith, Grant William, Vancouver, B.C.

Smith, Robert C., Toronto, Ont.

Smith, R. Munro, Toronto, Ont.

Smith, Samuel, Toronto, Ont.

St. Michael's College, Toronto, Ont.

Stapells, R. A., Toronto, Ont.

Tait, George Hope, Galashiels, Scotland.

Taylor, E. George T., Toronto, Ont.

Taylor, J. A. M., Toronto, Ont.

Taylor, J. W., Toronto, Ont.

Terrace, J. A., Toronto, Ont.

Thomas, Rev. William, Toronto, Ont.

Thompson, Norman H., Toronto, Ont.

Thomson, Rev. E. Archie, Elora, Ont.

Thomson, John M., Owen Sound, Ont.

Thomson, John W., Toronto, Ont.

Thomson, R. M., Toronto, Ont.

Thomson, Walter C., Pickering, Ont.

Toronto Public Library.

Totton, Joseph

Treacy, Rt. Rev. Mgr. J. P., Toronto, Ont.

Trinity College Library, Toronto, Ont.

Turley, W. E., Toronto, Ont.

Turnbull, W. G., Toronto, Ont.

Tuttle, The Rt. Rev. Dr. Aubrey S., Edmonton, Alta.

University of Toronto Library.

University of Toronto Schools Library.

Vaughan, J. J., Toronto, Ont.

Vesey, Rev. F. G., Toronto, Ont.

Victoria University Library, Toronto, Ont.

Vise, Bernard, Toronto, Ont.

Wagenhauser, W. A., Vancouver, B.C.

Walker, David I., Toronto, Ont.

Wallace, Dr. Malcolm W., Toronto, Ont.

Waller, Horace W., Toronto, Ont.

Ward, Rev. Canon James E., Toronto, Ont.

Wardley, T. C., Elora, Ont.

Wardrope, W. H., Hamilton, Ont.

Warren, H. R., Clarkson, Ont.

Watson, Rev. Thomas J., London, Ont.

Weston, James F., Toronto, Ont.

White, Sir Thomas, Toronto, Ont.

Will, William, London, England.

Wilson, Bishop A., Vancouver, B.C.

Wilson, Hartley P., Fernie, B.C.

Wilson, J. H., Toronto, Ont.

Wilson, Percy D., Toronto, Ont.

Wilson, Rev. Dr. R. J., Toronto, Ont.

Wilson, Mrs. Stafford T., Fernie, B.C.

Williamson, T. B., Toronto, Ont.

Wingfield, Dr. A. H., Hamilton, Ont.

Windsor Public Library, Windsor, Ont.

Wishart, George, Toronto, Ont.

Wood, Frank P., Toronto, Ont.

Woods, James Douglas, Toronto, Ont.

Woods, W. B., Toronto, Ont.

Woodcock, Rev. Canon, H.F.D., Toronto, Ont.

Wright, Dr. Cecil A., Toronto, Ont.

Wyllie, Hugh, London, England.

Young, Mrs. Isobel H., Toronto, Ont.

Young, John A., Toronto, Ont.

Young, J. Brownlee, Glasgow, Scotland.

Young, T. S., Toronto, Ont.

Young, Rev. Dr. W. Harold, Toronto, Ont.